THE SEA CHART

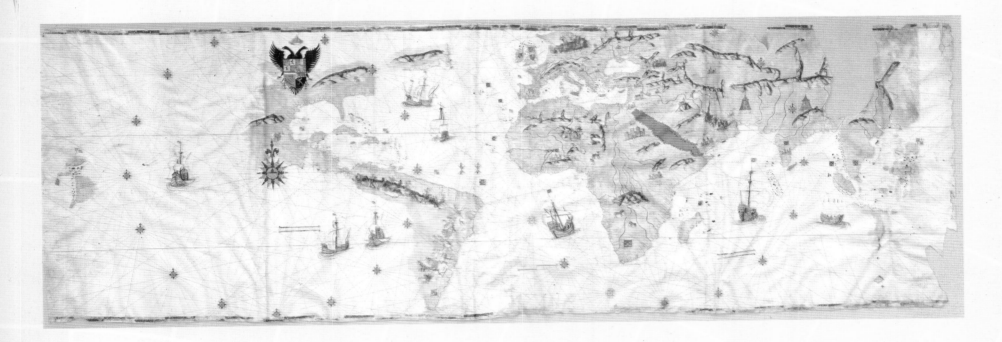

De voort van Tron
Oxefoort
Longen
Oost kiel
Conincx hauen

Mardou
Tron
Nieu bolmen
't ooster gatt van Mardou
't Eyland van Mardou
Tronfondt
't gatt van Oxefoort
't gat van Longen
Saut voort
't gat van oost kiel
Tiffer lendt
De baers
Conincx Eyland
't gat vers oost kiel

WEST

SOUTH

NOR

Englishe Leagues 20 in a degree
1 2 3 4 5 6 7
Spanishe Leagues 17½ in a degree
1 2 3 4 5
Dutche Leagues 15 in a degree
1 2 3 4

THE SEA CHART

THE ILLUSTRATED HISTORY OF NAUTICAL
MAPS AND NAVIGATIONAL CHARTS

JOHN BLAKE

Foreword by HRH The Duke of York

CONWAY

AUTHOR'S NOTE AND ACKNOWLEDGEMENTS

How inappropriate to call this planet Earth when it is clearly Ocean

Sir Arthur C Clarke, English fiction writer, Nature, 1990

Sailing the Seven Seas in the Royal Navy has given me an essential experience of our planet, which no amount of armchair research could have done. The story of mankind's expansion across the globe is bound up in the history of the sea, with the spectrum of emotions, good and bad, that drove the explorers to discover, understand or exploit the lands beyond. The tool was the chart. But dogma has no place in the face of Nature's elements. Galileo Galilei, after his enforced recantation in 1632 that the Earth moves around the Sun, reverted to his belief when he said '*Eppur si muove*' (but it moves). In understanding our world we can start to understand ourselves. As the historian Arnold Toynbee (1889–1975) noted 'Civilization is a movement and not a condition, a voyage and not a harbour'.

First, my thanks must go to my Editor, Alison Moss, for her untiring work and guidance, and to my Publisher, John Lee, for asking me to write, and his help in formulating the book.
I received considerable help from the maritime archives who supplied the images.

Matthew Sheldon, Head of Research Collections, at the Royal Naval Museum in Portsmouth. With a long-standing archive of its own, and access currently to the Admiralty Library Manuscript Collection, a small, but historically important collection assembled at the Admiralty from the early nineteenth century, it includes material on the development of charts, about 2000 manuscript and printed charts, chart atlases, remark books, sailing directions and accounts of voyages. In 2004 the Admiralty Library's printed material on hydrography and exploration (currently at the UKHO, Taunton) will be moved to Portsmouth creating a major resource on the history of navigation.

Adrian Webb, Archive Research Manager and Helen Breeze, Product Manager, The Admiralty Collection® at the United Kingdom Hydrographic Office that today produces navigational charts for the Royal Navy and Maritime community world-wide. All UKHO images are reproduced by permission of the Controller of Her Majesty's Stationery Office and the United Kingdom Hydrographic Office (www.ukho.gov.uk).

Dr John O'Neill, Curator of The Hispanic Society of America, New York. Founded in 1904 by Archer M Huntington to promote Hispanic culture and arts in North America, who collected representative examples of Spanish art and books, it is the largest single collection outside of Spain.

Ed Redmond, Curator of the Geography and Map Division of the Library of Congress in Washington. It keeps the largest and most comprehensive cartographic collection in the world, numbering over 4.8 million maps including 65,000 atlases, from the fourteenth century to the present day.

Brian Thynne, Curator of Hydrography at the National Maritime Museum, London where 40,000 loose charts from the fifteenth century onwards, 1000 atlases and 230 globes are housed.

Dr Richard Luckett, Curator, and Aude Fitzsimons of Pepys Library, Magdalene College, Cambridge, to Sarah Tyacke, Chief Executive of The National Archive (with help by Valerie Scott, Editor of the revised *Tooley's Dictionary of Mapmakers*) for the use of her chart photographs from the Pepys Library. Bequeathed in 1703, the material covers topics in which Pepys was interested, and many, including sea charts, reflect his involvement as Secretary of the Navy.

Francis Herbert, Curator of Maps at the Royal Geographic Society (with The Institute of British Geographers) and staff. The Map Room contains one of the largest private collections of maps and related material in the world.

Dr Tony Trowles, Librarian at the Library of Westminster Abbey, London. It was established at the end of the sixteenth century and houses the collections of printed books, manuscripts and other material made by the Dean and Chapter of Westminster since then.

Jeff Remling, Curator of Collections at the South Street Seaport Museum, New York. Founded in 1967, the Museum traces the history of the Port of New York, and its commercial and cultural impact on the city, and has, besides a maritime manuscript collection, the largest privately owned collection of historic vessels (in tonnage) in the United States.

My thanks to Keith Hammond, who photographed the chart on pages 36-37, and to Robin Brooks for the use of his painting on page 138, *The Triumph of the Navigators – Endeavour* July 13th 1771. Published as a limited edition print from the series of paintings entitled 'Captain James Cook; Son of the land, Master of the Sea'. (Black Dog Studios: Tel +44 (0) 1884 861313: Fax 861384: www.blackdog-studios.com)

My thanks too, to many who have helped me on the wider aspects, including Dr Andrew Cook, Map Archivist, India Office Records; Captain Martin Howard RN (previous Naval Attaché to India); Captain Rodney Browne CBE RN (former Captain of the RN Hydrographic Survey Squadron) and individual advice from Roderick Barron, Nobuko Somers, both Oriental Antique Map Specialists; Penelope Fussell, Archivist to the Worshipful Company of Drapers; Nicholas Courtney, who wrote Beaufort's biography and to Stephen Swann, Editor of *Traditional Boats and Tall Ships* magazine who set me on the road to authorship, and of course to all the authors whose books I have consulted, listed in the Bibliography. As this book is intended to appeal to the interested public at large, rather than the academic, I have left out specific references, which can be provided by me through the Publishers.

Lastly my thanks, and dedication of this book, to my wife Francine, who first gave me the idea and who suffered my absence in consequence (as have my family) but still encouraged and helped me.

John Blake

First published in Great Britain in 2004 by Conway Maritime Press

This edition first published in 2009 by Conway
an imprint of Anova Books Ltd,
10 Southcombe Street, London W14 0RA
www.anovabooks.com

Reprinted in 2010

A CIP catalogue record for this book is available from the British Library.

ISBN 9781844860630

Printed and bound by Imago, Singapore

Inside cover: Details from 'Coast of Portugal and Spain' by Captain Joseph Smith Speer, 1773. (Courtesy of The National Archives, SP112/101)

Contents

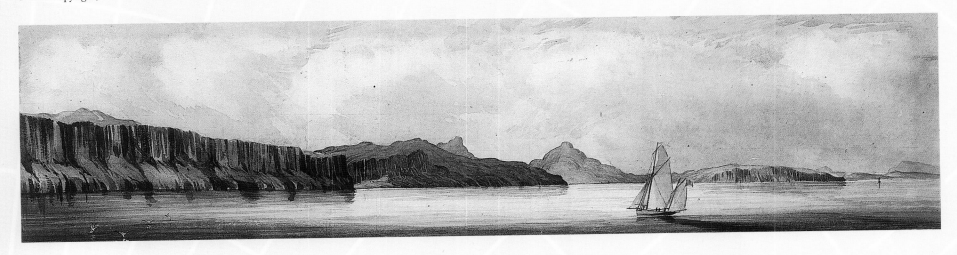

"As safe as an Admiralty Chart". This expression was coined during Rear-Admiral Sir Francis Beaufort's tenure as Hydrographer to the Royal Navy in the 19th century. Throughout my time in the Royal Navy and particularly when I commanded one of Her Majesty's warships, I understood and valued the reliability of the sea chart through personal experience.

We almost take for granted the safe and accurate transit of ships across and upon the oceans of the world that today's navigational charts give us. Two thirds of the world is covered by ocean and the oceans have been the means of discovery and trade of our planet over centuries.

Charts have developed, at a not inconsiderable cost to human life, through the courage, endeavour and experience of sea captains and navigators from all nations as they literally sailed into uncharted waters, in the roles of discovery, exploration, trade or conquest.

I recently opened the new Archive building at the UK Hydrographic Office in Taunton, from where many of the beautiful and intriguing charts in this book are found. With a selection of around 150 charts from ten major archives, such as the Library of Congress in Washington and the Admiralty Library in Portsmouth (many previously unpublished), this book visually accentuates the diverse international history of the evolution of the sea-chart and demonstrates their beauty from an age now past as the evolution of the Chart moves into the age of the electronic and computer generated image.

"The Sea Chart" is a work that exemplifies the rich skills and enterprises of our maritime nation.

Introduction

THE seas have been the arteries of trade, transport and conquest for man since he first fashioned the craft to sail them, an endeavour that needed immense courage, experience and skill. The sea chart became the indispensable tool with which to do this, changing from an aesthetic guide to a precise record for safe and timely navigation.

This account of how the sea chart developed outlines the historical background within a geographical framework to give a rich and interesting picture of the role of the chart, up to the time when the majority of the world's coastlines were surveyed, around the mid-nineteenth century. Starting with the earliest charts from the 'European cradle of civilization' – the Mediterranean – the narrative follows the opening up of the known world as it occurred to mariners over the centuries, through the Pillars of Hercules (Strait of Gibraltar), trading north to Britain, northern Europe including France, the low countries, and the Baltic, up beyond to the frozen Arctic with attempts to find the North-East or North-West passages across the top of the world, south down the coast of Africa, as the Portuguese discovered it, around the Cape of Good Hope and across the Indian Ocean. The lure of the Orient enticed sailors to China and Japan and the Spice Islands. In 1492 Columbus started the rush to the Americas, to the Caribbean, and south around the windiest cape in the world – Cape Horn. The hunt for the supposed vast counterbalancing continent around the South Pole, *Terra Australis Incognita*, was the catalyst that sparked expeditions to the South Pacific and Australasia, and, at much the same time, to find out what the west coast of North America held. The final chapter looks at the charting of the Antarctic and leaves the hope that mankind can, for once, benefit from its discovery, rather than its exploitation.

Two distinct reasons for voyaging developed very much in parallel; exploration leading to colonisation, and trade. The earliest voyages were undertaken to establish exclusive trading relationships with hitherto unknown lands and were sponsored by the monarch. The Portuguese and Spanish, through resolute explorers such as Magellan, Columbus, Vespucci and da Gama, set up trading monopolies with the Americas, Arabia, India and the Spice Islands, ratified, in principle, by the Pope's audacious Treaty of Tordesillas of 1494. This divided the world along a north-south meridian in the Atlantic, approximately 1770 kilometres west of the Cape Verde Islands. All lands falling to the west of this imaginary line were granted to Spain; all lands to the east were granted to Portugal.

This duopoly later came under attack from other fledgling European powers: the British with privateers and buccaneers, such as Drake, Raleigh, Sharp and Dampier in the Caribbean and South America, the French in the Caribbean and North America, and the Dutch, who later established pre-eminence in Indonesia. Some of these men produced manuscript charts of elegance, with elaborate cartouches, and wind roses at first, then compass roses of exquisite intricacy. The British, with the aid of accurate, but eloquent charts and views, were able ultimately to take India and Canada from the French and establish Australia and New Zealand and parts of the Far East and Pacific islands as their own. While manuscript charts were drawn by mariners of all maritime nations, after the advent of the printing press in 1450, printed charts were predominantly published in the country that held maritime supremacy; the Portuguese and Spanish in the fifteenth and sixteenth centuries, the Dutch in Amsterdam in the seventeenth century, then the British in London in the eighteenth century.

In medieval times sponsors would finance speculative oceanic voyages for profit, a captain was appointed, who would probably have invested in the venture himself but would not necessarily have the sailing skills to work the ship, relying on a sailing master to do this. Concurrently, the warship developed within a nation's maritime navy, and again the captain commanded the ship, but the master sailed it. In order to do so safely the master had to understand the art of navigation. Each master would have his own set of charts, but local knowledge was relied on from the harbour pilot. By the eighteenth century, for every ship lost to enemy action, an average of eight ships were grounded or shipwrecked, and a routine supply of accurate standardized charts to ships' captains became a matter of the utmost importance. As war and commerce became more sophisticated the need for a central organization to both prepare and supply reliable charts grew, and the emphasis for chart provision, following the invention of printing, and then engraving copper plates which would take the detail, slowly shifted from the individual navigator to more centralized chart-sellers. The French were the first to set up a Hydrographic Office in 1720, and the British, with much Admiralty vacillation but spurred on by the American War of Independence, followed much later in 1795. Other maritime nations did likewise; Denmark had preceded Britain in 1784, and then Spain in 1800, Russia in 1827, the USA in 1830 and Germany, Japan, Italy, Sweden, Norway, the Netherlands and Chile towards the end of the nineteenth century.

Once a central 'authority' for collating and printing charts was organized officers and sailing masters were asked to submit their own charts, along with comments on navigability, weather, and approach views to the seaports, or passing views along the coastline. To do this they were trained to draw, and views were often sketched and painted with great beauty, sometimes in the pursuit of naval intelligence or during actual surveys for inclusion in the definitive chart or pilot for that seaboard. Sometimes an artist was appointed as one of the ship's company for voyages of exploration. The gentle but beautiful watercolours by J T Serres of the north French coast with men-of-war sailing in the foreground are a fine example of British naval intelligence along the French coast during the Napoleonic Wars. He was appointed Marine Painter to King George III and to HRH Duke of Clarence, as well as marine draughtsman to the Admiralty.

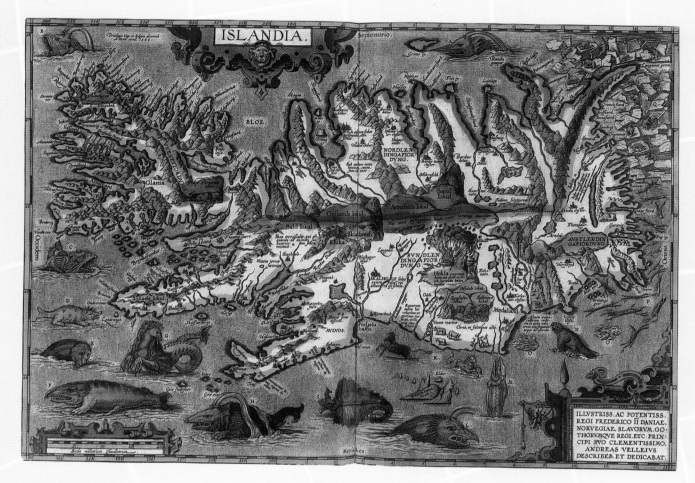

| **ORTELIUS'S MONSTER MAP, 1585** | The famous map of Iceland (Islandia) by Abraham Ortelius showing ghoulish monsters filling the surrounding seas, from an original work by Gudbrandur Thorlaksson. (UKHO © British Crown Copyright)

| THE ORIGINS OF THE SEA CHART |

What is a sea chart? Its essence lies in its informational orientation – it differs from a land map in that its accent is on the presentation of maritime information, such as depths, coastline and headlands, tides and the nature of the sea bed for the mariner looking from the sea towards the land. It enables the mariner to set his vessel in the direction he needs to achieve his destination, with a compass course, and then make adjustments to the progressive course when his current position, which will be changed by wind and tide, has been checked.

The chart has to reflect varying information in a fluid situation, whereas a land map is the opposite – it records fixed positional information and the only variable is to record progress across it. Once this fundamental difference is appreciated the need to record information to guide progress and to update position is understood.

Charts are needed for three different environmental situations: crossing oceans or large tracts of sea out of sight of land (the 'safest' part of a voyage), sailing along or approaching the coast, and entering or leaving harbour, anchorage or roadstead.

From the European perspective the oldest known map, a molded clay tablet depicting Babylon at the centre, the world as a flat disk and with a huge river referred to by Homer as the Okeanus, dates from the seventh or sixth century BC.

By the fourth century BC Pythagoras and Aristotle demonstrated the world as a globe, and Eratosthenes, who looked after the great library at Alexandria, demonstrated its circumference. Knowing the distance from Aswan, on the Tropic of Cancer, to Alexandria to be 5000 stadia – a stadium being 200 yards – he saw at the summer solstice that a gnomon casts no shadow, but that at Alexandria the sun's shadow gave him an angle subtended from the earth's centre of 7° 12' or 1/50th of 360°. He was able to assess the earth's circumference at 252,000 stadia, which is actually a remarkable 4 per cent more than today's satellite measurement.

Early charts filled unknown spaces with elaborate but beautiful artwork, even giving credence to fantastic sea-monsters and non-existent islands, rather as the ill-informed raconteur fills out his story with description. An example is the striking 'monster map' from Ortelius's Atlas of 1585 showing an island called Islandia, reputedly near Norway, with adjacent seas filled with ghoulish animals, complete with detailed descriptions of what they could do to unwary mariners. The necessity for, and availability of, more and more information on a chart, and the need for standardization, both as to production and interpretation, led to the chart becoming honed to a somewhat more severe style and serious execution. By the 1800s the fantastic was out, and the straightforward was in.

| THE PORTOLAN CHART |

Variously known as a Sea Carde, Sea Platte or just a Chart, the earliest known form of chart is the portolan by the Venetians and Genoese, who had a monopoly in the Mediterranean during the fifteenth and sixteenth centuries, providing the go-between for silks, spices and exotic fare from Cathay and the East. The word derives from *portolano* or *portulano*, an Italian pilot book with sailing directions, notes of headlands and navigational hazards.

The Greek Heroditus referred to the *periplus*, which gave sailing directions and later, drawings of the coasts and sketches in use up to the sixth century AD – this was much the same as the later Italian *portolano* and they, too, gave limited information such as a description of ports, anchorages, dangers on making a landfall, and wind and weather over wider areas, but they lacked one essential – the depth of water. The tradition of *periploi*, the plural of *periplus* and the Greek word for circumnavigation, continued over the centuries as sailing directions were developed in turn by the ascendant maritime power – Portuguese

| NAVIGATIONAL VIEWS BY J T SERRES OF LIGHTHOUSES AND HEADLANDS | In 1800 J T Serres embarked in HMS *Clyde* under Captain Charles Cunningham with the English fleet engaged in blockading French, Spanish and Portuguese ports. His spectacular views included the French, English and Mediterranean coasts, and were published with sailing directions in the book, *The Little Sea Torch*.

Two of his originals are reproduced here. The top view shows Cape Finisterre, off Corunna at the north-west tip of Spain, in the background, with HMS *La Nymphe* and a cutter giving perspective to the view. The lower view shows HMS *La Nymphe* underway and HMS *Triton* at anchor in an unusually calm Passage de l'Iroise (Iroise Gulf) off Île d'Ouessant (Ushant) at the approaches to Brest. (UKHO © British Crown Copyright)

Compare the stylized illustrations from the engravings in the published book, *The Little Sea Torch*, of this bevy of lighthouses, including the famous Eddystone (far left) and the approach to Leghorn (second from left) harbour in Italy. (Reproduced by courtesy of the Royal Geographical Society with IBG)

roteiros, French *routiers* and English rutters, and finally, universal pilots.

King Frederick II of Hohenstaufen (1194–1250) is obscurely given credit for instigating the portolan or compass chart. But this is not so surprising when one knows he was born in Sicily, spoke Sicilian as his first language and held his court at Foggia. As the last of the Holy Roman Emperors he felt a responsibility for this Italian kingdom and encouraged the navigational school. Modern charts derive more, however, from the Dutch charts of the 1600s onwards. But the portolan was essentially a compass chart, in use by ships from the beginning of the fourteenth century, and also an expensive work of art painted on parchment used in the cabin for a general appreciation of the voyage and for laying off a course to steer. At the time of the Crusades (the eleventh to thirteenth centuries) the tendency was to sail by day, hugging the coast, and anchor by night, although some might steer by the Pole Star. The portolan chart, with the use of the compass, had the ports written in a clockwise direction, red for safe, black for unfriendly, and enabled the cruise to be direct.

The oldest known surviving portolan, dated around 1290, is known as the *Carta Pisana* or Pisan Chart. It was drawn on what is probably goat skin in Genoa, Italy in the second half of the thirteenth century. The pilot or sailing directions that would have accompanied it are known as *Il Compasso da Navigare*.

Baron Nordenskiöld, the Arctic explorer, was probably the first to study the 180 or so portolans that have survived. Writing his great and painstaking book on the history of cartography (a copy is available in the British Library) in 1897, which he called *Periplus*, he put down many of the ideas regarding these charts that still hold true today, including the origins of the portulan chart, how they were constructed and how the distances between ports were exactly known from long experience. This is verifiable by converting the medieval units of length of various maritime nations, and allowing for these distances. Matching them up to a modern chart makes for a very satisfactory comparison between the portolan coastal outline and that of the modern chart.

Other surviving portolans include the first dated by Petrus Vesconte in 1311, who produced a set of the Mediterranean in 1320; and a set known as the Laurentian Collection, creator unknown but dated 1351, which has a remarkably accurate chart of the west coast of Africa; and a portolan of 1492 by the German cartographer, Henricus Martellus, which shows the voyage of Bartolomeu Diaz around the southern tip of Africa.

Portolans were usually constructed on vellum, made from calfskin, or on parchment from sheep or goatskins. These had to be soaked in alum and lime to remove the hair, and the damp skin was then stretched on a frame and scraped until it was the requisite thickness, sometimes adding chalk to whiten it. Then they were cut into the shape that would take the charted land outline. Weighting the skin on to a sloping writing board the outline could be pricked out, and the detail drawn with a sharpened quill using colours achieved with various natural materials or mediaeval chemicals. Yellow might be 'orpiment' (trisulphide of arsenic); red/orange toasted lead; green from verdigris, made by suspending copper over vinegar or with a blue/yellow mix (vergaut). White was achieved with chalk or crushed eggshell, and black from carbon. Ultramarine at

Wind Roses

This portolan chart by Battista Agnese dates *c.* 1550 and shows the Black Sea with eight wind cherubs lustily blowing their directions, each with the traditional names: *Tramontana*, *Greco*, *Levante*, *Sirocho* (*sic*), *Ostro*, *Garbin*, *Ponente* and *Maistro*.

A sonnet was written by the Venetian Captain Bartolommeo dalli Sonetti (recognizing his sonnet and poetic talents, although his real name was Zamberti), *fl.* 1477-85, in his *Isolario* (meaning island-book) that was designed to help the mariner remember the winds.

Written in mediaeval Venetian dialect it can be translated to read (with modern wind directions in brackets):

> Between Levant (E) and Sirocco (SE) it is called
> Eurus (ESE), as you see, in the middle,
> And Sirocco is between Eurus and its cousin
> Noto (SSE), which comes anonymously,
>
> And then between Ostro (S) and Garbin (SW) is found
> Libonoto (SSW) which comes close.
> And see in the middle of Ponente (W) and Garbin
> Is Aphrico (WSW), which has been noted between those.
>
> Between Ponente and Maistro (NW) you find Argesti (WNW).
> Between Maistro and Tramontana (N) you put
> Circio (NNW), as you see, between these.
>
> (Then) Aquilo (NNE) and then between Greco and Septentrio (N) Po.
> Between Greco (NE) and Levant is Cecias (ENE)
> Then as you expect is Pertrasone.
>
> And by writing this out
> One can believe the rules of the great authority.
> It is a great virtue to know these things.

The sailor needs to know both distance to go and distance covered, not just direction. Before the magnetic compass mariners used a rough and ready directional indicator, the wind; and symbols were used as wind direction. The older charts were often decorated with the winds as gods. The Greeks during the time of Homer (900 BC) and then the Phoenicians around 600 BC were using the four winds as directional references – *Boreas* from the north, *Euros* from the east, *Notos* from the south and *Zephuros* from the west. As voyages lengthened, more acute directions were needed and a further four winds were added; thus *Boreas* from the north, *Kaikias* from the north-east, *Apeliotes* from the east, *Euros* from the south-east, *Notos* from the south, *Lips* from the south-west, *Zephuros* from the west and *Skiros* from the

north-west. Navigators would have known the characteristics of a particular wind such as the temperature, dryness, saltiness and even smell and, knowing the sun's movement, the wind's relative direction could more or less be gauged. At night Polaris, in Ursa Minor, lying roughly due North satisfied the same purpose.

Taking over the Mediterranean trading from the Greeks, the Phoenicians and the nascent Italians, principally in Genoa and Venice adopted the same system, introducing their names *Tramontana* (over the mountains to the north), *Greco* (north-east), *Levante* (east), *Sirocco* (south-east), *Mezzodi* (south), *Garbino* changed to *Africus* or *Africone* (southwest), *Ponente*, (west) and *Maestro* (north-west). The Norse explorations and trading spread into the Baltic, Britain and Ireland, north and west coasts of France, Spain and further to the Mediterranean carrying their names for the four cardinal points, the north, south, east, west with them. As use of *Mare Nostrum* (the Mediterranean) grew, the need for directional refinement also grew and the rose was expanded to 16 points, then to 32. By 1250 an Italian pilot could name 64 directions or rhumb lines, and was even finding that number insufficient. The early portolans were very much wind rose directional charts with rhumb lines drawn to show these. The charts of the fifteenth and sixteenth centuries continued to show wind roses, although with the arrival of the far more accurate magnetic compass, referred to as being in use at Amalfi, Italy during the twelfth century, the compass rose superceded it. It was only natural that the existing wind rose designs should be used for the compass rose. Interestingly, an Italian ship inventory of 1294 included two charts, a pair of compasses and two lode-stones (magnetic needles).

(Reproduced by courtesy of the Royal Geographical Society with IBG, 265 C18)

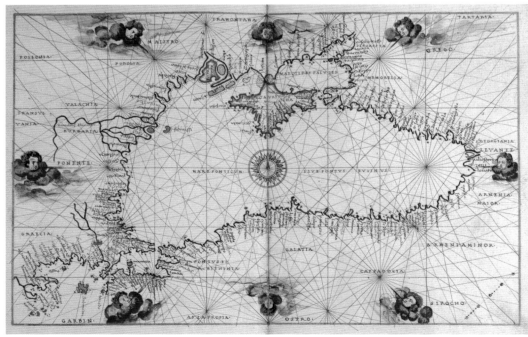

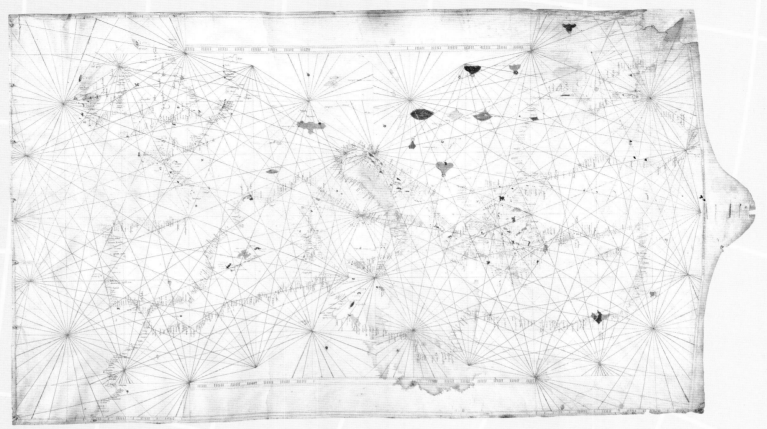

|JACOBUS DE GIROLDIS' MANUSCRIPT PORTOLAN CHART, 1447 | This is the oldest portolan chart in the collection of the Hispanic Society of America's archives. The place names are identical with the *Giroldis Atlas* of 1426 identified by Baron Nordenskiöld in his 1897 book, *Periplus*. It shows the Venetian understanding of the Mediterranean Sea, Black Sea and Atlantic covering from Ireland to Cape Cantin, Morocco, about 100 miles south of Agadir, and from Spain to the Near East. (Courtesy of The Hispanic Society of America, New York)

the time was obtained from crushed lapis lazuli brought from the Himalayas. Ink was mixed with an extract from oak galls and iron salts, which has never faded. And of course gold leaf and powdered gold ink was used to uplift flags and royal positions.

Printed portolans started to supersede the hand-drawn from 1569 with charts by a Dutch seaman and cartographer, Lucas Janszoon Wagenaer. A skilled navigator can judge the ship's speed up to 10 knots and distance measured by the thirteenth-century galley by the rhythm of the stroke of the oars and the length of the vessel. As such, a bank of knowledge of the distances between ports could be built up and charts were drawn. The average mariner was not familiar with a latitude and longitude graticule, although Gerardus Mercator was to find them in common use by the time of his towering solution to the problem of representing a line of longitude drawn on a sphere on to a flat surface, which he first published in 1569. Before his projectional solution they were used literally for plane sailing.

Providing a visual reference, the mariner did not need to know how to read, and portolans are made conspicuous by their radiating lines called rhumbs or lines of bearing (technically loxodromes), usually 32, representing, originally, the wind direction. Then, following the direction of the principal points of the compass, one convention was eight principal rhumb lines in red, green for the eight half-wind directions (half-way between each principal wind on the compass rose) and red for each of the sixteen quarter-winds (logically centred between each wind and half wind direction). Chart symbols were unvaried for centuries, the first black cross on the Pisan Chart denoted a dangerous rock; red dots showed shallow areas, islands and river deltas were shown in different colours; major ports and cities were highlighted in red, often with vignettes and national flags, with the cross or crescent indicating to the mariner, depending on his religious allegiance, whether to stop or sail on by. Place names were written at right angles, following around the coastline to be read from the direction of the coast. Nordenskiöld decided, after measuring many portulans from 1300 to 1600, that the 'portolano mile' was constant at around 5830 metres, nearly the same as a Catalan league. A Catalan centre of cartography was set up in Majorca, with the same style and symbols, but more beautiful compass roses. These, developed originally as the wind rose, were something of an art form in themselves, and were constructed using geometrical rules with dividers to mark out arcs and radii, and then coloured. Fleur de lys were incorporated, and conjecturally, as the rose in Europe, particularly in England, had religious and political/heraldic symbolic implications, it became something of the cartographer's trademark, besides the necessary function of giving the charts geographic orientation to North for the user.

Europeans colonized the world and this history of the sea chart is inevitably written from a European perspective. That the English language is filled with phrases from Britain's maritime heritage, metaphors such as 'the coast is clear'; 'plane sailing'; 'a square meal', 'nailing our colours to the mast'; 'the bitter end': 'pipe down!' and 'show a leg' to mention but a few, graphically conveying a meaning, albeit one that may deviate, but that derives, from the original, have become part of the English inheritance, and demonstrates the historical importance of the surrounding waters to the British island nation. The extraordinary expansion of European countries, coming out of the Dark and Medieval Ages into the Renaissance and the age of global exploration (as indeed with every other country that explored, traded and then often populated what was the unknown world by means of the sea) would have been impossible without the art of navigation, and one tool that became pre-eminent in this endeavour was the sea chart.

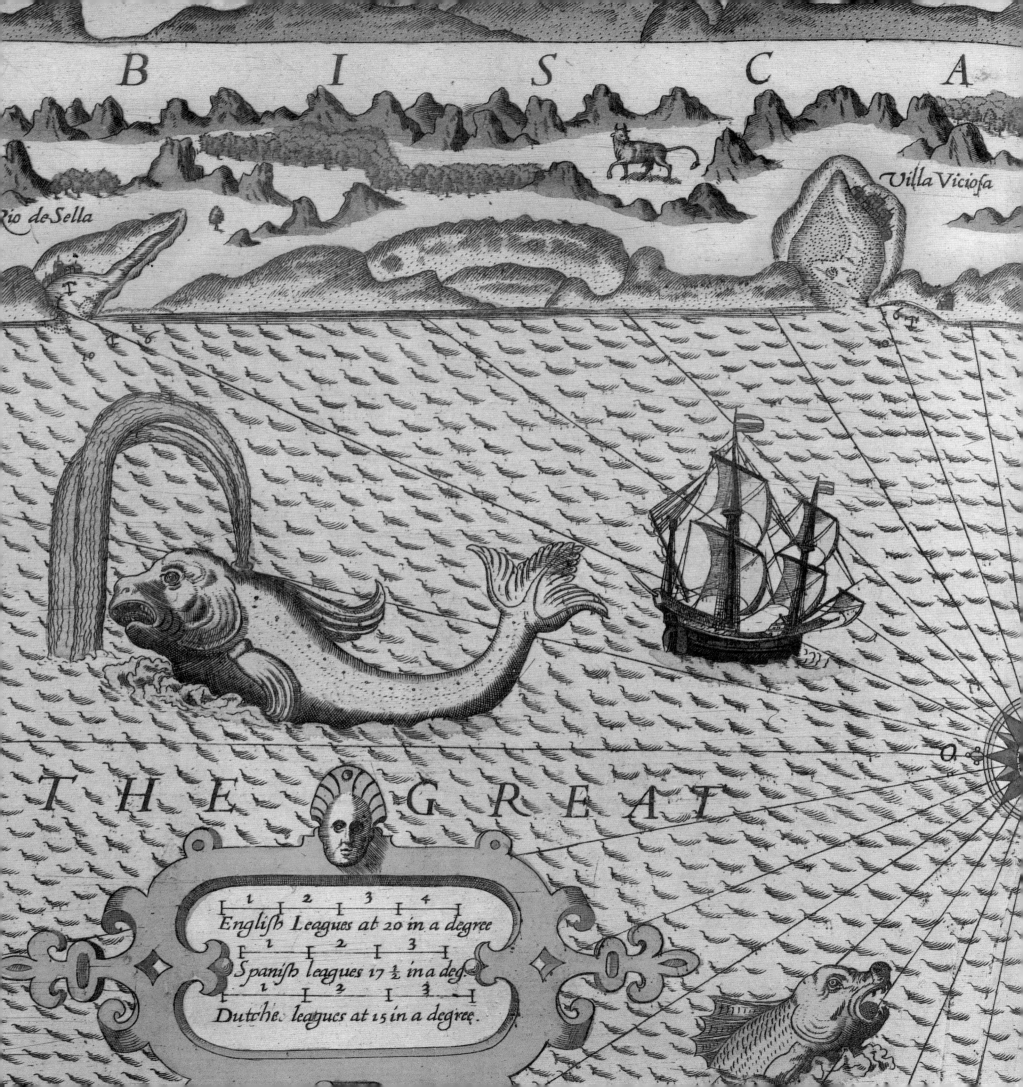

B I S C A

Villa Viciosa

Rio de Sella

THE GREAT

English Leagues at 20 in a degree

Spanish leagues 17½ in a deg.

Dutche leagues at 15 in a degree.

Navigation

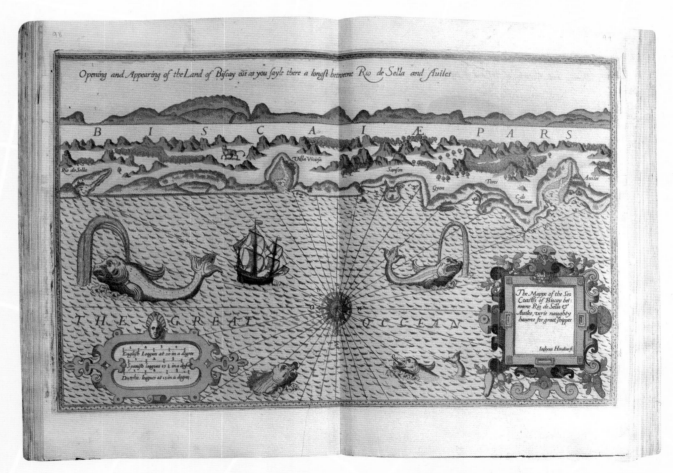

| **LEFT DETAIL & ABOVE** | **CHART OF THE BAY OF BISCAY FROM THE MARINER'S MIRROUR, 1587** | The orientation is with North towards the bottom of the page. The coast is the northern part of Spain to the west of Santander and shows Giyon (Gijon), Cape de Pennas (Peñas) and other ports along about 80 miles of the coast. Jodocus Hondius is given as the source of the advice that there are 'very naughtie havens for big ships'. It is understood that 'naughtie' in the mediaeval sense meant empty (naught), so indicating spacious natural harbours. (Reproduced by courtesy of the Royal Geographical Society with IBG, 264 G4 p.99)

SEAFARING, until the advent of the meticulous charts of the twentieth century, was an exceptionally dangerous profession. Although warships were usually safer than merchant ships, because they had more men, were bigger and better equipped, most vessels were square rigged and so could only sail up to six points off the wind. With high freeboard they were prone to drift to leeward, and if experiencing a strong current or tide were unable to make any ground to windward at all. Typically the route a sailing ship would sail, based on hard-won experience over many years, was determined by the prevailing winds and currents. If leaving the port of London or other ports in the Thames Estuary, an outward-bound vessel might have to anchor at the Downs, off the Kent coast, until the prevailing south-westerly wind backed sufficiently for a dash down Channel. This was the same prevailing wind that gave the British the windward gage to bear down on a French or Spanish ship attempting to tack out of their Atlantic ports during the successive wars over the centuries, and was a great aid to British blockade. At times the Downs, an open ground anchorage uncomfortably close to the Goodwin Sands, would have many merchantmen and men-of-war waiting even weeks for a favourable wind. One captain in February 1758 reported he had been beating up the Channel for four weeks trying to make port.

The dread of any sailing ship, merchant or war, was a lee shore. Square riggers in particular were vulnerable if embayed, and with an on-shore wind could make no headway. Worse was the tendency to make leeway (i.e. be blown sideways or even backwards), as they could be driven ashore and break up. This problem would be compounded by not knowing the position of the land. In 1760, the British warship *Ramillies*, having just relinquished Admiral Hawke's flag, was embayed off the Devon coast as the master had mistaken the landfall. A Davis or Hadley quadrant could fix the ship's latitude within 10 miles or less, but longitude at that time could be hundreds of miles out after a long voyage. Larger warships carried up to seven anchors, and the *Ramillies* dropped all hers, but they dragged and after many hours slowly drifting to the cliffs at Bolts Tail, the ship foundered, with tragically just 27 survivors from a crew of 800.

The safer option of running down a latitude until the ship sighted the shore was fraught during wartime as the enemy knew the ploy and waited for you to sail into them instead. The British applied this off Ushant, as did French privateers off the Windward Islands.

Marco Polo in the thirteenth century described and claimed to have explored the Silk Route, and this created trading aspirations in countries such as Portugal and Spain. Prince Henry the Navigator formalized the first effective School of Navigation, training pilot majors to take their caravels from Lisbon further and further down the African coast. These versatile sailing ships had adapted the lateen sail of the Arab dhows, which could sail into the wind, and added the rudder. This meant that with a lateen sail on the mizzen and mainmasts, and a square sail on the foremast, they could either sail as a square-rigged ship before the wind, or with the lateen sail close into the wind. In 1491 Bartholomeu Diaz dared to venture out of sight of land, and followed the trade winds out into the Atlantic, sailing south.

Sailing ships that had a fair wind and good visibility still needed constant vigilance of the sea state near to land. Seamen of all ages had the greatest respect for the power of the tides, as the English poet Charles Best in 1602 eloquently put it,

Look how the pale Queen of the silent night
Doth cause the Ocean to attend upon her,
And he, as long as she is in his sight,
With his full tide is ready her to honour.
Of the Moon

Care had to be taken to keep clear of the rapid infalls and outfalls of tidal seas, with some of the biggest tidal ranges around the Channel Islands and the notorious Île d'Ouessant, on a par with those in North America of 30 feet experienced at Cook Inlet, the route to Anchorage in Alaska, where the tidal sea pours in and out at a rate sufficient to test a motor-driven vessel, and beyond the ability of most sailing vessels of 10 knots.

Depending on their fresh water and provisions capacity, or the political alliance of the time, ships aiming to weather the Cape of Good Hope, even venture into the Indian Ocean and beyond could make directly for Madeira (Portuguese) at about latitude 33° North, or continue to the Canary Islands at about 28° North (Spanish) or even on to Cape Verde Islands at about 15° North, at 60 miles per latitude degree, distant 750 miles. By keeping reasonably close to the African coast they could use the favourable Canary current to cross the 'horse latitude' which is a belt of light and variable winds between the generally westerly winds of the higher latitudes and the trade winds, until they reached the wind belt of the north-east trade winds at around 30° North, the wind that helped Columbus to the Caribbean in 1492, and which Germanic sailors called the *Passat*. The name 'horse latitudes' came from the custom of throwing overboard an effigy of a dead horse after what was a usual passage of two months from the English Channel, which was sufficient time for merchant seamen to have worked off their advance of pay on signing on, and so giving rise to the expression 'to flog a dead horse' – to expect, in vain, to be able to get extra work from a crew while they were still working off the 'dead horse'.

The sailing ship then had to get across the calm in the equatorial zone between the northerly and southerly trade winds – the doldrums. The trade winds arise because the sun's heating of the air is stronger along the Equator with the consequent rising of the air to the upper atmosphere drawing in heavier air from the north and south. The resulting winds would be due north and south, but for the Earth's eastward spin, and the net result is north-easterly winds north of the Equator and south-easterly winds south of the Equator; called trade winds because of their regularity and the special benefit this gave to ships before the introduction of steam power. The 'intertropical convergence zone', i.e. the doldrums, is a belt extending 200 to 300 miles, although it can sometimes be reduced to nothing by a strong burst from one or both of the trade winds, and stays north of the Equator throughout the year. So, sailing south-west across the mid-Atlantic to the Brazilian current took the ships over the doldrums and the Equator further south to the roaring forties, where the wind blows strongly from the west, which gave them a swift passage across to the South Atlantic and to the Cape of Good Hope. The return voyage would take advantage of the south-east trade winds to sail past St Helena (British), on to Ascension Island (British) then picking up the north-east trades, to the mid-Atlantic until the ships met with the Gulf Stream and the North Atlantic Drift current which carried them towards the Channel.

| NAVIGATIONAL TOOLS |

Until the advent of the compass the seaman was reliant on local knowledge and generally kept to the coast. The commonly accepted birthplace of navigation is the Mediterranean, although pottery from the East and the Persian Gulf shows that these cultures had developed the idea of a sail to use the wind to move on the water.

The Polynesians, for example, had migrated across the Pacific spreading out from New Guinea eastwards through the Pacific islands whose names now resonate with eighteenth- and nineteenth-century European discovery and the idea of the noble savage and paradisiacal society; the Solomon Islands, New Hebrides, Fiji, Samoa, Tonga, Tahiti, Marquesas then north to Hawaii and south to New Zealand between roughly 2000 BC and AD 1000. But it is not known how they navigated, even though a nineteenth-century representation of the Pacific islands over a 500-mile area using a system of shells laid out on sticks was found on the Marshall Islands, which may have come from an earlier method.

Most probably they used a similar system as in the Mediterranean which, before the compass had arrived from China, relied on a system of 'dead reckoning', the term re-spelt by common usage from 'D'ed reckoning' and derived from 'deduced reckoning'. By estimating the vessel's speed and course through the water, an approximation of distance travelled could be assessed. If this was then marked on to the early form of chart, a vellum portolan, the navigator could estimate where he had got to, and adjust his course to steer in order to reach his final destination. Of course this was prone to error as any allowance made for the drift through 'crabbing' caused by the wind, current or tide could only be estimated, unless an accurate position could be taken.

The lead, with a small hollow at its base filled with tallow, and line marked off with fathoms – a fathom being the length of a man's outstretched arms (i.e. 6 feet) – would give the master a good indication of his whereabouts if he knew the nature of the sea bed, and increasing or decreasing depths would give an idea of the profile of the sea bottom over which he sailed. Edmond Halley, who was the first to attempt to chart the isogonic (lines of similar Earth's magnetic variation) contours of the Atlantic as an aid to navigation in 1698, summed up the seaman's stubborn approach to navigation as 'latitude, lead and line'. The usually predictable and steady winds of the Mediterranean provided a sense of direction, and early charts had a wind rose with the winds marked on, which, once the compass was understood, was replaced by the compass rose. Initially this was used, balanced on a piece of reed or wood in a bowl of water, to determine the wind direction and so the course to steer.

The idea of marking a card beneath the compass so that a direction could be taken was only developed around the late thirteenth and early fourteenth centuries. The simple portolan chart, little more than a beautifully presented list of coastal towns and ports, was more of use as a means of planning the strategy of the voyage than in laying on a course and position, but nonetheless had its place to play in navigation.

By the sixteenth century as well as portolans, coastal and island charts, manuscript charts for use at sea were produced, such as the Rotz Atlas, and early Portuguese charts of the coast of Africa. What is intriguing is the accuracy of the Rotz charts. Jean Rotz was appointed Hydrographer to the King by Henry VIII of England and had come from the Dieppe School of Cartography. As one of the leading cartographers of his day he was respected for the accuracy and careful preparation of his charts. It is thought that to have Antarctica and Australia shown on his charts with uncanny positioning, he must have copied them from earlier Portuguese charts. Similarly, the Turkish Admiral Piri R'eis, whose map of 1513 was dramatically unearthed in the old Imperial Palace in Constantinople in 1929, also shows Antarctica, and the positions of Brazil and Africa show longitude with considerable accuracy some 200 years before either lunar tables or John Harrison's chronometer provided the answer to establish longitude. The Piri charts are again thought to have been copied from earlier examples. In both cases Gavin Menzies persuasively argues that these must have been copied from the charts made by the Chinese during their four mammoth expeditions of the 1420s to various parts of the world, including the Atlantic and around Cape Horn to the Pacific. While Charles Hapgood argues that the Piri charts came from far earlier sources, the concept that the Chinese provided the material argues well. An eyewitness account from a Venetian, Niccolo da Conti, who was in Calicut and sailed in one of the ocean-sailing Chinese junks to South Africa, substantiates these events.

Along the coastline landmarks were built, such as lighthouses beacons, buoys and later lightships to warn ships about submerged rocks and other hidden dangers. In England these were set up by Trinity House, which still maintains them today, established by King Henry VIII in 1517, and 'fixes' were

| **SIR FRANCIS DRAKE'S POCKET TIDE TABLES, 1548** | Drake's original manuscript chart, part of his signed pocket tide table, shows the coasts of western Europe and, depending on the compass bearing of the required harbour, was used to determine the state of the tide from the tide tables for a particular date. (Pepys Library, Magdalene College, Cambridge)

obtained to draw as position lines on the chart by taking a horizontal sextant bearing of them.

Of growing use was the tide table. The seaman had no way of measuring time at sea until the introduction of the chronometer at the end of the eighteenth century. Ingeniously the related time of high water on the days of full and new moon, by the moon's compass bearing at the moment of high water, was worked out in the published tide tables of medieval times. For example, high water at Dieppe was expressed as 'Dieppe is NNW and SSE' (10.30 p.m. and 10.30 a.m.), which is fully expressed as 'High-water occurs at Dieppe on days of full and new moon when the moon bears north-north-west and south-south-east'.

One of the first tide tables was put together by a Breton from Conquest, Guillaume Brouscon in about 1548. He drew rough outlines of the coast between Biscay, the English Channel and the Irish Sea, noted the names of the principal ports on the coastline, drew a compass rose on the sea area, and linked with a line drawn from each port joining them to the compass point on the compass rose that related to that port's compass bearing of the moon at high water. By referring to a separate diagram made up of four circles, with the moon's 29-day cycle represented in the outermost circle, the phases of the moon and the tides (i.e. full and new moon and neap and spring tides) in the next circle, the time in hours and quarters of high water each day in the next circle, and for low water in the innermost circle, it was actually straightforward for the illiterate seamen to assess high and low water. Comparison of Brouscon's tides with The Admiralty Tide Tables of today gives a time of High Water at Dover just 13 minutes different. Brouscon's tide tables were very popular and a copy, signed by and belonging to Sir Francis Drake, and later in Samuel Pepys' ownership, is in the Pepys Library at Magdalene College, Cambridge.

The sailing master would use a sandglass for specific periods of time, measuring an hour for the changing of the four-hour crew watch at sea, and to measure the distance and course made good during the watch, recorded on a simple traverse board. Basic navigation involved sailing from cape to cape, called caping, keeping the coastline in view. Most rutters or sailing directions would note the features between the maximum distance a cape could be seen – about a kenning (20 miles). For example, carrying wine from Bordeaux, a seaman, if sailing to Portugal or into the Mediterranean would cut straight across the Bay of Biscay, as coast-hugging would be uneconomical. But during Elizabethan and Stuart times most English masters despised a rutter, and trusted a traverse board much more than a sea-card, relying on dead reckoning. The helmsman kept a record on the traverse board, as explained by one Captain Smith in his *Sea Grammar*:

> Upon the binnacle is also the Travas, which is a little round boord full of holes upon lines like the Compasse, upon which, by the removing of a little sticke, they keepe an account, how many glasses (which are but halfe hours) they steare upon every point.

Later boards had holes added to record speed. The master, at the end of each watch, would assess the mean course made good and the distance sailed, by now recorded in leagues, the more favoured measure of distance out of sight of land, which appealed to the pilot as most ships then sailed on average 3 miles (a league) an hour, noting it in chalk on the slate. He would then clear the traverse

for the next watch. (The expression wiping the slate clean comes from this).

Since the thirteenth century Italian and Catalan pilots used mathematics worked out as a traverse table, a more sophisticated way of assessing course and speed achieved. These could feature on the portolan chart,

It was the advent of charts with Gerardus Mercator's projection, published in 1569 with latitude and longitude, that slowly won over the navigator to use the chart as a measure of his daily progress, rather than a guide, since he could now lay his course on the chart and measure his distance achieved and to go, and make adjustments as necessary to maintain that course. But it took over a hundred years to become generally accepted by the seafarer.

| THE DEVELOPMENT OF ASTRONOMICAL NAVIGATION AND ITS USE OUT OF SIGHT OF LAND |

Called simply 'astro-nav' by yachtsmen and navigators alike, the understanding of the way the Earth, Sun, planets and stars interacted was essential to the development of a system of navigating out of sight of land.

By AD 100 we know that Marinus of Tyre was drawing sea maps with cylindrical projections making a grid of parallelograms centred on Rhodes. The Earth-centred (geocentric) view of the Universe is known as the Ptolemaic system, after the Alexandria-based astronomer Claudius Ptolemaeus (known today simply as Ptolemy) described by him in the second century AD. He lived from AD 127 to 151, and wrote about Marinus in his famous work, *Geographia*, one of the most significant books in the history of astonomy. His *Almagaest* was a great compendium of contemporary astronomical knowledge, consisting of Greek astronomy up to his own day. It drew on the work of Hipparchus (c. 190–120 BC), the most important Greek astronomer of his time. He observed the precession of the equinoxes (how the spring and autumn days of equal light and darkness change each year, important for accurate astro-navigation). Furthermore, dividing the world into 360°, Hipparchus put down a system of latitude and longitude to fix geographical positions in relation to the Pole Star with his prime meridian (base line of longitude running from the North Pole to the South Pole) positioned at the Fortunate (Canary) Islands. Perhaps as important was his foundation of trigonometry, essential in the accurate triangulation method of plotting coastlines, explained later, and his proof of the sphericity of the Earth. He suggested, too, the idea of time elapse between two points on the Earth to measure longitude, although the maritime world had to wait until John Harrison's invention of the chronometer in 1760 for a way of finding this out.

Ptolemy's *Geograhick Syntaxis* of 27 maps was the standard reference on geography through the Middle Ages. It provided the basis for our present-day system of constellations, listing 1025 stars visible to the naked eye around the Mediterranean Sea. These were formed into 48 constellations, which, with little modification, are still in use.

Ptolemy's system of the dominant, central role ascribed to the Earth with the known planets, the Moon and the Sun shown orbiting around it ruled European thought, becoming religious dogma, until Nicolaus Copernicus, a Polish astronomer published his book, *De revolutionibus orbium coelestium*, in 1543. It expounded his theory that the Earth rotates daily on its axis and

Mercator Solves the Course-to-Steer Conundrum

With the European discovery and desire to trade with, and dominate lands across the oceans of the world, navigators needed a means of sailing out of sight of land. There were actually two major problems: how to find the longitude of a position, and how to represent a ship's course on a plane (two-dimensional) surface which in reality it was one that went around the curvature of the earth, describing part of a circle.

Gerardus Mercator was the man who solved this problem. In 1544 he accepted the Chair of Cosmography at the university of Duisberg where he took forward the ideas he had studied of Ptolemy to create a projection of the world that allowed a navigator to lay off a straight course on a chart between his start point and destination. A navigator needs a chart from which to lay off his course, to plot his current position, to see how far he has got along his track, and to estimate how far (and how long) he still has to go. All previous projections meant that the drawing of the coastline on the chart was distorted, although on globes, which were cumbersome to take to sea and certainly inappropriate for smaller vessels, the ship's course could be laid out and adhered to. Mercator realised that the course the navigator wanted to steer, a line with a constant compass bearing called a rhumb line, needed, if he was to lay a straight edge on the chart, to cut all the meridians (lines) of longitude at the same angle. The problem did not exist with parallels of latitude which slice the world in, relative to a north/south axis, equal and parallel lines – hence the term plane (then to become plain) sailing, whereby the ship can sail the latitude and maintain a constant course across the ocean. This was particularly popular, for example, with voyages to Australia from the Cape of Good Hope, and was known also as 'sailing the latitude'.

But to sail on any other compass bearing was problematic, and Mercator (who never went to sea) solved it by distending the meridians. A chart using the Mercator Projection has the meridians of longitude and parallels of latitude crossing each other at right angles to form a grid. This projection works well until you near the poles, and is the reason why Greenland, the Strait of Magellan or Antarctica, for example, appear to stretch in size. In fact, at the poles the projection fails.

At the poles what is known as the 'gnomonic' projection is more appropriate. This projection is used for great circle sailing, where the parallels of latitude are curved, and the meridians of longitude are straight but converge towards the poles. The great circle track is the slightly changing course to steer to achieve the shortest distance between two points across the spherical surface of the ocean, and will appear as a straight line on the gnomonic chart. With a distance to cover of over 600 miles it is shorter to sail the great circle route. For example, the distance between Lisbon and Boston by the great circle route is 3170 nautical miles, but by the rhumb line is 3237 miles, and great circles appear as straight lines.

In the older portolans the scale can be seen set at an angle and this was an early but crude attempt to allow for the varying flat distance that the chart represented. It was this sort of distortion that had led Mercator to address the problem of a chart that could be plotted so that straight line courses could be laid off and the navigator assess the compass course for his vessel to steer.

Mercator introduced this projection in 1569 but it was nearly 70 years before it was fully accepted at sea. He almost literally squared the circle by his discovery.

| RIGHT | Portrait of Gerardus Mercator (1512–94).
(By courtesy of the Dean and Chapter of Westminster)

| BELOW |An early (1560) example of Mercator's world projection by Giovanni Francesco Camocio (*fl.* 1558–75).
(Reproduced by courtesy of the Royal Geographical Society with IBG)

revolves yearly around the Sun, that the planets also encircle the Sun, and that the Earth precesses on its axis (wobbles like a top) as it rotates.

Copernicus's heliocentric theory of planetary motion had the advantage of accounting for the apparent daily and yearly motion of the Sun and stars, and it neatly explained the apparent retrograde motion of Mars, Jupiter, and Saturn, and why Mercury and Venus never move more than a certain distance from the Sun. Copernicus's theory also stated that the sphere of the fixed stars was stationary. In his universe, unlike Ptolemy's, the greater the radius of a planet's orbit, the greater the time the planet takes to make one circuit around the Sun. But the concept of a moving Earth was difficult to accept for most sixteenth-century readers who grappled with Copernicus's claims; instead, parts of his theory were adopted, while the radical core was ignored or rejected.

There were but 10 Copernicans between 1543 and 1600, working mainly outside the universities in princely, royal, or imperial courts. The most famous were the Italian astronomer, Galileo Galilei (1564–1642), who was put under house arrest after appearing before the Inquisition and forced to retract the ideas published in his book on the movement of the Sun and planets (but he always thereafter signed his name with a circular symbol), and the German astronomer, Johannes Kepler (1571–1630). These men often differed in their reasons for supporting the Copernican system. In 1588 an important middle position was developed by the Danish astronomer, Tycho Brahe in which the Earth remained at rest and all the planets revolved around the Sun as it revolved around the Earth.

After the suppression of Copernican theory following Galileo's ecclesiastical trial in Rome in 1633, some Jesuit philosophers remained secret followers of Copernicus. Many others adopted the geocentric-heliocentric system of Brahe. The late seventeenth century saw the rise of the system of celestial mechanics put forward by Sir Isaac Newton (1642–1727), who also worked out the Sun and Moon's influence on the oceans to create tides, and who, through his work, perhaps developed an awe and humility of the magnitude and scale of the Universe. He wrote,

> I don't know what I may seem to the world, but as to myself, I seem to have been only like a boy playing on the sea-shore and diverting myself in now and then finding a smoother pebble or a prettier shell than ordinary, whilst the great ocean of truth lay all undiscovered before me.

By this time, most major thinkers in Britain, France, the Netherlands, and Denmark, with Newton amongst them, were Copernicans. But so strongly held were the ancient beliefs that natural philosophers in other European countries, however, held strong anti-Copernican views for at least another century. How much this hindered the advancement of 'astro-nav' is hard to assess, but it certainly held back the development of ways to measure longitude.

| PTOLEMY'S WORLD MAP, C. AD 150–160 | The world map illustrated, taken from Ptolemy's *Geographia* (*Theatri Geographia Veteris*) by Petrus Bertius (Bert) (1565–1629), who, in his words, 'improved' the original 1578 edition map by Mercator, is held in the Westminster Abbey archives. It shows the 12 cherubs blowing the navigational winds, pre-dating the compass rose, and has a zero meridian of longitude running through the Canary Islands. India and Ceylon have their relative sizes reversed, and in Ptolemy's original version, and copiously copied, Africa continues east as a huge continent, land-locking the Indian Ocean and then northwards joining China. (By courtesy of the Dean and Chapter of Westminster)

With the need for oceanic navigation, the master had to be able to determine the position of his ship on the globe. This could be achieved by measuring, as keenly as possible, the angular position North or South of the Equator (his latitude) and East or West of a zero (or prime) meridian (his longitude).

While the Chinese had perfected their own technique of measuring latitude and longitude centuries before Europe, unlike the compass, they kept this to themselves. The Arabs, adept at mathematics and familiar with sailing out of sight of land in the Mediterranean, Persian Gulf and Indian Ocean, had perfected the art of the noon-day sun sight. Using a wooden brass measuring instrument known as a quadrant, the maximum height of the sun at noon each day could be accurately recorded. Although the sun's maximum height overhead varies daily throughout the year, the Arabs knew it would give the navigator a latitude position line. Knowing the latitude position of his home port the navigator could subtract one from the other, and after taking into account his estimated speed of advance, he could deduce his distance sailed.

The surest guide at night was the Pole Star – often known by sailors as Stella Maris or star of the sea – so easily identified by its position at the tail, the pointers, of the Little Bear (Ursa Minor). But on a cloudy night the lodestone had the strongest claim on the seaman: 'I guide the Pilot's course, his helping hande am I. The Mariner delights in me, so doth the Marchaunt man.'(R Norman, *The Newe Attractive*, 1581)

It was realized that using the Pole Star had an inbuilt inaccuracy because it precesses, or wanders, predictably around the position of the true North Pole, and a table was devised, called the Regiment of the North Star, by the Portuguese navigational school, and published in Martin Cortes landmark book *Arte de Navigar* in 1551, which allowed the calculation.

Altitudes were taken in the fifteenth century with the back-staff, then the astrolabe and the cross-staff, which was greatly improved by the quadrant, invented by John Hadley, an English mathematician and scientist, in 1731, and followed by the sextant, which is still the instrument used to measure a star's angle (altitude) in relation to the horizon today.

A commission formed by the Portuguese King John II in 1484 solved the problem of position finding further south than the colonized Azores, where the Pole Star would start to disappear below the horizon, by measuring the declination of the sun, and 'The Regiment of the Sun' (i.e. Sun's altitude tables) and putting a position line on to the chart.

Interestingly, the compass could be used as an approximate timepiece as well as a direction finder. This was explained by John Davis, the famous Elizabethan seaman and Arctic explorer who invented the back-staff or Davis Quadrant in the 1590s, in his important book on navigation, *The Seaman's Secrets*, of 1594.

| THE DEVELOPMENT OF SURVEYING AND CHARTING TECHNIQUES |

With the knowledge of the compass from China around the mid-thirteenth century the placing of the land's outline in a meaningful directional relationship was possible, but with little accuracy, except over small areas on a chart. Small islands and promontories were exaggerated, no soundings recorded, although shallows and shoals were sometimes shown. There was usually no latitude and longitude nor any type of grid reference. With the advent of copper plate engraving on charts by 1560, and Gerardus Mercator's 'Universal Map' published nine years later with a grid that incorporated for the first time the two dimensional representation on a flat surface (i.e. the chart) of a three-dimensional sphere (i.e. the Earth), accurate outlines of the coast and navigational features were at last possible. Huge numbers of charts were produced based on sketchy information and were remarkably inaccurate. Even though published privately by individual captains and sold commercially the titles and letterpress resumé trumpeted the accuracy of the work.

The method of drawing up a chart today has developed as a series of 'breakthroughs' over the centuries. In fact, it is impossible to accurately represent large parts of the globe on a small-scale chart without distortion, and charts are really a compromise. With large scale charts, covering a small area of land and sea, the amount of distortion is minimal, and a course for the ship to steer taken off the chart, or compass bearings of points of land to fix a position drawn on the chart to check progress, are of sufficient accuracy.

So the surveyor today has to choose the type of projection, of which there are many, but Mercator and 'gnomonic' are the most favoured. The essential feature of the Mercator Projection is that parallels of latitude and meridians of longitude form a rectangular grid, with scale becoming exaggerated with distance away from the Equator towards the poles. The cylindrical projection of the Earth's surface allows the mariner to lay off the ship's course to steer as a straight line (rhumb line). However, this doesn't hold good in the polar latitudes, so the gnomonic chart is better used in the polar regions, and for laying off a course between two far distant points, say across the ocean.

Next the surveyor needs to decide the scale; the proportion (of distance) between the real distances and the representation of the same distance on the chart, with the larger scale enabling more detail to be shown. Merchant ships are interested in small scale charts, so that they can get from A to B as economically as possible – warships the converse, requiring large scale charts giving details world-wide to allow for operations in any unexpected area. Rivers and harbour approaches clearly need large scale charts, with closely run contour lines giving a depth profile, and accurate positions of rocks and any known position of wrecks, too. Earlier charts would have depths recorded along the ship or more likely small boat's track as they were taken.

A major breakthrough was the concept of triangulation to plot key positional points on the chart (see Chapter IV). Professor Murdoch Mackenzie used this method to create the first reasonably accurate charts, starting in the Orkney Islands in 1744. This now seems an irrelevant place to start a survey of the British Isles which, after 26 years, took Mackenzie to Pembroke and retirement, but the seas to the north of Scotland in the eighteenth century were the gateway for European shipping into the Atlantic. Somebody had the brilliant idea of turning the quadrant, and later the sextant, sideways to measure angles horizontally between selected shore-side features to gain their exact position for plotting on the chart. It had previously only been used to measure the vertical – angle of the stars and sun above the horizon.

The compass is used actively and passively. 'Passively' allows the ship to steer the course obtained from the chart, and to measure the angle or bearing of prominent land features, draw them on the chart so that where, say, three bearings cross it gives a fix to plot the ship's position on the chart. 'Actively' allows the mariner to measure the actual angles for plotting the land features needed to create the embryonic chart in the first place. Mackenzie also first grasped the idea of a station-pointer, whereby three simultaneous bearings of land features represented by three adjustable straight-line arms, which met at the centre of the instrument, gave the single position of the ship.

Other surveying methods used the gun to measure distance, timing the flash of the gun and hearing the report on firing. This was being taught at the Naval Academy at Portsmouth in the early eighteenth century as part of the navigation curriculum and was a technique used by Captain Cook. He would have preferred to use the triangulation method in his survey of the islands of New Zealand, but continuous bad weather mostly prevented him from setting up the shore points needed. His running survey, carried out with remarkably well-judged dead reckoning positions in stormy seas with horizontal sextant angles, is one of the most extraordinary surveying feats ever achieved. The lead and line were used as well to record the nature of the seabed, nowadays measured to within half a metre by the echo sounder. Massey's patent log, utilizing three brass fins rotating inside a copper tube with distance run out recorded on board was developed in 1802, and was used to get the distance covered during a running survey.

| LONGITUDE |

But perhaps the biggest breakthrough in navigation was the invention of a time-piece by a Yorkshire carpenter, John Harrison, which could be used to find out longitude.

Out of sight of land, across the vast oceans, the means of pinpointing position was haphazard and many ships were lost with their men and their valuable cargo. In 1707, for example, Sir Clowdisley Shovel, with his fleet of men-of-war returning home after sinking French ships of the line off Gibraltar, had reckoned he was by the Île d'Ouessant off north-west France, only to be sharply updated as to his position when his flagship, HMS *Association*, and three more of his ships struck rocks by the Scilly Isles and went to the bottom. Nearly 2000 men drowned, and only two men reached the Cornish shore, one of whom was Shovel. He was relieved of his emerald ring on the beach by a woman, who killed him in an attempt to ensure she was not found out.

An answer to the longitude problem became so acute that a Board of Longitude was set up by Act of Parliament in 1714, with a prize of £20,000 offered to anyone who could devise a satisfactory method of finding longitude at sea.

Latitude and longitude have been the grid lines that mark out the globe for centuries before Christ was born, and Ptolemy used them to grid his first maps of the known world in AD 150. Latitude lines run parallel to the Equator, marked 0°, and advance pole wards North and South, ending at the relevant pole at a point of 90°. Lines of longitude run north to south and converge at the poles. They fan out like segments of an orange (in that the distance between them is greatest at the Equator) East and West from a zero or prime meridian (180° is therefore on the opposite side of the Earth to the zero meridian). Since the Meridian Convention in Washington, D.C. in 1884 the Prime Meridian has been standardized for the world as the one used by the astronomers at the Royal Observatory in Greenwich. Before then different countries used a local meridian from which to measure longitude.

Finding longitude involves the comparison of the local time at two places and converting them to distance. If the time the sun passed directly overhead (its meridian) at, say, Greenwich could be carried accurately for long distances at sea, and the local time of the sun passing overhead could be noted, then the two times could be compared. Astronomers knew that the Earth revolves at a constant rate once every 24 hours, hence that one hour equals 15° of longitude. Comparison of the two times would give the longitude position. So if the time in New York harbour was 7.00 a.m., and the 'base' time at Greenwich, London, was 12.00 noon, the time difference of five hours means that New York is 75° of longitude West of Greenwich.

Many methods of finding longitude were put forward. Some were completely impractical, such as mooring ships across the Atlantic Trade Route that would fire guns at certain times. Others were simply lunatic. A wounded dog on a ship in the Atlantic would bark when, at noon in England, a special powder was applied to a bandage. The astronomer, Edmond Halley (1656–1742), went on two sea voyages to compile data showing the variation of the magnetic needle over the entire Atlantic Ocean in an attempt to enable a navigator to know his longitude by the lines of magnetic variation drawn on a chart. Halley made a third voyage recording the tidal currents on both sides of the English Channel partly with a view to using these as a possible positional guide. Lunar tables had been painstakingly recorded, and the idea here was to find longitude by measuring the Moon's position against certain stars, but it took at least four hours to calculate. This method was for some time the one supported by the Board of Longitude.

The key was to design a timepiece that could keep the time at Greenwich accurately at sea, and it was a Yorkshireman, John Harrison, who eventually did so. Born in 1693 he succeeded with the last of a series of clocks that ran to time, needed no lubrication or cleaning, was impervious to rust, and with moving parts that were perfectly balanced in relation to one another, regardless of ship movement, changes in magnetic field, humidity, temperature or air (barometric) pressure – and this without a pendulum. It was called H4.

His Yorkshire tenacity was needed, however. It took him a lifetime (40 years) to achieve the solution in the face of obstruction by the scientific elite of his time, with vested interest in their own methods, or plain downright bias and snobbism. It needed the support of King George III himself to overcome the prejudice before Harrison was ultimately recognized and awarded the Longitude Prize in 1773.

Seafaring men such as William Bligh, well known for his captaincy of the mutinied ship, HMS *Bounty*, and the great circumnavigator James Cook, who made three long voyages of exploration across the Pacific, took the more promising methods to sea to test their accuracy. Much of their charts and other work is held in the United Kingdom Hydrographic Office archives. Cook was clearly impressed by K1, the exact copy of H4 made by Larcum Kendall on the instructions of the Board, for he referred to 'our trusty friend the watch' and 'our never failing guide'.

The East India Company issued new log books for use by its captains with specially printed instructions for 'finding longitude by chronometer'. It was actually Alexander Dalrymple, appointed as the first UK Hydrographer in 1795, who coined the word 'chronometer' and who said, 'so valuable a machine deserves to be known by a name instead of a definition'.

It is sobering to think that today Global Positioning System (GPS) will fix a ship's position to within a few feet, day or night, within a fraction of time. All the more admiration goes to those early explorers, discoverers and voyagers, men such as da Gama, Magellan, Columbus, Cook, Bligh, Vancouver, and Flinders who all achieved so much with relatively blunt tools. It would not be too extravagant a statement to say that without Harrison's pioneering work, Britain's foreign trade would not have developed so extensively, and its overseas influence, then bundled together as the Empire, could not have expanded as rapidly as it did.

The next two centuries were mainly ones of refinements to the range of tools and methods already available. The compass points to the magnetic North Pole, which varies year on year, and is anyway at a differing point at the top of the Earth than the true geographic North Pole. The difference needs to be allowed for when plotting positions and steering a course by the compass. Thanks initially to the work by Halley on the variation across the world of the Earth's magnetic influence on the compass, and Flinders' on the integral magnetic effect of metal in the ship's hull on the compass this became better understood, and applied as a correction to bearings and courses steered.

During the twentieth century Sperry invented the gyroscopic compass which, spinning freely in its own small space, was unaffected by any magnetic influence and points to the *true* North Pole; wireless telegraphy spawned the invention of radio direction finding aids, and today satellite navigation has taken over the mathematical dexterity and visual skill of the pilot.

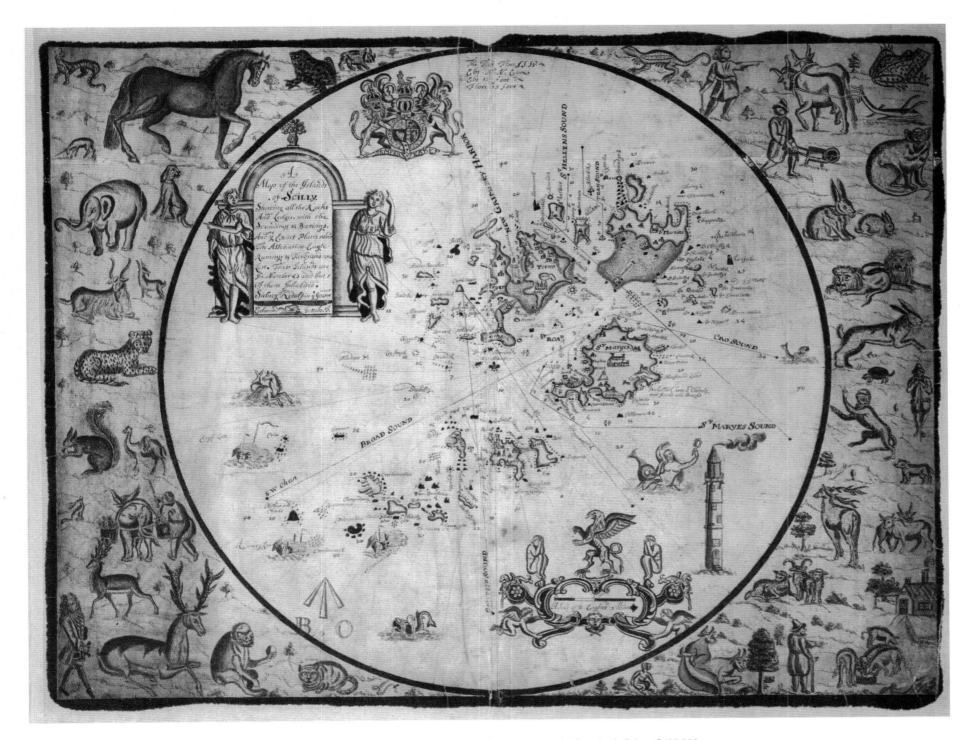

| ISLES OF SCILLY, C.1707 | It wasn't enough for the Commander-in-Chief of the Mediterranean squadron, Admiral Sir Clowdisley Shovel, to rely on his charts, or even on Divine Providence, to keep his 21 ships clear of the dangers of the south-western approaches as he sailed to England. In 1707 he had skilfully supported Prince Eugene's campaign in southern France with the near capture of the main French naval base of Toulon and the subsequent scuttling of the French fleet. But as he neared home with a hopelessly inaccurate assessment of his position, an unsuspected northerly current swept his squadron on to the rocks. The Admiral's flagship, *Association*, and three of his ships of the line, *Eagle, Rumney* and *Firebrand*, sank with all hands except one seaman and, ironically, Sir Clowdisley, who was later killed on the beach. It was the loss of so distinguished an Admiral with so many men – 1647 – that finally prompted Parliament to set up the Longitude Prize of £20,000.

Dated to around 1707 this contemporary chart shows where the four ships of Sir Clowdisley's squadron sank, but doesn't give longitude at all, or even latitude; although it does show where he was washed ashore on St Mary's Island. This is a whimsical chart with some fantastical beasts that could inspire heraldic devices or even cast iron firebacks of the time, surrounding the perimeter, which seems, unusually, to have been constructed on a 320° circle. It does, however, have useful navigational information such as tidal streams, clearing bearings to head safely towards marked anchorages (but only viable with good visibility) or avoid the marked rocks, as well as the positions of the lost ships. (Courtesy of The National Archive, United Kingdom)

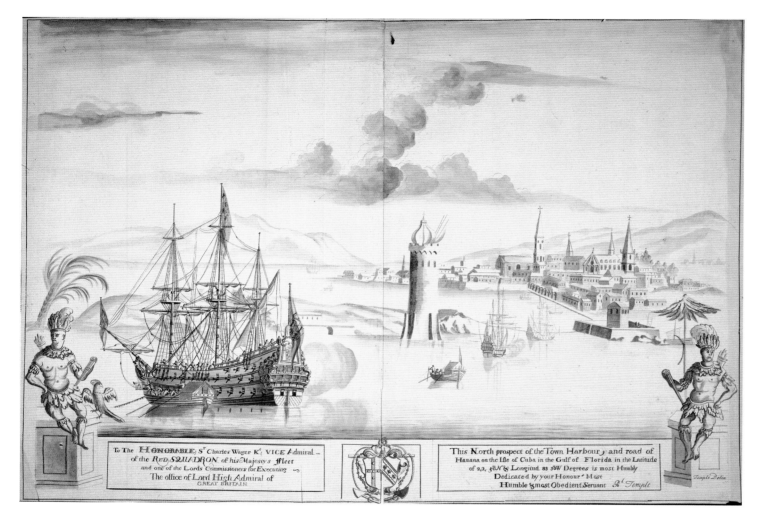

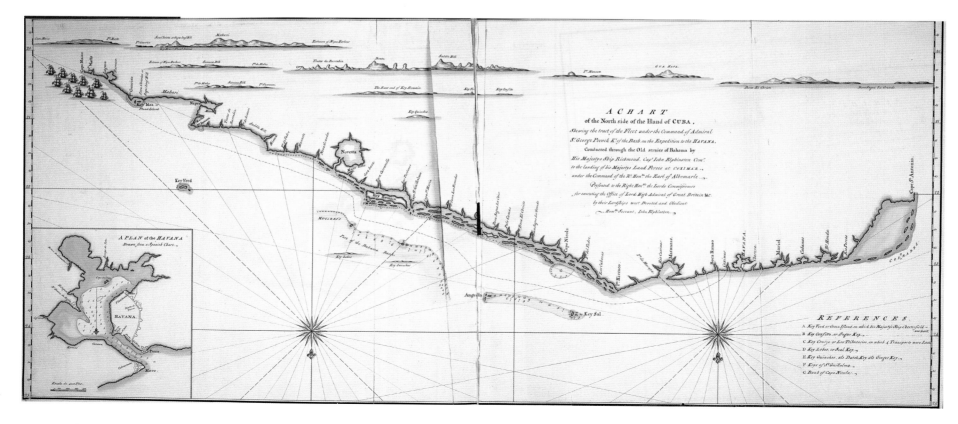

| LEFT | **HAVANA HARBOUR, C. 1730** | An English illustration of Havana Harbour in Cuba, which was Spanish at the time and constantly under attack during the seventeenth and eighteenth centuries. It not only shows the fortifications, but also has a fine illustration of a Spanish man-of-war in the foreground. (Admiralty Library Manuscript Collection VZ 10/11)

| BELOW | **CAPTAIN ELPHINSTONE'S CHART OF THE NORTHERLY PASSAGE, THROUGH THE NARROW BAHAMA BANK, AND THE ATTACK ON HAVANA OF 1762** | As the Commanding Officer of the *Richmond*, Captain John Elphinstone's chart shows how critical was the safe navigation of the fleet, which he led, that attacked Havana in 1762 for the successful and surprise landing at Coximar, adjacent to the port of Havana. With the Fleet's track pecked in red, the chart is orientated with north to the bottom of the page, and to the right are shown Elphinstone's sailing directions. (Admiralty Library Manuscript Collection VZ 10/15)

| RIGHT | **HAVANA HARBOUR, 1741** | From the written note it can be seen that this chart of Havana Harbour in 1741 was copied by Captain Spry (later Rear-Admiral Sir Richard Spry) while a prisoner of the Spanish during the 1740–45 war and that he was able to get this chart back to the Admiralty. This would have provided useful intelligence from which to plan the 1762 attack (below left), during the Seven Years War. The scale of 'milla Castillano' is an example of the almost bewildering array of differing national distance measurements. (Admiralty Library Manuscript Collection VZ 10/18)

| BELOW | **MINORCA** | Although undated, this beautiful, detailed and hand-drawn map of the island has notes in English advising 'good land for corn' and 'good land for wine', an English cartouche announcing the purpose and 12 British warships (with flags flying), which date this to the first part of the eighteenth century. The author had a delicate touch with the brush and the ships are accurate portrayals of ships of the line, frigates and smaller Mediterranean sailing vessels. Whilst a map, it is compiled with a nautical eye as it has fine detail of the harbours and coastline, rivers, 'sandi bays' and small islands and would have been useful at the Admiralty for strategic decisions. (Admiralty Library Manuscript Collection VZ 4/16)

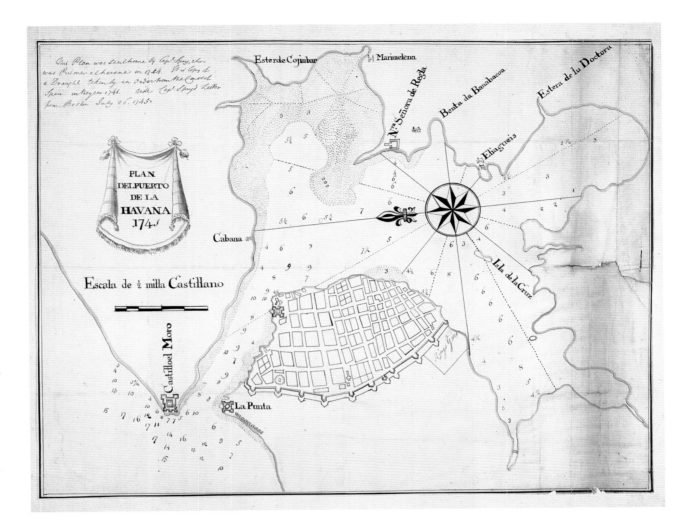

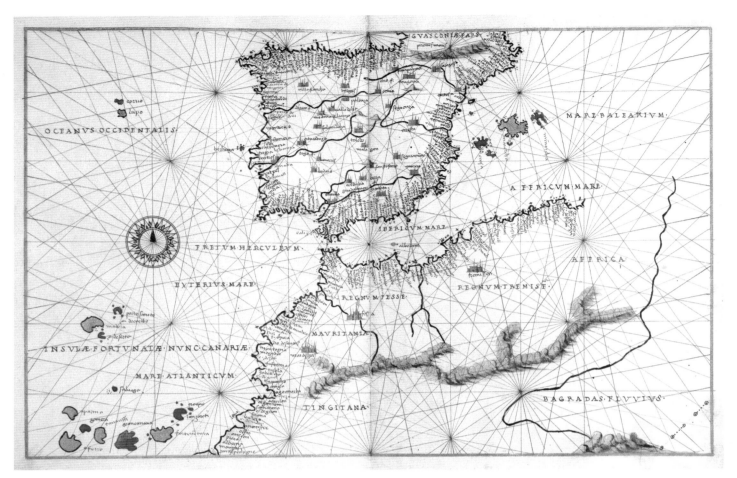

| PORTOLAN OF SPAIN, PORTUGAL AND NORTH AFRICA BY BATTISTA AGNESE | Battista Giovanni Agnese was a Genoese who worked in Venice. One source names him as 'the son of the daughter of Titian or Tintoretto'. True or not his work has high artistic merit. He was one of the most prolific creators of portolan charts, designed to help navigators and sailors, although their ornamental and beautiful execution indicated that they were more likely to grace the libraries of the wealthy or be used for planning a voyage on board, than to 'chart' a vessel's progress.

This chart of Portugal, Spain and North Africa dates to *c*.1550, when Spain and Portugal were under the reign of King Ferdinand and Queen Isabella. The Atlas Mountains are prominent, as is the believed route of the River Niger. The Fortunate Islands (Canary Islands) and the Cape Verde Islands, are haphazardly placed, but the coastlines of Spain and North Africa are surprisingly accurate. Names of principal ports en route are written at right angles and Latinized versions of the seas are used. (Reproduced by courtesy of the Royal Geographical Society with IBG, 265.C.18.16)

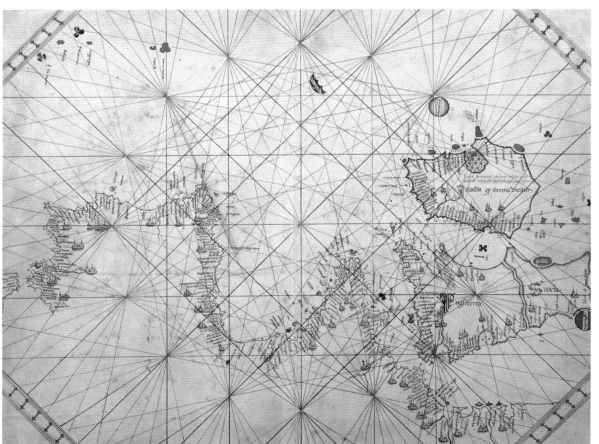

| PORTOLAN CHART OF THE ATLANTIC OCEAN FROM NORTHERN SCOTLAND TO GIBRALTAR, 1537 | The author of this portolan chart, Conte Hoctomanno Freducci, from the port of Ancona on the Adriatic Sea in Italy, has unusually drawn it without a compass rose. Bearings could still be assessed from the rhumb lines, and this chart would have been used to navigate the western European shores. The British Isles and Ireland have still to mature to the real coastline, especially as Scotland is shown (as some may wish it now) as a separate island. (Courtesy of The Hispanic Society of America, New York, K14)

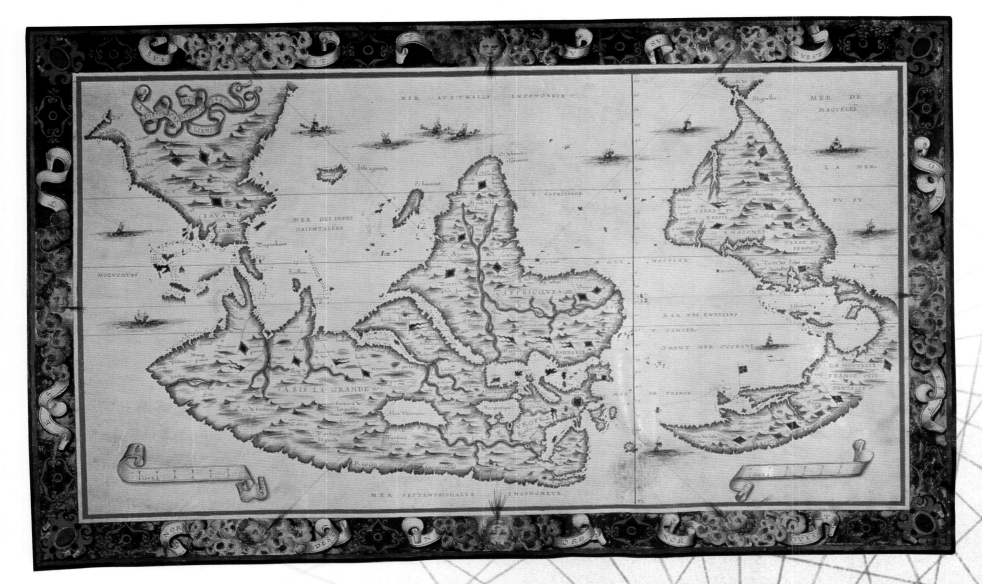

| **WORLD MAP FROM THE DIEPPE SCHOOL, *C.1542*** | Jean Rotz started and, after a period in England as Hydrographer to King Henry VIII, returned to, the Dieppe School of Cartography, bringing with him much knowledge of English waters that, history surmises, he willingly shared with Henri II of France, perhaps even contributing to the loss of Calais, England's last territory in France, in 1558.

Nicholas Desliens was a member of the school and drew up this chart *c.*1542. Apart from placing the known continents of the world, from our perspective, upside down, with North pointing downwards, a large portion of the continent of Australia is shown, which was thought to be unknown at that time, and the tip of Antarctica reaching towards South America. Were these relatively accurate parts charted by the Chinese expeditions of 1521? (© National Maritime Museum, London, A7244)

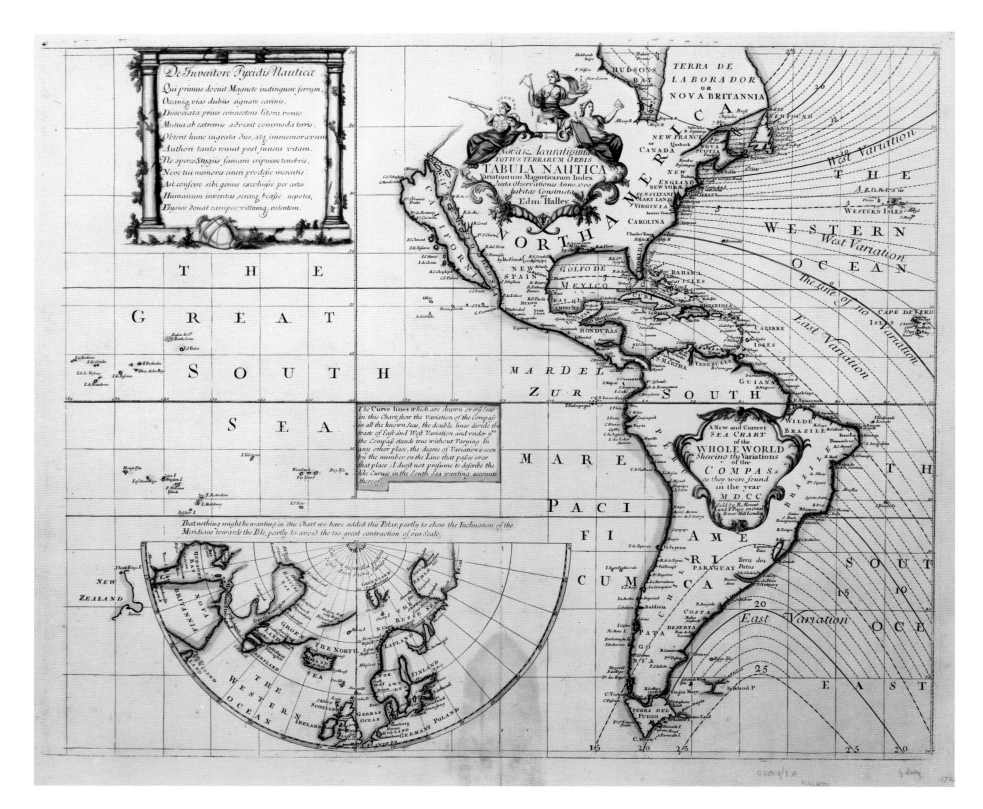

| EDMOND HALLEY'S 1700 CHART OF THE WESTERN ATLANTIC AND THE
AMERICAS | Edmond Halley's chart shows the lines of magnetic variation that he measured
while in command of the pink, *Paramour* (a pink was a small, square-rigged sailing ship with a
large overhanging stern, often used to carry ships' wooden masts). He covered the 'Old World'
and Asia with a correlating chart showing lines of magnetic variation. It is interesting to note the
mistaken charting of California as an island. (See also page 130) (© National Maritime Museum,
London, C508)

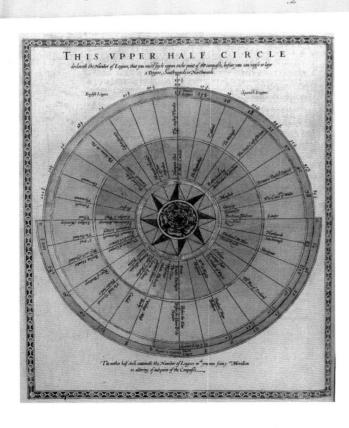

THIS VPPER HALF CIRCLE
declareth the Number of Leagues, that you must sayle vppon eache point of the compasse, before you can rayse or layre a Degree, Southwards or Northwards

English Leagues   Spanish Leagues

The nether half circle contenteth the Number of Leagues w.ᶜʰ you can fayng ᵗʰᵉ Meridian in altering of eache point of the Compasse.

| TOP LEFT | **EXTRACT FROM LIEUTENANT SPENCE'S ADMIRALTY SAILING DIRECTIONS OF THE ISLE OF WIGHT, 1805** | Nautical Description of the east part of the Channel between the Isle of Wight, and Hampshire, covering Cowes harbour in detail, hand-written by Lieutenant Graeme Spence in 1805. (Admiralty Library Manuscript Collection MSS 340)

| TOP RIGHT | **EXTRACT FROM A ROYAL NAVAL ACADEMY NOTEBOOK** |
The Royal Naval Academy at Portsmouth Naval Dockyard was started in 1730 to take young gentlemen under Admiralty patronage to train them for the navy. Numbers compared to the more normal method of entry under the patronage of a captain, joining as a captain's servant, or joining the quarterdeck through merit having entered as a rating foremastman during boyhood. The notebook of one student, later Lieutenant Mark Whyte (*fl.* 1749–1756) includes arithmetic, geometry, trigonometry, navigation, astronomy, fortification and gunnery. This extract discusses the method of estimating range by timing the difference between sight of the gunfire explosion and hearing it by counting the 'pulsations', the heartbeat of a fit man at rest (as 75 beats a minute) and then computing the distance. (Admiralty Library Manuscript Collection MSS 336)

| BOTTOM LEFT | **NAVIGATION CIRCLE FROM THE *MARINER'S MIRROUR*** |
Part of the navigational guidance from the *Mariner's Mirrour*, the English translation of Lucas Janszoon Waghenaer's *Spieghel der Zeevaerdt* 1584, by Sir Anthony Ashley, explaining, in the upper half circle how much further distance (in English, Spanish and Dutch leagues) to add to each compass course for various points of the compass to achieve a degree of latitude (which is 60 nautical miles). The 'nether half' allows the converse. (Reproduced by courtesy of the Royal Geographical Society with IBG, 264n.G4.p44)

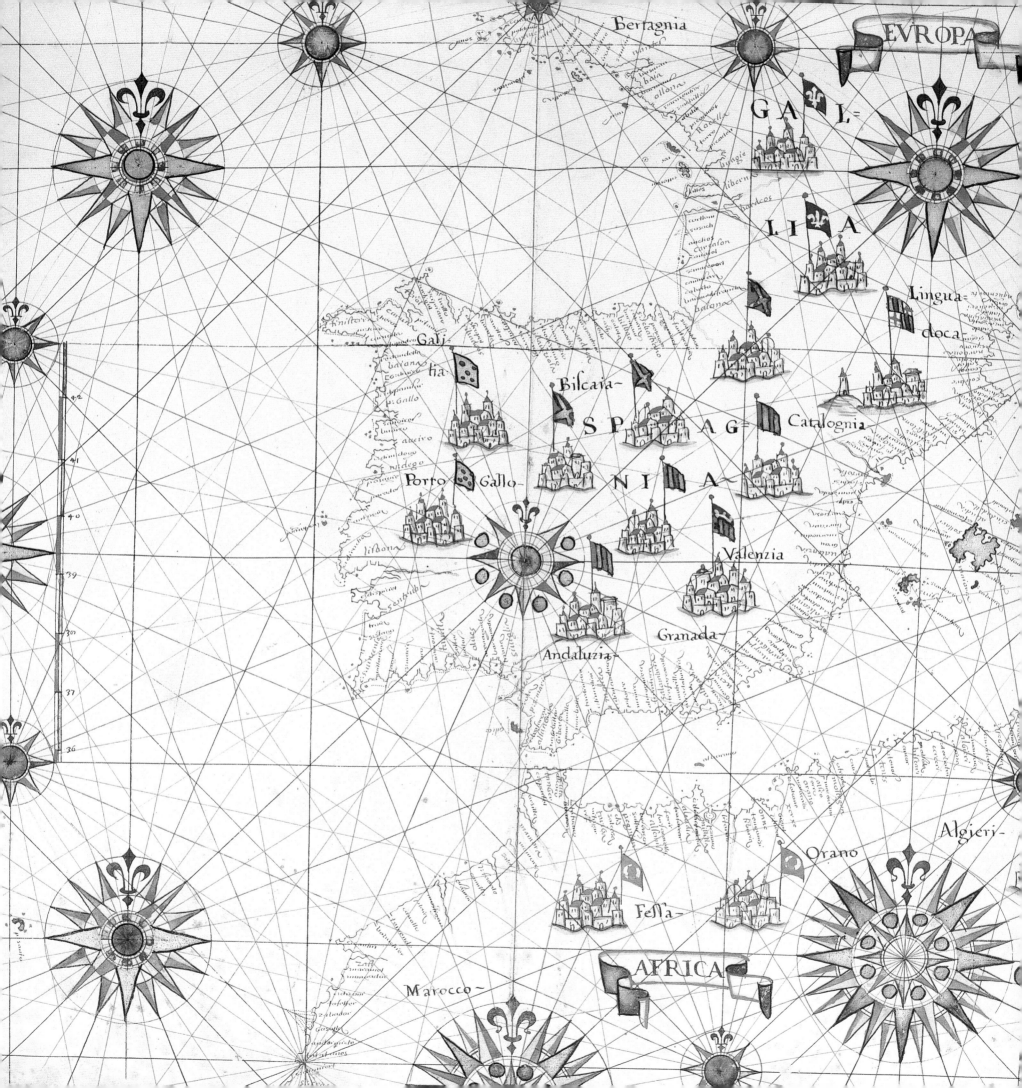

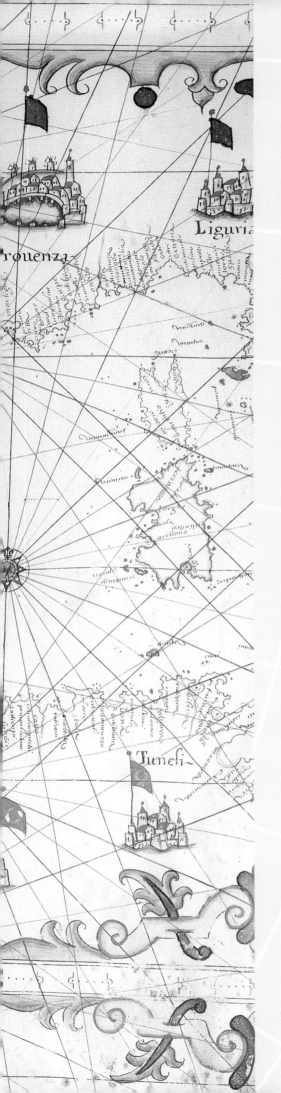

CHAPTER II

The Mediterranean

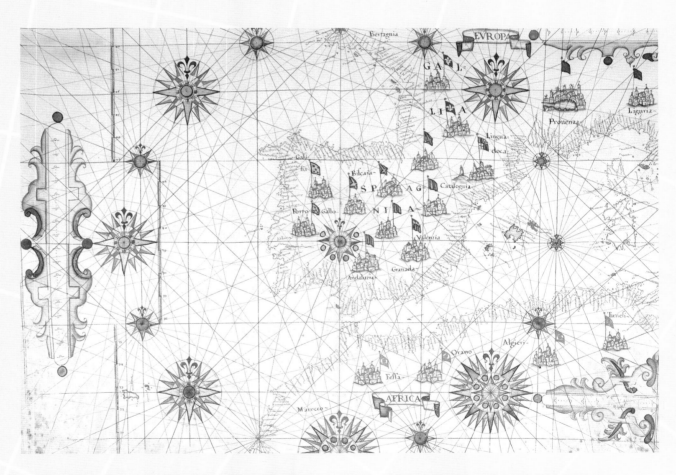

| LEFT DETAIL & ABOVE | **NORTH AFRICAN AND EUROPEAN COASTS BY HIERONYMUS GIRAVA, 1567** | A portolan chart showing the prevailing familiarity with the North African and European coasts, from Brittany to S. Croce (probably Agadir), Morocco. Purportedly by Hieronymus Girava (*fl.* 1556) from Tarragona, cosmographer to Charles V of Spain, and dated 1567, the cities have the relevant Portuguese, Spanish, French, Moor or mid-European state flags, and the author has drawn his beautiful state of the art compass roses. The worth of a cartographer seems to have been judged by the excellence of their completion. (Courtesy of The Hispanic Society of America, New York, K47)

THE Mediterranean is the birthplace of European navigation. Almost completely enclosed by land, the Sea has just a narrow entrance at the Strait of Gibraltar. At about 10 miles wide, the constriction of the Strait prevents the 6-hourly tidal ebb and flow of the Atlantic affecting the level within, as water is unable to gain momentum before the gravitational pull of the sun and moon reverses. As such, the Mediterranean tidal level only has a range of about 2 inches.

Egypt is regarded as the first Mediterranean nation to achieve the art of shipbuilding, about 5,000 years ago, spreading out from river transport sailing to coastal voyaging, sailing by day and anchoring by night, then more confidently making direct voyages rather than hugging the coast, as trade and power demanded more distant markets. Rowing galleys, powered by slaves, evolved as the predominant war vessel to protect, maraud and conquer, particularly with the unreliable Mediterranean winds. As Egyptian power waned the Cretans, Persians and Greeks fought for supremacy of the sea, with Greece dominating in the east until the inevitable clash with Rome, when the Greeks were utterly defeated in 260 BC at Mylae, off the north coast of Sicily. Against this historical background the Greeks developed the art of astronomy and charting, which peaked in the first and second centuries AD with the works of Ptolemy and Marinus of Tyre.

It has been said that if the Greeks were the first true chart-makers then the Phoenicians were the first true navigators. They built ships that excelled in trade and for war. Centred to start with on their ports of Tyre and Sidon in today's southern Syria, they built up a huge trade, and developed their navigational understanding in the use of the Pole Star to make a course to steer, and to offset the effect of wind and current on the course made good. A Phoenician fleet reputedly went around Africa in the seventh century BC, and they had set up a successful trading centre at present-day Tartessus in southwest Spain, with large sailing ships of a comparable size to the eighteenth-century East Indiamen, even sailing as far north as the Scilly Isles to bring back tin.

Over the centuries the centre of sea power moved westwards to Spain and Portugal, and once the means of voyaging across the Atlantic to America, and round Africa to the Orient was acquired, the Mediterranean became a relative backwater, although piracy flourished along the Barbary Coast, and the Levant Coast in the east for over 1000 years, with nations living off the sale of slaves and captured goods. The pirates' reach was renowned. In 1631 they sacked the town of Baltimore in Ireland and carried off the populace to sell as slaves in Algiers. But piracy in the Mediterranean was finally stamped out by the French conquest of Algiers in 1831, although various previous attempts had partial success: Admiral Blake with the Dutch in 1655, two French operations in 1682 and 1683, American operations from 1801 to 1805 and 1815 and a British-Dutch operation in 1816.

During the Napoleonic Wars, the British found themselves using the much more reliable French charts while maintaining fleets in the Mediterranean to blockade French seaports such as Toulon and Marseilles in order to prevent Napoleon's plan of joining the French Mediterranean fleet with the Atlantic one to a combined fleet strong enough to hold off the British navy, to allow his invasion fleet of barges to make their way across the Channel. Nelson even used a French chart on board *Victory* at the Battle of Trafalgar in October 1805.

With the ending of the French threat over Europe in the nineteenth century the more benign aspects of British maritime supremacy emerged, and Rear-Admiral Sir Francis Beaufort, the Navy's Hydrographer for 26 years, planned the complete charting of the Mediterranean to update and supercede the earlier charts of the French and Spanish, together with those manuscript charts compiled by individual ship's masters and captains and sent in to the Admiralty, as often as not to lie in piles unexamined until the Hydrographic Office had put in place the necessary systems for recording and archiving this information.

Beaufort himself had produced an excellent survey of Karamania, the southern coast of Turkey in Asia Minor when commanding the survey vessel *Frederickssteen* in 1810, the same year that Captain William Smyth, known ever after for his formidable surveying achievements as 'Mediterranean Smyth', started a task which he continued until 1824 – the charting of much of the Mediterranean coastline, including those along the Adriatic and Aegean seas, Italy and Sicily, Corsica and part of Sardinia, Tunis and Morocco.

First, using the Spanish Don Vicente Tofino's *Atlas Maritimo de Espana* published in Madrid in 1789 through Cayetano Valdés who had worked with George Vancouver on his British Columbia survey 20 years earlier and the work of Alcalá-Galiano, who had died a hero commanding a 74-gun Spanish ship, *Bahama*, at Trafalgar, Smyth corrected some errors in the Strait of Gibraltar and the Mediterranean coast of Spain. In 1813 he joined the Anglo-Sicilian flotilla defending Sicily, and he started a detailed survey of the island.

But in surveying circles Smyth was also known, as were others, for his artistic talents, and he decorated many of his charts with archaeological views and Roman coins as well as navigational views.

His appointment to conduct a full Mediterranean survey came out of his Sicilian survey, published in 1823 as the *Hydrography of Sicily, Malta and the Adjacent Islands*. Next he was granted clearance from the ruler of Tripoli to survey the North African coast, which he did after the more urgent survey of the Ionian islands, where ships were continuously running aground. In 1818 Smyth negotiated an agreement with the Austrians to carry out a joint survey of the whole of the Adriatic, Smyth in *Aid* and the Austrian ship *Velox* under his command.

He also co-operated with the French, in Malta in 1816 with Captain Gauttier. Lord Melville at the Admiralty sent him to Paris to avoid duplication. The French surveyed the Greek archipelago and the British concentrated on the Western Mediterranean and North Africa, which Smyth conducted in HMS *Adventure* from Tripoli to Alexandria. Captain Frederick William Beechey, newly returned from the Arctic with Captain William Parry, surveyed the coastline walking with his brother dressed as Arabs. Smyth surveyed the remainder of the African Mediterranean coast, parts of Sardinia and the west coast of Italy, while the French surveyed Corsica.

The Mediterranean was re-invigorated by the opening of the Suez Canal in 1869 when it became the quickest route to India and the Far East, with each of the bigger maritime nations maintaining a large fleet to protect its trade passing through. The small island of Malta came into its own astride the relatively narrow channel between the tip of Italy and the northernmost part of Africa.

The Junior Hydrographer's Revenge, 1903

A lieutenant surveying in the Royal Navy, 'Tubby' Lockyer, had worked under one of the navy's most demanding officers, Captain Alvin Coote Corry. He was a brilliant officer, but a tartar and disciplinarian who, as a captain on the China Station, had more officers courts-martialled than all the other captains put together. So many officers had suffered that they were referred to as having been awarded the Corry medal. Years later Vice-Admiral Sir John Edgell, one of the navy's chief hydrographers, tells the story that Lieutenant Lockyer had wanted to shoot partridges at Mudros over a weekend, but that Captain Corry required the harbour survey of Port Mudros (now spelt Moudhros), to be completed. Port Mudros and Mudros Bay are part of the Greek island of Lemnos in the Aegean Sea at the eastern Mediterranean.

Lieutenant Lockyer, drawing out the survey on board, exacted eternal revenge on his unpopular captain, unbeknownst to him, by naming the four hills on the chart, which was printed and sold world-wide, at the easterly headland by the entrance to the bay, Yam, Yrroc, Eb and Denmad. If you read these names backwards you will understand why! He also named one of the hills after his pet name for the girl he married, Nulma.

The chart itself shows how refined the techniques of surveying had become by the turn of the century, and had the look of the standard style of charts up to the 1980s. The hatching gives the main topographical features such as the hills that can be seen from seawards and two leading bearings. These are shown so that a ship can take a safe compass heading to run into the bay between the two islands in the middle, based on a left- and right-hand edge of two distinctive hills remaining 'closed' to each other. Comprehensive soundings give a good 'feel' for safe depths for any ship and isobath (fathom) lines are shown around the shoreline. The nature of the seabed is shown (with the code on the cartouche) to indicate the potential holding ground for the anchor. Magnetic variation is given on each compass rose as standard, and they are positioned to enable a navigator to run his parallel ruler across from the course he would draw on the chart, to keep clear of marked navigational dangers, on to the compass rose to read off the course to steer. Navigational views of significant land features, as seen from typical courses into the bay, are shown at the foot of the chart.

(UKHO © British Crown Copyright)

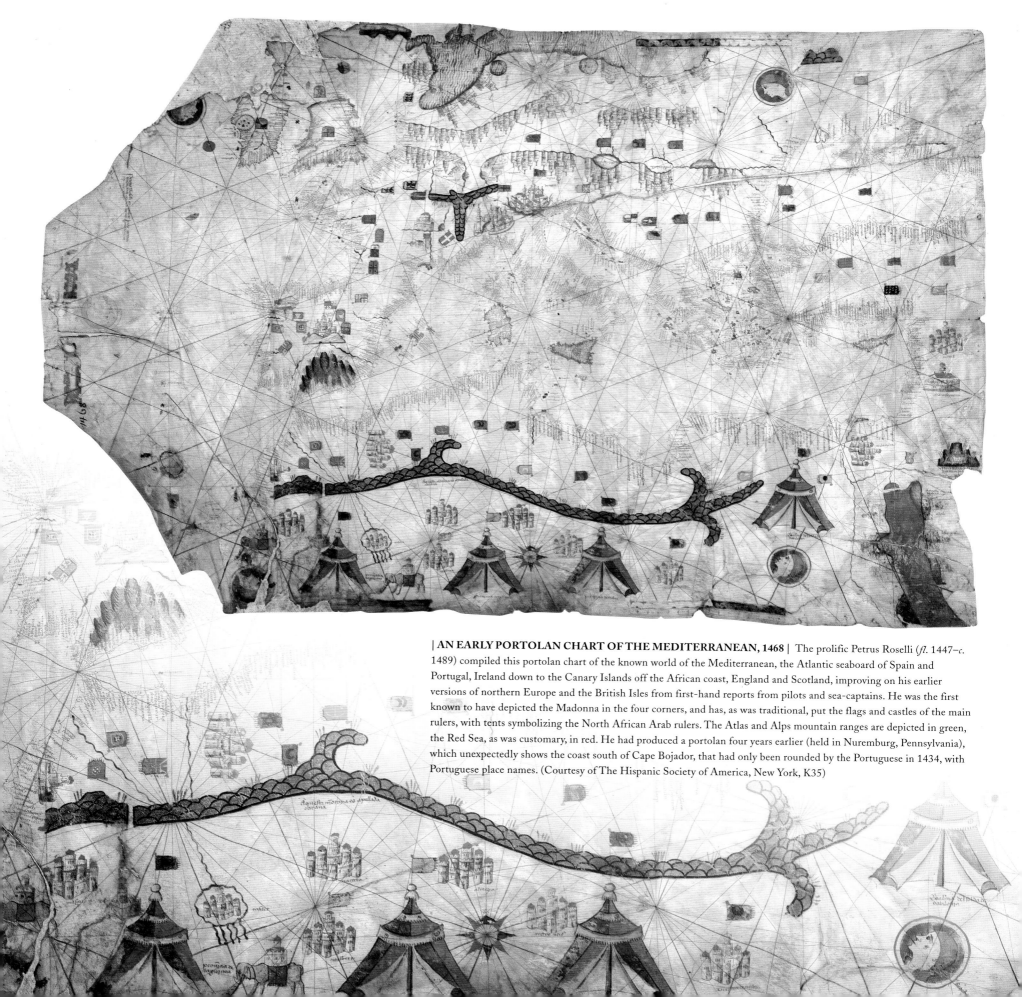

| AN EARLY PORTOLAN CHART OF THE MEDITERRANEAN, 1468 | The prolific Petrus Roselli (*fl.* 1447–*c.* 1489) compiled this portolan chart of the known world of the Mediterranean, the Atlantic seaboard of Spain and Portugal, Ireland down to the Canary Islands off the African coast, England and Scotland, improving on his earlier versions of northern Europe and the British Isles from first-hand reports from pilots and sea-captains. He was the first known to have depicted the Madonna in the four corners, and has, as was traditional, put the flags and castles of the main rulers, with tents symbolizing the North African Arab rulers. The Atlas and Alps mountain ranges are depicted in green, the Red Sea, as was customary, in red. He had produced a portolan four years earlier (held in Nuremburg, Pennsylvania), which unexpectedly shows the coast south of Cape Bojador, that had only been rounded by the Portuguese in 1434, with Portuguese place names. (Courtesy of The Hispanic Society of America, New York, K35)

| RIGHT | **BARTOLOMMEO ZAMBERTI, *ISOLARIO*, 1485** | Sonetti, whose real name was Bartolommeo Zamberto, was something of a poet as well as a Venetian shipmaster, for he wrote his navigational guidance in verse, it is thought to make it easier to remember. He compiled the first *printed* sea charts in 1485, 49 of them bound as a book called *Isolario* (the Island-Book) covering Crete, Cyprus and the Greek Archipelago. He states that he constructed them with the compass, and each chart has the eight-pointed compass rose with the traditional symbols for the directions. Off-lying rocks are indicated by +, the symbol still used today. The instructions to get to Rhodes ('per Rodi'), written in sonnet form alongside, are in Venetian dialect. At the time, the Knights of St John of Jerusalem were based in Rhodes, until they were ousted by the Turks, and eventually settled in Malta. (Reproduced by courtesy of the Royal Geographical Society with IBG, 265.f.1.p9)

| FAR RIGHT | **PER RODI (TO GO TO RHODES)** | The second illustration shows the island of Caloiero, a rocky islet in the Aegean, supposedly near Kos, surmounted by a chapel where two Christian monks reputedly lived and would help sailors who called by, giving water as sustenance, indicated by the derrick and basket to hoist and lower supplies. (Reproduced by courtesy of the Royal Geographical Society with IBG, F.1.p34)

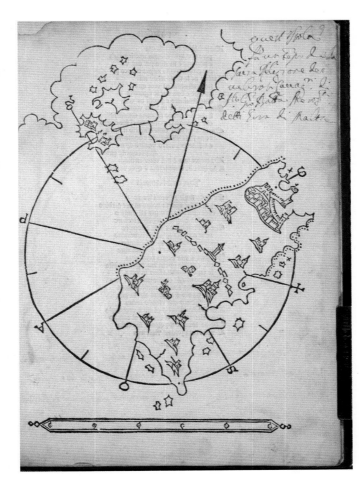

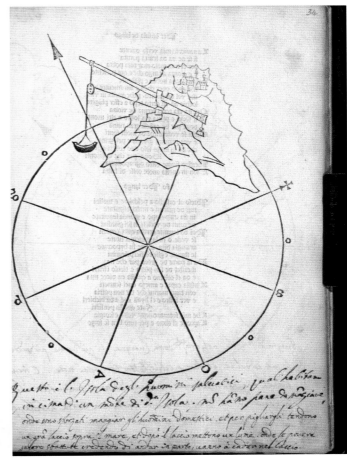

| RIGHT | **SIR ROBERT DUDLEY'S CHART OF TUNIS AND SICILY, *C.* 1646** | Covering Tunis and Sicily, this chart is an example of Sir Robert Dudley's fine chart work, which comes from his epic work *Dell' Arcano del Mare*, the first English sea atlas, published in Florence in 1645–46. It was also the first atlas composed on Mercator's projection and incorporating the entire known world. His work is immediately recognizable for its beautiful calligraphy, and the excellent engraving by the Italian Antonio Lucini. (© National Maritime Museum, London, C4117)

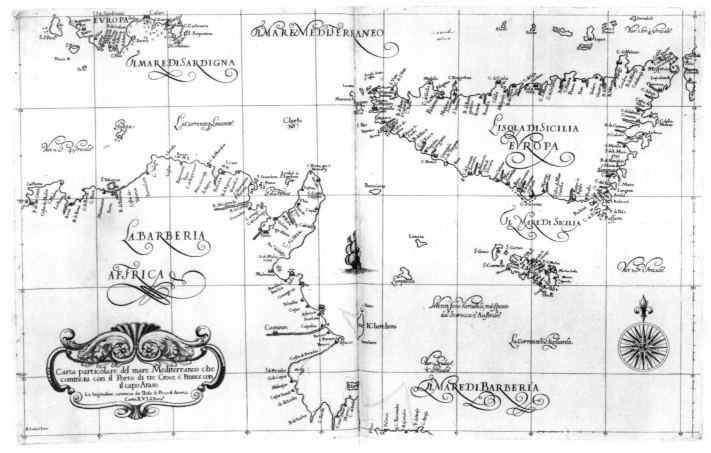

APPEARANCE OF THE CHANNEL BETWEEN THE ISLANDS OF LIPARI AND VULCANO.

VIEW TAKEN FROM THE ANCHORAGE ON EXMOUTH BANK.

THE ÆOLIAN ISLANDS AS SEEN FROM THE PENROSE ROCKS.

THE CHANNEL OF MESSINA FROM THE ANCHORAGE AT THE FARO POINT.

| LEFT | **CAPTAIN SMYTH'S NAVIGATIONAL VIEWS AROUND SICILY** | William Henry Smyth was a founder and then President of the Royal Geographical Society, a Fellow of the Royal Society and President of the Royal Astronomical Society. He rose to the rank of Rear-Admiral. Before he finished sea-service in 1824, his Mediterranean surveys were highly acclaimed for their pictorial and cartographical elegance and accuracy. His interest in antiquities was reflected in his drawings, for example, of ancient Greek coins, and his pictorial views won him an exceptional Admiralty award of £500.

These four evocative navigational views, engraved from Smyth's originals, fulfilled a navigational function, but more, show his artistic expertise, detail and sense of mood, such as the skies, the birds flying off the stack rock in the first view, the smoking volcano of Stromboli in the second and third, and the local fishermen spearing a swordfish in the fourth. (© National Maritime Museum, London)

| RIGHT | **MEDITERRANEAN HARBOUR CHARTS OF 1707** | This trio of delightful but crude charts are from a set of 53 French manuscript charts held in the Admiralty Library covering the Mediterranean and dating from 1707.

The top chart is painted to achieve a naïve three-dimensional view of the Gulf of Naples and harbour. With a few soundings it would have been useful as a guide or in a presentational sense only.

In the same volume is the plan of Marseilles which has 10° lines of bearing drawn in red from prominent headlands as gun emplacement arcs of fire, and working pencil notes, too.

The plan of Alexandria harbour in Egypt, nearby the site of Nelson's victory at Aboukir Bay nearly 100 years later in 1798, has extensive soundings and a plan of the outside fortifications of the town. All three are probably by the same hand, although the compass roses, indicating North as best fitted the page, are of a different design. The modern convention of North to the top of the page came at a later date. (Admiralty Library Manuscript Collection MSS 353)

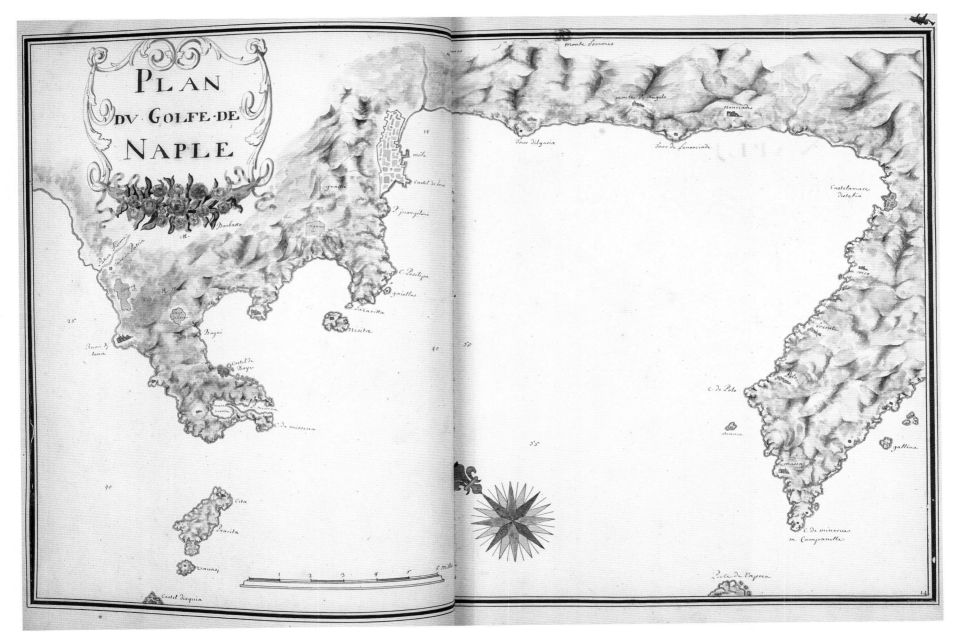

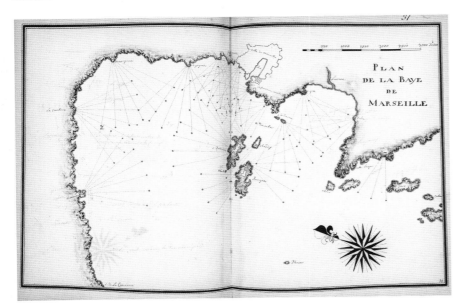

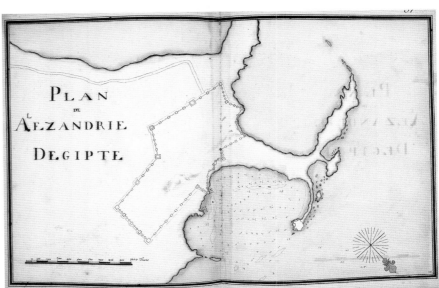

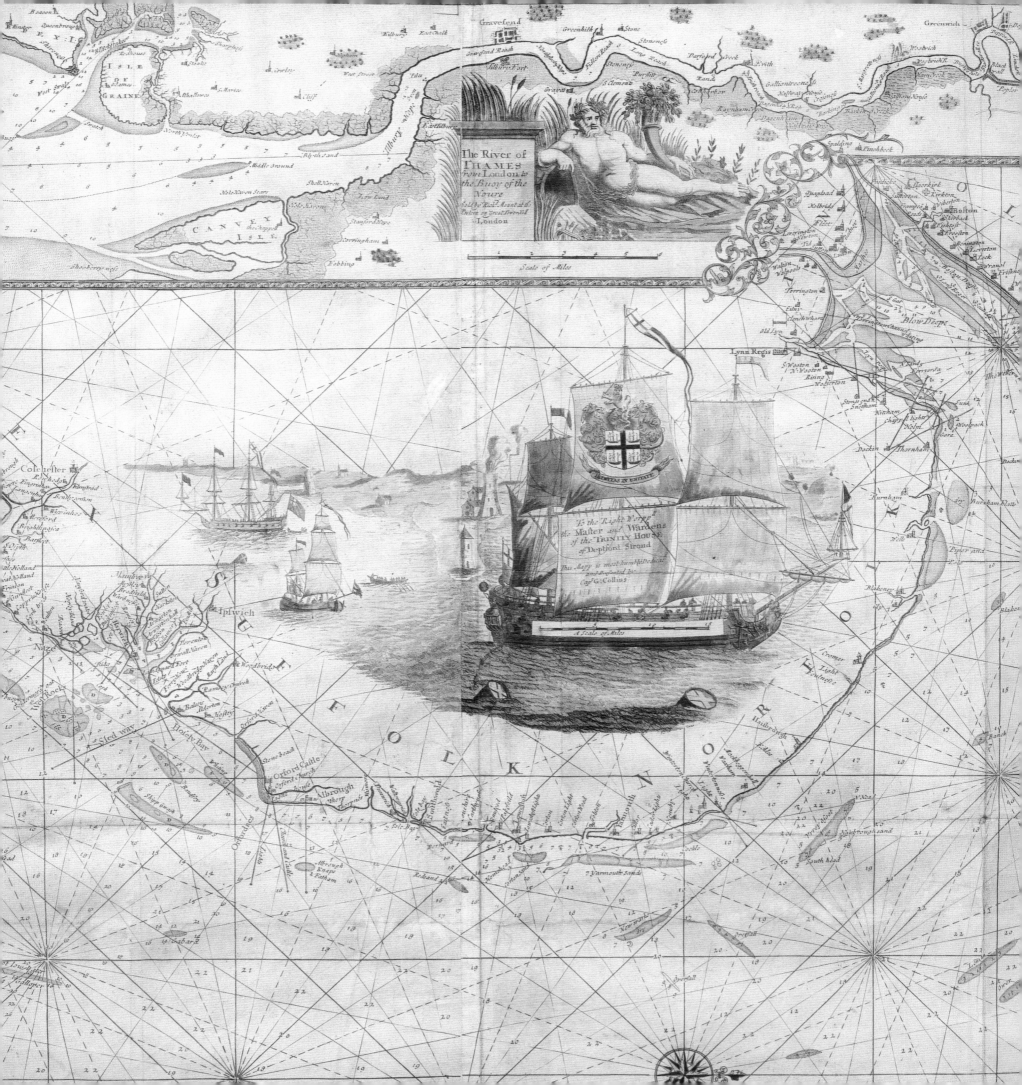

The River of
THAMES
from London to
the Buoy of the
Nore
Sold by Rich.d Mount at the
Postern on Great Towerhill
London

Scale of Miles

To the Right Worp.ll
th.e Master and Wardens
of the TRINITY HOUSE
of Deptford Strond
This Mapp is most humbly Dedicated
and Presented by
Cap.t G. Collins

A Scale of Miles

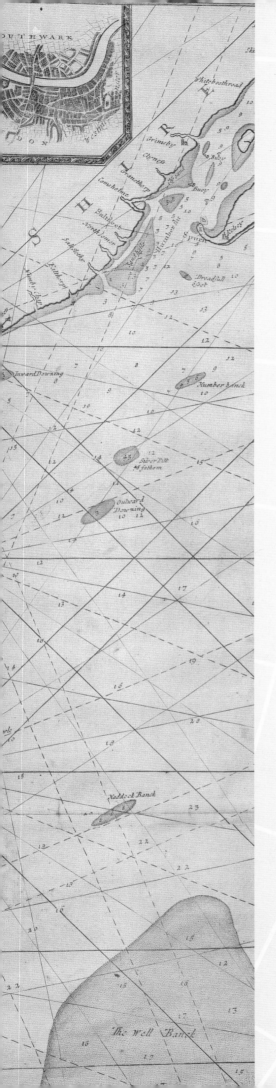

The British Coasts, the North Sea, Northern Europe and the Baltic

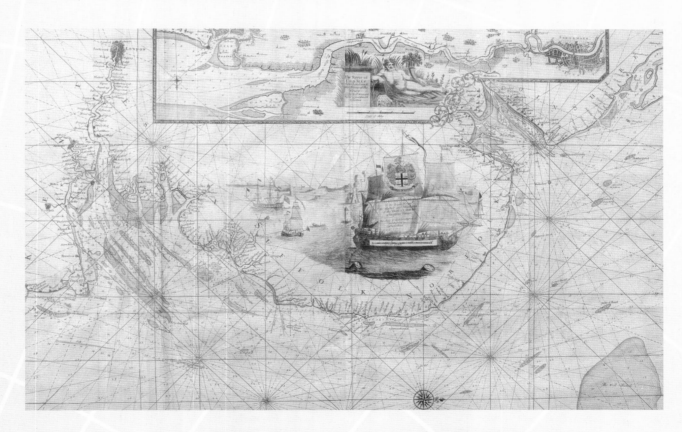

| LEFT DETAIL & ABOVE | **CAPTAIN COLLINS' CHART OF THE RIVER THAMES** | This beautiful chart by Greenvile Collins shows a wonderful eye for detail and presentation: he dedicated it to Trinity House, originally a guild of English 'shipmen and mariners' started by Henry VIII in 1517. Elizabeth I extended its original responsibilities for the 'relief, increase and augmentation of the shipping of this our realm of England' to include the erection of sea-marks. Richard Mount (1684–1722) sold this chart in London as part of Collins' *Great Britain's Coasting Pilot*. William Page joined the company which continued well into the nineteenth century selling charts as Mount and Page. (Courtesy of The Worshipful Society of Apothecaries of London)

BY the sixteenth century the Dutch held a virtual monopoly on the coastal west European trade, carrying the riches of the East and newly discovered America from Lisbon and Spanish ports to Holland, the Baltic and British Isles. The Dutch seaman and cartographer, Lucas Janszoon Wagenaer, published his well-known, two-volume set of charts of the northern waters between 1584 and 1585, as the *Spieghel der Zeevaerdt*, a manual of navigation, pilot book and a series of nautical charts covering from the Zuider Zee to Cadiz. They included the first coverage of the English coastline from the Wash to Cornwall. The *Spieghel der Zeevaerdt* was euphorically received and appeared in Dutch, French and German editions. The Earl of Effingham, Lord High Admiral to Queen Elizabeth I, was so impressed that he commissioned Sir Anthony Ashley to publish an English edition, with entirely re-engraved charts in London in 1588, the year of the Spanish Armada, as the very popular *Mariner's Mirrour*. Still in use over a century later, Wagenaer's name, anglicized to 'Waggoner' became the generic term for sea charts of all kinds, supplanting the old term, rutter, taken from the French *routier*.

The Dutch continued their lead in the publishing of sea charts with the Blaeu family who created a number of sea atlases based on Wagenaer's work. The irony for the English was that during the Anglo-Dutch Wars of the 1650s they were

| THE *MARINER'S MIRROUR*, 1587 | Chart of the Sea Coast of Andalusia with Cadiz and the approach to the 'straight of Gibraltar' taken from the *Mariner's Mirrour*. There are naïve coastal elevations of the Granada Mountains (optimistic as they are about 100 miles eastward) and the aspect of Gibraltar as approached from the west. Augustine Ryther, who engraved the Armada charts, engraved the English version, keeping symbolic details such as the donkey near the salt pans, and the Spanish galley (with oarsmen) and galleon. (Reproduced by courtesy of the Royal Geographical Society with IBG, 264 G4 p.127)

using Dutch printed charts, although there was one important exception.

In the turmoil of Elizabethan politics, where so many tried to impress the Queen to gain land and power, the court was a place of intrigue and changing allegiances. Affairs were disapproved of, but happened, and the son of a dalliance between Robert Dudley, Earl of Leicester and Lady Douglas Sheffield, the daughter of the Lord High Admiral, the Earl of Effingham, was, through historic accident, to produce a collection of important charts of the period. The young Robert Dudley sailed with Francis Drake on his expedition to Cadiz in 1596 to 'singe the beard' of the King of Spain and was knighted for his distinguished service. Marrying Elizabeth Southwell, the sister of Thomas Cavendish, who was the second Englishman to circumnavigate the world, and inheriting two large fortunes, from his father and from his uncle, the Earl of Warwick, he approached James I to grant him legitimacy to inherit the titles of his father and uncle, but fell out of the court's favour. When in 1605 he sailed to Italy with his bride, he refused the King's order to return and was outlawed. He settled in Florence and worked for the Grand Duke of Tuscany, Cosimo II, directing the construction of the important port of Leghorn, draining the marshes, and fighting Barbary pirates.

But he will be chiefly remembered for his production of three volumes of charts, all beautifully and painstakingly prepared, engraved by an Italian, Antonio Lucini, and published in Florence in 1645 and 1646. *Dell' Arcano del Mare* (Secrets of the Sea) was the first comprehensive series of 130 charts drawn on the Mercator Projection, along with details of all the navigational instruments of the time, mounted in *volvelles*, which are discs mounted centrally to show how the instruments worked, examples of shipwork, and a plan for a naval force with five rates of ship. These he wrote himself in Italian.

Many captains still preferred manuscript charts to printed charts, and, while there was nothing produced in England to rival the Dutch printed charts, a group of 'platte-makers' as they were then known, combined under the patronage of the Worshipful Company of Drapers. The Drapers took a pragmatic view of the rules of membership of the Company at this time when there was a certain amount of rivalry with the Stationers' Company. This, coupled with the phenomenal growth in demand for charts by the increase of British trade around the 1600s with the burgeoning East India Company and activity in the West Indies, found a marriage between the chart producers and the Drapers. Dubbed the Thames School by the well-known historian, Helen Wallis, they were active from around 1600 through to the early years of the eighteenth century. Probably the best known are William Hack (*c.*1680–1700), who produced about 1600 manuscript charts, Nicholas Comberford and John Thornton, who also went on to print maps and charts. Others who took on apprentices, and who were in turn

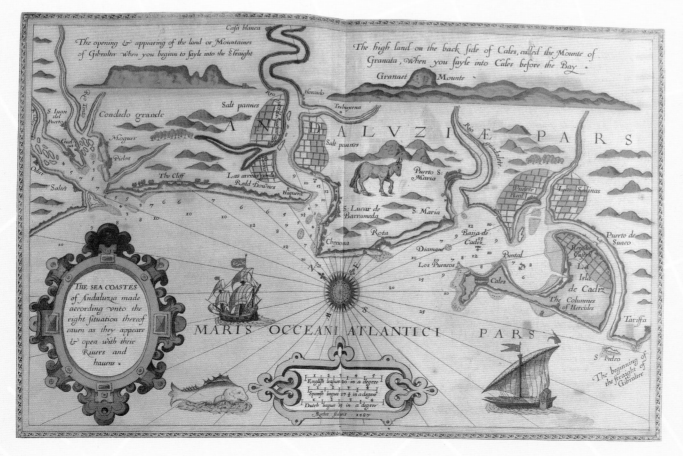

made Liverymen of the Drapers, included Gabriel Tatton (*c.* 1600), John Daniell (1614–42), described in the Drapers' archives as in 1622 taking on six 'Apprentice Patternmakers' at the Irongate, including William Hanman 'seacard drawer at S Katherine by the Tower', and John Burston (1638–65). Between them, their manuscript charts covered almost the entire known world and provided an important starting point for the next phase of charting, which was accelerated by the Dutch attack on Chatham and the British fleet in the River Medway in 1667, adding to the misery already experienced by the Plague and the Great Fire of London. John Seller's *The English Pilot* published in 1671, still relied heavily on Dutch plates.

Samuel Pepys, a talented musician and famous for his diaries, was also a gifted administrator and rose through his merits, surviving political swings from Commonwealth to Monarch, to become First Secretary to the Admiralty in 1673, having reformed the navy while Clerk of the Navy Board. In 1681 he commissioned the first real survey of British harbours and coasts and was instrumental in the appointment of Captain Greenvile Collins to undertake the work, with the title Hydrographer to the King. Collins had gained his sea-going experience in the navy, sailing under Sir John Narborough as master of the *Sweepstake*, during a voyage instigated by Charles II to break through the Strait of Magellan and into the Spanish monopoly in the Pacific. Collins' mammoth survey took seven years and he published his results in 1693, the same year as *Le Neptune François*, described below, was published in France, as *Great Britain's Coasting Pilot* of 48 charts. The first edition sold out by 1728 but, reprinted by chart-sellers Mount and Page, it was sold until 1792, with 19 further editions.

In 1698 Edmond Halley, sometime Savilian Professor of Geometry at Oxford, Secretary of the Royal Society and Astronomer Royal, had set a precedent, which was to be the first and the last civilian appointment in the Royal Navy, as Captain of HMS *Paramour*. The purpose was to carry out an astronomical and magnetic survey in the Southern Hemisphere to ascertain a method of finding that most elusive of navigational information – longitude. His lunar tables did work, but were extremely time-consuming and mathematically complex. His first lieutenant, Edmund Harrison, thought he had a better answer, but Halley dismissed it. The upshot of the argument was insubordination almost to the point of mutiny, and Halley had his first lieutenant arrested and court-martialled. After this experience the Admiralty vowed never to put a civilian in charge of a navy ship again.

During the seventeenth century France was as interested in establishing trade and opportunities overseas as the Dutch and English. Louis XIV, in encouraging science and the arts, had the Royal Observatory set up in Paris in 1667, and an ambitious survey of the French coasts, set up by the King's Chief Minister, Jean Baptiste Colbert, was completed using triangulation which gave considerable accuracy. The resulting set or atlas of charts was published in 1693 by Hubert Jaillot as *Le Neptune François*. These beautiful charts, which covered from Norway to the Strait of Gibraltar in 29 coastal charts and included depths along suggested coastline routes, ports, sandbanks and rocks, gave France the cartographic edge over Britain. Their Hydrographic Office, set up in 1720, maintained this lead well into the eighteenth century, with a revision to the *Neptune* by J N Bellin coming out in 1753. Jean Picard, a French astronomer of the time, used the longitude coordinates derived from the times of the eclipses of Jupiter's satellites first observed by the Observatoire Director, Jean Dominique Cassini, to fix the land coordinates of France accurately. Louis XIV

| SAMUEL PEPYS BY SIR GODFREY KNELLER, *C.* 1684 | Samuel Pepys was instrumental in appointing Captain Greenvile Collins to carry out the first full coastal survey of the British Isles. The artist's studio copy of Sir Godfrey Kneller's portrait of Samuel Pepys is held in the Pepys Library. Spanning 50 years, Kneller was 'Court recorder' from Charles II to George II. (Pepys Library, Magdalene College, Cambridge)

exclaimed that his geographers were losing him land in the west as fast as his armies were gaining land in the east. As with the Anglo-Dutch Wars, the British found themselves using French charts when planning attacks on the French at La Rochelle, and even into the Revolutionary and Napoleonic Wars.

But the British were making significant progress on the charting of their own coastal waters. Murdoch Mackenzie, already at 30 a mathematics professor, was appointed by the Navy Board in 1742 to carry out a geographic and hydrographic survey of the Orkney Islands. He used new surveying principles to do this, which he wrote up in a treatise, and they became the standard for the next hundred years or so. The Navy Board loaned him a plane table, a theodolite and a measuring chain for the work. He measured a 3-mile base line across a frozen lake, and observed its direction relative to his magnetic compass. He then took bearings from a suitable hilltop at either end of the base line with the theodolite to previously placed beacons, and then extended these triangles across the Orkneys. As an aside, Greenvile Collins advised Pepys in a covering note of the potential of Scapa Flow as an anchorage for ships of the line – a pre-cursor of the First World War battleship refuge from which to strike out at the Germans. Mackenzie checked the scale by measuring latitude with a fix of the noon-day Sun using Hadley's quadrant on Kirkwall and North Ronaldsay. Taking a small boat he was able to delineate the coastline and off-lying rocks by taking intersecting compass bearings to two or more of his triangulated bearings ashore. He was able to perfect this method, publishing the results in an atlas in 1750 entitled *Orcades*. He then spent the next 20 years surveying around the whole of Ireland and along the west coast of Britain finishing in 1770 at Pembroke, typically using beaches or coastal plains for his 10-mile base when possible, otherwise observing the latitude of two positions.

His nephew, a lieutenant in the navy, and also named Murdoch Mackenzie, learned his craft when he sailed with Admiral John Byron, grandfather of Lord Byron the poet, on his hasty and unproductive circumnavigation of the world in HMS *Dolphin* in 1764, searching for *Terra Australis Incognita*. He took over where his uncle had left off, moving through the Bristol Channel, south-west to Lands End and thence to Plymouth. The Admiralty ordered him to survey the Thames Estuary in 1775, and, keeping the family connections, with his cousin Graeme Spence, assisting, it is known

The UK Hydrographic Office

Alexander Dalrymple was appointed as the first Royal Navy Hydrographer in 1795. He contributed many of his own charts that he had already published during his time in the Far East, but so huge was the task that he didn't actually get any charts organized and out into the navy during his tenure. Dalrymple did much with a small staff and little money from the Admiralty, introducing a more defined system for captains to submit their Remark Books. With one copper printing press by 1808 he had engraved 30 large-scale charts of the English Channel, based on French charts to the south and those of Murdoch Mackenzie and Graeme Spence to the north, along with Lieutenant John Murray, back from surveying Australian coasts.

Dalrymple recommended setting up what became the Admiralty Chart Committee in 1808, which was to review and recommend procedures for getting charts out urgently into the navy. Captain Thomas Hurd was appointed to re-chart the Bay of Brest after, in March 1804, the 74-gun second-rate battle ship *Magnificent*, part of the blockading fleet sailing back and forth around the confusion of rocks and islets, struck an uncharted rock and was a complete loss. Hurd worked in Dalrymple's office drawing up his observations and became one of the members of the Chart Committee. He became Dalrymple's successor in 1808.

The hydrographic peace dividend that resulted after the British victory at Waterloo in 1815 was an ambitious plan to fill in all the gaps in a world sea survey. The Royal Navy, reduced from 145,000 to 20,000 men, was to fulfil a peacekeeping role; capturing slavers, and attacking piracy. The blue-print Hurd laid down was highly ambitious, aiming to cover the whole of China and the eastern seas from Kamchatka to Van Diemen's Land (Tasmania), the east and west coasts of Africa, the now much frequented trade wind sailing route from the Cape of Good Hope to New Holland (Australia) which had uncharted islands and shoals, the coastlines of 'our Dominions', of South America, the southern shores of the Mediterranean and the Grecian Archipelago and in British waters the Firth of Forth, north and west coasts of Scotland and much of Ireland.

Hurd also realized the need for a corps of specialist officers who were proficient in the art and science of hydrography, and the Royal Naval Surveying Service was set up in 1817, with better pay and ships allocated for the job. This was an important event for world trade as Hurd planned to sell the printed Admiralty charts to the general public, perhaps more with the motive of raising money to be able to increase the wages of Office staff, but also to be sold through a number of chart agents, not just through the so-called 'King's Geographer', William Faden. Their charts quickly became accepted as the last word in accuracy and reliability. By 1821 there were sufficient Admiralty charts to warrant the first catalogue, drawn up by Hurd, who died in 1823.

William Parry was appointed as the next Hydrographer in 1823, although he was as keen to pursue his Arctic exploration as he was to carry out his duties as Hydrographer. He had an able assistant in Lieutenant Alexander Becher, who was able to keep the Office ticking over during his absences, with John Walker running the administration. The long-serving Secretary to the Admiralty, Sir John Croker, had an almost personal detest of the Office. He put such difficulties in the way that Captain Peter Heywood and Captain William Smyth left the Office, hounded by Croker's unreasonable demands for weekly reports. Smyth left with all his Mediterranean material where he had made outstanding surveys. The Office of Lord High Admiral was in 1827 given to HRH the Duke of Clarence, who became the Sailor King, William IV. He took a personal interest in charting, and overruled Croker by upping the department's manpower by six extra draughtsmen. Parry retired aged 40 to take on the job of Commissioner of the Australian Agricultural Company.

In 1829, aged 55, Sir Francis Beaufort took over as Hydrographer and, with the resignation of Croker, the way became clear for him to organize naval surveying very much as he saw fit.

Naval needs were not merchant needs. Warships needed to be prepared to go to any part of the world, following unexpected courses, and put into minor ports as well, so the charts they used had to cover all coastlines in great detail, and have a modern appearance, finely engraved, undecorated.

He sent surveyors around the world – Robert Fitzroy to South America, William Fitzwilliam Owen to Africa. The survey of the British Isles, initiated by Hurd, and pushed forward by Beaufort, was finally completed in 1855, the year of Beaufort's retirement.

During Beaufort's aegis of 26 years, his team created 1437 charts in 113 surveys world-wide, a prodigious average of one a week. Chart information became standardized under Beaufort: the Hydrographic Office seal on each chart carried the Hydrographer's initials (e.g. F.B.); tidal heights (e.g. high water springs) were given, then tidal ranges, ebb and flow directional arrows. Buoys were shown with a small symbol; nautic miles became sea miles; compass roses were shown with true directions, and the magnetic variation as an arrow to one side; a 5-fathom line was marked from 1835, with depth in feet within, and many other refinements were drawn with which navigators are familiar today and which set the pictorial trend to chartmakers around the globe.

The conditions of service at that time could require dedication as shown by the master commanding HMS *Investigator*, George Thomas, an appointment he held for 25 years. He was employed surveying the English Channel, the Thames approaches, the North Sea, the east coasts of England and Scotland and the Orkneys and Shetlands continuously for 35 years. He died on board the brig *Mastiff* returning from working the Orkneys in 1846.

that he used the surveying methods devised and described by his uncle in his important book *Treatise on Maritim* (sic) *Surveying*. Spence was later to make an important advance in the instrumentation that facilitated surveying – the station pointer, which was soon adopted as standard naval equipment. Written of by Murdoch senior and almost certainly used by Murdoch junior and Spence it was, in essence, a three-armed protractor which, when lined up with the three angles measured by the Hadley quadrant, gave a position point where the three lines intersected.

Spence was appointed Chief Surveyor to the Admiralty in 1788, having worked with Mackenzie to sound out and chart a new and deeper sailing channel into the Thames Estuary that was named the Queen's Channel, and which was then buoyed by Trinity House in 1775. They then went back to Plymouth to complete the work, resulting in the channels being buoyed, and also important shore batteries sited to control the approaches. Spence also worked for Trinity House advising them on the siting of lighthouses, such as Portland and Owers lightship, then to survey from South Foreland to Beachy Head, with special attention to the feared Goodwin Sands, then back to the Thames Estuary to work on surveying the shipping route south-westwards through the Kings Channel and East Swin, and over the swatch-way into the West Swin, thence north-eastwards to Orfordness and Harwich. In 1801 he piloted Admiral Nelson returning to England from his successful battle at Copenhagen in HMS *Medusa*, which he had discovered and buoyed shortly before: it is still called the Medusa Channel today. Spence was an important continuation of the Mackenzies and he retired to the Hydrographic Office to write up his and their work until he died in 1812.

The invidious situation for a British naval captain, who was expected to buy his own charts, and would often make and have his own published, could not continue if hydrography was going to be used strategically to win sea battles. The Earl of St Vincent had, as Lieutenant John Jervis, during a 14-year 'lull' in his naval career from 1761 embarked on cheap voyages to the Baltic, to Swedish and Russian waters to make his own charts and to put right some of the deadly errors prevailing in contemporary charts. When, at the age of 60, he took over as Commander-in-Chief of the Mediterranean Fleet, during which he achieved his crowning glory in defeating the Spanish fleet off Cape St Vincent in 1797, he could look back on a lifetime in the navy without an official naval organization for providing charts. He, like Admiral Anson before him, had been vociferous in the setting up of the British Hydrographic Office to pull together the ramshackle system of providing charts for commercial and military British shipping, which was finally granted by George III by an Order in Council in 1795.

The Baltic Sea is one of the world's 'inland' seas and gives access from the North Sea through the narrow necks of the Kattegat and Skagerrak to Finland, Russia, Sweden, and Germany. In medieval times it was the centre of the European herring industry, until the fish moved to the North Sea (perhaps to enjoy saltier waters), and in the seventeenth to nineteenth centuries, before the advent of iron-hulled ships and steam prolusion, it was the centre for their tim-

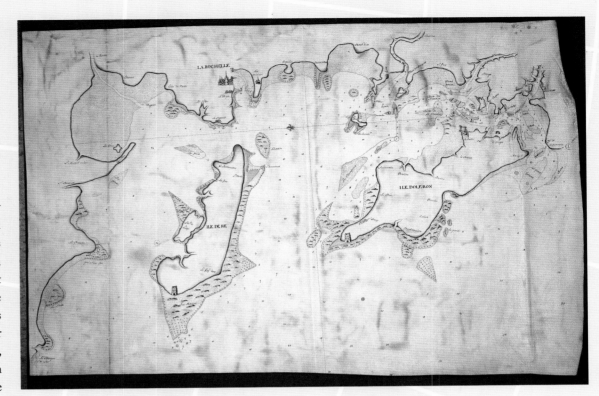

| CHART OF LA ROCHELLE AND ROCHEFORT | Rochefort was an important French naval base with a dockyard and arsenal up the River Charente and near La Rochelle, and this area was the setting for many British pre-emptive attacks. Admiral Hawke's had failed in 1758. The Aix Roads are the approaches and the scene of Lord Cochrane's famous fireship attack against the French fleet during the Napoleonic War of 1809. This captured French chart is earlier, hand-drawn in the late seventeenth or early eighteenth century and is possibly a basis of the chart incorporated in *Le Neptune François*. The detail is finely worked; note the drawing of the town of La Rochelle. The achievement of Cochrane's attack can be appreciated when the complexity of shoals and narrow channels is considered on the Aix Roads and approaches to Rochefort; the entrance to the River Charente is between Île Day (Isle d'Aix) and Île Madame – using the spelling of that time. (Admiralty Library Manuscript Collection VZ 5/40)

ber for masts and hulls, tar for shipbuilding and flax for sails. The constricted entrance and shallow average depth of 36 fathoms (about 140 metres) precludes any real tide, maintains an unsaline sea, which (and without the warming influence of the Gulf Stream) readily ices over in winter. Northern navigators felt little need for charts; knowledge was handed down from father to son and navigation was along the lines of 'caping' and the use of lead and line. English charts of this area survive by captains and pilots of the Muscovy Company made in the sixteenth and seventeenth centuries. Wagenaer produced the first charts of northern waters, influenced by the Mediterranean portolans carried by the Flemish wool merchants, covering up to Norway. The Russians, as described on page 43, then became the prime surveyors of these seas. Their charts should have been used by the British in naval operations in the Baltic against them during the Crimean War of 1854–57, rather than relying on Swedish pilots, although detailed surveys were made of the approaches to the main Russian naval ports such as Kronstadt and Bomarsund (on the Aland Islands commanding the approach into the Gulf of Finland), by such as Captain (later Admiral) Bartholomew James Sulivan who had sailed with Robert Fitzroy and Charles Darwin in the *Beagle* as a young officer.

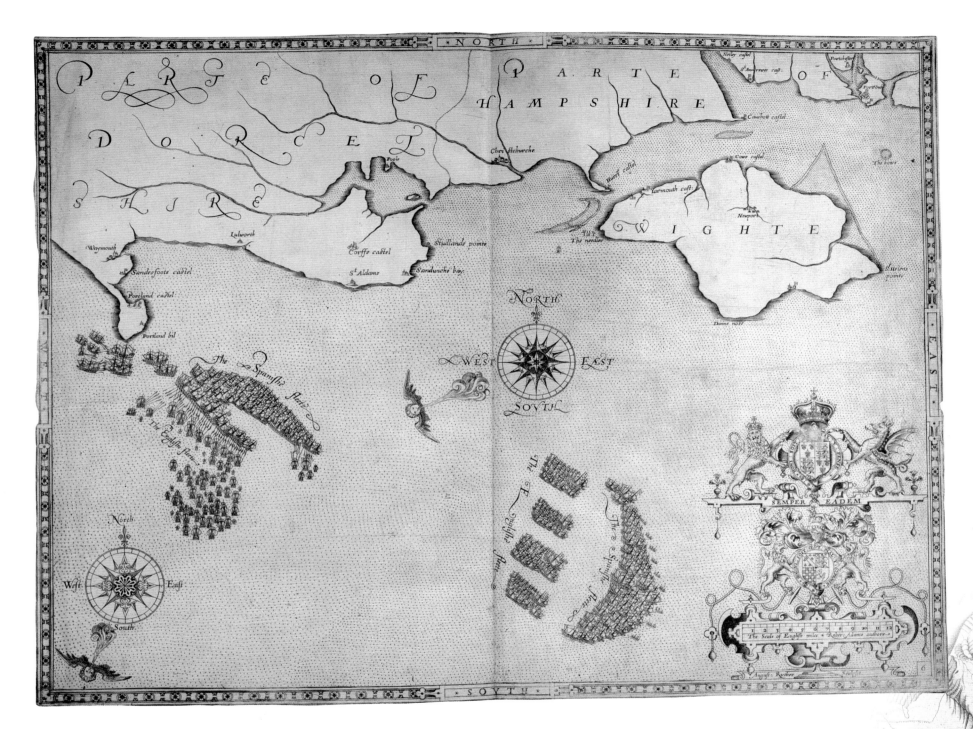

| **SPANISH ARMADA CHART** | An example of an historic chart, reporting the event in hindsight, engraved by Augustine Ryther from a chart by Robert Adams to illustrate the account of 1590. This was an event of momentous significance for Britain and Spain. One hundred and thirty Spanish ships sailed to invade England as Spain, the superpower of the day, was determined to crush English maritime competition and Protestantism. Sailing in a large crescent formation, having been harried by the English fleet from Plymouth under Lord Howard of Effingham, with Drake and Hawkins, the Spanish fleet is shown passing the Isle of Wight. It had then anchored off Calais, giving the English the opportunity to send in eight fireships. In confusion, the Spanish ships cut their anchor cables and sailed north around the British Isles. The 'Protestant wind' drove nearly half the fleet ashore off the Irish coast and Britain was spared invasion. The loss foreshadowed the decline of Spain's Empire and maritime superiority. (Reproduced by courtesy of the Royal Geographical Society with IBG, Plate 6, print 265.G.26)

| RIGHT | **DETAIL FROM MORDEN AND LEA'S CHART OF THE EUROPEAN COAST,** *C. 1693* | Detail of a printed chart of about 1693 showing Europe's coast, from the map publishers Morden and Lea in Cheapside, London. It is dedicated to Admiral Edward Russell, Earl of Oxford, who commanded the combined Anglo-Dutch fleet that beat the French at the Battle of Barfleur in 1692, and was appointed First Lord of the Admiralty for some years after. Pepys inserted this chart into his copy of Greenvile Collins' *Coasting Pilot* as part of his investigation into the accuracy of Collins' surveys. (Pepys Library, Magdalene College, Cambridge)

| BELOW | **CHART OF THE GULF OF FINLAND BY CAPTAIN NAGAEV, 1750** | Captain of the Russian Navy, Alexei Nagaev, made the strongest contribution to the hydrography of the Baltic Sea with his atlas of 15 charts published in 1750, during the reign of Empress Elizabeth (1709–62), daughter of Peter the Great, as *The Atlas of the Baltic Sea*.

The chart shows the Gulf of Finland, covering from St Petersburg west towards Helsinki. The naval base and fortress on the island of Kronstadt, built in 1710, guards the approaches to the Russian capital. The port of Vyborg is up the gulf to the north, although normally shut off by ice during the winter, as is much of the Baltic. Soundings are in Russian fathoms (7 English feet), and the scale is also in Russian fathoms, English feet, and German and Italian miles. The cartouche is magnificent, as befits an empress, and glorifies the Russian State and her dominion over the seas. No latitude or longitude is given, but orientation was obtained from the radiating rhumb lines. The use of isobaths, marking out the extent of shoals, was a sophisticated advance, as their systematic use was not on charts until the nineteenth century. The rapid introduction of charting and cartography in Russia in the eighteenth century indicated her rise to importance in the world, although some would say at the expense of her populace. (Reproduced by courtesy of the Royal Geographical Society with IBG, MR:14.B.89)

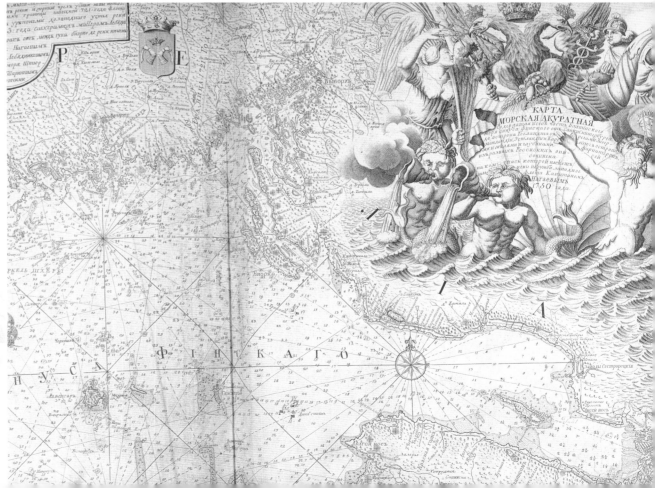

| CAPTAIN COLLINS' CHART OF THE
ORKNEY ISLANDS | As part of his awesome task
of surveying 'the sea coast of the Kingdom', Greenvile
Collins prepared 120 plans of harbours and stretches
of the British coast, of which 48 were published. He
was unable to find longitude and used a quadrant to
measure latitude. Laboriously obtaining his
soundings, in fathoms, at low water spring tides,
plotted by compass bearing of land marks and a
measuring chain, he had no topographical (land) map
against which to relate his own charts. The chart
illustrated here, from Collins' *Great Britain's Coasting
Pilot*, completed in 1692, is of the Orkneys which
were on the important but dangerous route from the
Baltic and Scandinavia across the top of England to
the west Atlantic fishing areas and the new northern
American settlements. The cormorants on the
cartouche are typical of his decorative dedications, in
this case to Captain Will Bond, a local 'bigwig'.
However, Pepys compared the *Pilot* less favourably
with *Le Neptune François*, even though it continued to
be published until 1792. (UKHO © British Crown
Copyright, Va40)

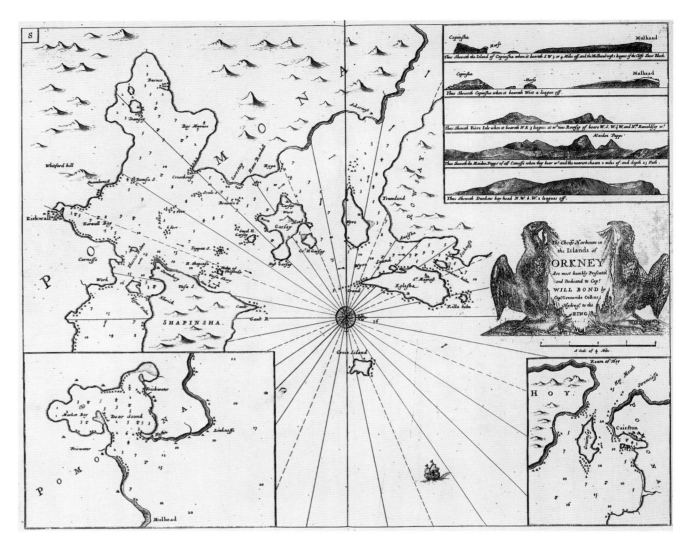

| MILFORD HAVEN BY LEWIS MORRIS,
1748 | Milford Haven is a superb natural harbour.
Lewis Morris (*fl.* 1737–48) drew this chart of
Milford Haven which was published in 1748 as one
of the charts of St George's Channel and the
Pembrokeshire coast. His notes of the tides and tidal
streams were a useful addition. His son, William,
revised the charts and re-issued them in 1801. (By
courtesy of the Dean and Chapter of Westminster)

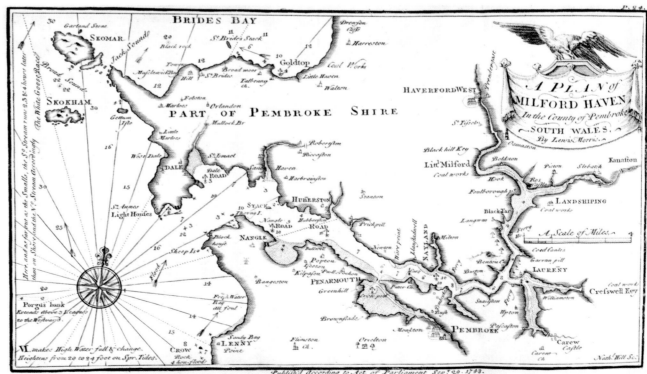

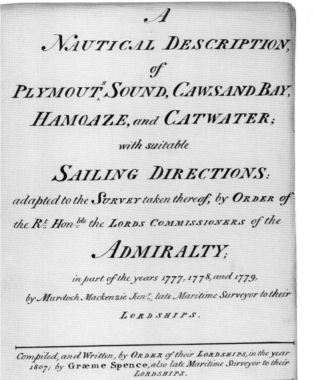

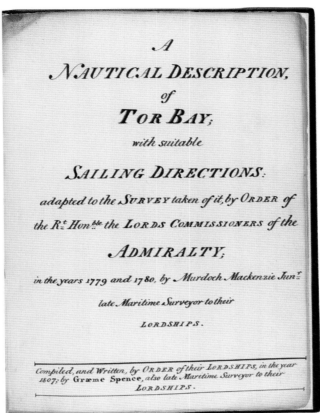

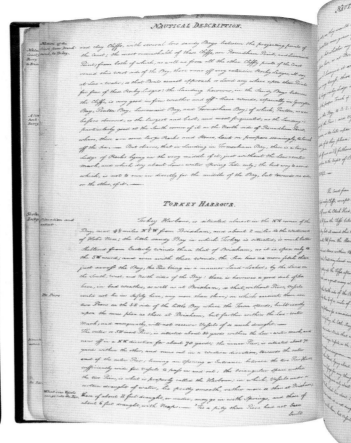

| SAILING DIRECTIONS BY LIEUTENANT MACKENZIE |

The two-page extract (right) is from Lieutenant Murdoch Mackenzie's hand-written sailing directions, forerunner of the *Admiralty Sailing Directions*, now issued in 72 volumes, and similarly by the USA and other maritime countries, focusing on shoals and harbours between the Lizard and Falmouth, surveyed in 1772–73. It describes the navigational features from Barnstaple Bay in Devon, around Land's End to Polkerry's in Cornwall. The corrections to the compass bearings were annotated by Graeme Spence in 1808, who worked with Mackenzie and was appointed Admiralty Surveyor in 1788.

The title page (above) is of Graeme Spence's 1807 sailing directions adapted from Mackenzie's of 1777–79. The careful and pleasing hand-written titles set another precedent for the standard of chartwork of hydrographers to follow.

A second volume of Spence's sailing directions (above right), of which the title and a two-page extract are shown, describes Tor Bay and, in particular, Torkey harbour (Torquay). An example of advice given states, 'the triangular open space within the two piers, is what is properly called the harbour, in which vessels under a certain draught [hull depth] lie pretty smooth, rather more so than at Brixham'. (Admiralty Library Manuscript Collection MSS 65(2) 66 & 67)

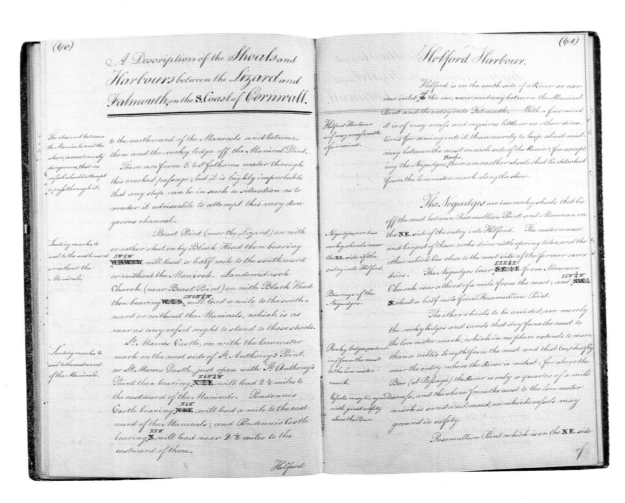

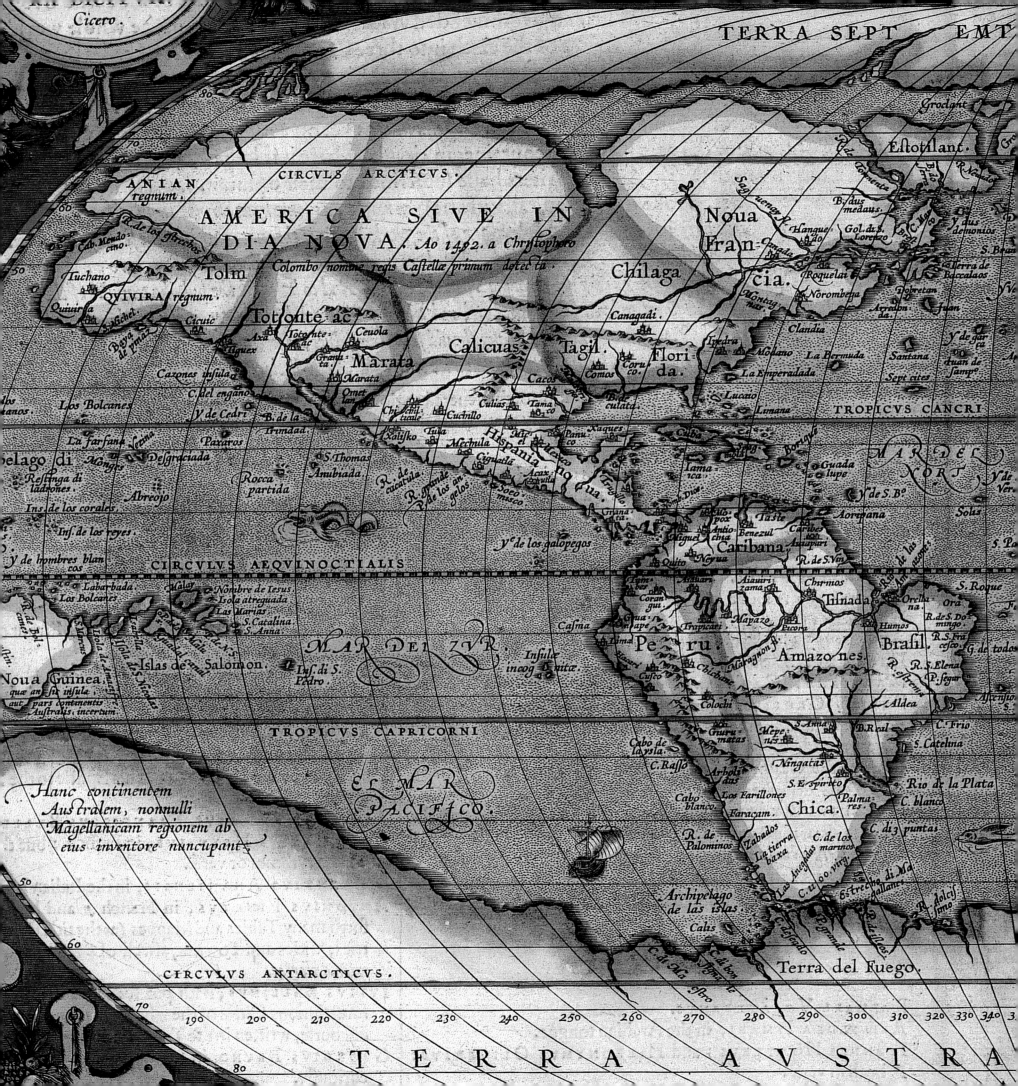

CHAPTER IV

The Arctic and Attempts to Find the North-East and North-West Passages

| LEFT DETAIL & ABOVE | **WORLD MAP BY ABRAHAM ORTELIUS, 1587** | Abraham Ortelius from Antwerp was one of the foremost mapmakers of his time, and his heirs published 42 editions of the *Theatrum Orbis Terrarum* between 1570 and 1612. The first book, consisting of uniformly sized maps systematically put together, can be called an Atlas, although it was Mercator who coined the phrase some 20 years later. This world map of 1587 shows the understanding of the time of the great North-East and North-West passages across the 'top' of the world; that to the west by 'Anian'. Canada is Noua Francia (Nouvelle Francais), and amongst other geographical inaccuracies Japan is just a large island and the northern part of Australia merges into a vast Southern Continent. Magellan's strait is firmly established, however. (By courtesy of the Dean and Chapter of Westminster)

THE Arctic region is internationally known as that area within the Arctic Circle at latitude 66º 33' N, where the sun never sets below the horizon in summer, nor rises above in winter. Vast tracts of land at the northernmost parts of Asia, North America and Europe cut into the Circle, but on the whole the Arctic is covered with sea-ice, which varies between 5 feet and 30 feet thick (1.5 to 9 metres). In winter this is a solid mass, but breaks up in summer into ice floes with long 'leads' between. (Leads are described in the Admiralty publication *The Mariner's Handbook* as 'any fracture of passage-way through sea ice which is navigable by surface vessels'.) Strong winds push these floes together dangerously into large hummocks with a huge pressure that will crush ships entrapped. This ice drifts generally north easterly from the middle of Siberia round towards the north-eastern tip of Greenland. The warmer Gulf Stream flowing northwards between Greenland and Norway, cools, sinks and reverses southwards down the Davis Strait between Greenland and Baffin Island carrying icebergs which pose a great danger to North Atlantic shipping, as RMS *Titanic* found to her total cost. This then sets the scene for the exploration and charting of this cold and complex area which held such promise of quick trading routes across the roof of the world, but which literally crushed the hopes and endeavours of so many expeditions.

| MAP OF ASIA BY ABRAHAM ORTELIUS C. 1570 | The excitement of a northerly route to Cathay and the Spice Islands from Europe was fuelled by the study of maps of Asia executed by explorers such as Henry Hudson and the Muscovy Company, like this one published by Ortelius *c*.1570, which showed clear water past Russia and the northern coast of China. (By courtesy of the Dean and Chapter of Westminster)

It is known that the Greek navigator Pytheas, as written by Pliny, headed north in 320 BC and discovered an island six days sailing north of the Orcades (Orkneys) which he called Thule and which may have been either Iceland or Greenland. The Russians are reputed to have sailed around the White Sea and by AD 800 Irish monks had established themselves in Iceland, which the Norsemen colonized 200 years later along with Greenland.

There seems to have been little activity for almost 600 years until the concept of sea-routes from the Atlantic past the north of Canada to the Pacific, or north of Russia, through the Bering Strait and south to Japan and the Orient took hold. The lure of trading the riches of the East from Cathay (China), the Spice Islands and Cipangu (Japan) by sea and the recognized difficulties of sailing to them, either by rounding the Cape of Good Hope or beating for perhaps weeks to weather Cape Horn or negotiate the tortuous Strait of Magellan, would have been reason enough to seek out new routes. But when, following the discovery of America, Pope Alexander VI divided the world between Portugal and Spain by the Treaty of Tordesillas in 1494 this denied the eastern route to any but the Portuguese and the western route was legitimized only to Spain. It encouraged the English, finding their oceanic maritime feet, to explore new trade routes – the North-West and North-East passages. These are names that evoked the wish rather than the actuality, as 350 years of optimistic geographers, who hypothesised an open sea to the north, and tragic failure were to show.

Couple this with the Ottoman Turks fifteenth-century conquest of the eastern Mediterranean which closed off the ancient caravan routes over which the spices and silks of the Orient had previously been brought to the European markets, and the British involvement, and to a lesser extent the Dutch, with a maturing system of offering merchant investment opportunities into voyages of exploration, as opposed to the continental method through Royal Patronage, and the desire to find either a North-West of North-East passage intensified.

However foolhardy and fruitless the repeated attempts to find the 'Strait of Anian' seem to us, with hindsight we have to admire the fortitude and courage of those explorers, most of whom were from Britain, as the North-West passage became a peculiarly English obsession. The strait bearing this name first appeared on charts and maps in the 1560s after the Italian mapmaker, Giacomo Gastaldi, whose work was copied in turn by many such as Abraham Ortelius and Gerardus Mercator, drew the strait relying on reference to it in Marco Polo's *Travels*. It became, over time, portrayed as a broad channel flowing into the North Pacific from somewhere in the interior of North America, plausibly from the Great Lakes.

Conditions so far north are extreme. Typically there are only two brief summer months in the year when the northern seas are free of ice. The compass becomes less and less reliable, with wild variations as you near the North Pole. There are tidal overfalls that run swifter than a ship can sail and the build up of ice on the rigging made handling a ship an exhausting ordeal. Everything touched gives frost nips and cold burns. Foraging on the ice for fresh water leaves a person exposed to attack from polar bears, which can move surprisingly quickly.

The Gulf Stream

The Folger family of Nantucket Island were both Quakers and Whalemen. Many captained their own ships and whaling was the key livelihood in the eighteenth and nineteenth centuries. Benjamin Franklin's mother, Abiah, was a Folger, and was born in Nantucket and it was to her Nantucket cousin, Captain Timothy Folger, that Franklin (1706–1790), later to become one of America's most famous statesmen, turned for the practical seaman's view of an important matter he had observed on his first transatlantic crossing from London to Philadelphia as a young man in 1726. He mentioned in his Journal the 'Gulph-weed' he collected that spread all over the Atlantic from the Western Isles (the Azores) to the coast of America. He mentioned the 'hot damp winds' and again the next day that 'the water is now very visibly changed to the eyes of all except the Captain and the Mate, and they will by no means allow it; I suppose because they did not see it first.'

His memory of what he had observed came back to him some 40 years later in 1768 when he was Deputy Postmaster-General for the American colonies. Customs in Boston complained that the mail packets from Falmouth, England were taking a fortnight longer to make the voyage to New York than from London to Rhode Island. Franklin sought out Folger who described how the Nantucket whalemen 'cruise along the edge of the Stream in quest of whales' and 'have opportunities of discovering the Strength of it when their Boats are out in pursuit of this Fish, and happen to get into the stream while the Ship is out of it … For then they are separated very fast, and would soon lose sight of each other if care were not taken'. Franklin later recollected in a letter to Alphonsus le Roy in 1785 that Folger told how English packets were stemming the current of 3 miles an hour, while the Rhode Island captains, acquainted with the Gulf Stream, advised the packet captains to 'cross it and get out of it: but they were too wise to be counselled by simple American fishermen.'

In 1768 Franklin worked on a chart of the North Atlantic with Folger and they produced their first idea of how the Gulf Stream flowed. He 'procured it to be engraved by order from the general post-office, on the old Chart of the Atlantic, Mount and Page's, Tower Hill: and copies were sent down to Falmouth for the captains of the packets, who slighted it however; but it is since printed in France, of which edition I hereto annex a copy.' Both the French and English charts are rare, and the Library of Congress has a copy of each, the French chart presented by Franklin Bache, a direct descendant of Benjamin Franklin, in 1935.

Franklin was still experimenting to expand his theory on the cause of the Stream, when he made water temperature observations on three transatlantic crossings in 1775, 1776 and 1778. His premise assumed that the north-easterly trade winds piled the Atlantic waters into the Gulf of Mexico so that the warm water flowed north up the coast of America and was then blown across toward northern Europe by the prevailing south-westerlies.

We know today that the Gulf Stream actually starts in the Caribbean where the water is expanded by the heat of the sun and escapes into the Gulf of Mexico. Warmed still further it expands hugely and escapes through the Florida Strait and to the east of the Grand Banks off Newfoundland, continuing as a deep stream of water across the North Atlantic to northern Europe, ensuring a temperate climate by such as Newcastle, England which, at the same latitude as Moscow and the northerly end of Lake Superior, would otherwise have the same climatic extremes! With a velocity calculated at 80 miles a day, a counter current flows to the south of it westwards across the Atlantic to the Caribbean, as the water becomes cooled in the higher latitudes and reverses down the Davis Strait carrying its deadly cargo of icebergs.

There is a current argument that as global warming speeds up the rate of melting at the North Pole, it could affect the character and behaviour of the Gulf Stream to such an extent that a Siberian climate could replace the temperate climate enjoyed by the shores of northern Europe.

Benjamin Franklin's chart of 1768, showing his investigations into the actions of the Gulf Stream. (Library of Congress)

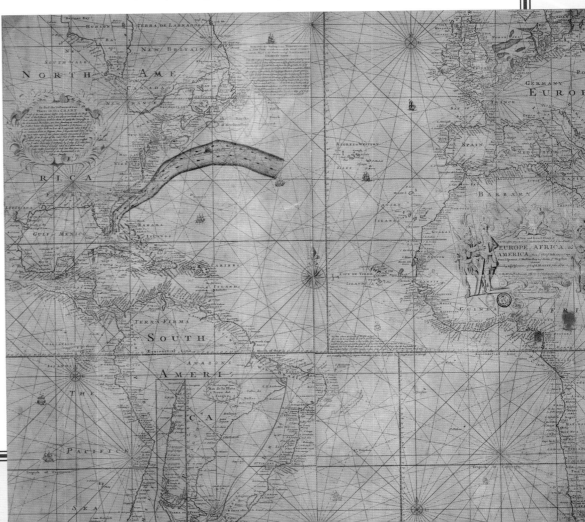

There were two concentrated periods of English involvement. The first, sparked by the jealous regard towards the expansion of Spanish and Portuguese trade following Columbus's discovery of America in 1492, started when a company of Merchant Adventurers, formed in London in 1551, sponsored an expedition of three ships under Sir Hugh Willoughby to find the North-East passage. Starting out in 1553 with great hopes and in grand style, the three ships were towed past the Royal Palace at Greenwich to salute the King, all dressed to impress in sky-blue.

Two of the three ships, with Willoughby, were lost but Richard Chancellor, the second-in-command, reached the White Sea and, enduring a lengthy trip overland, met the Tsar of Russia, Ivan the Terrible, and negotiated trading rights which lead to the formation of the Muscovy Company in 1555. On his second voyage, calling at Arzinia in Lapland Chancellor re-covered the body of his erstwhile Commander along with his papers and charts, but he died on his third voyage when his ship was wrecked off Aberdeen. Over the next 20 years several voyages were undertaken to expand the Russian trade, but little more exploration of the North-East passage was attempted.

More ambitious were the efforts to find a North-West passage. The first was set in motion by Sir Humphrey Gilbert, who petitioned Queen Elizabeth I in 1555 to undertake 'the discovering of a passage by the Northe, to go to Cataia [Cathay], & all other east partes of the worlde' providing of course he and his backers could have a monopoly on all derived trade. Although nothing came of it, his now famous letter to his brother, Sir John Gilbert, inspired the first attempt by Martin Frobisher in 1576, and again in 1577 and 1578. Frobisher made two major errors. He thought that the bay today named Frobisher Bay, which extends north west into Baffin Island near the Hudson Strait for about 150 miles, led on to a North-West passage and into the Pacific, and named it Frobishers Straightes. The cartographical error, drawn by his sailing companion, George Best, who published an account of the voyage, was perpetuated by geographers for two centuries. Secondly, he excitedly brought back what he thought was gold but which to the anger of his backers, proved to be iron pyrites, or fool's gold.

John Davis made three voyages in 1585, 1586 and 1587, making a valuable contribution to the knowledge of the Arctic. One of the greatest of Elizabethan seamen, he not only discovered Davis Strait which is the 700-mile stretch of sea between Greenland and Baffin Island, and made a thorough exploration of Greenland, but also contributed to the art of celestial navigation through his invention, the back-staff, to be known as the Davis Quadrant, used until John Hadley's reflecting quadrant was introduced in 1731.

Henry Hudson's four voyages between 1607 and 1611 increased knowledge in that area. He got to 80° 23' N, a record at the time, discovered Jan Meyen Island and sailed up the Hudson River, which he explored as a possible route to the Pacific, and Hudson Bay where he was thanklessly cast adrift by his mutinous crew and perished with his son and loyal crew members.

William Baffin endured five voyages between 1612 and 1616, pushing to the northern part of the bay that bears his name. Proving that there was no passage, Luke Fox's and Thomas James's efforts have been commemorated by Fox Channel and James Bay, and the latter's account gave inspiration to Samuel Taylor Coleridge's *The Rime of the Ancient Mariner*.

The Russians, too, made considerable exploratory contributions to the potential North-East passage following on from the Dutchman, Willem Barents'. His objective, occasioned by a Spanish ruling denying the Netherlands trade with Portugal, was to discover a northern route to India. During his three voyages he explored the west coast of Novaya Zemlya, two large islands to the north of the Russian steppes around longitude 60° E, found the strait leading beyond them into the Kara Sea from the sea which bears his name, and discovered Spitzbergen and Bear Island. In 1648 Semyon Dezhnev sailed round the northern tip of Siberia and through the strait later named after Bering. Samuel Pepys, as a member of the Royal Society, was keen to see a north-easterly passage to China and the Far East, and John Wood took the *Speedwell* in another attempt in 1676. Between 1733 and 1743 the 'Great Northern' expedition organised by the Russians charted the larger part of the Siberian coast.

While no North-West passage was found, the explorations led to the founding by Royal Charter, along the lines of the East India Company, of the Hudson Bay Company in 1670. This began the opening up and development of Canada. The Company was perhaps understandably more interested in an immediate return on capital through fur trading than on exploration, which its charter bound it to do. The resulting criticism eventually stimulated voyages around the Hudson Bay, the most important of which was Samuel Hearne's overland expedition in 1771 to the Coppermine River. Sir Alexander Mackenzie, for the rival North West Company, discovered and reached the mouth of the after-named Mackenzie River, giving two points of contact with the Arctic.

With Captain Cook's third voyage (1776–79) and his careful charting of the west coast of North America, and around Alaska through the Bering Strait north to Icy Cape, to discover, if it existed, the route from the Pacific, the shape of northern parts of North America began to take their modern form.

The second 'period' of intensive exploration was stimulated by an Act of Parliament of 1745 along the lines of the Longitude Prize, to grant £20,000 to any British subject who discovered the North-West passage. By 1765 Royal Naval expeditions were included and the first such voyage, with the purpose of reaching the North Pole, was started in 1773 under Commodore Constantine Phipps with HMS *Racehorse* and HMS *Carcass* (which had Horatio Nelson on board as a young midshipman). They got to 80° 40' N before ice stopped them.

In 1817 John Barrow, Second Secretary to the Admiralty for 40 years, whose ambition was to have British explorers fill in all the gaps in the world chart, so easing the rate of naval reduction of strength after the defeat of Napoleon, was initiating explorations to the Arctic. This 'peace dividend' ran alongside the navy's other roles of enforcing slave trade abolition during nearly a century of *Pax Britannica*, and the first of a succession of Royal Naval expeditions commenced under Commodore John Ross in 1818. With two later famous naval explorers on board, William Parry and Ross's nephew, James Clark Ross, as a midshipman, Commodore Ross got north to Davis Strait and Lancaster Sound. He decided any further progress was barred by mountains, which he named after Barrow's boss, the First Secretary to the Admiralty, Sir John Croker – a devious man to whom naming a mountain range was too little to maintain his favour. Barrow, himself well travelled and as a young man part of the three-year Embassy voyage to China under Lord Macartney, was not convinced, however, and sent a second expedition under Parry with two ships, HMS *Hecla* and HMS *Griper*.

Barrow ensured that each expedition, following on from Captain Cook's first voyage, was scientifically fulfilled with an expert in astronomy, navigation, hydrography, meteorology and magnetism. Queen Elizabeth I had said that 'knowledge is power'. Ross's reputation was dented when Parry, the first to successfully over-winter in the Arctic broke through Lancaster Sound, the mountain range Ross claimed to have seen disappearing from sight, to Melville Island, named inevitably after the First Lord of the Admiralty. Parry's success assured him a second chance and he sailed in 1821 in command of a two-ship expedition in HMS *Fury* with HMS *Hecla*, under Commander George Lyon. This expedition showed the value of a close relationship with the local Eskimo while they over-wintered as, after familiarising them with 'boxing the compass' (literally a sailor's term for the ability to name all 32 points of the compass both clockwise and anti-clockwise, but in this context giving the Eskimos the understanding of how direction is indicated at sea) they were able to draw a 'chart' to help direct the expedition. A third expedition sailed in 1824 with the same ships, but HMS *Fury* was wrecked. In 1825 Captain George Lyon in HMS *Griper* and Captain Frederick Beechey in HMS *Blossom* followed Cook's third voyage route to try to join from the Pacific through the Bering Strait working to the east.

In 1829 John Ross was keen to salvage his reputation and took a privately funded expedition in *Victory*, wintering four years when his ship was wrecked on the Boothia Peninsula. His nephew James Clark Ross, who later rose to Admiral, sledged north and discovered the north magnetic pole.

Admiral Sir John Franklin made considerable contribution to the exploration of the Arctic in three voyages. The first, with four ships, explored many thousands of miles of the north Canadian coastline and the Mackenzie River in the Beaufort Sea. Franklin's second voyage, following Parry's of 1824, set out in 1825 and further successfully charted the Northwest Territories coast, for which he was knighted. In 1836 George Back, who served under Franklin's expeditions between 1818 and 1827, saving the lives of his companions in the second, further explored and charted the Northwest Territories. The final voyage of this period is perhaps the best known because of its tragic ending under Franklin, who had, in turn, sailed under Flinders as a midshipman and then as Governor of Tasmania, followed William Bligh to Australia (who was appointed Governor of New South Wales). In May 1845, as a relatively elderly officer, Franklin took command of the expedition to find the North-West passage in HMS *Erebus* and HMS *Terror* (under Captain Francis Crozier), which became trapped in the ice in Victoria Stait by King William Island. Many of the crew survived into a third winter when they tried to sled south to find a settlement. Their attempts to return home were extraordinary, but all perished and Franklin's loss sparked the biggest and longest search ever undertaken at sea, starting with James Clark Ross in HMS *Enterprise* with HMS *Investigator* and some 40 more following, two of them financed privately by Lady Franklin. The inadvertent result of this was the fullest exploration and charting of the Arctic and North-West passage. Robert McClure, who in turn was fortuitously rescued by another British expedition under Rear-Admiral Sir Edward Belcher (one of the Navy's more difficult officers to serve under – his querulous reputation was well known during his China surveys) after he had to abandon his ships, actually discovered the passage's existence in 1850, although Francis McClintock in HMS *Fox* finally found the site of Franklin's demise in 1857. Disappointingly this showed that the passage was not commercially realistic and nothing more was attempted for 50 years, when ironically, Roald Amundsen, the first to reach the South Pole, navigated it over three years in 1903 in a small fishing sloop with a crew of six.

Today with the onset of global warming, it has been possible for large ice-breakers to make the passage and, if this trend continues, for better or worse, the dream of earlier centuries may now become a practical circumstance.

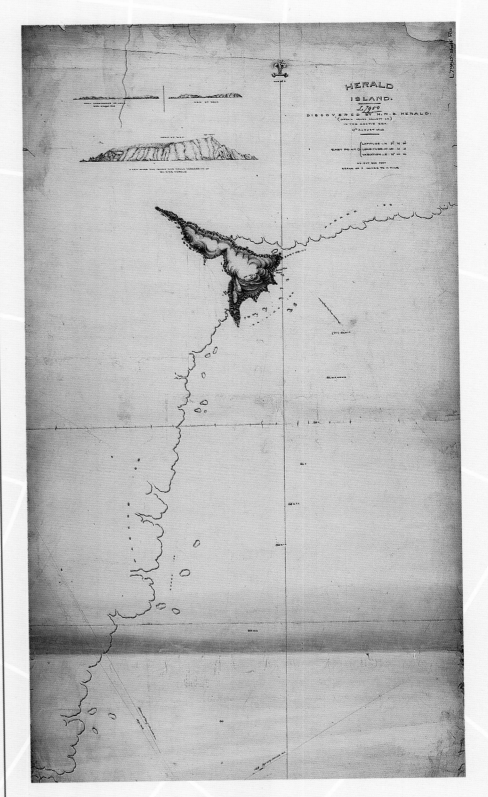

| CHART OF HERALD ISLAND, NORTH OF THE PACIFIC OCEAN IN THE CHUKCHI SEA | Captain Henry Kellett had learned his surveying techniques under Captain W F Owen on his African coastal survey in the 1830s and was then involved with Captain Edward Belcher in the attacks on Canton in 1841 during the Opium Wars. In command of HMS *Herald* from 1845 he made three voyages to the Arctic, and was a part of the multi-ship search for Franklin, but from the west. He produced this chart of the island he discovered in the Chukchi Sea, at above 71° N of the Bering Strait, naming it Herald Island. As an example of painstaking work carried out under extreme conditions it shows the edge of the 'packed ice', the ship's track and survey bearings. (UKHO © British Crown Copyright)

| RIGHT | **CHART OF THE WHITE SEA AND NOVAYA ZEMLYA, 1676** | John Wood's chart shows the extent of the ice which defeated his purpose in attempting the North-East passage in the *Speedwell* on her voyage of 1676, with Greenvile Collins as master. Wood had been encouraged by the conclusions of Joseph Moxon and others that Novaya Zemlya was not an island and the White Sea (Barents Sea) was a bay. As always, Wood followed the custom of naming new lands after sponsors and patrons – King Charles Snow Hills, Cape James and York Point – although a glance at a modern atlas shows these names, unsurprisingly, did not survive. (Pepys Library, Magdalene College, Cambridge)

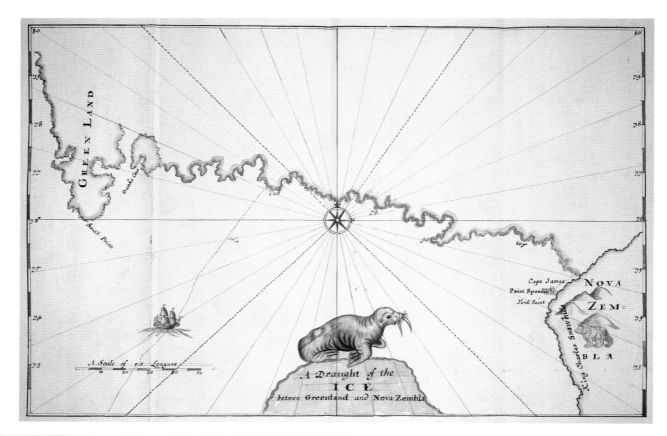

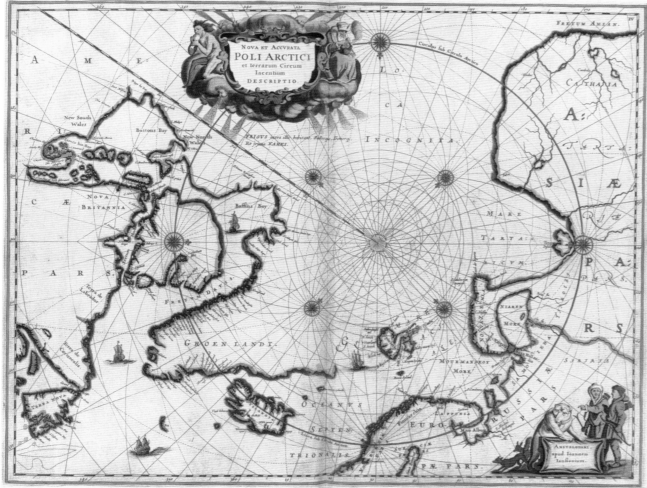

| RIGHT & LEFT | **THE ARCTIC BY JOHN WOOD, *C.*1676 AND BY JAN JANSSON, *C.* 1650 |** John Wood's chart of the Arctic after the *Speedwell's* voyage of 1676, shows that he believed the White Sea (Barents Sea) to be a bay with Novaya Zemlya a peninsula. It shows that little had been learnt since the view of the Arctic by Jan Jansson, a mapmaker publishing in Amsterdam, with a distinctively decorative and flamboyant style. He published his Sea Atlas as Volume V in 1650 as part of the eight volume *Atlas Novus* between 1638 and 1666. (Pepys Library, Magdalene College, Cambridge)

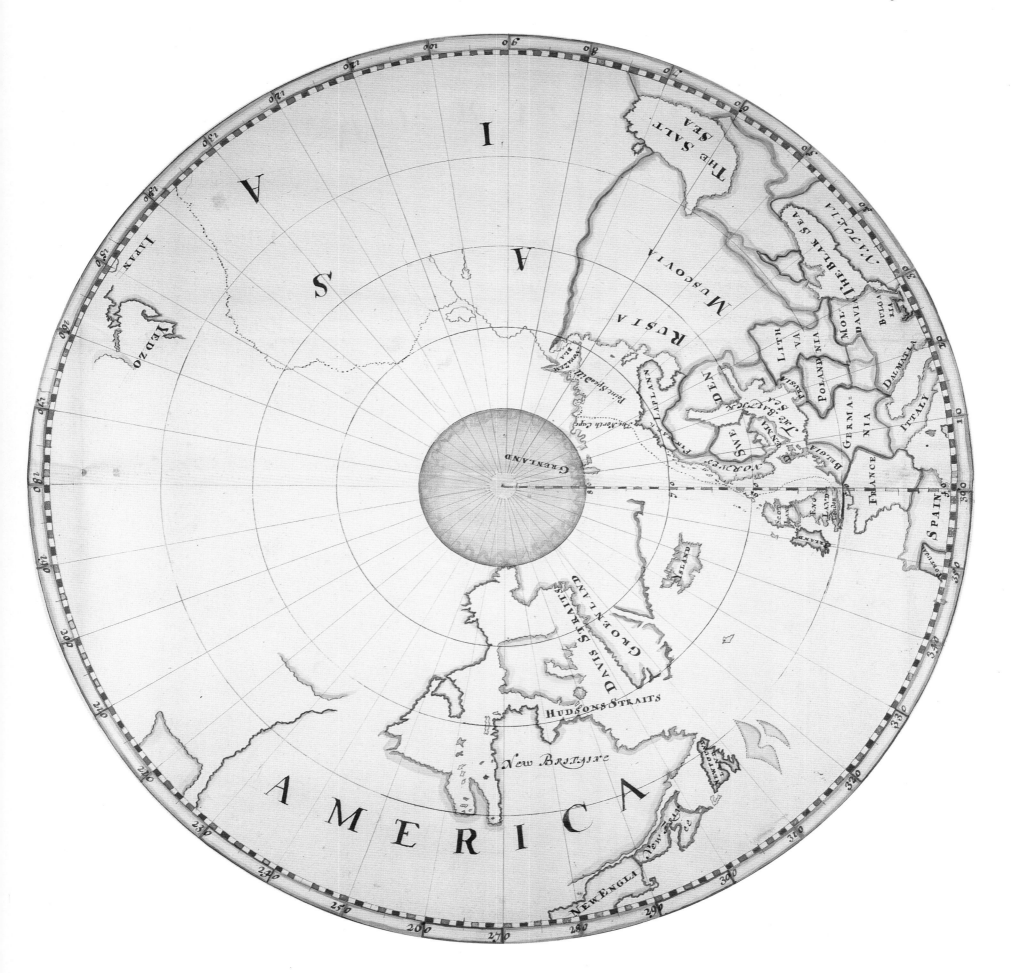

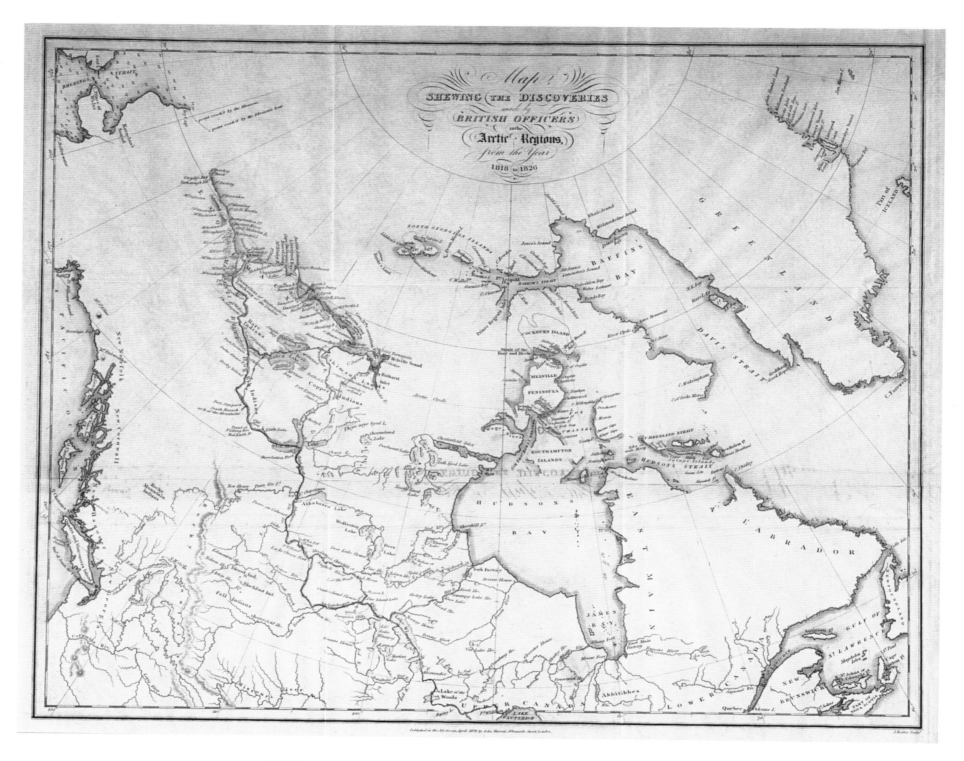

| **DISCOVERIES IN THE ARCTIC BY BRITISH NAVAL OFFICERS 1818–1826** | This map shows the discoveries of expeditions organized by the Admiralty in collaboration with other institutions of the time – such as the Royal Society – between 1818 and 1826. As of that date there was no known passage through to the Pacific. The attempts thus far showed the most promising route to be through Baffin Bay to the north of Baffin Island and subsequent expeditions concentrated on trying to force a way through Lancaster Sound. In fact the chart-makers at the Admiralty had to wait 30 years after Parry's farthest journey west of 1819 when he had got to within 80 miles of Richard Collinson's farthest east from the Pacific of 1850–51 to complete the picture with this chart. Collinson (known for his China surveys) spent three winters in the Arctic after his ship HMS *Enterprise* was separated from Captain Robert McClure in HMS *Investigator*. (UKHO © British Crown Copyright)

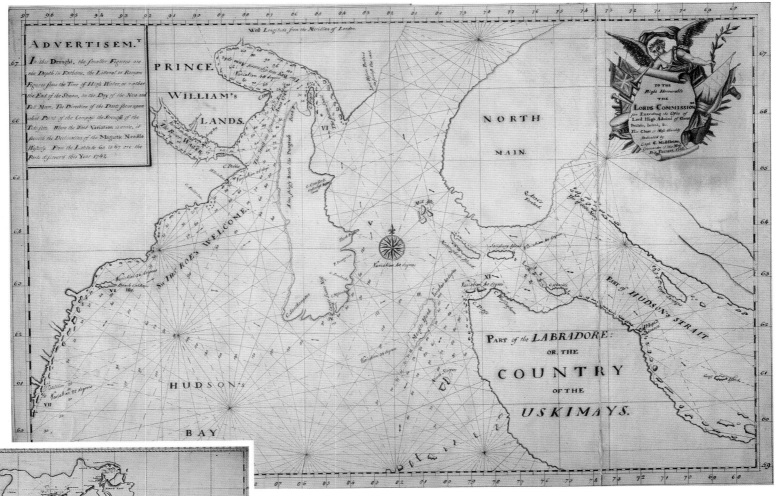

| ABOVE | **CHART OF HUDSON BAY, 1742** | The first attempt at an accurate survey of the west coast of Hudson Bay, and a conspicuous advance on any previous charts of that region, is an original hand-drawn chart by Captain Christopher Middleton, commanding HMS *Furnace,* in 1742. It is a professional chart with explanations and times of the tides, early use of the directional arrows for currents, and an elaborate cartouche with which to dedicate the chart (to the Lord High Commissioners of the Admiralty). He names two of his discoveries as the River Wager and Dobbs Point after his two most important 'sponsors', Sir Charles Wager, First Lord of the Admiralty and Arthur Dobbs, an Irish MP under Walpole and instigator of the Admiralty's decision to order the voyage. Twenty years earlier in 1722 John Scroggs, a captain in the Hudson Bay Company, had led a probing voyage in the *Whalebone* to the north of the Churchill River in search of copper. He reported strong tides from what came to be named Chesterfield Inlet, about 65° N. Middleton sailed in company with HMS *Discovery* on the orders of the Admiralty to follow up the report. A Hudson Bay Company captain, he was given a special commission try to find the North-West passage. The curiously named Sir Thomas Roe's Welcome was after a career diplomat who skilfully negotiated trade arrangements for the East India Company in India in 1615.

Controversy dogged Middleton's exploratory achievement, as he stood accused of not fully investigating the strong tides from Chesterfield Inlet by Dobbs, his sponsor and an armchair zealot of the existence of the North-West passage – a dream he pushed for 20 years. A very different version of this chart was concocted by a couple of Middleton's dissatisfied crew showing Chesterfield Inlet as opening to the west. Middleton had to fight to clear his name for some years through volumes of tracts he published and sent to those in Office – hence the immediate importance of the tidal streams he showed on this chart. (Admiralty Library Manuscript Collection MSS 368/1)

| LEFT | **TRACK CHART OF *CARCASS* AND *RACEHORSE* TO SPITZBERGEN** | The chart shows the track of these two specially adapted bomb vessels, fitted with double bottoms and strengthened bows, between 28 June and 23 August 1773 under the command of Commodore the Honourable Constantine Phipps, to try to find the North-East passage to the Pacific, and take in the North Pole *en route*. It is interesting to see references made in the 'explanation' to the different methods of fixing the ship – i.e. lunar observations and dead reckoning, and 'the watch', which would be one of the earliest uses of Arnold's and Kendall's copy of Harrison's chronometer, especially as Arnold's first three copies and Kendall's K1 had only been taken by Cook on his 1772–75 voyage to the Southern Ocean. But as Phipps recorded in his journal, after sailing north of Spitzbergen, his course was blocked by 'one continued plain of smooth unbroken ice, bounded only by the horizon' which is shown on the chart. (UKHO © British Crown Copyright)

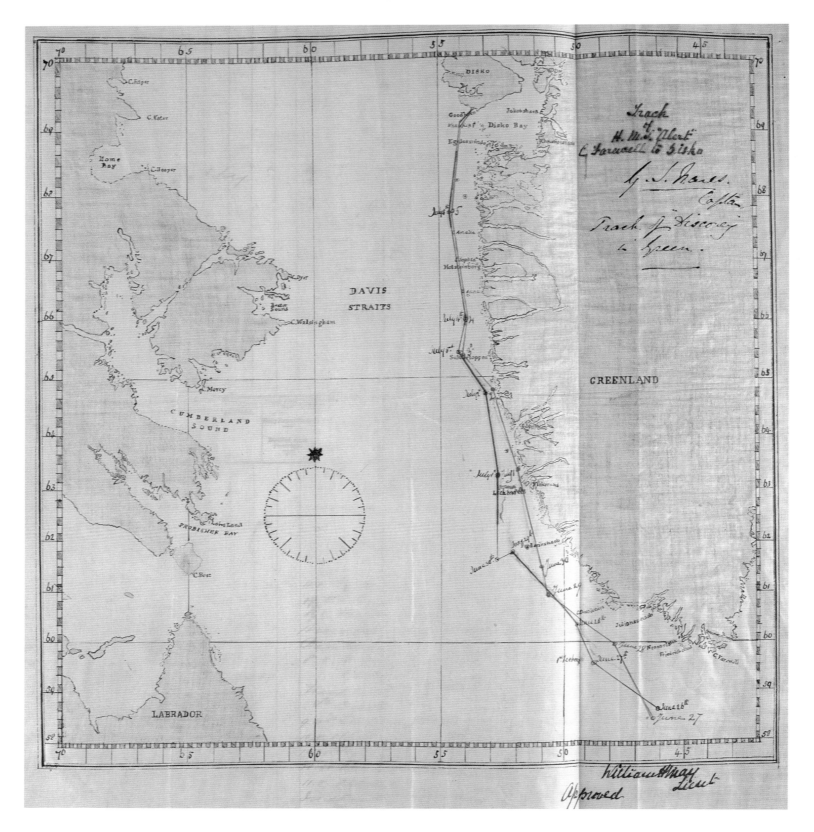

| **CHART OF THE TRACKS OF HMS *ALERT* AND *DISCOVERY* IN THE ARCTIC** | A manuscript chart of the tracks of *Alert* and *Discovery* showing progress up the west coast of Greenland during the 1875–76 expedition into the Arctic Circle north to the island of Disko, drawn up by the ships' surveying officers and signed as approved by Captain George Nares. The fjord-like inlets along the Greenland coast are relatively accurate, but the surveys of the Baffin Island coast, just as indented with fjords, is shown as a bland straight line giving some indication of the amount of survey work still to be done. (Admiralty Library Manuscript Collection)

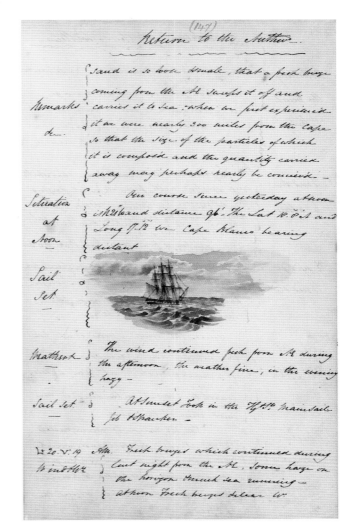

| SHIP'S LOG OF HMS *DISCOVERY* FROM BANTRY BAY TO DISCO | For some 20 years Britain remained disillusioned after the last of 40 expeditions, under Captain Francis McClintock, had found the papers, tucked under a cairn in King William's Land, which explained the tragedy of the loss of Admiral Franklin, his crews and ships *Erebus* and *Terror*. The American attempt on the North Pole by Captain Charles Francis Hall in USS *Polaris* attained a *plus ultra* of 81° 38'N in 1871–72 which encouraged renewed interest in a British attempt. The Arctic Committee worked closely with the Hydrographer to the Navy and appointed Captain George Nares, fresh from commanding the circumnavigation expedition of HMS *Challenger*, to lead a two-ship expedition to the Arctic in HMS *Alert* with Captain Henry Stephenson in the back-up ship HMS *Discovery*. *Alert* got closer to the Pole than any other ship before her, at 82° 24'N off Cape Sheridan, Ellesmere Island. The small town at the north end of what is now called Nares Strait is named Alert, where the ship was icebound for 142 days, while *Discovery*, as pre-arranged, wintered further south at 81° 44'N. Despite four deaths and 60 out of a crew of 120 unexpectedly suffering from scurvy (the navy had substituted cheaper lime juice, with only a quarter of the Vitamin C of lemon juice), the positive outcome was the knowledge that the Pole could not be reached by this route; ice was solid around the pole and not, as hitherto believed, melted. Invaluable information on the earth's magnetism in the region was recorded, including an unsuspected diurnal variation, and 300 miles of ice-bound coastline was charted.

This page from the official log of *Discovery*, signed on every page by the Captain, Henry Stephenson, shows the formalization of recorded information by now required at the Admiralty, and it is interesting to contrast this with a Remark Book of one hundred years before (above right). It is 30 June 1875, and *Discovery* is on passage to Disco (called Disko today), having left Portsmouth on 29 May, at approximately 70° N to rendezvous with *Alert* if they had become separated. *Discovery*'s 'Remarks' section in the ship's log records increasing ice such that they had to 'commence steaming' to supplement the sails. Weather is recorded at every watch change (i.e. four hours except the two two-hour 'dog watches' between 1600 and 2000) and ship's course and speed hourly with a noon-day actual or estimated position. The straightforward language of the record contrasts and understates the endurance and determination of these early explorers fulfilling a peacetime role for patriotic gain. (Admiralty Library Manuscript Collection)

| REMARK BOOK OR SHIP'S LOG OF A BRITISH NAVAL FRIGATE, *C.*1790 | The captain reports the weather, sails set, sea state, noon position in latitude and longitude off Cape Blanco (Cape Blanc is on the coast of west Africa at the border between Mauritania and the Western Sahara) and the phenomenon of sand being blown so far – 300 miles – out to sea, and adds a delightful vignette watercolour of the ship sailing. (UKHO © British Crown Copyright)

MARE MAIVS

ASIA

ISPANIA

MAVRITANIA

AFRICA

AEGIPTVS

AETHIOPI

TROPICVS CANCRI

C. DE S. AGOSTI

BRAZIL

RV PROVINTIA

VNDVS NOVVS

RIO DE LA PLATA

C. DE BON

elstreto d maglanes

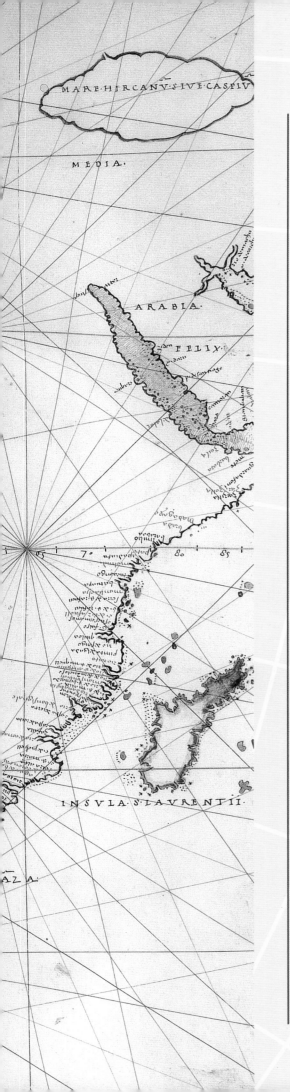

CHAPTER V

Africa

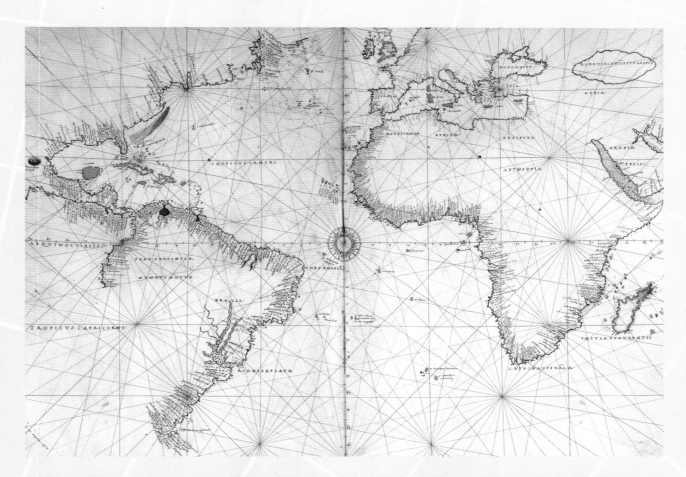

| LEFT DETAIL & ABOVE | BATTISTA AGNESE'S PORTOLAN CHART OF EUROPE, AFRICA, ATLANTIC OCEAN AND AMERICA, *C.* 1550 | One of Battista Agnese's beautiful but, by the standards of the time, unembellished and simple portolan charts shows that by 1550 the coastline of Africa was well understood, with Portuguese place names proliferating along the trade route to the Red Sea and India. Across the Atlantic the Rio de la Plata (River Plate) is shown with large inland estuaries, and north of Florida, conjecturally there is the first indication of the swiftly flowing Gulf Stream shown in green. Other Spanish and Portuguese settlements are named along the American coasts, but the west coast of South America is completely unexplored. There are virtually no Spanish or Portuguese charts of this time that have survived. (Courtesy of The Hispanic Society of America, New York)

ALTHOUGH Africa is the second largest of the earth's seven continents, comprising 22 per cent of the world's landmass, its regular coastline, measuring about 19,500 miles (30,500 kilometres) has comparatively few indentations and so is short in relation to its land area. Nonetheless, the charting of the coastline cost more lives through disease, as did the exploration of the interior, than any other part of the world. Essentially, Africa is a vast rolling plateau – 90 per cent of the land lies over 500 feet above sea level – albeit with large mountain ranges, to the north the Atlas range and to the south the Drakensburg. Height differences in other areas were caused either by the continental drift fault creating the Rift Valley or the five vast river basins of the Congo, Niger, Nile, Volta and Zambezi that gouged through the rock and met the sea through a fan of deltic tributaries. The plateau descends sharply through escarpments to the narrow surrounding coastal plain and all the rivers except the Niger-Benue and Zambezi-Shire systems plunge dramatically to the coast in a series of waterfalls and cataracts over the escarpment, giving little opportunity or access for river navigation inland from the sea.

While the Mediterranean coast of Africa was well understood by the early civilizations of Egypt, Phoenicia, Greece and Rome, their understanding was fanciful on what happened to the south of the Sahara, of which Ptolemy's second-century AD view is representative. He drew the African contour so that the continent distended east and west into a huge landmass that stretched around the world and covered the southern part of the globe. This was adapted to the belief that Africa extended eastwards joining up with Asia to enclose the Indian Ocean as a vast inland sea. Islamic scholars knew from Arab traders of the shape of the east coast of Africa and the Sahara, but little of the west. At that time gold was brought across the Sahara into Western Europe, along with ivory, slaves and salt. If these goods could come across the Sahara, the thinking went; then surely they could be obtained by going south and then somehow into the interior by sea?

Don Henrique, Duke of Viseo and Prince of Portugal (1394–1460) has been described as the Father of Navigation and the greatest man that Portugal ever produced. Immortalized afterwards as Prince Henry the Navigator, he had set up a court and observatory in 1418 at Sagres in the Algarve, of which he was Governor. This attracted Jewish and Arab mathematicians, navigators, shipbuilders and scientists and, with the proselytizing zeal he had used to drive the Moors out of the Iberian peninsula and capture Ceuta in 1415, he inspired expeditions to head southwards 'off the edge of the world'. They also set out to solve the problems of navigation out of sight of land, and together with the spread of Portuguese exploratory interest in the fourteenth century that it stimulated, pieced together the West African coastline.

A century of tentative thrusts, each one building on the experience of the previous voyage, started in 1420 with the re-discovery of the Madeira group, (previously known to the Romans but uninhabited and forgotten) and then the Azores. By 1434 Cape Yuby and Cape Bojador, about 500 miles south of Tangier and of the latitude of the Canary Islands, were reached by Gil Eannes. This was significant because the area was at that time the most southerly point on European maps. Their tenacity is the more appreciated when considering that the 'usual' difficulties of navigation through unknown waters were aggravated by the mists and the prevailing south-easterly current that sweeps between Fuertaventura Island and the Moroccan coast. In 1443 Cape Blanco was reached, and a year later the Senegal River, thought to be the Nile; then Cape Verde and the Gambia River. By 1460, the year Prince Henry died, the Portuguese had reached Sierra Leone: the hope was always of finding a navigable river they could use to get into the African interior.

Giving the Portuguese the edge on discovery over other European countries, the Roman Catholic church legitimized Portuguese ambitions to the east with a Papal bull, *Pontifex Romanus,* in 1455, which gave them a trading and navigation monopoly from Cape Bojador to the Indies. With a fort and trading post built in 1448 on the island in Arguin Bay (Bay du Levrier), at Cape Blanc just south of the Western Sahara by Mauritania and gold first minted as the *cruzado* (the cross bearer) in 1457, the motivational and trading stepping-stones were in place. Gold was being traded in 1471 from Mina and that winter Fernao do Po and Pero de Cintra explored the island of Fernando Po, placed between the Bights of Benin and Biafra by the part of the African coastline that renews its southward trend again. In 1472 the Equator, near Cape Lopez was crossed for the first time. By now the night sky was looking uncomfortably unfamiliar as the Pole Star had disappeared below the northern horizon, and a different icon, the Southern Cross, was seen. It was of little navigational value as, unlike the juxtaposition of Polaris to the Celestial Pole in the Northern Hemisphere, is well away from overhead the South Pole. The star that is readily identifiable in the Southern Hemisphere is Canopus, a yellow-white supergiant positioned quite near to the Celestial South Pole.

The Portuguese/Spanish war temporarily put a stop to further exploration, but by 1482 King John II had taken on the patronage once more, after a period of leasing the exploration rights to 'private' hands. Convinced now of the viability of a route to India to the east, and rejecting, perhaps regrettably with hindsight, an approach by Christopher Columbus in 1484 to sponsor a voyage westwards, the King appointed Diogo Cam (also recorded in history as Diego Cão) to carry the Portuguese flag southwards. He sailed past the Congo River and during his second voyage in 1485–86 got to Walvis Bay, just 500 miles north of the Cape of Good Hope. He marked his progress intermittently with tall marble columns, called *padroes*, and inscribed with details of his voyage, at Shark Point at the mouth of the River Congo, Cape Santa Maria, Monte Negro and Cape Cross. Only the one at Shark Point, fragmented, is still in position; two others are at the Lisbon Geographical Society and one is at Kiel on the German Baltic coast.

King John already knew that a passage to India was feasible from Arab sources and Bartolomeu Diaz de Novaes was given a three-ship expedition in 1487. He sailed to the cape that bears his name at 26° 38' S where he, too, as became the custom, erected a commemorative pillar; but from there he was swept south by gales for 13 days. As soon as the weather permitted he headed west, but finding no land turned back north and hit the African coast at Mossel Bay on the south coast. He coasted eastwards noting that the trend of the land was turning north before his crew, greatly alarmed, forced him to turn back.

Nine years later King John chose Vasco da Gama to command a squadron of four ships to follow up Diaz's discovery of a great ocean to the east of Africa, with the hope that this would provide a route to the Orient. He rounded the southern tip of Africa and headed up the East Coast as far as Malindi, near Mombasa, and was fortunate to be able to engage a Gujerati pilot to guide him to India. There da Gama was able to erect another Portuguese pillar at Calicut on the Malabar Coast, although Arab traders encouraged local Hindus to resist his setting up a trading post. Instead, he had to be content with loading up spices showing a 600 per cent profit: he got back to Lisbon in 1499. This encouraged another voyage of 14 ships, quickly set up in 1500 in which Diaz, to his regret, was appointed second-in-command to Pedro Cabral. They sailed further to the west than intended, touching land at Brazil at 17° S. Although Cabral is credited with its discovery, there is documentation to show that the Spaniard, Vicente Yañez Pinzon, had reached it three months earlier. Back on course Diaz perished in a violent storm off the distinctive cape he had sighted on his home journey in 1488, and with unfortunate foresight had called *Cabo Tormentoso* (Cape of Storms), and which King John had optimistically re-named *Cabo da Bona Esperanza* – the Cape of Good Hope. Across the Indian Ocean Cabral established a trading post, known as a factory, at Calicut. This was savagely attacked and the factors killed.

In response, a much bigger expedition was organized. A fleet of 10 ships under da Gama, now titled Admiral of India, took advantage of the trade winds in a bold sweep out towards the South American coast and then back to Africa. By sailing 96 days out of sight of land, they proved that this was possible with implications for further long-distance exploration. The bombardment of Calicut was ruthlessly followed through. Da Gama then sailed on to Cochin where he loaded up with an immensely rich cargo.

Portuguese exploration and trading activity had, by the end of the fifteenth century, described the general shape of Africa. Athough the charts that they must have produced are not to be found, perhaps destroyed, maps such as Martin Waldseemüller's *Carta Marina* (Marine Chart) of 1516 and others by Italian chartmakers, recording a string of Portuguese names along the coasts that are still in general use today, suggest they had access to what were at the time secret Portuguese charts. An Italian diplomat, Alberto Cantino, smuggled a chart, to be known as the famous Cantino chart, in 1502, which he gave to the Duke of Ferrara and which became the source of maps and charts for decades, and a testimony to the Portuguese discoveries, clearly showing Africa and its physical relationship to India.

The potential from oriental trade was much stronger than that from the interior of Africa, apart from slaves. With scant knowledge of the interior, much was guessed, and charts that appeared were, in compensation, embellished with wonderfully imaginative beasts, cities, and kings such as Prester John, the mythical priest-king of central Africa. Jonathan Swift (1667–1745), who based *Gulliver's Travels* on what was assumed to be parts of Africa and Australia, pithily wrote:

> So geographers, in Afric-maps,
> With savage-pictures fill their gaps;
> And o'er unhabitable downs,
> Place elephants for want of towns.

The sixteenth-century cartographer, Willem Janszoon Blaeu, was providing an elegant but fanciful depiction of Africa with sea beasts frolicking in off-shore waters and inaccurate depictions of elephants, ostriches and monkeys inland.

With the decline of Portuguese trade in the East, caused to a large extent by the emergence of the Dutch, who took over the Javanese and Spice Islands, a Dutch presence at the Cape of Good Hope under Jan van Riebeek was started in 1652. It became very important as a 'staging post' both to the Far East and to Australia, as Britain was to realize when it decided to purchase the Cape

from the Dutch in 1814 for £6 million. Essentially though, the main European interest in Africa between 1500 and 1800 was for the slaves, who were captured and transported to America to work the cotton fields, and Portuguese influence, built up on the east coast of Africa around the Zambezi River, was in the hunt for gold, until Mozambique was made a colony in 1891.

Various English attempts to establish trade out of West Africa were made starting in 1553 and typically these were similar in form to various other trading ventures to the Orient which eventually culminated in the East India Company. These voyages added to the pool of navigational knowledge of the African coastline. In the same year Captain Thomas Wyndham, with a Portuguese navigator, Anes Pinteado, took his ships to the mouth of the Benin River, and was able to trade 80 tons of pepper – however, not without a cost as only 40 of the 140 who sailed out survived. The Bight of Benin had started to earn its notorious name as the 'White Man's Grave'.

In 1554 a second voyage of three ships stood out from London and brought back 400 pounds of gold, 250 elephant tusks and 36 butts of Guinea pepper. This was profit on profit and the Captain, William Towrson made two more trading voyages, the last one with greater loss of life than Wyndham, just six crew and six merchants were available to work the returning ship. By this time Sir John Hawkins, cousin of Sir Francis Drake, recognized the potential profit in slaving and in 1562 took the first English human cargo to the West Indies, setting the trend and selling to Hispaniola. In doing so, he managed to upset both the Spanish and the Portuguese and, after two more voyages, had started a long quarrel which finally lead to open war between England and Spain.

In 1618 King James I granted a royal charter to 'The Company of the Adventurers of London trading into Africa' with exclusive trading rights along the Guinea coast, but having to fight the other European countries of France, Holland and Portugal for the privilege. Ill health took such a toll that these companies were never going to make the sort of profits, or to grow to the size of the East India Company. The Dutch were founding joint stock companies at the same time as the English and established themselves along the coast in 1621 with the 'Netherlands West India Company'. By the time Antigua and Barbados were colonized around 1623–1625 slave trading had a ready market and blossomed. Another chartered company was set up in 1672, 'The Royal African Company', which having interest from the Duke of York and the King, was a powerful enterprise and had a concession from South Barbary to the Cape of Good Hope, building ports at Accra, Secundee and Kommenda, and bought Fredericksborg, Cape Coast, from the Danish. Further slave trading rights were set up through the 'Assiento Company' to supply Spanish colonies in America in 1713, which lasted with more or less financial success until 1752 by which time Spain was demanding more of the profits as a royalty than the company could sustain.

In 1788 the President of the Royal Society, Sir Joseph Banks, backed up by a passionate interest in Africa, formed the 'Association for Promoting the Discovery of Africa', which gave encouragement and money to explorers, in particular to explore the Niger basin. The source, direction and the nature of its delta had perplexed geographers from the early sixteenth century onwards. Its parameters became important because it was seen as the route to the gold and slaves that were hitherto brought over the northern barrier of the Great Sahara Desert to the north by Arab traders. The impassable rain forests south of the Sahara combined with a European propensity to malaria gave the impression of an impenetrable curtain that was only broken through by consistent, mainly British, explorations from 1805 onwards. The expeditions of the interior by Victorian household names such as Mungo Park, the Lander brothers, and John Laird – from the well-known family of Scottish shipbuilders who subsequently formed his own African shipping company that became the Elder Dempster Line – to find the gold, or the source of the Niger, believed for a long time to emanate from the Nile, further inspired coastal surveys at the river mouths from where these men started their expeditions. In fact the Niger originates just 200 miles from the Atlantic but winds eastwards and then south for 2600 miles before flowing out into the Bight of Benin in a comprehensive spread of tributaries, which for many years were thought to be the mouths of many separate rivers, until they were properly surveyed in the nineteenth century.

By the eighteenth century cartographers became more honest and left gaps for areas they did not know, exemplified by the French cartographers, Guillaume De L'Isle and Jean Baptiste Bourguignon D'Anville. How much this 'truthful' approach with large blanks marked as *incognita* motivated Europeans to explore, claim and colonize these lands is hard to assess, but the Victorian explorers and missionaries relied on the coastal surveys to deliver them to the start point of their expeditions into the dark interior. David Livingstone was supported by the Royal Navy, who provided the ship and crew to take him out. Typically his exploration, and others like it, paved the way for the European 'scramble for Africa' of the 1880s and 1890s so that by 1914 only two states did not fly a European flag: Liberia, set up by philanthropists as a refuge country for freed slaves, and Abyssinia, now Ethiopia.

Captain Matthew Flinders' unhappy six-year incarceration from 1804 by the French on the island of Mauritius (after the island's governor refused to accept that Flinders had been granted immunity) with mainly his surveying knowledge and charts garnered from his survey of Australia for company, was joined in the last two by another prisoner, Lieutenant William Fitzwilliam Owen. He had carried out surveys in the Maldives, and was able to learn a lot more from Flinders between 1808 and 1810 which was to stand him in good stead for his five-year African survey, which he started in 1821.

However, the first British Admiralty expedition to the African continent was to have disastrous results, which became, sadly, typical. With Commodore James Tuckey in charge in the schooner *Congo*, he and his team were to explore and survey the river of that name. They got 280 miles upstream where Tuckey and five of the surveying officers developed malaria and died. The efficacy of quinine had been known from about 1640 by the Jesuits in Peru, where it was extracted by the Indians from the bark of the Cinchona tree. Although it had been brought to Europe, its use by Europeans in middle Africa, in parallel to the slow acceptance of citric fruits as an anti-scorbutic measure to prevent the condition of scurvy, was slow to develop, and many surveying expeditions were to be aborted in consequence.

Along the African east coast the Portuguese were content to build a chain of forts up into the Arabian Peninsula, culminating in Muscat, while leaving the Sultan of Oman to claim sovereignty over the entire coast south to Cape Delgado, at the border between what is now Mozambique and Tanzania. Most ships sailing to India avoided this coast, using the friendly Comoros Islands about 200 miles off Cape Delgado. The East India Company made a small survey in 1810 of a minor part of the east coast, but too small to be useful.

Consequently, there was little hydrographic information of this coast in existence, but with the abolition of the slave trade in 1807 Britain started to suppress it on the east coast as well as the west coast, and to develop trade there, too – this made for more and better surveys.

Good charts were now essential and in 1821 Captain Owen was chosen by the British Hydrographer, Captain Thomas Hurd, to survey the whole of the east coast from the Cape of Good Hope north to Cape Guardafui at the northeastern tip of Somalia, a coastal distance of well over 6000 miles. He set off with two survey ships, HMS *Leven*, a ship-sloop, and *Barracouta*, a small brig. These were later supplemented on the trade wind sweep across the Atlantic to Rio de Janeiro by the local purchase of an American steamboat, the *Cockburn*, and in Cape Town, by the *Albatross*, which, with a shallower draught, could work close inshore and up river. Owen had a team of officers who, surviving the fever, were all in their turn to make their mark in surveying, and some would later have survey ships named after them. Alexander Vidal, later to become a vice-admiral, was noted for disproving the existence of the worrying vigia (the hydrographic term for an unproven rock or shoal marked on a chart) in the eastern Atlantic known as Aitkin's Rock. Also in Owen's team were William Mudge, who did considerable work later along the Irish coast, with Thomas Boteler along the West African coastal region and Richard Owen, his nephew, who did much valuable work in South America, prior to Robert Fitzroy with Charles Darwin in HMS *Beagle*.

Surveying techniques were continually appraised, and Owen was keen to try new ideas. He had calibrated rockets of different magnitude, based on an earlier design by Sir William Congreve, so that he knew at what height a given size of rocket would explode, and he fired two at once vertically from different stations, calculating the meridian distance by measuring with the chronometer the time of each explosion, a 'rough and ready way to measure longitude difference'. It could well have been that the rockets were more useful fired horizontally, for example when Lieutenant Vidal was attacked by Hollontonte natives at Delagoa Bay. Captain Cook had learned from army surveyors in North America of the idea of using guns and measuring the time between seeing the flash and hearing the report, and this method is still valid today, but during the African surveys the local chief was pleased to accept this as a personal salute.

Owen started the five-year enterprise with a previous survey of the Cape Verde Islands, which, given to the authorities in Lisbon, became the currency exchanged for permission to survey Portugal's African territory. In 1822 Owen surveyed southwards from Delagoa Bay. As so many of his crew died from malaria, so points of significance along the coast gained a name *in memoriam*, and, with the season's work done, the squadron retired to Simon's Bay to draw up their surveys and recuperate.

The squadron divided to complete the survey north from English River to Cape Delgado, then sailed to Mozambique to present the Portuguese governor with a set of charts. For example, a small group were landed by Lieutenant Vidal from the *Barracouta* who tried to explore the Zambezi from Quelimane. Next they tackled the coast to the north of Delgado Bay, while Owen sailed to Bombay to recruit merchant sailors, send his ready charts to England, re-provision and then call at Muscat to get the Imam's approval to survey in his area. Every attempt at any inshore surveying and exploration resulted in fever. Surveys were made from Cape Guardafui, although Owen himself fell ill, along the inhospitable Somali coast to Mogadishu. Mombasa

Slavery

Given the opportunity to own vast tracts of land in the Americas, the prospect of farming on a grand scale invited the means to plant and harvest the produce. Mix this with an ideological sense of superiority and you had the formula for acceptable slavery. By the eighteenth century this was the scene. The Portuguese had started enslavement as they explored down the coast of Africa. The Spanish in South America used the indigenous population until it was all but wiped out by European disease and excruciating work. Black Africans seemed a better alternative as they were physically stronger and seemed to adapt well to the Caribbean climate. With the development of the plantation system in the American South during the 1750s the traffic in slaves grew apace. Their status in America changed from indentured servants to absolute slaves, and by the end of the eighteenth century they had no legal rights. The moral tide started to turn when Denmark became the first European country to abolish slavery in 1792, and England, led by the rhetoric of William Wilberforce MP, followed suit on 1807, with the USA outlawing it a year later. Brazil was the last country to emancipate slaves in 1888.

The British were vigorous in stamping out slavery and established a large squadron to patrol the West African coast, particularly around the Bight of Benin, and blockade the ports from which the slavers would sail. The USA was slower to act to enforce the abolition. Even by 1859–60 at least 100 American-built slave ships sailed from New York harbour, and the American anti-slave patrol never had more than four or five ships on the job.

Policing the 'Slave Coast' around West Africa was not easy – the blockade needed to cover a coastline 2000 miles long. Slave ships were adept at tricks such as false colours and papers (America was a popular choice of pretence as she would not allow her ships to be searched on the high seas) and some slavers had false decks built where slaves were packed in like sardines, back to belly, so that one could only turn over if all turned over together. Once a slaver was arrested, the ship and her cargo had to be dealt with. This was difficult as the slaves were usually sent to an uncertain fate in Liberia or Sierra Leone, and the ships, initially, were auctioned off in their country of origin, and would likely end up in the hands of the previous owner again. Later the British solution was to burn the slavers. The fate of the captain and crew was, in America, draconian on paper, with the death penalty. In practice, however, in America during the period 1837–62 only one crew was executed, and just two-dozen imprisoned – little deterrent.

One man who commanded British anti-slave patrols was Captain William Buck, who wrote, 'Here we are in the most miserable station in the world, attempting the impossible – the suppression of the slave trade. We look upon the affair as complete humbug … So long as a slave worth a few dollars here fetches £80–£100 in America, men and means will be found to evade even the strictest blockade.'

With the slave trade still flourishing in Cuba, Brazil and the American South, Buck was in the Gulf of Benin for a total of eight years during two commissions. In 1846–49 he was master's assistant in HMS *Grappler* during which they had moderate success in capturing 15 slavers, mainly Brazilian, with euphemistic names such as *Felicidade* and *Esperança*. Before 1839 a slaver could only be detained if she had slaves actually on board, which lead to horrific scenes of the evidence of human cargo being thrown overboard. With the change in the law, the presumption of guilt hinged on the 'equipment clause' and arrests were made on this evidence.

Buck's second commission was as commanding officer of HMS *Medusa* in 1856–60. A side-wheel paddle steamer with auxiliary sails, she was bigger and quicker than the *Grappler*, but captured few slavers, partly because the demand from the Americas was reducing as the demographics of the now resident slave population grew.

Buck was a keen amateur painter and recorded his experiences, giving us today a unique reference (see illustration below). Buck finished his seatime after the *Medusa*, and looked after a coast guard station at Winchelsea, Sussex in England until 1870.

Capture of the cutter from the slave schooner *Secunda Andorinha* (seen in the background, which had 500 slaves on board) by HMS *Grappler* in April 1848. The warning shot splashes astern. (Courtesy of the South Street Seaport Museum, New York, 81.42.12)

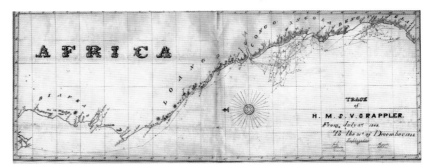

This chart shows the monthly track of the *Grappler* between 2 July and 31 December 1848. Buck was the sailing master. It covers from the River Volta round the coast of the Bight of Benin to Cape Formosa. (Courtesy of the South Street Seaport Museum, New York, 81.42.18)

north to Mogadishu had already been surveyed by Vidal. Royal Navy survey ships were quite often involved in the drive to eliminate slavery and at Mombasa the Sheikh agreed to abolish it if Owen gave him protection from the Muscat Imam. They remained there to draw up the completed charts covering the 6000 miles so far surveyed and on their conclusion split to survey the islands of Madagascar, Mauritius and the Seychelles, where Owen thankfully dropped anchor on Christmas Day 1824 with the idea of returning to England. His instructions from the Admiralty, however, told him to carry out a survey of West Africa from the Congo to the Gambia Rivers, another fever-ridden area. He was to complete the Madagascar survey before leaving, and during this was involved in further anti-slavery work, capturing a slaver near St Augustine's Bay bound for Brazil with 172 slaves on board: amongst the crew was a deserter from one of Owen's ships. Mombasa, from which many slave traders operated, was re-taken some years later, vindicating Owen's agreement to put the port under Britain's protection when threatened by the Imam of Muscat, which had been expediently over-turned by the government after another turn of the political tide to appease the Imam. Mombasa became an important British naval base in the fight against slavery.

The squadron left the Cape of Good Hope for home in October 1825, but would do some coastal work *en route* to the Congo River, where they intended to carry out a full survey. They passed and noted the marble crosses left by

Diaz, like milestones on the road, at Angra Peguena (near Luderitz Bay), at Cape Negro and then to Benguela, checking positions with the theodolite. The *Leven* and the *Barracouta* split here, making for Sierra Leone and the Gulf of Guinea respectively. By 1817 a Court of Mixed Commission, a vice-admiralty court, was set up to deal with the slavers captured by naval warships and Britain had also acquired control of Ile de Los and the Banana Islands, which needed surveying. But Owen's homecoming was delayed again because the new governor of Sierra Leone needed help in stamping out a notorious slaver, James Tucker, up-river along the coast. Owen led the squadron, navigating the River Kittan, and combining a running survey. Success in overwhelming the slave station was tinged with, as with every expedition, death from malaria, including the governor and many of the crew.

Vidal had been promoted Post Captain and after five years the squadron finally sailed for home. An astonishing achievement was the accurate surveying of 30,000 miles of coastline over a five-year period. Surveyors had experienced far more than simple charting. They had played the roles of ambassadors and anti-slavers, sorted out local wars, dined with the fading colonial power of Portugal, enjoyed the civilized hospitality of Cape Town, and survived malaria. Owen was sent once more to the Bight of Benin to survey Fernando Po Island, as it was to take the anti-slavery court there. He survived, was offered the post of Hydrographer to the Navy, and had it denied him in the same despatches. (It was given to Francis Beaufort.) Owen retired to Canada where he had spent his earlier years surveying the Great Lakes, dying a vice-admiral at 83. So many men had died during the survey that when John Washington reported the completed African survey to the Royal Geographical Society, of which he was Secretary, in 1838, he remarked '… (it) may be said to have been drawn and coloured with drops of blood'.

| THE ENTRANCE TO THE RIVER CONGO, SURVEYED BY CAPTAIN BUCK, ***C.1857*** **|** Whilst on anti-slavery duties, as was asked of all naval officers by the Hydrographical Office at the Admiralty, Captain William Buck made surveys. Here, we have one of the charts he made of the River Congo's mouth and up the river for about 60 miles. (Courtesy of the South Street Seaport Museum, New York, 81.42.24)

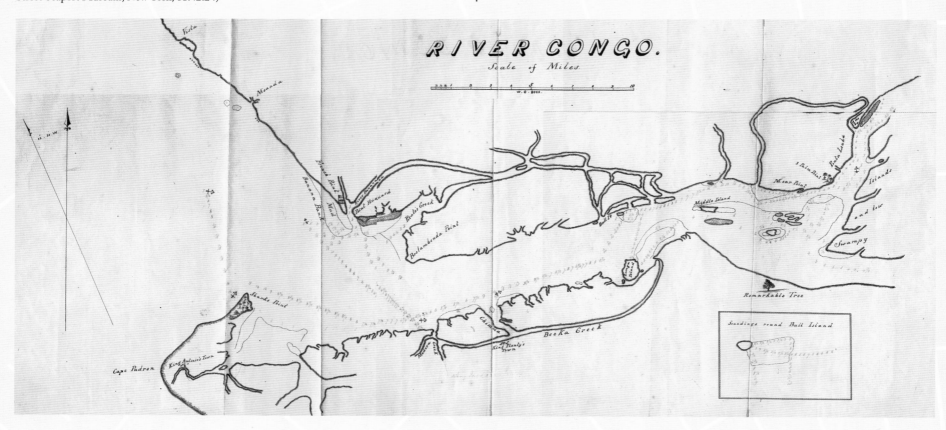

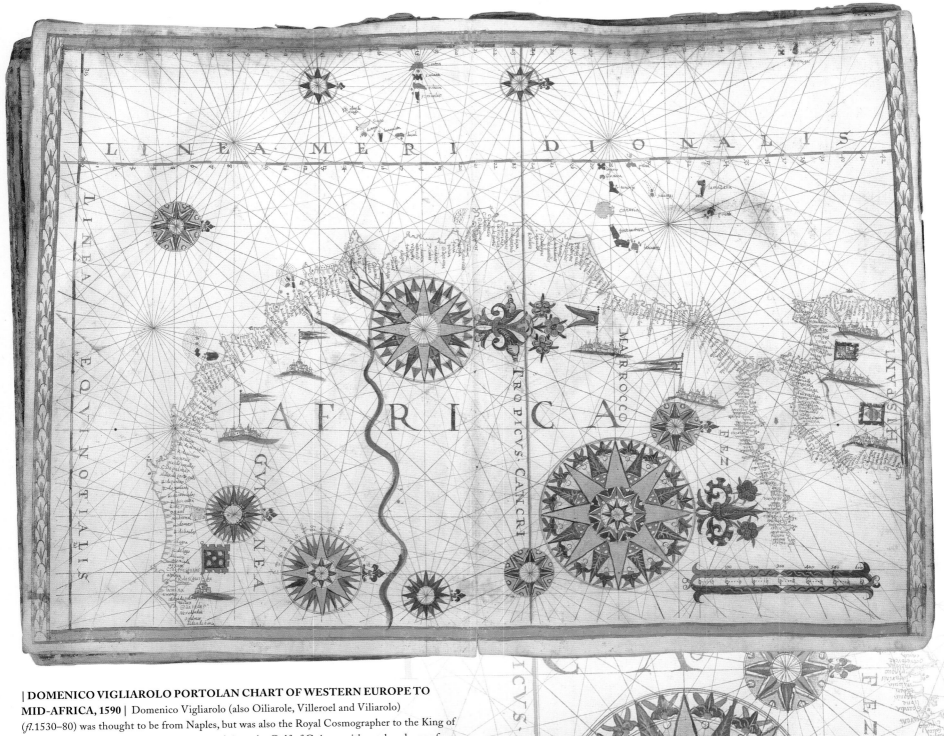

| DOMENICO VIGLIAROLO PORTOLAN CHART OF WESTERN EUROPE TO MID-AFRICA, 1590 | Domenico Vigliarolo (also Oiliarole, Villeroel and Viliarolo) (*fl.*1530–80) was thought to be from Naples, but was also the Royal Cosmographer to the King of Spain. His portolan chart of 1590 covers south into the Gulf of Guinea, with an abundance of named ports, culminating with the Portuguese flag near to the Bight of Benin, and beautiful and flamboyant compass roses. (Courtesy of The Hispanic Society of America, New York, K18)

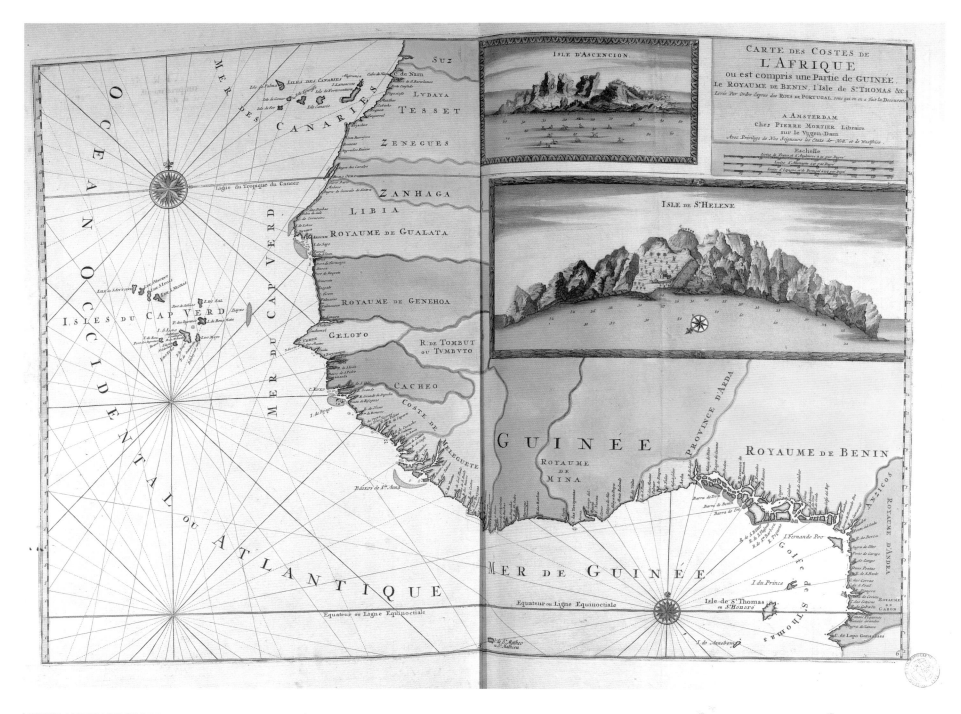

| WEST AFRICA FROM *LE NEPTUNE FRANÇOIS*, 1693 | *Le Neptune François* was published in 1693, and was the result of the collaboration of a national French effort of hydrographers, mathematicians and astronomers. The coastlines had been tied to various points of land by triangulation and, using Mercator's projection, latitude and longitude were used to anchor the coastline to a fixed grid. This chart, which covers round to the Congo, is a copy by an astute map-seller from Amsterdam, Pierre Mortier, who pirated the original *Neptune* and published editions in French, Dutch and English.

The elevations of St Helena and Ascension islands – the two important watering stops and dead reckoning updates on any sailing passage through the South Atlantic to South America or to the East Indies – are shown complete with soundings. (Reproduced by courtesy of the Royal Geographical Society with IBG, 14.c.73)

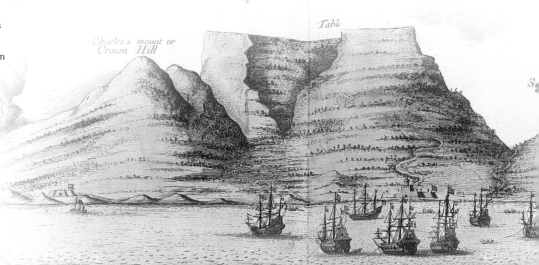

| PAULUS VAN HUSUM'S MANUSCRIPT CHART OF THE CAPE OF GOOD HOPE, C.1670 |

The Dutch cartographer Paulus van Husum worked for a time for Joan Blaeu (1596–1673), son of Willem Janszoon Blaeu who was Hydrographer to the Dutch East India Company, and used an engraved base of Blaeu's with rhumb lines to draw out this chart of *Cabo da Bona Esperanza* of *c*.1670, where there had been a Dutch settlement for around a hundred years. John Seller copied this chart for his *Atlas Maritimus*. (Pepys Library, Magdalene College, Cambridge)

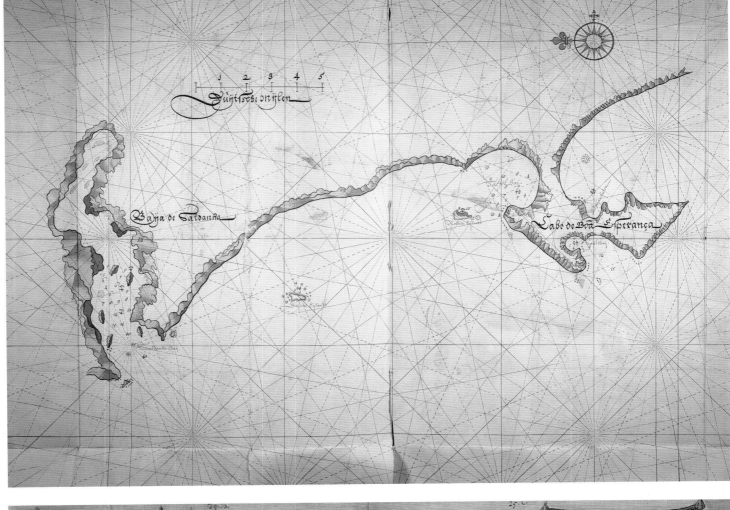

| JOHN SELLER'S CHART OF THE CAPE OF GOOD HOPE,

1675. | From Pepys' personal collection of charts at the Admiralty the elevation shows warships and merchants ships of the contemporary maritime powers nestling in the shelter of Table Bay not long after the conclusion of the Third Dutch War with England of 1672–74. John Seller had copied many of the charts that appear in his *Atlas Maritimus* from Dutch sources as much as 50 years old, with doubtful accuracy. As a consequence, Pepys was instrumental in having Captain Greenvile Collins appointed to produce his *Great Britain's Coasting Pilot*. (Pepys Library, Magdalene College, Cambridge)

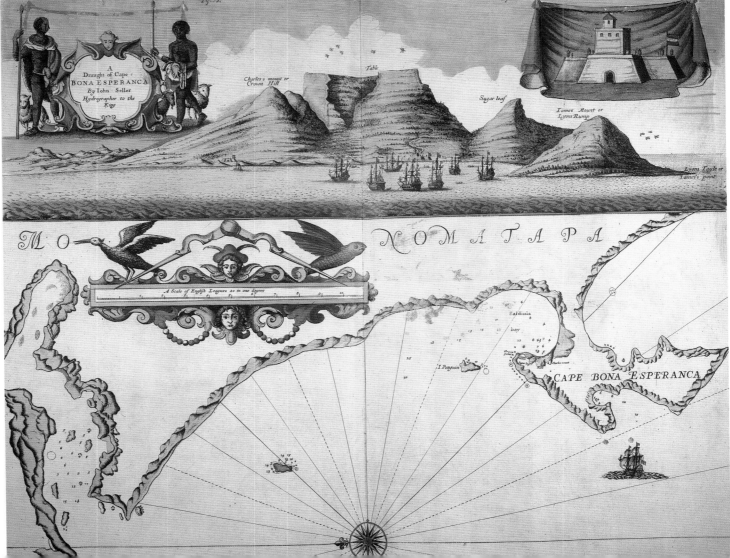

| RIGHT | WORKING SURVEY OF THE WEST AND SOUTHERN COASTLINES OF AFRICA, *C. 1825* | The graticule lines on this working survey, the style and details of which are commensurate with the techniques of the early nineteenth century, show how the coastline from Cape Santa Clara, Gabon, south and around the Cape of Good Hope to Cape Agullas in South Africa has been worked up. The depths along the coast and compass variation are noted, along with the names of the premier rivers and coastal settlements. This working chart is probably part of Captain W F Owen's survey of the coastline of Africa carried out between the years 1820 and 1828. Once received in the Hydrographic Office, it would be re-worked so as to accord with the instructions written across the top: 'Mr Harrison Pray reduce by squares this Mercator Chart where the Latitudes are unequal and the Longitudes equal (which is the hall mark of a Mercator projection) to a Plane chart where lat & long are both equal. The scale of Long. Is 4/10 = 1d. It is to come into this Branch.' A plane chart is one where the squares formed by 'lat and long' have sides of the same length, which, apart for the Equator where this holds true, because of the spherical shape of the Earth, will lead to inaccuracies in a ship's position because this way of projecting the land has to assume that the earth is flat. Plane sailing remained the preferred method of navigating for a long time after Mercator published his projectional method in 1569. The gnomonic projection is the other main type where a great circle, the shortest distance between two points on the curved surface of the earth, appears as a straight line. Measuring the latitude and longitude of suitable points along this line, which could be used to represent the course a ship wants to steer, positions can be transferred to a Mercator chart and the course to be steered sketched in. In practice the ship will sail a series of straight (i.e. rhumb lines) that join up the position points, altering course slightly for each one, and making good a curved course across the surface of the earth's oceans which will be the shortest distance between departure and landfall. (Admiralty Library Manuscript Collection VZ 8/36/2)

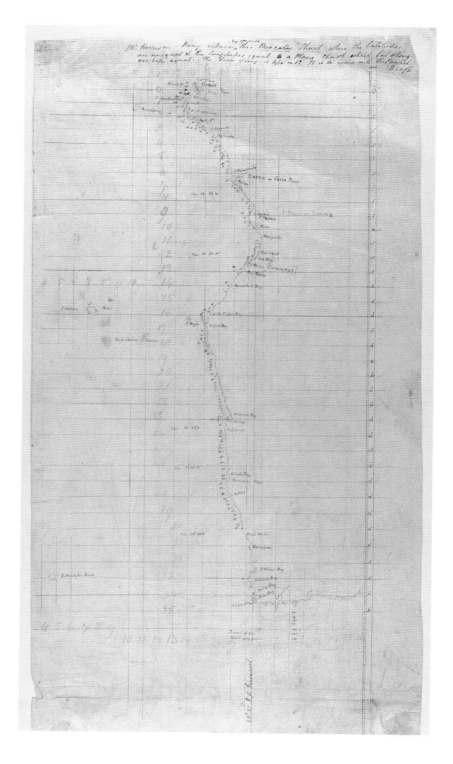

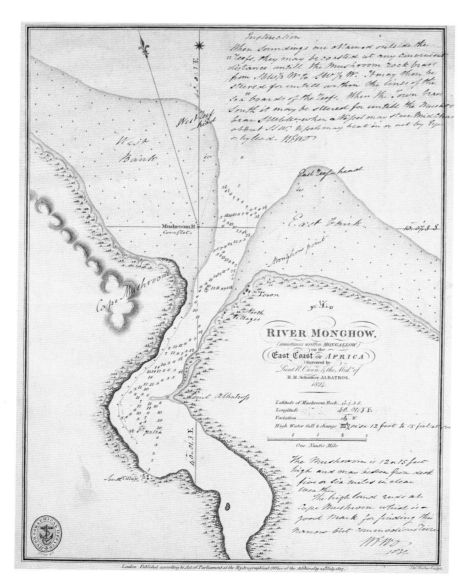

| LEFT | PRINTED CHART OF THE RIVER MONGHOW BY LIEUTENANT OWEN | Richard Owen, nephew of Captain W F Owen, carried out this survey with the midshipmen of HMS *Albatross* of the River Monghow about 50 miles north of Cape Delgado, in the south of Tanzania, between Lindi and Mikindani, in 1824. The original chart, published in 1827, was engraved in Holborn, London by John and Charles Walker. The brothers, who ran their own copper engraving company, were the eldest and youngest of four sons of John Walker who had worked with Dalrymple in the East India Company and followed him to the Admiralty. Captain W F Owen carried out the colossal task of surveying in detail the African coastline and here has made his own manuscript notes to update this chart in 1834. The notes would have been incorporated in the relevant Sailing Directions, the African Pilot and issued by the Admiralty as a chart correction. (Admiralty Library Manuscript Collection VZ 8/35/1)

| ABOVE | **VIEW OF FERNANDO PO ISLAND** | Part of the view of Fernando Po Island, a former colony of both Portugal and Spain in the Bight of Biafra, painted from Maidstone Bay by the captain of HMS *Barracouta*, Thomas Boteler, in 1827. Although it measures 11½ feet long by 1 foot high, it would form the basis for an elevation or navigational view for inclusion on charts of the area. The island, being quite high, was a useful navigational mark and base for the slave patrols that sailed in the area. Note the six seabirds flying atop the mountain. Surveyors marked important points on a chart or view with sea birds to key the written notes instead of numbers. So the first prominent point, such as a headland or church might have one bird, and so on. (UKHO © British Crown Copyright)

| RIGHT | **PRAIA PORT, CAPE VERDE ISLANDS FROM PETER FANNIN'S REMARK BOOK, 1772** | Peter Fannin was the sailing master in HMS *Adventure* under Captain Tobias Furneaux, the back-up ship to Captain Cook in HMS *Resolution* on his second voyage of Pacific exploration. This delightful chart of the harbour of Cape Verde's main island port of Praia in St Tiago comes from his Remark Book that he kept as a record of the voyage. Perhaps the monkey wielding the navigational dividers is symptomatic of some of the mathematical difficulties navigators had to grasp. (UKHO © British Crown Copyright)

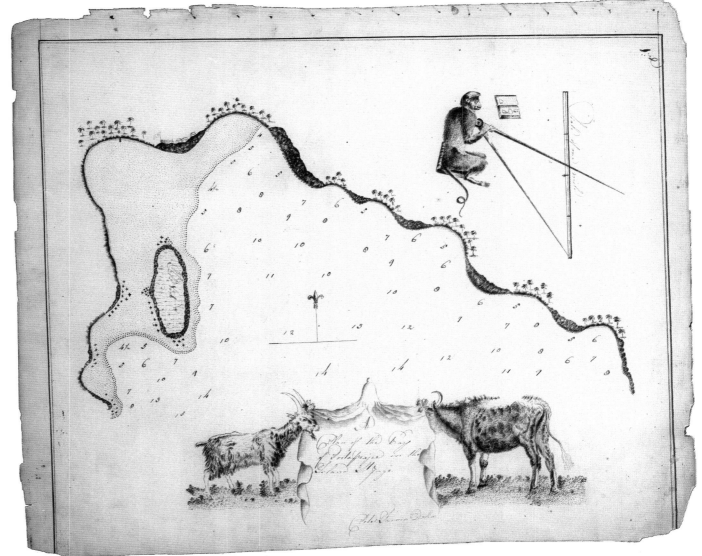

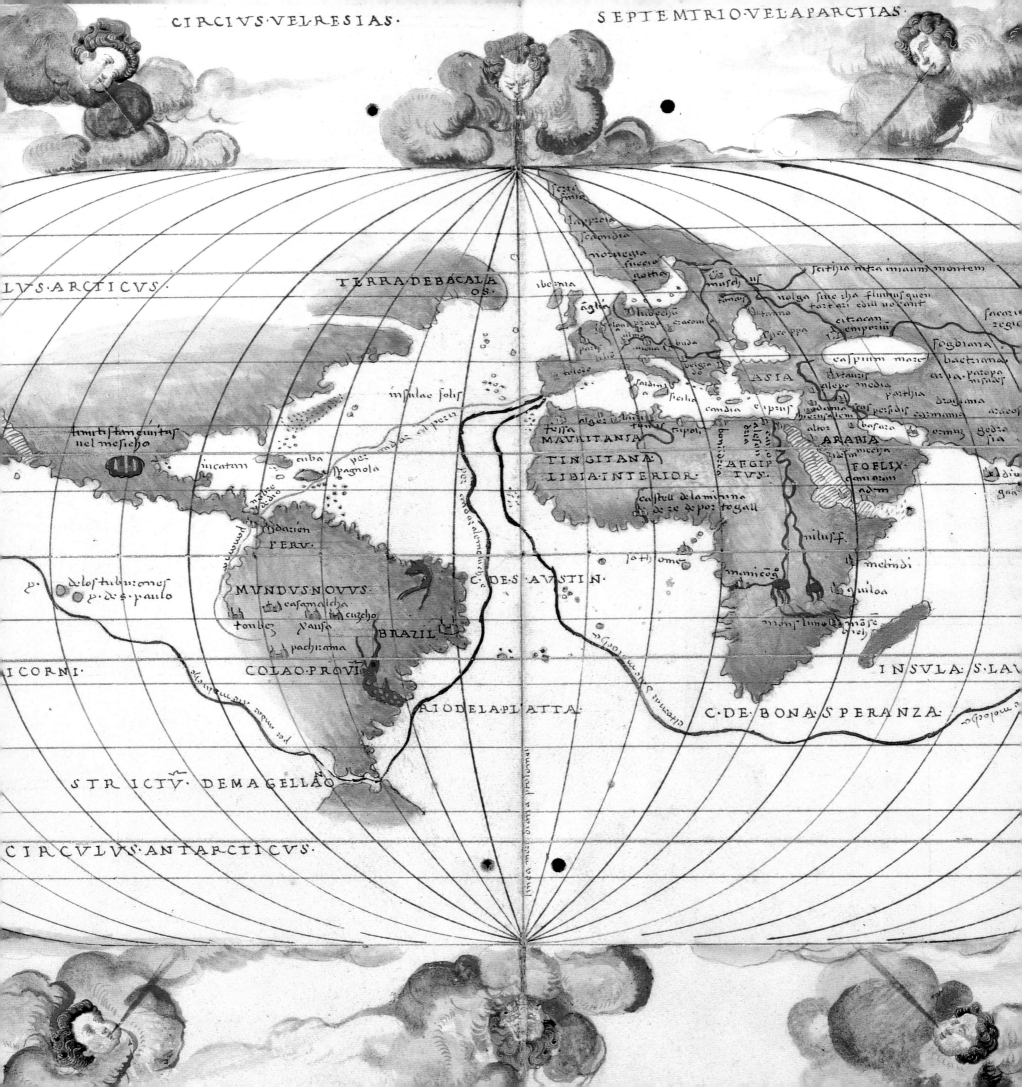

India, Ceylon and the Persian Gulf

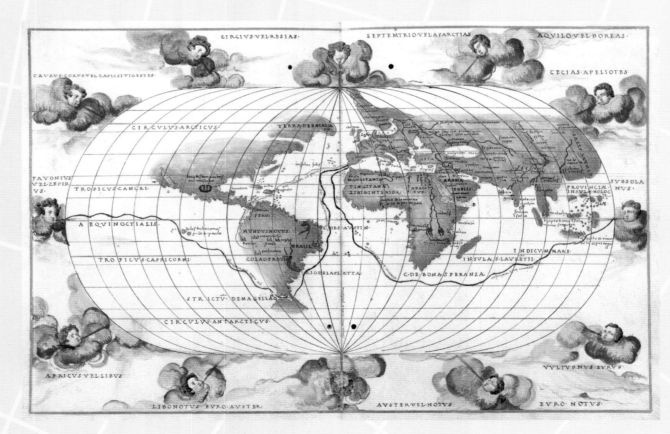

| LEFT DETAIL & ABOVE | **MAP OF THE WORLD BY BATTISTA AGNESE FROM A BOOK OF PORTOLAN CHARTS, _C._ 1550** | This map depicts much of the old and new worlds defined by Magellan's circumnavigation track. The continents are starting to look familiar, yet strange, with Africa too wide, North America too large and India too small. The zero meridian follows Ptolemy and centres along the Fortunate (Canary) Islands with lines of longitude every 15°. Contemporary convention shows the Red Sea in red; the supposed sources of the Nile, the River Plate in South America and the Ganges in China feature strongly. Mythological Mediterranean wind gods puff their cheeks from twelve traditional directions. (Reproduced by courtesy of the Royal Geographical Society with IBG, 265.C.18)

THE charting of the coastline of the Indian sub-continent, the Indian Ocean and into the Persian Gulf to the north west, the Spice Islands to the east and thence to China and Japan, was inexorably bound up for 250 years with the development of a small joint stock company comprising 218 investors from the Merchants and Aldermen of London and Royal Courtiers.

Protected by a royal charter, giving it a monopoly of trade, granted by Queen Elizabeth I in 1600, it was called the Honourable East India Company (later affectionately and colloquially known as John Company). From a tiny foothold on the continent of India at the port of Surat in 1611, it had become the absolute ruler of an oriental empire by 1857, even though as a private company it faced fierce competition from French and Dutch 'East India companies' owned and run by their national governments during the formative years. Only after the Indian Mutiny was John Company taken under government control.

Navigation of the Indian Ocean, however, goes back as early as the records of mankind. Accounts of trading in the Ocean are found in ancient Indian and Chinese texts. Early Sumerian inscriptions allude to shipbuilding in Oman for this purpose and are substantiated by Indian wood found at Sumerian sites. The Greeks, in the first century AD used the *Periplus* of the Erythrean Sea, which were simple sailing directions for the Red Sea and known parts of the Indian Ocean. – the Greek word '*euthera*' means red. The Romans, too, wrote about sailing the Indian Ocean, and we know that the Greek navigator Hippalus understood how to time the use of the Monsoon winds to sail direct to India.

Much of our understanding of Arab navigation during medieval times, which was sophisticated, comes from the writings of the navigator and pilot Ibn Majid. He is quoted in Arab texts as the navigator who was paid to guide Vasco da Gama to India. He later died a broken man for having revealed his knowledge and methods, thereby bringing the invader to the Arabian Sea.

His lengthy treatise on navigation, written as poetry and perhaps in consequence easier to learn, shows that the Arabs understood the use of the Pole Star to determine latitude. They had guiding pilot books that gave distances between ports, descriptions of all the coasts with compass bearings and knew the winds and their seasons. The word 'monsoon' comes from the Arabic *mausim*, indicating their understanding of the use of the monsoon winds.

Gavin Menzies in his meticulously researched book *1421* shows how the Chinese had sailed along the coasts bordering the Indian Ocean in that year with one of four huge fleets that sailed across the world (and makes a persuasive case that they discovered America in that year, too).

The insatiable European demand for spices from the Orient represented more than just a status symbol for the wealthy. Pepper masked putrid victuals; nutmeg and mace sweetened food and were regarded as a cure for sickness; cloves, only grown in the Banda and Molucca Islands in Indonesia, were used for flavouring, medicines and toothache; and perfumes disguised poor drainage and personal hygiene. Cinnamon bark, ginger root, galangal and cardamom were used for culinary and medicinal purposes.

For up to four centuries these and other exotic oriental merchandise, such as silks and porcelain, had been brought overland via the slow Silk Route, so well described by Marco Polo. When the Ottomans blocked this route in the fourteenth century, it was supplanted by discovery of the route around the Cape of Good Hope and across the Indian Ocean. Fortunes were then made by bringing back nutmeg, mace and pepper from the Spice Islands of Java and Banda.

Companies, such as the Muscovy Company, set up in 1555 to trade through the Baltic to Russia, and the Levant Company in 1580 to the Ottomans, were forerunners for the fledgling East India Company. While the captains and crews of all the European maritime nations had served their apprenticeship in northern European waters and the Atlantic, the English company in particular faced ferocious competition from the Portuguese, sailing in purpose-built carracks, and who had taken a technological leap forward by using the metal nail to secure a ship's planks to better face the rough Atlantic seas. They set up a chain of coastal settlements from Goa to Lisbon, the focus of trade into Europe from Asia for a century until ousted by the Dutch in the early seventeenth century, who handled the trade thereon into northern Europe, and then, in turn, the British established their trading organization in the eighteenth century.

In general terms the evolution of oriental trade during the sixteenth century was set against a background of European wars, with contenders becoming co-conspirators, and changing political alliances. The eventual outcome of a war would depend as much on a peace treaty and marriage settlement as on business acumen and military prowess in the orient.

After King Sebastian of Portugal's disastrous invasion of Morocco, Philip II of Spain (instigator of the Armada of 1588) united Portugal and Spain in 1580. Subsequently, Portugal's overseas trading settlements and shipping were targeted by Spain's protestant enemies from England under Elizabeth I, and from Holland, fighting for independence from Spain. The vulnerability of Portugal's monopoly in the East, sanctioned with a line of demarcation between Spain and Portugal in the Treaty of Tordesillas of 1494, was gradually exposed: Drake's circumnavigation brought news of the Spice Islands where he touched *en route* also in 1580, and Portuguese carracks had been captured in 1587 and 1592 off the Azores and their oriental cargoes very profitably auctioned in London.

However, it was the Dutch who first contested the Portuguese monopoly. During previous years they had been involved as intermediaries between the Portuguese and the other northern European countries, and slowly put together the charts and sailing directions that were crucial for successful navigation to India and on to the Spice Islands. Dirk Gerritszoon's notes on navigation were published in Leiden in 1592. The Dutch explorer, Jan Huygen van Linschoten, had worked with his brothers in Seville and sailed to India in 1583 remaining there for seven years. He sailed with Willem Barents to try to open up the North-East passage to China, wrote an account under the title *Itinerario* of routes, countries, peoples and products as well as maps and charts that inspired the Dutch and English penetration of the East Indies. A record of the first Dutch trading voyage returning from Bantam in 1595 with a cargo of pepper was published in 1598 by Willem Lodewijckszoon as an illustrated *Historie van Indien*.

These accounts, and others, had enormous influence on the Dutch who formed their own East India Company, called *Vereenigde Oostindische Compagnie*, and known as the VOC, in 1602. They reached Bantam six years before the English in 1596, and were to beat them to almost all the Asian ports by that sort of margin, arriving with more men, ships, money and a stronger national intent. They shattered the Portuguese monopoly in a naval engagement off Bantam (north of modern day Djakarta) in 1601. This was part of the ruthless Dutch take-over of the supply of spices to Europe by snatching control of the means and place of production – the Banda group of islands, consisting of Amboyna, where large forts were built, Buru and Ceram.

When, in 1616, the ruler of the island of Run (where mace and nutmeg grew naturally) ceded the island to England, the Dutch moved in, capturing seven English ships. The Dutch consolidated their position making Batavia, present day Jakarta, their new headquarters, fully fortified. A century of strife between the two countries with intermittent periods of half-hearted co-operation countered with the three Anglo-Dutch Wars of 1652–55, 1665–67 and 1672–74 in the North Sea, combined with ruthless actions in the Asian theatre, which the English rarely won, such as the torture and execution of the English factors from Amboyna in 1623 (although the claim on Run was given up by the Dutch in exchange for Manhattan), meant English access to spices was denied.

Instead, the pepper trade was developed by the English at Benkulen in Indonesia. Enormous quantities were shipped by the East India Company to Europe, with more from Malabar, and later from Madras throughout the eighteenth century, with as much as one to two million pounds weight (453,600 to 907,200 kilograms) per year to London. In 1825, in a sort of international geographical rationalization, the settlement was exchanged with the Dutch for Malacca.

Throughout the seventeenth century the VOC was at the height of its success and had 40 warships, 150 merchant ships and 10,000 soldiers operating from its main base in Batavia, with subsidiary capitals in Malaya, Ceylon, Java, Malacca, Amboyna and Ternate (in the Molucca Islands), and a fortified post at the Cape of Good Hope.

Towards the end of that century power shifted to the British. With William of Orange on the British throne as William III, Britain became the more aggressive country, and Dutch corruption, complacency and lack of competitive edge in shipbuilding contributed to the VOC decline. It was further weakened by the catastrophic fourth Anglo-Dutch War of 1780–84. The Company was dissolved in 1795 after the invasion of Holland by the French Revolutionary army.

The British were much more successful in India than in Indonesia where the Dutch maintained their dominance. From Surat, where textiles were exported from Gujarat, the most important centre for trade for the Mughal Empire, trade was taken up into the Persian Gulf and the Red Sea.

The East India Company's centres of operation grew up in a more haphazard way than the Dutch. 'Presidencies' were based at Bantam, Surat and then nearby Bombay (fortunately acquired through Charles I's marriage to the Portuguese Catherine of Braganza as part of her dowry in 1661), Madras and later Calcutta in 1690, which took over as the 'senior' organization from Bombay. In its infancy the venture was risky. High capitalization was needed to build and run expensive ships and find skilled and willing crew. Investment would have a three-to-four-year lag before any return, and only such as London City Aldermen and others in the Royal Court could afford to invest. But profits from a successful voyage could be huge – 400 per cent or more. The English were more successful in getting a toehold into the Indian continent than the Portuguese who were less tolerated, partly because of their proselytizing zeal to convert the mogul's subjects to Catholicism. With a more patient approach, sometimes Company men were kept waiting for an audience with a mogul for up to three years, Britain gained footholds on the sub-continent at strategic seaports, and interestingly the seventeenth-century paintings of the

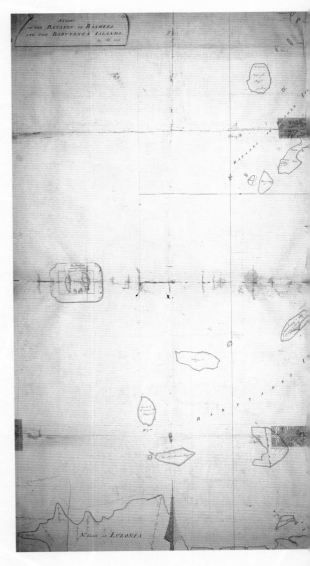

ALEXANDER DALRYMPLE'S ORIGINAL MANUSCRIPT CHART OF LUZONIA (LUZON) AND THE BATAN (BASHEES) ISLANDS, 1759 | While this chart of the Luzon Strait and the Philippines, dated 1759, is, of itself, perhaps dull to glimpse, it is a very important milestone in the history of charting and it was one of Alexander Dalrymple's first and original charts given by him to the British Hydrographic Office when he started in office in 1795. It covers the Batan Islands to the north Luzon coast, although most of the latitude graduations are now missing. A nice touch by Dalrymple is the small navigational views of island peaks placed within two of the islands and as, for us, a taster of his later cartouche designs, with the inset: 'The Bashees according to Dampier'. (Admiralty Library Manuscript Collection VZ 7/20)

Company's officials all reflect this with a coastline background. The British soon learned to make alliances, which made initial inroads with the moguls and slowly got a military grasp on the country by negotiating the right to self protection with a small number of armed Company soldiers at trading ports. Local British bureaucrats took pains to learn Persian, understand local culture and customs, even intermarried and integrated, but there was no grand scheme for an imperial project.

By 1609 the East India Company had built its own dockyard at Deptford on the Thames and there they constructed the magnificent ships that formed the Company's fleet – the East Indiamen – armed to fight the Malay pirates and competing rival ships of Holland, Portugal and France. Later, in 1656, the Company changed policy to hiring vessels from other builders, but the style of ship was continued. Ownership and management were separated, a precursor of today's joint stock company, and by 1677 it had evolved into a permanent company with annual dividends and shares that could be sold, rather than with investment and speculation for each voyage. To start with, one of the conditions stipulated by the Crown in allowing the Company to maintain its monopoly was that it support the English manufacture of broadcloth by exporting it to India. To sell this and even the lighter cloths such as kerseys, serges and baize into the hot climates of India and south-east Asia was bizarre and in fact wool didn't sell well;

it was no match against the beautiful designs of Indian textiles. Initially only pepper and cotton (allowing, it is said, the British clean underwear for the first time!) were exported to England until the silk textile trade from Bengal developed, along with salt-petre and indigo dye shipped out of Calcutta. The only other medium of exchange the English had was silver or *real de plata* (pieces of eight), either captured, or bought on the European bullion market.

On the voyages, beside surviving the cramped conditions on board, illnesses contracted in Asian ports, poor food, and scurvy, the greatest danger was from shipwreck, either from violent storms or from unforeseen shoals and rocks, and reliable charts became a priority which was not really systematically tackled until 1779 when Alexander Dalrymple became, in actuality although never formally appointed, the East India Company's Hydrographer.

Over the whole period of the Company's trading history from 1600 to 1833 approximately 4600 voyages set out from the River Thames, averaging eight ships a year up to 1720 and growing to 42 a year from 1800. Of these, 231 ended with total loss, of which 110 were wrecked, 32 lost at sea in storms, and 89 during sea battles with the Dutch or French, or some through carelessness with explosives or galley fires.

The voyage from Europe to the East Indies was probably the most complex of routes compared to those across the Atlantic, and round Cape Horn to the Pacific. For the first leg a ship used the Atlantic currents and winds to best advantage, and this is described in Chapter II. With a stop at the Cape of Good Hope to water, re-provision, repair ship and rest the crew, the passage to India took a north-westerly heading parallel to the East African coast through the Mozambique Channel, later stopping at Anjouan, one of the Comoros Islands between Mozambique and Madagascar to take on water, avoiding the south-westerly flowing Agulhas and Mozambique currents and across the northern Indian Ocean, taking advantage of the summer south-westerly monsoon wind. Or, taking a different route, the ship chased along the southern latitudes known as the roaring forties, before altering course north based on a dead reckoning position to India, or sailed further west to head through the Indonesian islands via straits such as the Sunda Strait, between Sumatra and Java, to run to Bantam, Batavia or further across the Gulf of Tonkin to China.

The need for charts to build up a safe means of navigating to the East and to safely tuck their ships into harbour at the end of their long voyage was well appreciated. While the French and Dutch East India companies tackled this by setting up hydrographic offices, the British and its East India Company during the eighteenth century expected their captains to purchase charts from commercial sources such as London chart-sellers. At the end of the return voyage they were then expected to leave the ship's journal, which included the log with daily entries of the ship's (probably estimated) position, hourly sea state, notice of any dangers to mariners, such as shoals, wrecks, rocks, currents and tidal streams, at the Company's London offices. The sailing master or captain would include a navigational view, an elevation of the land profile as seen from the sea to help identify the ship's position, along with hand-drawn harbour and anchorage sketches. But this invaluable information was not exploited properly although English captains would pass on their knowledge (for a stipend) to the commercial chartmakers in London. The resulting folio of charts and pilots, paradoxically, 'owed more to commercialism than to any systematic analysis'. One pioneering publication was the *English Pilot for Oriental Navigation* compiled by John Seller with the help of John Thornton, who was appointed

Native Indian Chart

This unusual Gujarati chart actually covers the Red Sea and the Gulf of Aden, although the illustration shows approximately from 'Mocha' (Al Mukha) around the distinctive right-angle bend of the strait 'Babool Mandeb' (Bab el Mandeb) to 'Maculla' (Al Mukalla). Its significance lies in the approach taken to solving the problem common to all maritime cultures, navigating from one landfall to another. Just as the Japanese found the answer to striking a bell with a clapper from the outside, this chart gives Asian pilots as effective a means of navigation that is diametrically different in execution to the European solution. It was drawn, it is thought, in the 1790s but has a stylistic similarity to Indian charts at least 100 years earlier, and may well show the schematic chart style going back yet much further.

Stylistic clues to its age lie in the stellar rhumb lines with constellation symbols at each end indicating sailing directions, and the attitude of the Pole Star regularly placed along the African coast of the Red Sea, and at selective positions elsewhere. No great importance was placed on the apparent direction and length of these rhumb lines, as their compass direction was indicated to the pilot by symbols and their distances in *zam* of sailing time. The characteristic Red Sea right angle bend at the strait of Bab el Mandeb that links the Red Sea to the Gulf of Aden just doesn't appear, but is not a problem to the pilot brought up on the schematic 'straight line' approach to charting.

Contemporary Southern Indian charts give more emphasis to on shore features whereas the Gujarati chart stresses sea features such as islands, shoals, reefs, and shallows. Perhaps this emphasis relates to the scales used and thus the size of ship; the larger-scale southern India charts for smaller vessels sailing short distances from port to port, and the larger vessels that would use the small-scale Red Sea chart to cross the Arabian Sea from, for example, Gujarat ports to Arabia and the horn of Africa. Perhaps, too, these ships would carry pilgrims to the northernmost port of Jiddah, Mecca, for the religious Hajj festival. Even so the chart still has room to show selected shoreline profiles, symbols indicating rare forested coastline, major mosques and other coastal monuments and flags of local rulers.

This chart was given to Sir Alexander Burnes by a local pilot in 1835, and then presented to the Royal Geographical Society, where it is now kept, and, although Gujarati pilots knew of European charts at least a hundred years earlier, it seems they saw no advantage in 'converting' to the European charting approach.

(Reproduced by courtesy of the Royal Geographical Society with IBG)

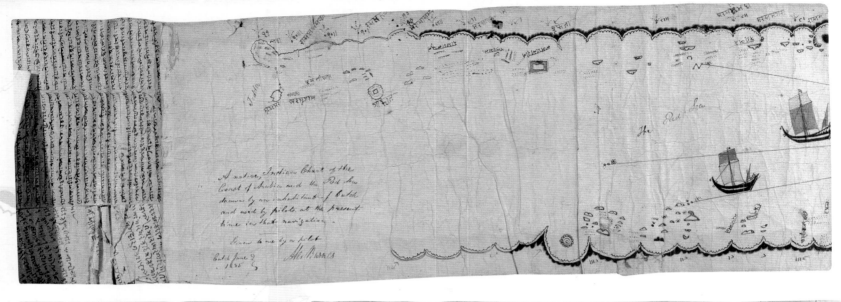

A native Indian Chart of the
Coast of Arabia and the Red Sea
drawn by an inhabitant of Cutch
and used by pilots at the present
time for that navigation.

Given to me by a pilot

Cutch June
1835   Alex Burnes

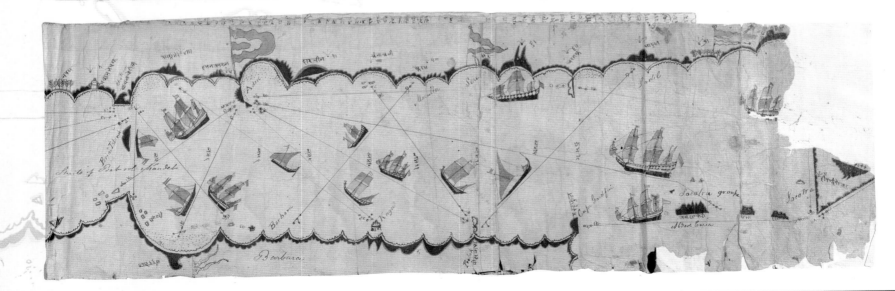

Hydrographer to the Hudson Bay Company and the East India Company. It was published in 1703 as Book III of *The English Pilot*. Captains used this in conjunction with H Cornwall's *Observations on Several Voyages to India*.

The Dutch company secretly supplied their captains with manuscript charts until Johannes Van Keulen published the Indian Ocean and Far East sea charts in *De Nieuwe Groote Lictende Zee-Fakkel* in 1753. The Dutch produced a remarkable number of map and chartmakers such as Blaeu and Jansson, but not even they could rival the extraordinary vigour of the Van Keulen family whose business was started by Johannes grandfather in 1680, continuing until 1823, and with other names until 1885. Until the Dutch Hydrographic Office was started in 1856, the Van Keulen charts were regarded as the 'offical' Dutch sea charts. Chart workshops in Amsterdam produced many coastal pilot charts of the East Indies, which were issued to captains and had to be returned at the end of each voyage, or paid for. The French had set up the *Dépot des Cartes et Plans de la Marine,* in 1720, and under it a retired French naval captain, D'Après de Mannevillette, was the French East India Company's hydrographer with an office at Lorient where he organized charts for the French ships until he died in 1780. His 1745 edition of *Le Neptune Oriental* was often used by British sea captains, more so after William Herbert translated it in 1758 as *A New Directory for the East Indies*.

It may seem surprising that the British did so well at sea, given the unprofessional state of chart and navigational provision up to the latter half of the seventeenth century. Charles Noble wrote a pamphlet in 1755 describing the difference between English and French charting by saying that

> the French have been at pains to improve their Navigation and their Charts; Those of the Indian Seas, by Monsieur D'Après de Mannevillette, a Captain in their Service, exceed everything of the kind in Europe. It is a pity they are not translated into English, for the benefit of the Navigators. Those who understand the language, and have seen them, must have a despicable opinion, of our Indian Pilot, with which Messrs Mount and Page have long imposed on, and picked the pockets of our Countrymen, and which are fit only for the Grocers and Chandler Shops, or posterior uses.

Damning words indeed for the charts which 25 to 30 ships a year in four or five fleets of the East India Company used.

After the loss of their North American territories in Canada and Louisiana the French focussed their ambitions in the east and in the south Pacific. Skirmishes between Britain and France along the Coromandel Coast, down the east coast of India, escalated into a hot war by the latter half of the eighteenth century as the conflict in home waters, precipitated by French support for the Americans in their War of Independence and progressing into the Napoleonic Wars, extended around the globe. By having three bases – Madras, Calcutta and Bombay – the British had a triangle of military advantage. They became skilled at playing one Indian ruler against another and very good at organising their military, with better uniforms, food, and welfare than the French. On a national level the East India Company learned to build up an indigenous soldiery who were relatively well paid and well armed, important in ousting the French from the Indian continent. By the early nineteenth century the Company had a quarter of a million troops in India – a fiscal and military complex supported by a naval fleet backed up by the British State.

At a personal level company servants were allowed to trade in their own right. By the 1750s ship owners and officers could set themselves up for life with the profits from one trading voyage, and retired company servants could set themselves up to trade between Asian ports nearby to the Company factories. Thomas Pitt was one such successful businessman who acquired a rough diamond which he sold to (and literally for) the French Crown, giving him the nickname of 'Diamond' Pitt plus the profits to buy large estates throughout England and to create progeny who provided two later prime ministers.

The turning point in Britain's dominant presence in India was undoubtedly the Battle of Plassey of 1757 after which Robert Clive (to be given a peerage as Baron Clive of Plassey), became the *de facto* ruler of Bengal, as its nawab. He had already beaten the French in 1751 near Madras and this, with subsequent victories, broke French power in southern India by 1753. At Plassey he directed his mainly indigenous Indian army of 3000 in a decisive defeat of the Mogul's Nawab of Bengal army of 10,000. By the 1770s and 80s the Company saw their opportunity and decided to secure and link the borders between the different states. With the loss of the American colonies, the emphasis of interest shifted to India. Swollen armies crossed Mysore in the south, mopped up the Maharats in central India and conquered the Punjab to the north, unifying the rule of India and changing the stature of the East India Company from company to empire. By 1773 with William Pitt the Elder as Prime Minister, India was ruled by the Company under Warren Hastings, the first Governor-General of Bengal, who built India into a homogenous British State, but whose methods were sometimes dubious. He was attacked at home by Edmund Burke, a Member of Parliament appointed to a Parliamentary Select Committee to investigate the Company, and was impeached in the House of Commons. This became an axis for debate as to what Britain was actually trying to do in India, and what India might do for Britain.

The Company's position in India had been achieved by the strength of the British naval warship and the determination of its merchant ships, in spite of poor charts. The problem was that there was no central collation of charts and navigational information, and those charts that were available were privately published, albeit commercially, and had little peripheral information on sailing routes, ocean currents, prevailing winds, distances between key landfalls and so on. With the Atlantic traverse taking four or more of the seven to eight months' average passage time to get to India, navigational knowledge was vital, and, in addition to the prosaic methods such as how the profile and nature of the sea-bed changed, the rate of rise and fall of the barometer, the use of the sextant to assess latitude, and later the complex lunar observations and then the chronometer to obtain longitude, every subtle clue was needed to gauge the right moment to change course to gain the advantageous current and wind (the oceans' circulatory patterns weren't shown on charts) such as the changes in sea-water temperature and salinity, sightings of seaweed, floating vegetation or land birds, changes in air temperature, or land smells and even intuition based on experience.

Alexander Dalrymple was to change all this. Joining the East India Company, and most did, as a writer in 1752 in Madras, he became the foremost geographer of the eighteenth century and the first Hydrographer to the Admiralty in 1795. With a vision of extending the Company's trade eastwards he was given permission by the Governor to (secretly) sail in the Company's schooner *Cuddalore,* setting out after the siege of Madras in 1759, for a two-and-a-half-year cruise around the East Indian (Sulu) archipelagos, through the Philippines and the China Sea, learning seamanship and surveying. The

Company couldn't break into the rigid Dutch monopoly of spices and trade east of India. By 1762 he was voyaging via Palembang and Sulu to Canton attempting to find routes to China for the East Indiamen. He returned to England in 1765 and published charts on the East Indies for the next 11 years, including *An Account of the Discoveries made in the South Pacific Previous to 1764*, a copy of which he presented to Joseph Banks. In it he argued strongly for a vast southern continent and hoped that he would be chosen for a voyage to find and survey it. The Admiralty had resolved never to appoint a 'civilian' in charge of one of HM Ships again after the difficulties experienced with Edmond Halley's captaincy of the *Paramour*. To Dalrymple's enduring disappointment, Lieutenant James Cook was given the job, ostensibly to measure the transit of Venus from Tahiti in 1769 but secretly to find *Terra Incognita Australis* before the French did.

By 1777 Dalrymple had developed a system to abstract information from the East Indiamen captains' journals which 'will be very conducive towards explaining the currents, that most curious and important phenomenon in nautical history'. He issued blank charts with a common scale (5° to the inch) on which captains were to record the ship's track, along with a standard journal to record positional fixes and so on. Although few captains responded, it was a start that was to lead to the collation and publishing of *Notices to Mariners*. In August 1778 the Company ship *Colebrook* sank after hitting the Anvil Rock in False Bay by the Cape of Good Hope and in 1779 the Company seemed glad to confirm Dalrymple's suggestion that he publish Nautical Directions and charts based on the examination of the Company's ships' journals when the Chairman, Sir George Wombwell, was said to have remarked that Dalrymple 'had timed it very well' and that 'the loss of the *Colebrook* was more than the expence [*sic*] of such an Office to all eternity'. Dalrymple was able to style himself 'Hydrographer to the East India Company', although this was never actually confirmed by the Company.

In 1782 he compiled a memorial concerning the passages to and from China, secretly distributed to Company ships. But his ambition to issue a full set of charts needed up-to-date surveys based on chronometer observations and only John McCluer, as a commander of the Bombay Marine, had made a survey of the western coast of India. His surveys were of such accuracy that he was sent to survey the Pelew Islands and New Guinea where, in breach of all naval regulations, he 'went native'. The Bombay Marine was formed at the beginning of the eighteenth century to protect its merchant ships from, amongst others, the predatory Mahratta states along the Konkan coast between Bombay and Goa. It soon built up to a strength in 1857 of 43 warships with 270 European officers, encouraged to develop surveying skills. It could go into action anywhere between the Red Sea and China and helped to establish Bombay as the first real power base in India.

The lack of confirmed accurate longitude positions thwarted Dalrymple's plans to issue a comprehensive set of charts, although by the 1790s he had produced over 450 harbour plans, 28 charts and 40 navigational views. Laurie and Whittle's *East India Pilot* was still the standard reference. James Horsburgh who took over from Dalrymple in the Company, published his own charts of the China Sea in 1805 and Dalrymple's one success in getting an East India Company ship, the *Vansittart*, to carry out a survey ended in disaster. The captain, Lestock Wilson, had previously navigated the shorter route to Canton through the difficult Gaspar Strait, with countless small islands to the east of

Banca, a large island off Sumatra, rather than the usual but longer route to the west of Banca. Dalrymple considered him 'to be a proper person to make the necessary observations' and he was directed in 1789 to carry out the survey on his way to Canton. Unfortunately the ship struck the very shoal she was trying to survey, and sank. Most of the crew survived, including one signed on as a captain's servant, Francis Beaufort, who was to top a distinguished career at sea with his appointment as the Royal Navy's fourth Hydrographer. After three nights in the ship's boats, they came across two East Indiamen at anchor in the straits, who agreed to return to the wreck to salvage the discarded treasure (for a third of the value of £90,655).

The English Company then expanded by invading Dutch Ceylon in 1796, previously taken from the Portuguese in 1658, and in 1811 fought the Dutch for Java. Thomas Raffles, who served as Governor, with acute business foresight was convinced of the appropriateness of the site of Singapore as an Asian entrepôt and founded the settlement there in 1819.

By the 1800s emphasis of trade switched to tea and opium so that the Company could make inroads into China. The Chinese demand for opium was encouraged and pushed, against the edict of the Chinese Emperor, as part of the Company's trade triangle with China and India – Opium from India, the Bengal area, to China, silks, porcelain and tea to England. The Company did not want to have any public profile in carrying opium to China, and independent shipping firms developed in the three main ports of Bombay, Madras and Calcutta. The captains of these ships developed, through their weight of experience, the knowledge needed to sail through the islands and waters of the South China Sea to Canton and back. James Horsburgh, a sailor from Fife, had been shipwrecked on Diego Garcia in 1786 and coincidentally rescued by a surveying party from Bombay who were assessing the island for settlement, and from them he developed an interest in survey work. Dalrymple published the charts he had compiled in 1796, and Horsburgh was encouraged by Sir Joseph Banks and Neville Maskelyne (the Astronomer Royal). By 1805, he was able to bring a set of charts covering the whole navigation to China, both in the Atlantic and Indian Oceans. He published these as the *East India Pilot* with the assistance of Captain Peter Heywood, whose varied naval career had started with exoneration by court martial of any involvement as a midshipman with the *Bounty* mutineers. As a senior Royal Navy captain he had been appointed to advise the Hydrographer, Thomas Hurd, on the formation of the Royal Naval Surveying Service in 1816. These finally provided the charts that the East India Company needed and Horsburgh was appointed their Hydrographer in 1810. His job became one of publishing others' manuscript surveys as the work of other Company surveyors from the Persian Gulf and China Sea, and after 1830, Indian Navy surveyors came in.

From 1834 the Company's monopoly on the China run was ended, and Horsburgh died in 1836, to be succeeded by his engraver, John Walker, who issued charts from East India House until, following the shock of the 1857 Indian Mutiny, it was realized that control of the vast sub-continent of India could not be left to a joint stock company, and the Company's responsibilities in that country were taken on by the British Government in 1858. The Indian navy surveys were thereafter published by the Hydrographic Office, although the *India Directory* continued in publication until 1864, by which time the essential charting of these waters was complete, and further surveys were, in effect, to fine tune what had been achieved.

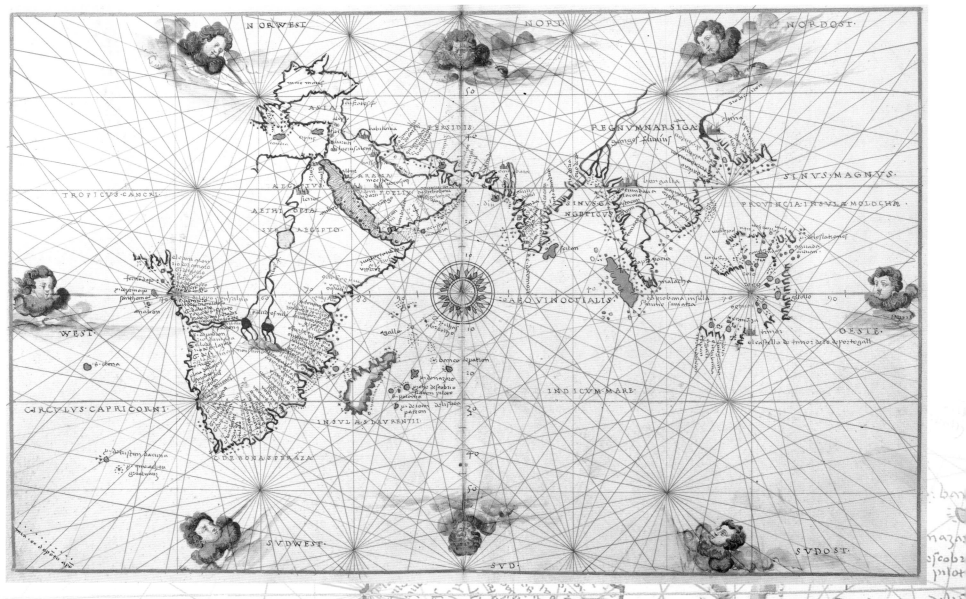

| **PORTOLAN CHART BY BATTISTA AGNESE, C. 1550** | It shows the Red Sea, in red, and the juxtaposition of the Mediterranean, the Persian Gulf and India as seen through the eyes of the merchants of the time. The supposed sources of the Nile figure strongly, the wind cherubs have names we use today, the Ganges drains China, but Canton is named in red and prominently marked with a large stronghold as are other important cities including Cochin, Calicut and Goa in India and Babylon in the Middle East. (Reproduced by courtesy of the Royal Geographical Society with IBG)

| MAP OF THE OTTOMAN EMPIRE, C. 1650 | This map, published by Jan Jansson in Amsterdam, shows the extent of the Ottoman Empire, established in the fifteenth century, which extended from Turkey into the Holy Land, Arabia, Egypt and Eastern Europe, and was therefore pivotal in the access to trade from the Far East. Ships would sail between Gujarat and ports in the Persian Gulf loaded with silks and ceramics from China, cottons from India and spices from the Moluccas and Spice Islands around the Philippines. (UKHO © British Crown Copyright)

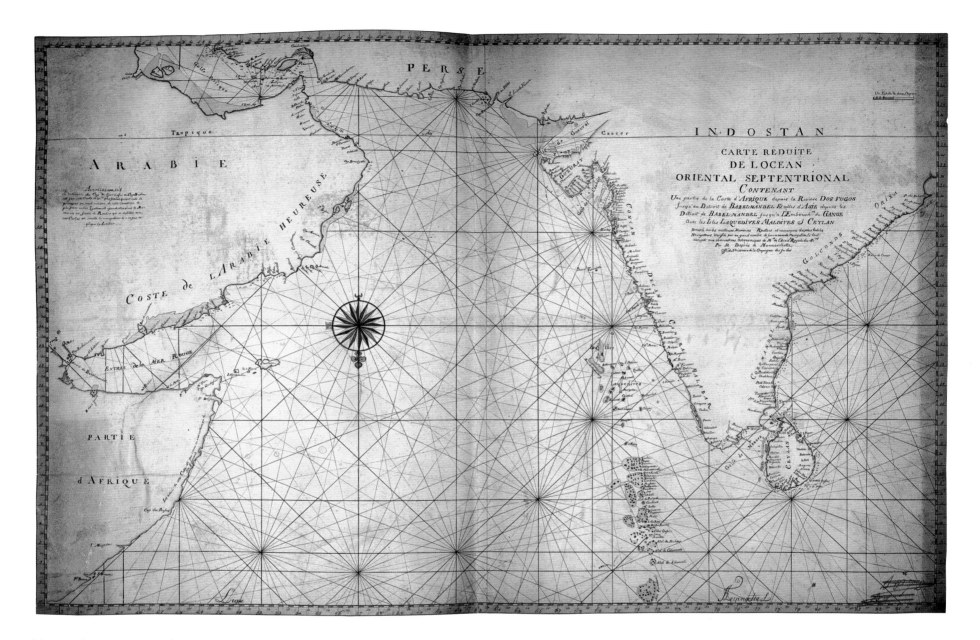

| ABOVE | **FRENCH CHART OF THE INDIAN OCEAN FLANKED BY AFRICA, INDIA AND CEYLON** | D'Après de Mannevillette, a captain in the French East India Company probably drew this chart before 1720 when he was appointed their Hydrographer. He verifies it as from the best records (*memoires*) taken from a number of navigators and ship's captains who had habitually sailed these waters and using astronomic observations from the French Royal Academy to fix the latitude and longitude. He had an office at Lorient, Brittany, and compiled *Le Neptune Oriental*, which was greatly respected at the time for navigational use over and above British charts.

French interests were centred mainly along the Coromandel Coast. Britain had established a trading base at Bombay; Ceylon (Ceylan then, and Sri Lanka today) was Dutch. The chart extends from the *Ligne Aeyinoctial* (the Equator), the names are in French, and three distinct sets of grid lines are drawn, latitude and longitude and diagonals, and each set of rhumb lines extending from a point on an equidistant circle centred on the compass rose, which appears at first glance to be pointing southwards, but pointing to the north is the old medieval symbol for this. (Admiralty Library Manuscript Collection VZ 7/1)

| RIGHT | **CHART OF CALCUTTA AND THE RIVER HOOGHLY, 1757** | Rivers also need to be navigated using charts. In January 1757 Robert Clive recaptured Fort William (shown on the chart with the British flag flying) in Calcutta from the Nawab, Siraj-ud-Dawlah, who became notorious for his treatment of the British he incarcerated in the notorious, but perhaps exaggerated 'black hole of Calcutta'. At the time the River Hooghly was surveyed in March 1757, following the re-taking of Calcutta, Clive was able to beat the Nawab on 23 June and became the de facto ruler of Bengal, further increasing the opportunity for trade out of Calcutta.

Delightful details are shown of Callacutta waterfront, and up-river an important local's house is shown – 'Mulla Fackadin' – clearly a useful navigational mark to key the turn, with a bearing checked by compass, around the bend approaching it. The survey continues north farther than reproduced here. The full caption reads 'Plan of the River Hughly from Calcutta to Chandernagar – Survey'd by Order of Admiral Watson – done by the Pilots and Masters of the Men of War in March 1757. Presented to the Right Honourable the Earl of Egmont, by His Most Respectfull, and faithful; Humble Servant. W. Brereton.' The Earl of Egmont was First Lord of the Admiralty, and the best person to whom such a chart should be presented. From there it was deposited into the Admiralty chart archives.

Chandernagar was a French settlement that was subsequently captured by Clive and the charting of the river played its part. Some historians, whilst acknowledging Clive's military brilliance, recognize the role of Admiral Charles Watson in supporting Clive. Watson was perhaps one of Britain's best, although least known, of the eighteenth-century admirals. Without his naval campaigns as Commander-in-Chief of the East Indies in support, which stopped all movement of the French navy and kept them at bay, Clive could not have won. (Admiralty Library Manuscript Collection VZ 7/8)

| CHART OF THE BAY OF BENGAL, *C.1750* | Captain William Lisle (d.1752), by whose orders this chart was compiled, was the Commander-in-Chief of all British ships in the East Indies. Taken from the Equinoctial Line (the Equator) as the base line, this chart, with English men-of-war depicted across the seas, is a confident expression of the British presence in the Orient and extends to Calcutta in the north. It is put together from a number of other larger scale charts dating around 1751. The names used for Bangladesh, Burma and Thailand are unfamiliar to us now. The confrontational situation between Britain and France in India, to be resolved by battle at sea and on land some five years later, is demonstrated by the mix of French and English flags flying by the ports and cities along the Coromandel Coast. (Admiralty Library Manuscript Collection VZ 7/5)

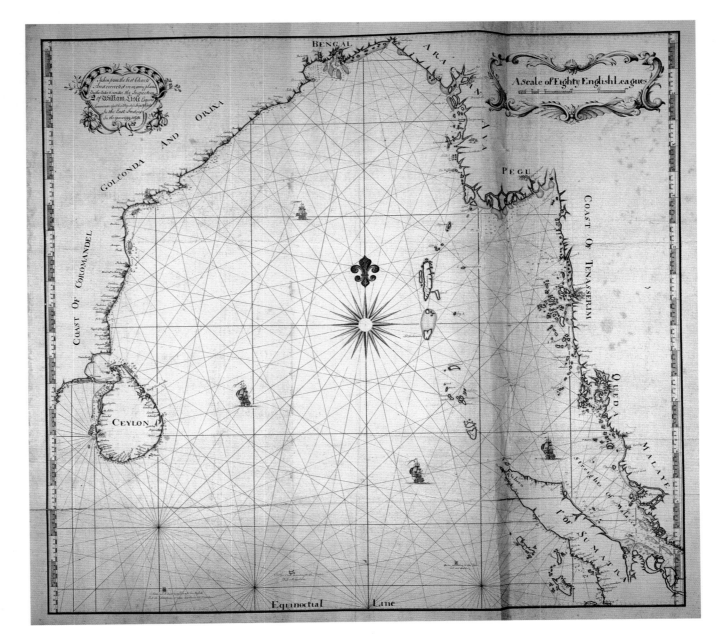

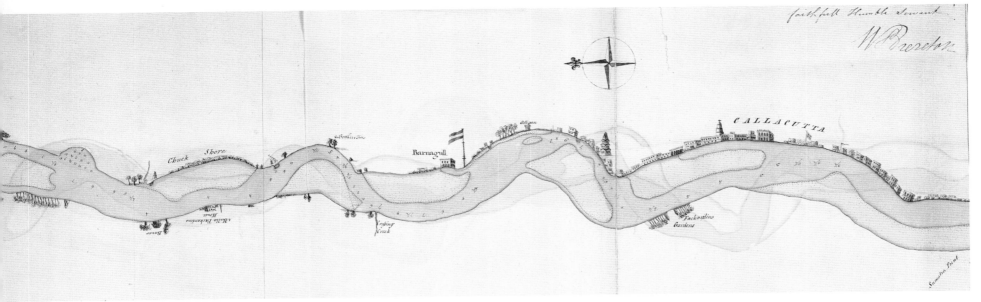

| **DUTCH CHART OF THE BANDA ISLANDS, *C.*1750** |

This simple but attractive Dutch chart of the Banda Islands belies the bitterness of their contested ownership between the rival colonial powers of Holland and England. The island of Run is to the east, with Nailaka to its north; then the island Ai, Gunung Api with the Banda Islands' volcano (which was in the habit of erupting when the Dutch fleet hove to), Neira with Fort Nassau, the main island of Banda itself with Fort Hollandia and a line of representational trees which could well be nutmegs, and finally to the west Rozengain. (Admiralty Library Manuscript Collection VZ 8/51)

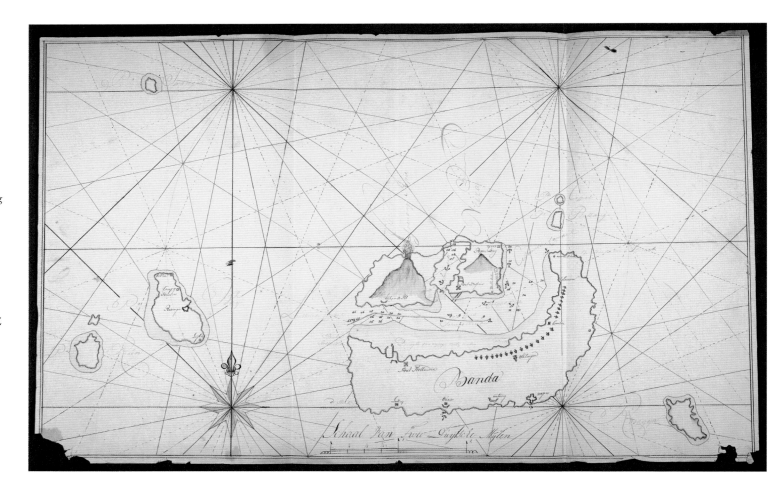

| **CHART OF MALAYA AND SINGAPORE BY GERARD VAN KEULEN, C.1700** | A gracefully hand-drawn, coloured manuscript chart by the talented engraver and mathematician Gerard Van Keulen. He was from the prolific Van Keulen map-making dynasty of Amsterdam and was Hydrographer to the Dutch East India Company (VOC). With north orientated to the right it covers Mallaya (Malaya), Sinkapura (Singapore) and Sumatra with two inset charts of Branca and Sabon Islands and has soundings in the straits and channels with the scale in Dutch miles. (Admiralty Library Manuscript Collection VZ 7/28)

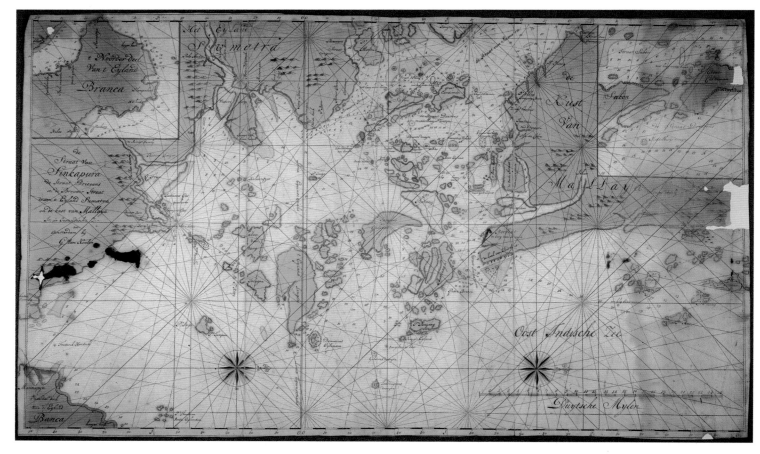

| RIGHT | **MAP OF SRI LANKA (CEYLON)** *C.* **1618 FROM** *GEOGRAPHIA* (*THEATRI GEOGRAPHIA VETERIS*) **BY PETRUS BERTIUS (BERT)** | It shows a 'Portuguese' Ceylon with a Portuguese caravel sailing by and a number of named islands whose existence, whilst not in doubt then, must be so now. (By courtesy of the Dean and Chapter of Westminster)

| BELOW RIGHT | **CHART OF SINGAPORE, C.1820** | The island of Singapore is in a key position at the southern tip of the Malay Peninsula and between the Far East and the Spice Islands, and India. Its commercial importance accelerated with the opening of the Suez Canal in 1869, and it became a major port along the route to Europe. This must be one of the earliest charts of the island, dating to *c.* 1820. A collaboration between the army and navy, the land was surveyed by Lieutenant Colonel Farquhar, and the strait with clearing bearings for the approaches by Captain Franklin and soundings from the charts of 'Captain Ross and Mr Horsburgh', respectively Daniel Ross, superintendent surveyor of the East India Company, who did much work in the Red Sea between 1823 and 1833, and James Horsburgh, Hydrographer to the East India Company in 1810 following Dalrymple. (Admiralty Library Manuscript Collection VZ 7/51)

| BELOW | **CHART OF SELAT BANGKA (BANCA STRAIT), 1750** | Alexander Dalrymple, as a hydrographer with the East India Company, was understandably anxious to put together a folio of charts that assisted safe navigation for the East Indiamen. This chart is of the dangerous Selat Bangka or Banca Strait that separates Banca Island from Sumatra, but provides the shortest route between Batavia (Djakarta) and Singapore. He inherited many charts like this one, drawn, according to the title, by Christian Kemsitt for Captain Stauter of the East India Ship *Triton* in 1750. Although the latitude is quite accurate, it has no longitude base, so drawing one meaningful chart from disparate longitude charts was an impossible task, until land-based longitudes were 'locked' in. Nonetheless, the navigational advice written on this chart as to clearing navigational hazards, the soundings and shoals, was extremely useful and Dalrymple would have added this to the Pilot. (Admiralty Library Manuscript Collection VZ/7)

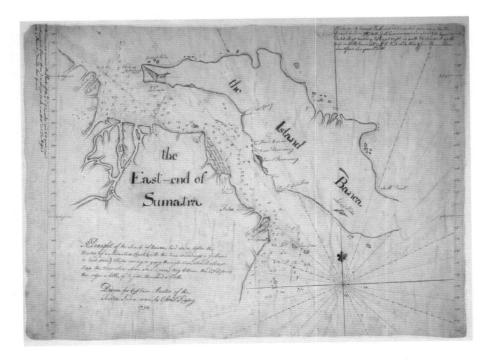

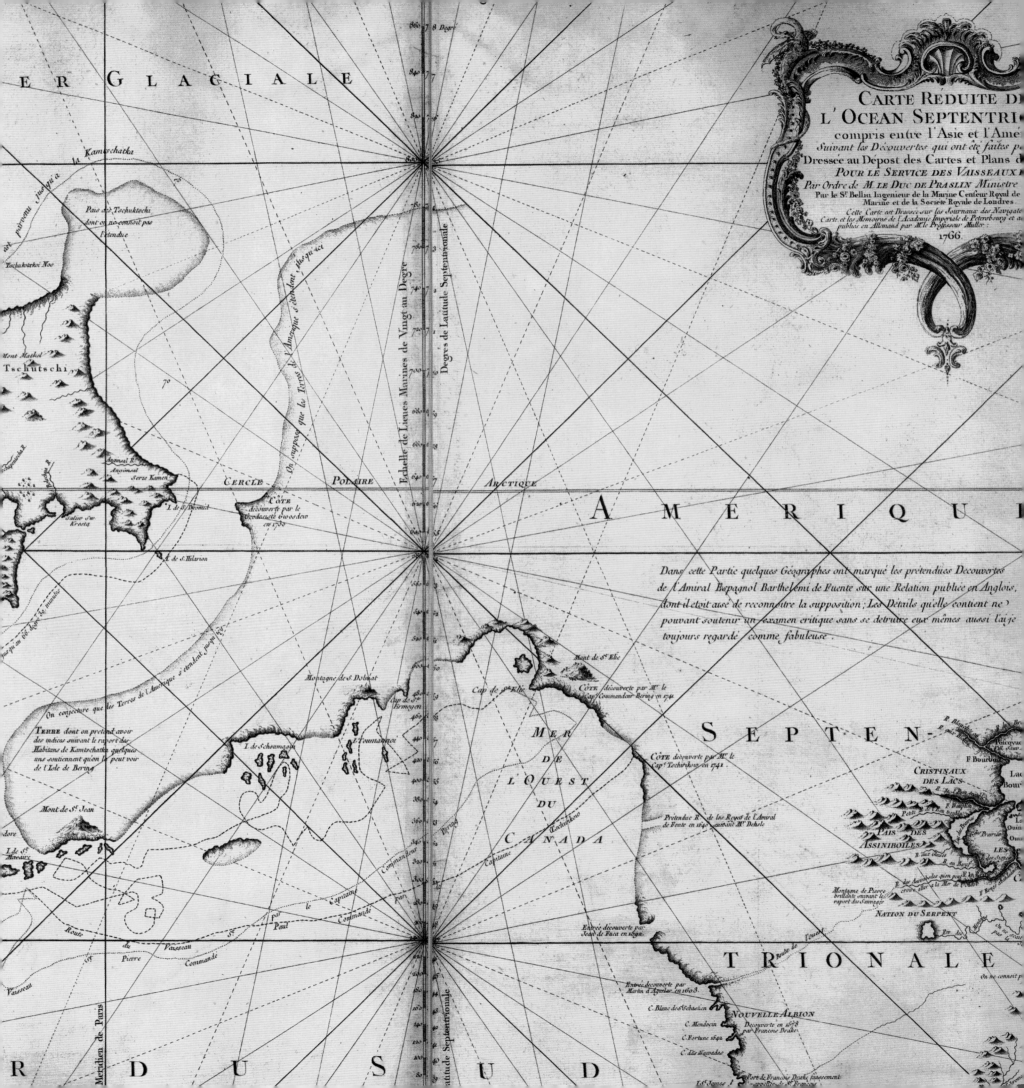

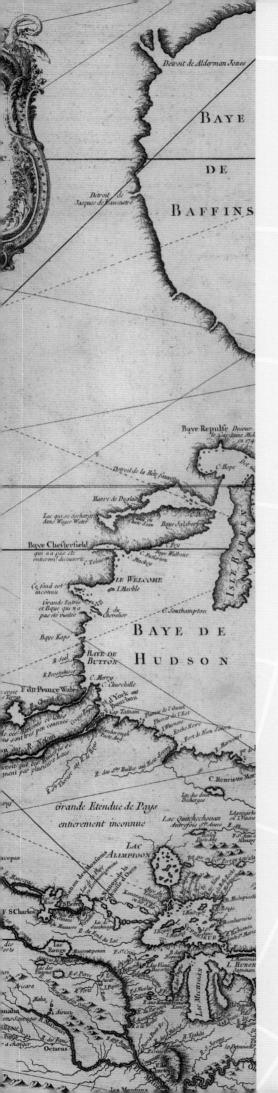

CHAPTER VII

The Pacific and the East Indies

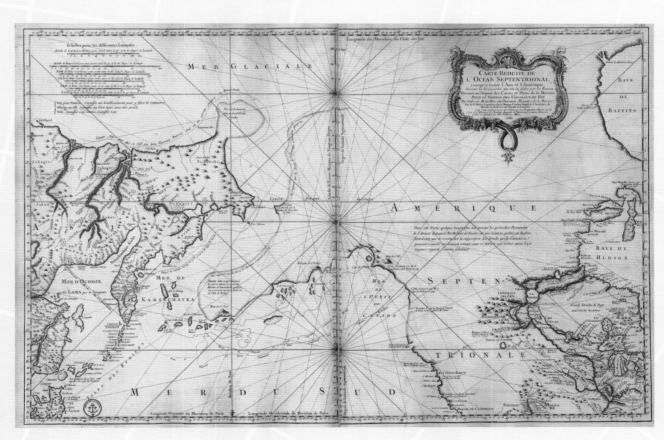

| **LEFT DETAIL & ABOVE** | **FRENCH CHART OF THE NORTHERN PACIFIC ASSEMBLED AND PUBLISHED BY J N BELLIN FROM VARIOUS CHARTS DATED BETWEEN 1737 AND 1765** | The efforts of Vitus Bering on behalf of the Russians after their occupation of the Kamchatka peninsula in 1720, and others, had, as this French chart dated 1766 of the northern Pacific shows, delineated the Asian coastline. However, conjecture as to the shape of North America towards Asia, where islands had been joined together to construct a coastline reaching towards the eastern Russian coast, would only be dispelled by the voyages of James Cook and George Vancouver in the latter part of the eighteenth century.

It shows the tracks of Bering's 1728 voyage, when he discovered the strait that bears his name, and Alaska, and his 1741 voyage in the ships *St Peter* and *St Paul* across to Canada. It also marks Francis Drake's furthest position north during his raiding circumnavigation of 1577–80, at Cape Mendocino, California – he named the area 'New Albion'. (Library of Congress)

THE Pacific Ocean covers more than a third of the Earth's surface, contains more than half of its free water, and is substantially larger than the entire land surface. Stretching from the west coast of the Americas across 11,000 miles of almost uninterrupted sea to the coasts of Asia and from the Bering Strait in the north, where North America and the USSR are within 50 miles of touching, 9600 miles south to the Southern Ocean, it was the largest of the five great oceans to be discovered and explored. Its total area is about 55 1/2 million square miles, of which over half lies below 2000 fathoms (3900 metres) depth, and between Guam and Midway Islands the Mindanāo trench has a depth of more than 7 1/2 miles. Most of the 30,000 islands are volcanic in origin, with many topped by coral atolls, and lie in the southern part. The largest islands form volcanic island arcs that rise from the broad continental shelf along the eastern edge of the Eurasian Plate. They include Japan, Taiwan, the Philippines, Indonesia, New Guinea, and New Zealand.

Along the American edge of the Pacific, the continental shelf is narrow and steep, with few island areas. The major groups are the Galapagos at the Equator, which rise from the Nazca Plate, the Aleutians in the north, which are part of the North American continental shelf, and the islands of Hawaii, which rise some 18,000 feet (5550 metres) from the seafloor of the central Pacific, reaching in Mauna Kea a height of 13,796 feet (4205 metres) above sea level.

Equatorial currents caused by the prevailing winds carried the Polynesians on great migratory explorations so that they peopled most of the islands in Polynesia over a 200-year period, arriving in New Zealand in the seventeenth century. The judicial use of the water highway of currents that flow to-and-fro across the Pacific Ocean enabled them to cover vast distances in their outrigger canoes. The north Pacific current running eastwards around 30° N, the north equatorial current running west around 15–20° N, the counter current heading east at around 5–10° N, and the south equatorial current running west at about 0–5° S in conjunction carried them, while they navigated by a form of chart based on a sea shell and stick representation of the islands' bearing and distance, using the sun and the predictable westerly wind direction between 30° N and 30° S as direction finders.

Early European geographers, however, thought that the east coast of Asia bordered on to the western Atlantic Ocean. The discovery of America by Columbus in 1492 dented this idea, and when the Portuguese reached China in 1517, and the Spanish got to the western coast of America it was realized that there was a lot more water in between than had at first been supposed. Vasco Nunez de Balboa first sighted the Pacific from the mountain range when he crossed the Isthmus of Darien (present day Isthmus of Panama). In fact Ferdinand Magellan, a Portuguese but in the service of Spain, made his circumnavigation between 1519 and 1522 to claim the Spice Islands for Spain, naming the Ocean, unusually calm as he entered it, *Mar Pacifico*. This was a particularly inept name for that part of the Ocean bordering on the Antarctic where the sea averages a 'significant wave height of thirty-six feet' – the height of office blocks.

The Spanish had sailed west from South America and, despite the territorial division of the world between Spain and Portugal by the Treaty of Tordesillas giving lands to the east to Portugal, they were to take and keep the lands named after King Philip, the Philippines. These were just a few hundred miles from the Banda Islands, which the Portuguese had occupied for the remarkable spice that grew there, the nutmeg. This medicinal spice, highly regarded for its believed ability to cure the plague, that 'pestiferous pestilence' that entered the body with a sneeze and left it at death, cost under a penny for ten pounds in the Banda Islands, but fetched £2.10s, which was a markup of 60,000 per cent! Men would form an East India Company for profits like that, and England and Holland acquired charters to do so in 1600 and 1602 respectively.

Circumnavigations, with piracy rather than the interests of science and knowledge for a motive, gradually added to the knowledge of the Pacific. Notable names are Sir Francis Drake in 1577–80, Thomas Cavendish in 1586–88 – who also captured one of the annual Spanish treasure ships, discovering St Helena (in the Atlantic) on the way home, but, having got through the prize money, died on a second attempt – and Olivier van Noort in 1598–1601, the first Dutch circumnavigator who attempted to buccaneer his way up the west South American coast raiding Spanish territories, but with little success. Truly exploratory voyages were made by Pedro Fernandez de Quiros and Luis Vaez de Torres in 1605–06 who discovered the New Hebrides and Tuomotus Island Groups, and of course the dangerous strait that bears Torres's name between New Guinea and the north of Australia. Antony Van Diemen, the Dutch Governor of New Guinea, authorized Abel Tasman to explore to the south in three voyages of 1634, 1642 and 1644 when he touched Australia.

But the next hundred years were given over to voyages of plunder by adventurers who called themselves privateers or buccaneers, such as Bartholomew Sharp, William Ambrose Cowley and Woodes Rogers. Between 1680 and 1720 they so harried the Spanish that their monopoly was shattered. William Dampier, perhaps the first educated pirate, was both a buccaneer and man of science. Described succinctly by a contemporary as 'the mildest mannered man that ever scuttled ship or cut a throat', his circumnavigation of 1683–91 resulted in *A New Voyage Round the World*, which was published in 1697 and became a bestseller. He was commissioned as a naval officer commanding the *Roebuck* in which he made another voyage in 1699. On a third voyage to the Pacific, 1703–07 he had trouble with his crew and famously put his lieutenant, a Scotsman, Alexander Selkirk, ashore (for insubordination) on Juan Fernandez Island, providing Daniel Defoe with the inspiration for the story of *Robinson Crusoe*. He sighted western Australia and passed New Guinea in 1700. His chart recording this is one of the first to try to show the prevailing south Pacific winds and currents.

Woodes Rogers, similarly, was engaged by a syndicate of British merchants to lead a privateering expedition to the South Seas, legalized by a letter of marque, during the War of the Spanish Succession in 1708. With two frigates, the *Duke* and *Duchess*, and with William Dampier as his navigator, they sailed round Cape Horn to Juan Fernandez Island for replenishment, collecting Alexander Selkirk, and had the good fortune to meet up with the Spanish treasure galleon, *Nuestra Señora de la Encarnación Desengano*. She struck her colours after a short engagement, and Rogers completed a circumnavigation home via Guam and the Cape of Good Hope arriving in the Thames in 1711. His entertaining account *A Cruising Voyage Around the World* supplemented the knowledge and fascination of the South Seas engendered by Dampier's earlier accounts of his voyages.

By the War of the Spanish Succession Commodore George Anson combined plunder with exploration, capturing the Spanish treasure ship during his circumnavigation of 1740-44.

Genuine voyages of exploration began to supercede buccaneering and men of ability such as James Cook and Louis Antoine de Bougainville, Compte de La Pérouse, Philip Carteret and Samuel Wallis set out on well-equipped research expeditions. The Pacific became yet another arena in the competition for land, trade and influence between France and Britain. Samuel Wallis filled in some of the earlier gaps in the Pacific chart when he commanded HMS *Dolphin*, in company with HMS *Swallow*, on their voyage of discovery in 1766–68. They separated passing through the ever-restless Magellan Strait, and *Dolphin* completed a circumnavigation, remarkable for the time in being free of scurvy and a forerunner of Captain Cook's three Pacific voyages. George Robertson, *Dolphin*'s master, wrote an account of the voyage, later published by the Hakluyt Society.

| JAPAN AND THE NORTH PACIFIC |

The Venetian traveller, Marco Polo, who journeyed overland reaching the court of Kublai Khan in Peking in 1275, wrote from hearsay that the great island of Japan – Cipangu as he called it and Zipangri by others – lay 1500 miles east of Cathay (China). His account of his 10 years in Peking and the two-year return journey by sea from Changchow via Sumatra and southern India, excitedly reported, 'the quantity of gold they have here is endless, for they find it in their own islands'. Such reports fired the Elizabethan adventurers to set off explorations. Gerardus Mercator's 1569 map of the world showed a logical route atop Asia – the North-East passage. It did not show the ice bound sea that would crush a wooden vessel and block her voyage. Dr John Dee, Queen Elizabeth's astrologer, claims to have been a close friend of Mercator's and using his empirical cartographic knowledge wrote a persuasive treatise expounding a complete format for the Queen to build an English Empire.

The Japanese were largely inward looking for many centuries, warring amongst themselves and forbidden to travel overseas, and so there was little contact with Europe. In 1534 the Portuguese set up a small trading settlement, and missionaries introduced the Christian religion. The first Portuguese had rounded the Cape of Good Hope in 1488, moved on to agree trading rights with Goa in India 10 years later and in 1511 had established themselves at the Malay port of Malacca. The Portuguese were keen to extend their trading activities beyond the Spice Islands and having drawn a blank to the south, knowing enough of Australia to convince them that any more of that land was the same uninhabitable tract, they looked to the North Pacific. A trading post was set up in Macao to deal in Chinese silks and a carrack set sail in 1555 to trade silver with Japan. By 1571 they had set up a trading post confined to a small island by Nagasaki.

In 1598 an expedition of five Dutch carracks set sail from the Texel bound for India. The pilot of the squadron was an Englishman, William Adams. His ship, the *Charity*, was the only survivor of the expedition, washing up exhausted on the shore of Japan. Adams's knowledge of shipbuilding and pilotage made him valuable to the Japanese rulers, who refused to allow him to return home, but presented him with an estate and a Japanese wife. Within 10 years, he had risen quite extraordinarily to the position of shogun, writing back regularly to his wife and children in England and to the Court of King James I. The King was sceptical of the wonderful description of the Japanese denouncing

Adams's letters as 'the loudest lies I have ever seen'. The English sent out an expedition in 1611 to capitalize on his position and set up a trading post, convinced that the Japanese, used to the finest of silks from China, would welcome the coarse English woollen broadcloth. It seems that the only product successfully introduced was the potato. The English were kicked out within a few years and the Dutch likewise. Japan battened down its territorial hatches for the next 200 years.

The lure of a strait from the Pacific to the Atlantic through the Strait of Anian across North America was sufficient to persuade the Dutch to follow Abel Tasman's attempt to chart these waters by sending another expedition under Maarten Vries in 1643. His distortion of the coast along Japan by the Kurils and Yezo was followed by chartmakers for the next 100 years showing a huge shadowy Dutch empire extending even to the North American coast. Japan was always misleadingly shown with two main islands, not four.

The Russians dispelled these inaccuracies with the expansion eastward pushed by Peter the Great. The Russians in 1720 occupied the whole Kamchatka peninsula and charted the area more accurately. Vitus Bering was a Dane appointed to the Russian navy who explored for the North-West passage, and discovered the strait that bears his name. He established that America and Asia were not joined, and on a return voyage in 1741 explored Alaska, sighting Mount Elias that later would so impress Captains James Cook and Vancouver, opening the way for the Russians. Bering wrote of Alaska,

> The land was here very much elevated; the mountains, observed extending inland, were so lofty that we could see them quite plainly at sea at a distance of 16 Dutch miles. I cannot recall having seen higher mountains anywhere in Siberia and Kamchatka. The coast was everywhere much indented and therefore provided with numerous bays and inlets close to the mainland.

Also in 1720, the Japanese re-awakening interest in overseas culture was acknowledged when Shogun Yoshimune repealed the proscription on European books and study. By the early nineteenth century visits from Europeans, mostly traders and explorers, became comparatively frequent, although the ban was still officially in force. The USA was particularly anxious to make a treaty of friendship and, if possible, one of trade with Japan. One object behind this US policy was to secure the release of American whalers from ships wrecked on the Japanese coast; another was to open up Japanese markets. In 1853 the US Government sent a formal mission to the Emperor of Japan headed by Commodore Matthew Perry, who arrived with a squadron of ships. Following extended negotiations, Perry and representatives of the Emperor signed a pact on 31 March 1854, establishing relations between the USA and Japan.

| CHINA |

China was almost as coy as Japan in opening trade with Europeans, but an East India Company trading post was opened at Amoy in 1685. Arab traders had long traded with the Chinese at Canton, up the Pearl River from Hong Kong and Macao. Silks and ceramics were manufactured well inland, and brought to Canton – the Chinese wanted the benefit of trade without the chance of

Bligh and the *Bounty*

William Bligh's navigational skills and contribution to charting in the Pacific is important to note. In 1787 he was given command of the *Bounty* to take breadfruit seedlings from Tahiti to the West Indies. He arrived in Tahiti on 26 October 1788 having attempted to round Cape Horn, but forced by continuously contrary winds and bad weather to sail via the Cape of Good Hope instead. Once there he stayed on the island for nearly six months, which gave the crew plenty of time to forge strong relationships with the beautiful Tahitian women, and more than half decided to take the ship and start a new life, led by Fletcher Christian. The mutiny occurred on 27 April 1789, 23 days out of Tahiti off Tofua in the Friendly Islands. Bligh and 18 loyal crew were cast adrift in a 22-foot open boat with few provisions, little water and a sextant. Bligh managed to sail the boat 3618 miles in 41 days to Timor in the Dutch East Indies without losing any of his men and living only on water, fish and birds that they caught either at sea or when they navigated past one of the few islands en route of which he knew from his exploration with Cook. In spite of the obvious difficulties, he was still able to survey the islands he passed and even discovered the Fiji Islands. The whole voyage, which included negotiating the dangerous Torres Strait, was an outstanding achievement by any standard.

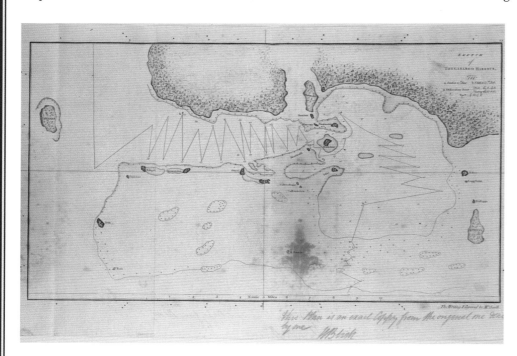

| LEFT | As Cook's sailing master on his third voyage, Bligh was responsible for the navigation of the ship, a highly responsible job for which Bligh was selected at the young age of 25, a tribute to his navigational and surveying skills. He drew this chart of the Tonga Tapoo island (previously Amsterdam Island) sighted by Abel Tasman on his 1642 voyage, and part of the more than 100 islands in the Friendly Islands Group some 400 miles east of Fiji in the Pacific Ocean. Bligh lost his original charts, which he had to leave on board the *Bounty* after the mutiny, but possessively, and to refute that they were produced by others, he wrote on a number that are in the UKHO archives, including this one, that they are an exact copy of his own and, in fairness to Bligh, the Hydrographic Office, once formed in 1795, always acknowledged the chief surveyor of a chart by name. (UKHO © British Crown Copyright)

| RIGHT | Captain William Bligh FRS RN, painted by J Russell RA in 1792. (Author's collection)

| BELOW | The courage, stamina and navigational ability of Bligh can be better understood from this contemporary chart from Bligh's own, made on the incredible voyage in the open boat, from nearby Tofua, in the Friendly Islands, to East Timor in 1789. (UKHO © British Crown Copyright)

European merchants travelling inland and subverting the Chinese populace, and a system developed with goods sold only to Chinese traders by licence at the port, with the Portuguese first utilizing it, and other European nations following. By 1729 all foreign trade was restricted to Canton and the waterfront became a united nations façade with East India companies from Holland, Sweden, Denmark, France, even the Holy Roman Empire, and Britain to be joined later by the new fledgling country of the USA, but with Britain at the time the largest.

In 1793 Lord Macartney, as Governor of Madras, had tangled with Warren Hastings, the first Governor-General of Bengal, and made himself diplomatically unpopular in many ways, lead an expedition on behalf of the East India Company to 'rationalise matters of trade'. The mission failed as Macartney refused to 'kow-tow' to the Emperor and his gifts were refused. A similar 'embassy' was bungled under Lord Amherst in 1816.

As part of the expedition Sir Joseph Banks had asked Sir Edward Staunton to observe the way the Chinese cultivated and scented their tea, with the hope of growing the herb in India. Lord Bentinck, Governor-General of India, set up a tea committee in 1834 to find out how to grow the tea bush (*Camellia sinensis*) within the British Empire, so as to circumvent the Chinese monopoly. Robert Fortune finally solved the mystery in 1848 managing to go inland to the tea-growing areas north of Shanghai disguised as a Chinese merchant to observe at first hand how green tea was cultivated, and again to the black tea areas disguised as a Mongolian mandarin visiting factories. Travelling back to Calcutta, down the River Yangtze to Hong Kong and thence by boat with 85 Chinese specialists, he set to work in the newly cleared plantations in northwest India sited where tea can only successfully be grown at an altitude of about 6500 feet. Enormous tea-growing estates had been started earlier in Assam where naturally growing wild tea plants were found. A Scot, Charles Bruce, developed a successful technique of cutting and burning the jungle to create plantations, and in 1838 the first consignment of 12 chests of Assam tea in the *Calcutta* left for London.

Ceylon had become another jewel in the British Empire's crown in 1802, and a strong coffee bean growing industry had developed, with tea as a minor activity until, in 1869, an outbreak of a parasitic fungus (*Hemileia vastatrix*) destroyed the entire crop. Tea took over.

During the American War of Independence the need to out sail the comparatively tubby, over-masted sloops and brigs of the Royal Navy brought about the introduction of a slim and fast-type of sailing ship – the Baltimore clipper. With a great beam, placed far forward, giving a very fine run from a high bow with plenty of sheer to a low stern, and stem, sternpost and mast very raked, they had a profile which made them easily distinguished. These long, low, flush-decked brigs and schooners were the first sailing ships to be built with speed rather than cargo capacity as their chief design feature, and many were privateers, slavers or carried the skull and crossbones flag. Their style spawned the opium clippers (1830–1850), the American clippers (1846–1860) and the British tea clippers (1850–1875) until steam displaced sail and the magnificent sight of these sleek, fast greyhounds of the oceans disappeared.

Sailing out of Calcutta with their cargo from Patna and Benares bought at the government opium sales in India, these vessels were manned to a high standard often by ex-Royal Naval officers and crewed by deserters, and made passage round China under racing canvas in all weathers and seasons, especially during the north-east monsoon, when they would thrash their way to the Chinese Ladrones Islands against a heavy head sea and strong current, taking either the open route or, by way of the Palawan Passage to Linton off Macao. Their cargo was transferred to smaller receiving ships to be transhipped to smugglers up lonely estuaries and creeks. The Emperor of China had outlawed opium, to which the British response was to send warships to Canton (Guangzhou) in 1840, and force the Chinese to sign the Treaty of Nanking whereby a large indemnity was paid to England, five ports opened for trade to Europeans, and Hong Kong ceded to Britain. Again in 1857, in response to Chinese police action, the French and British occupied Beijing, and importation of opium was legalized by the Chinese.

Until the expiration of the East India Company's charter in 1834, the tea trade was entirely in their hands. The tea clippers, so called because they 'clipped' time off the regular sailing times, were a development from the opium clippers. Prior to that date, Chinese silks, lacquered furniture, porcelain and tea were carried in the East Indiamen, known from their slow performance as 'tea wagons'. As the tea trade expanded in the late 1840s, these ships of 500 tons were outmoded and with the abolition of the restrictive British Navigation Acts in 1849, the American tea clippers dominated the tea trade from 1850 to 1855 having built up expertise and numbers during the Californian Gold Rush where everything was carried around Cape Horn. They carried more and faster, loading up in Canton and making racing passages to New York and Boston. The British built a different style known as the Aberdeen clipper, and a tradition of races between American and British clippers, and between each clipper, ensued.

Loading up at Whampoa or Canton, huge wagers were placed as to the outcome, and probably the most famous was the great tea race of 1866. The captains were expected to back the outcome with much more than just their beaver hat. Sixteen clippers assembled at Foochow, with names such as *Fiery Cross*, *Ariel*, *Flying Cloud*, and *Taeping*. The partakers needed a tug to steam them through the racing tidal waters of the Min River. Five of the early starters formed the main race; the remainder didn't have a chance to catch up. The usual route was down the China Sea, through the Formosa Channel to the Paracels, relying on the fickle squalls of the south-west monsoon of June or catching the coastal breezes along the Cochin Coast, then across to the Borneo coast to similarly catch coastal breezes. Great skill was needed to get the best of the land and sea breeze as they changed direction. Constant awareness was required for faultily charted or uncharted rocks and reefs, and currents that were misreported in the sparse sailing directions.

Once through the Sunda Strait between Sumatra and Java, the captain could take a few minutes off the quarterdeck, and take advantage of the southeast trade wind across the Indian Ocean to Mauritius with every sail set including the auxiliary 'kites'. The best day's runs shown for this year were *Fiery Cross* 328 miles, and *Ariel* 330 miles. Stormy passage was experienced on the run to the Cape of Good Hope from light airs to heavy storms. They could take advantage of the Agulhas current or stand out to sea and hope for stronger advantageous winds.

The next landmark was the island of St Helena, then past Ascension Island, crossing the Equator. The *Taeping* and *Ariel* arrived at London within 20 minutes of each other, but as there were delays with the tugs, it was agreed that they should both share the prize money – a dead heat. *Serica* came in to the

West India Dock one and a half hours later at 11.30 p.m. It was an extraordinary result with the first three leaving the Min River on the same tide, and arriving 99 days later, covering 16,000 miles, in the River Thames on the same tide. The *Fiery Cross* and *Taitsing* arrived two days later.

With the opening of the Suez Canal in 1869 steam ships could make the journey in half the time. The clippers turned to the Australian wool trade, using the westerlies along the latitude of the roaring forties.

Accurate charts were needed for all these activities and Lieutenant Richard Collinson charted the Chinese coast from Chusan to Hong Kong in an old Calcutta pilot brig HMS *Plover* with a small schooner, *Young Hebe*. His work culminated in some 30 detailed charts, with full sailing directions, published separately in the Chinese Pilot. As part of his project to chart the world, Sir Francis Beaufort, Hydrographer of the Navy, appointed Captain Edward Belcher to this area of the Pacific. For three years Belcher surveyed the islands of the eastern seas from Japan to the Celebes, and an extensive part of the north-east coast of Borneo, too, at the same time joining with HMS *Dido* in anti-pirate operations along the Borneo rivers. Captain Richard Bate surveyed extensively off the China coast following on from his involvement in the taking of Canton in 1842 until he was killed by a musket shot while surveying from the top of a tower in the second opium war in 1857.

| THE GROWING FRENCH INTEREST IN THE PACIFIC |

Dutch maritime activity declined after the Anglo-Dutch wars, the last of which was fought out in 1667. The French and English were to become the more powerful navies fighting in theatres across the world from India to Canada, and competition in the Pacific and Australia became heated, the French forming the *Compagnie des Indes Orientales* and the *Compagnie Royale de la Mer Pacifique*. Various islands bear testimony to the French explorers who discovered them – Bouvet, Crozet and Kerguelen. But many islands were inaccurately plotted, hardly surprising with the difficulties of finding accurate longitude.

One example is the Solomon Islands, which the Spanish navigator, Alvaro de Mendaña, discovered in 1567. He sailed from Peru anticipating finding the Southern Continent as near as 600 leagues (1800 miles) from the South American coast. He sailed across 120° of longitude a few degrees south of the Equator, believing what he found to be the islands of King Solomon. In 1595 he was finally permitted to return to found a colony, but he greatly underestimated their distance. He discovered the Marquesas group of islands *en route* and continued on to Santa Cruz at 167° E, some 200 miles short of the Solomons, where he decided to set up his colony. But Mendaña's death and the men's general disrespect towards the natives made colonization impossible, and the chief pilot, Pedro Fernandez de Quiros, sailed back to Peru with the survivors, after first visiting Manila in the Philippines and discovering Ponape in the Caroline Islands on the way.

In 1605 Quiros got together two ships and a launch, with Luis Vaez de Torres as his second-in-command, and sailed from Callao, Peru in search of the Southern Continent. Had he continued to head west-south-west, he would undoubtedly have come upon New Zealand. In the event and against the remonstrations of Torres he headed through the Duff group, found the New Hebrides group, thinking them to be *Terra Australis Incognita*, but his crew mutinied and his ship returned to Peru. Torres, with the two other vessels, headed through the strait between New Guinea ad Australia that now bears his name.

Philip Carteret sailed as a lieutenant under John Byron's voyage around the world in HMS *Dolphin* between 1764 and 1766. On his return he was appointed to command HMS *Swallow* with Captain Samuel Wallis in command of *Dolphin* on a second circumnavigation. Separated, Carteret made discoveries of previously unknown Polynesian and Melanesian islands and completed valuable surveys of the Philippines, and probably passed through the Solomon Islands, earning him the right to be considered one of the greatest explorers of his time.

The name of Bougainville lives on in the mind of every gardener, for it was he who brought the flower named after him as Bougainvillea back to Europe. Compte Louis Antoine de Bougainville was the French equivalent to James Cook as a mathematician and a seafarer. He was also a French aristocrat, soldier and diplomat, serving with distinction under General Montcalm during the Seven Years War fought between the British and French between 1756 and 1763. After this he founded a colony in the Falkland Islands. In 1766 in command of *La Boudeuse*, with the back-up store ship *L'Étoile*, he withdrew from the Falklands colony and sailed through the Strait of Magellan, crossed the Pacific driven by the trade wind to Tahiti, which he formally annexed, although the British naval explorer Samuel Wallis had visited there six months earlier. He continued around the world with assembled scientists, naturalists and artists,

Yves Joseph de Kerguelen-Tremerac, another French aristocrat, as a navigator was commanded by the King to head an expedition to find *Terra Australis Incognita*. He headed south from Cape Horn and came across a desolate group of islands close to the Antarctic in 1772 giving them his family name – the Kerguelen Islands. On his return in 1774, unable to penetrate the ice barrier, he confirmed his conclusion that such a vast continent as was shown on the old maps and charts was unlikely to exist.

Like many of the French explorers of the time Compte de La Pérouse had learned his craft serving with distinction helping the American colonies in the War of Independence. In 1785 La Pérouse was given command of a two-ship expedition – the *Boussole* and the *Astrolabe* – with instructions, like George Vancouver, to find the North-West passage from the Pacific. He was driven back from Alaska by atrocious weather in June of that year, discovered Necker Island, one of the Sandwich or Hawaiian group, then crossed the Pacific as instructed to explore the north-east coasts of Asia, China and Japan, the Solomon Islands, and then Australia. He surveyed up the coast of Korea, gave the strait dividing Japan and Sakhalin his name, and sent his charts and records to France from Petropavlovsk. He then sailed south reaching Mauna in the Samoan group on 8 December, but the captain of the *Astrolabe* was murdered. Staunchly sailing on, the expedition stopped at the Friendly Islands and Norfolk Island and on to the British settlement at Botany Bay in January 1788. They left in February and were never heard of again until some wreckage was found years later on the reefs of Vanikoro Island, part of the Santa Cruz group. The artistic studies of the flora and fauna that were sent back from Australia were published in Paris and exemplify the French abilities; beautiful drawings and studies in colour.

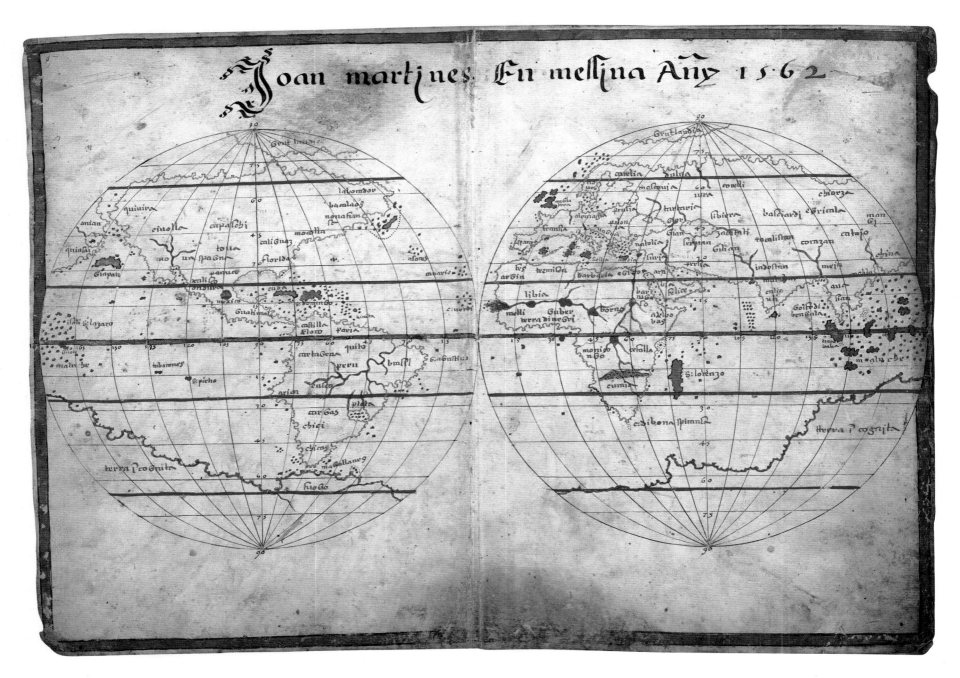

Joan martines En messina Any 1562

| **DOUBLE HEMISPHERE WORLD MAP BY JOAN MARTINES, *C.1560*** | The world's shape and the juxtaposition of the continents was becoming understood by the time of one of the first manuscript maps showing the Old and New Worlds as separate hemispheres. It is considered as dated 1560 (there is an erasure under the 2 of 1562) in which case it pre-dates Girolamo Ruscelli's double hemisphere world map of 1561. A maritime map rather than a navigational chart, the portolan is by Joan Martines, a prolific Spanish master cartographer from Catalan who worked in Messina, Italy. In the Pacific hemisphere it shows Japan as one island off the China coast, the Maluchi (Moluccas) and innumerable islands in the Pacific, with surprisingly, as it wasn't known until Bering's voyage in 1728, a strait between the continents of Asia and America. (Courtesy of The Hispanic Society of America, New York, K20)

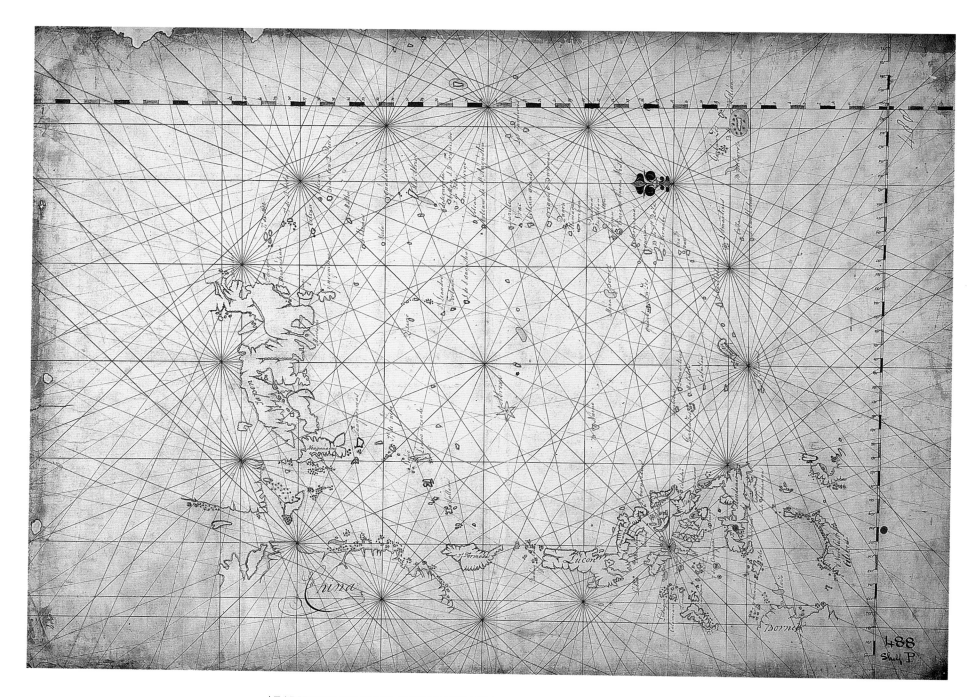

**| EARLY EIGHTEENTH-CENTURY SPANISH MANUSCRIPT CHART OF THE
NORTH PACIFIC |** Rear-Admiral Sir Thomas Troubridge was one of Nelson's 'Band of
Brothers' who fought with distinction at the battles of Cape St Vincent and the Nile. He gave
this early eighteenth-century Spanish manuscript chart of the North Pacific to the Admiralty. He
had served (with Nelson) in HMS *Seahorse* in the East Indies returning to England in 1785.

It shows the sphere of Spanish influence between the Equator and 45° N that was to wane
after the last major effort of Spanish exploration by the 1605 voyages of Torres and Quiros. Her
Treasury had suffered from continuous successful attacks against her treasure galleons, such as
Anson's, and she did not have the manpower to continue expansion. (UKHO © British Crown
Copyright)

| CHART OF COMMODORE ANSON'S PACIFIC OCEAN TRACK |

Commodore George Anson's circumnavigation of the world, during which he lost four ships from his squadron but gained the annual Spanish treasure ship also benefited the explorers who came after him into the Pacific such as Byron, Carteret, Wallis and Cook. This contemporary track chart shows his route from Acapulco to Tenian and from thence to China, and how he sailed too far south to catch the trade winds. The track of *Nuestra Señora de Covadonga*, the Spanish galleon, shows the great circle route she followed from Manila to Acapulco, from Acapulco to Guam and from thence to the Philippine Islands, where she was taken with a fortune on board by Commodore Anson in the *Centurion* on 20 June 1743. (UKHO © British Crown Copyright)

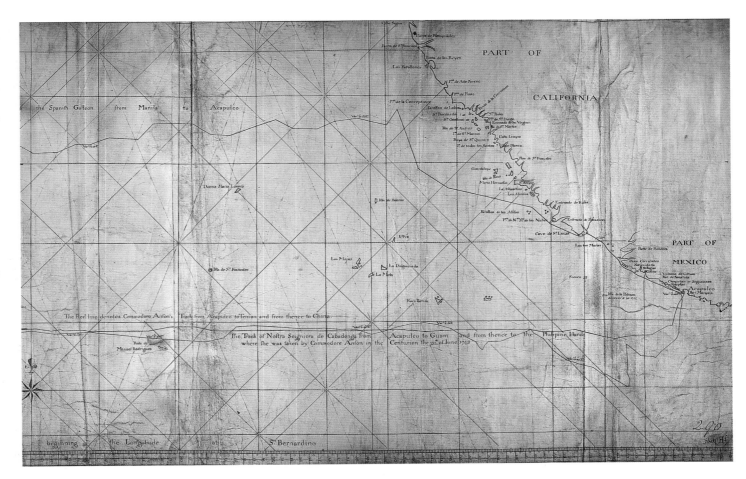

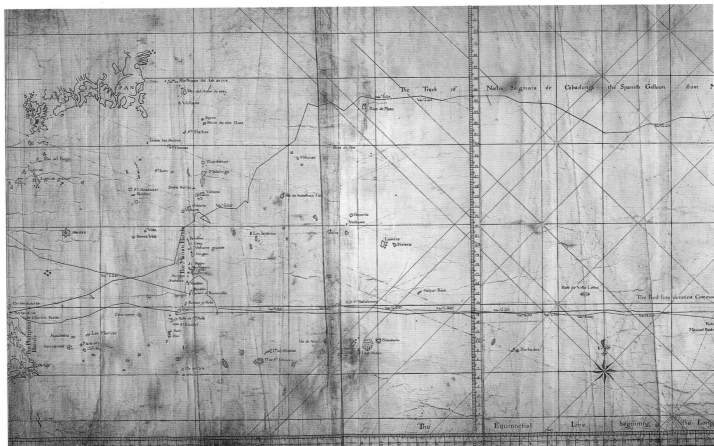

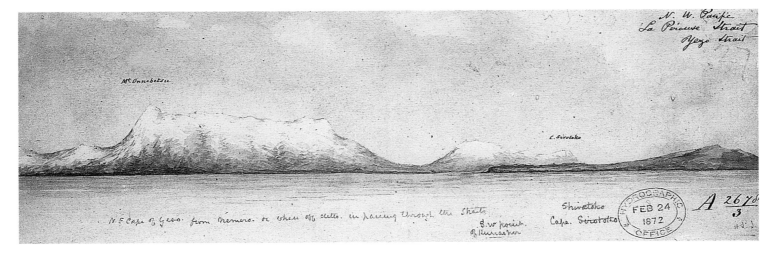

| NAVIGATIONAL VIEWS OF HOKKAIDO AND SAKHALIN | These views of La Pérouse and Yezo Straits, between the northernmost island of Japan, Hokkaido, and the Russian island of Sakhalin, are fine examples of the high standard of watercolour paintings that could be achieved by naval officers in the line of duty. They are then stylised and engraved to be incorporated into charts as navigational views. Compte de La Pérouse was the famous French explorer and naval officer who took a French expedition into the Pacific to try to find the North-West passage. (UKHO © British Crown Copyright)

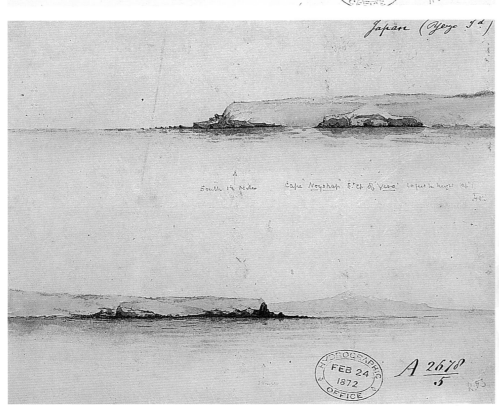

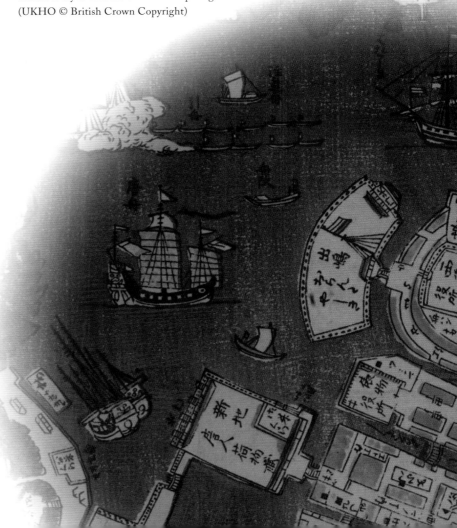

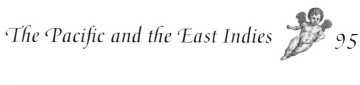

| LEFT | **JAPANESE CHART OF NAGASAKI, 1801** | The Japanese stylistic approach to charting in this 1801 chart of Nagasaki by the Japanese chart-sellers Baikido is not dissimilar to the Chinese charts of that time, showing the cultural influence that migrated over the sea. This woodblock print shows the trading island of Deshima (where cargo was checked and unloaded in quarantine without contact with the mainland) a Dutch man-of-war and a Chinese *karabume* (sailing junk). The characters in each corner identify the four geographical directions with Japanese north at the top right of the illustration. The characters bottom left show sailing distances to other Japanese ports. (© National Maritime Museum, London, FO308)

| BELOW | **NAVIGATIONAL VIEW OF NAGASAKI** | Once Japan was officially 'opened up' to the West, sea views of Japan were needed back in London to complete the new charts of the area. This painting, which would form the basis of the engraved view at the edge of a chart, is a particularly beautiful example showing the entrance to Nagasaki drawn by the Master, Mr E Wilds, from HMS *Swallow* in 1866. (UKHO © British Crown Copyright)

Entrance to Nagasaki Harbour – Japan.

| ABOVE | **CHINESE CHART OF THE YELLOW SEA** |
This delightful, rare and unusual Chinese manuscript chart
probably dates from the early nineteenth century and almost has
the air of a Chinese painting. China always had a strong tradition
of sea trading of which charts were a fundamental part. Cheng-
Ho, in the fourteenth and fifteenth centuries had commanded
seven long voyages of Chinese Imperial fleets to East Africa,
Arabia, the Persian Gulf, India and, it has been argued, to
Australia and America. By the sixteenth century Chinese
cartography was strongly influenced by Jesuit missionaries, and
they were appointed by the Emperor to organise Chinese charts
and mapmaking from the seventeenth century.

It covers from Chusan to the Gulf of Pe che le and the border
with Corea – shown by a 'stockade'. The names are in Chinese
characters and the chart is embellished by drawings of junks
sailing across the Yellow Sea, with the Great Wall of China shown
at the top right. (UKHO © British Crown Copyright)

| LEFT | **CHINESE CHART OF CANTON** | This is the
central part of a Chinese chart that probably dates from the early
eighteenth century. It shows the Quangdong (Canton) Province
and the Pearl River estuary, with the city of Guangzhou (Canton).
As a city that was to become one of the major European ports in
the nineteenth century there is little depicted of the waterfront
that was to develop. The sailing route pecked out is that used by
sailing ships going up and down the estuary to and from Canton.
The lower part was heavily defended at the narrows, the so-called
Boccas-Tigris with the twin Anunghoi forts, where a chain could
be drawn across if danger threatened. Shipping would then
continue upstream to anchor at Whampoa, by the Pagoda shown
on the chart; its height was a useful seamark for navigation.
(Admiralty Library Manuscript Collection VZ 6/7)

| CHINESE CHART OF THE COASTLINE OF FUKIEN PROVINCE | Drawn on many sheets of thin paper this interesting colourful chart, of which three parts are shown here, is a Chinese representation of the Fukien Province coastline, today called Fujian, opposite the island of Formosa (Taiwan), dating between the late eighteenth century to early nineteenth century. The Dutch factory and settlement at Fort Zeelandia, on the west coast of Taiwan, had been driven out after the great siege of 1661–62 by the Fujiang leader, Koxinga. Thereafter, Westerners were only tolerated in the foreign 'factories' of Guangzhou (Canton) and the Portuguese outpost at Aomen (Macao), and European influence on maps and charts, although accepted from the Jesuits in the seventeenth century, was rejected by 1724 when the Emperor banned Christianity. This chart has its own cultural development with an emphasis on a three-dimensional, almost block representation, of hills, mountains and islands. These would typically detail such necessary information for military and trade purposes, concentrating on the more southern Chinese ports where Western trade was prolific, and foreign intervention and piratical attacks more likely. The red line of demarcation, with a note written in English, is shown between Fu Kien (Fukien) and Chekiang Province to the north and deep water is also noted in English. (Admiralty Library Manuscript Collection MSS 360)

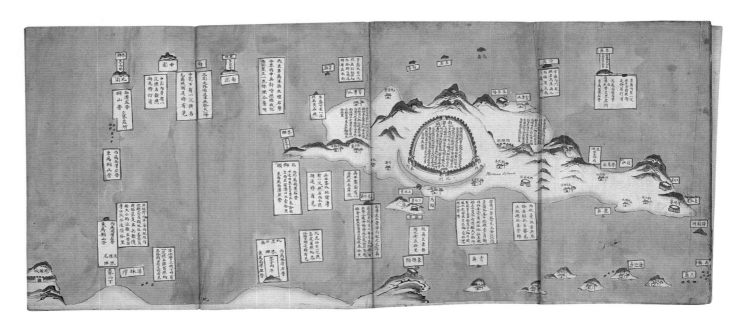

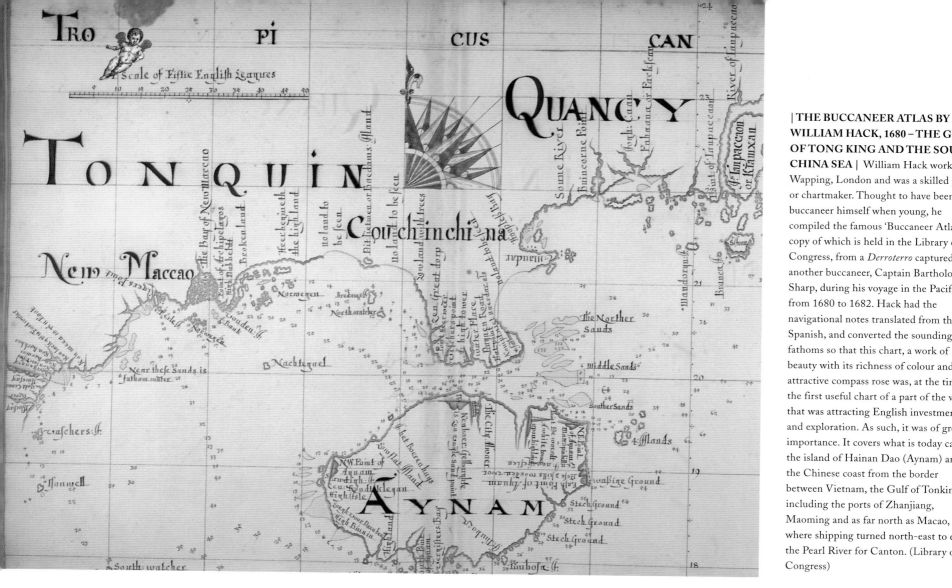

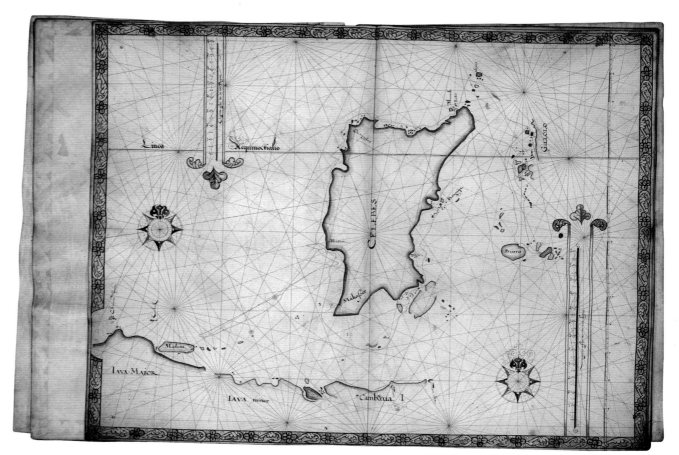

| A HAND-DRAWN SURVEY OF MANILA BAY AND HARBOUR, *C.*1762 | The latitude on this manuscript chart of the approach through the bay, shown by a line of soundings, to Manila harbour is written as 'Latt'd of the City 14 35 North', which differs little from the actual latitude noted today. The scale is in leagues and the pencil notation shows that it was 'received from Major Rennell 20th June 1802 formerly belonging to Adml. Richard Kempenfelt'. This would have been when he was flag-captain to Admiral Cornish at the capture of Manila in 1762 from the Spanish during the Seven Years War (1756–63). We can safely assume, and the style of the survey supports this, that the chart dates from then. The key gives '1. Landing Place' and this may indicate where the force landed to capture the city.

Admiral Kempenfelt brought an innovative approach to the navy and gave so much on strategy, health, gunnery, signalling, and a divisional structure that is still in use today to manage sailors. He tragically lost his life with the majority of the crew of the *Royal George*, in which he was flying his flag, when she took on water through open gunports at Spithead after a sudden gust of wind and capsized on 29 August 1782, inspiring William Cowper's poem, 'Toll for the Brave'. (Admiralty Library Manuscript Collection VZ 7/39{2})

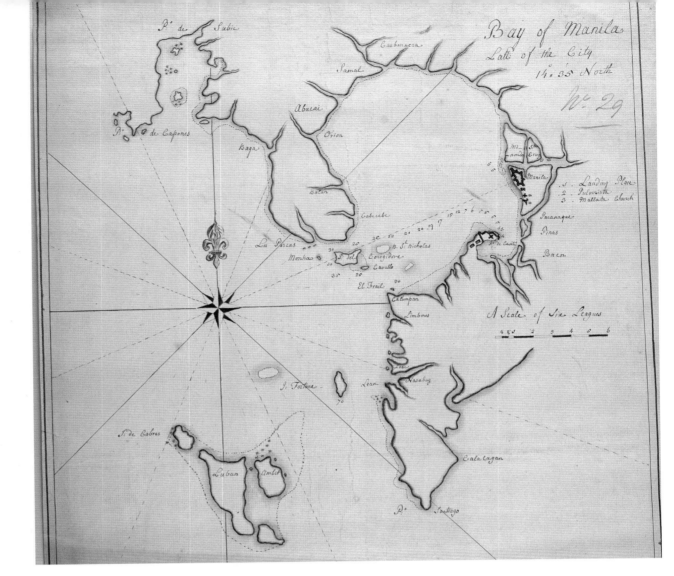

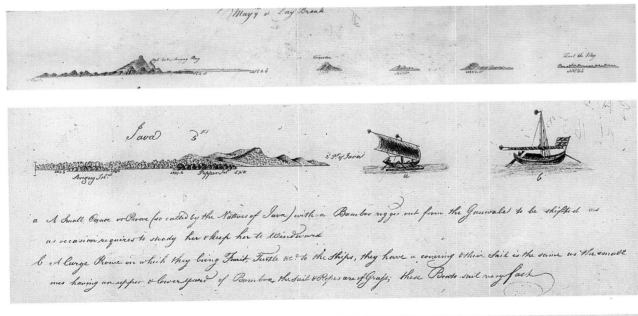

| NAVIGATIONAL VIEW OF JAVA, *C.* 1878–89 | An attractive elevation preparatory to a navigational view for inclusion in a chart of Java by the East India Company ship *Mars*, *c.*1787–89, it shows the entrance for a landing from her anchorage, and a description of the unfamiliar outrigger that the natives used in their Prowe canoe to bring fresh fruit and provisions out to the ship. The name of one of the islands as Pepper Island gives an indication of the importance of this spice. (UKHO © British Crown Copyright)

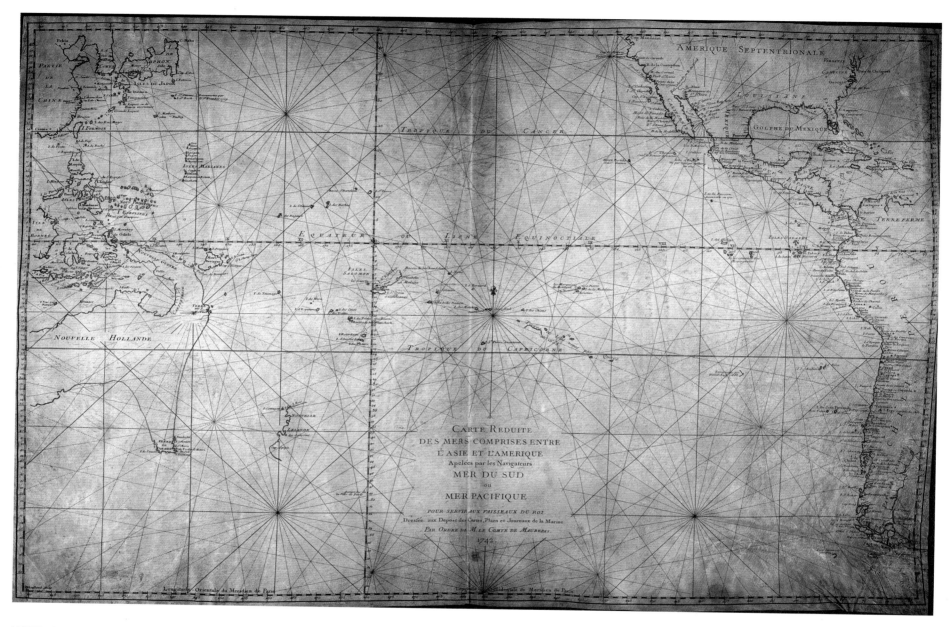

| FRENCH CHART OF THE PACIFIC FROM *LE NEPTUNE FRANÇOIS*, 1742 | *'Pour servir aux vaisseaux du Roi'* ('for the use of the King's ships') announces this maritime map drawn on vellum to endure and form part of the folio of charts in *Le Neptune Francois* engraved by 'D heulland Sculp'. As a French chart, the zero meridian of longitude is naturally based on Paris, and the immense scope of the coverage must have emphasized the confidence of French explorers and adventurers to find for *La France*.

With a series of rhumb lines radiating from the centre, and subsidiary rhumb line azimuths in an outer circle based on the inner one, and covering the immensity of the Pacific Ocean between 61º S and 41º N, including the known Pacific islands and spreading into the Caribbean islands, this is a chart giving graphic expression to what had been, but more interestingly, to what still could be, discovered. Australia was still thought to form an unbroken chain of land from New Guinea, obliterating the Torres Strait that separates New Guinea from Northern Australia, to Tasmania with no room for the Bass Strait. New Zealand, pre-Cook, is a whisper of land that was thought to be a peninsula from the anticipated great Southern Continent. The Spice Islands and East Indies are better understood, but Japan is just an unfamiliar embryonic shape of three main islands, not four. The last voyages for gain, such as Anson's circumnavigational raid on the Spanish Acapulco treasure ship, were happening, but the great, late eighteenth-century voyages of exploration by such as Cook, Vancouver, Wallis and Carteret and others that would finally shape the Pacific into what we know today were still to come. (Admiralty Library Manuscript Collection VZ 7/16)

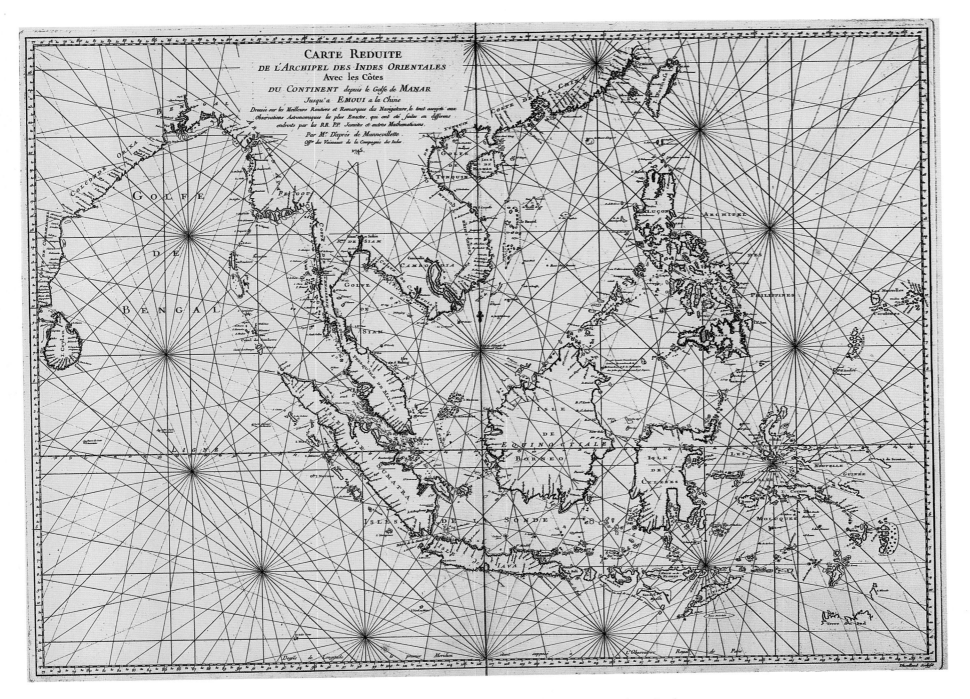

| **FRENCH CHART OF THE EAST INDIES, 1745** | Drawn with the portolan style of a circle of radiating rhumb lines, this French chart of the period was compiled and published in 1745 by D'Aprés de Mannevillette from a number of manuscript charts which formed *Le Neptune François*. Although becoming more accurate in parts such as India and south-east Asia, it shows the need to explore and chart the lesser exploited areas. The coasts around New Guinea, Australia (where just a few parts of northern Australia are laid down) and the Sunda Islands, with Timor, are sketchy and have yet to be defined, while the Mekong delta in Vietnam is greatly exaggerated into a large bay. (UKHO© British Crown Copyright)

The Caribbean and Northwards Along the East Coast of North America

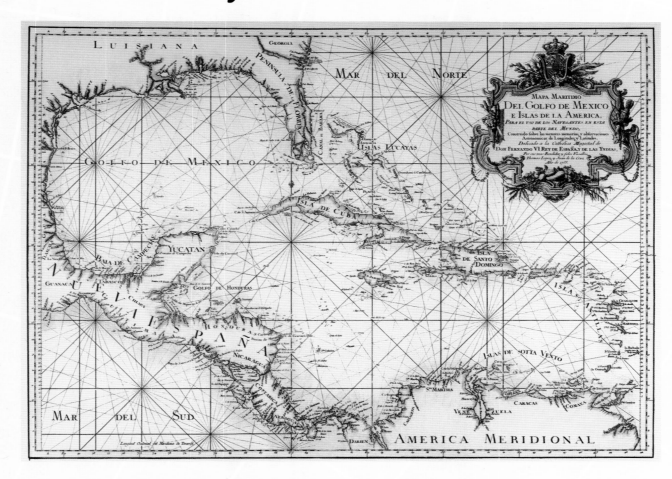

| LEFT DETAIL & ABOVE | **SPANISH MARITIME MAP OF THE CARIBBEAN, 1755** | This splendid Spanish maritime map encompasses the entire Gulf of Mexico, for which Spain still felt territorial ownership, but already wars and buccaneering were tearing away large parts of her American Empire. Florida and Mexico still belonged to Spain, as did the equatorial American countries of Honduras, Nicaragua, Costa Rica and others.

It is one of the earlier works of Tomas Lopez (de Vargas Machuca), who worked copiously in Madrid as Geographer to the Spanish King, Don Fernando VI, compiling and publishing atlases and maps, many of Spanish possessions. (Library of Congress)

Up until October 1492 the continent of America did not exist – at least not to the peoples of Europe. For a while after that it was in the way – the way to the fabled East. There is evidence that the Vikings had voyaged to Newfoundland and the northern coasts of America, and may have settled there, perhaps using feldspar quartz to diffract the sun's rays through the ice fog to get a course relative to the sun's bearing. According to Norse sagas, Lief Ericsson sailed from Greenland to follow up earlier sightings of new lands to the south-west. He landed in succession at Helluland (meaning country of flat stones, probably Baffin Island), Markland (country of trees, probably Labrador) and Vinland, also named after the wild grapes found growing there, (probably northern Newfoundland). Controversy continues as to whether a map of Vinlandia, reputedly dated 1440 and held at Yale University, is a forgery or not.

Coastal navigation by the close of the fifteenth century was well understood, it was known as caping and the pilot's rutter gave the main features such as coastal headlands the distance apart of the normal distance of visibility – 20 miles. Venetians traded through the Strait of Gibraltar and into the Atlantic ports of Spain, Portugal, France and up to Flanders; English fishermen and wool traders brought back wine from Portugal and the Mediterranean; Iceland was fished by northern European countries, and, venturing apprehensively into the Atlantic, the Spanish settled the Canaries in the fourteenth century; the Portuguese in the Madeira archipelago about 1420 and the Azores by 1440.

For a 6-foot, red headed, Genoese-born Cristoforo Colombo, known to us as Christopher Columbus, the idea of sailing west to Cathy (China) became an obsession. Initially running a mapmaking firm with his brother, he looked for the best form of sponsorship available – a royal court. In 1484 he was turned down by the King of Portugal, and his brother by Henry VII of England and again by Louis XI of France. Columbus pursued the Royal Court of Spain for nearly eight years before securing King Ferdinand and Queen Isabella's approval, with his vision of outflanking the Turkish Empire to get to the riches of the East. He relished the prospect of converting every prince and pauper he encountered to Christianity, having himself proclaimed governor of every land and island he discovered, along with a useful 5 per cent of the pickings. Eratosthenes in the third century BC had put forward the idea that one could sail from Iberia to India. Columbus made a calculation from older texts that the world's diameter was 20,000 miles and decided that he need only sail for 30 days to get to Marco Polo's Cipangu (Japan) and thence to Cathay.

His 'Enterprise' of three ships, the *Santa Maria*, and caravels *Pinta* and *Niña*, set out on 3 August 1492, and touched land on the Bahamian island of Guanahani on 11 October. Columbus was convinced that he had discovered the short route to India, and the name given to the locals has stuck to this day – Indians.

The tide of Europeans flowing to the New World had started, and one of the first to represent it was Martin Waldseemüller in 1507, whose atlas map had the name Americus, after Amerigo Vespucci the florentine merchant-adventurer who claimed to have discovered the mainland itself, on the southern continent: the name of the continent stuck too. Columbus' next voyage was a fleet of 17 ships with 1500 soldiers, sailors and adolescents to start to people the Americas, and take the spoils – gold in particular.

The first known published chart to show America, as discovered by Columbus was the Spanish navigator, Juan de la Cosa, in 1500.

Giovanni Caboto, known through history as John Cabot, a Venetian or Genoese like Columbus, would have known of his discoveries in Central America and won the approval of Henry VII of England to explore west. Granted a royal charter in 1496, and with Bristol Merchants' backing, he sailed the *Mathew*, a 50-ton square-rigger, across the North Atlantic and landed at what is now assumed to be Belle Isle. He claimed 'New Found Land' for England and his reports of the codfish soon attracted fishermen to follow him.

By the time Francis I assumed the throne in France in 1515, Breton fishermen were already making massive catches of fish on the north American coast around the cod banks of Nova Scotia and, probing inland, began to trade fur. Francis wanted to find the North-West passage, famously dismissing the Pope's edict of Tordesillas with the rebuke, 'We fail to find this clause in Adam's will'.

To this end, he enlisted the skills of Florentine-born navigator, Giovanni da Verrazano. He tried to find a new passage to the Pacific from the Atlantic coast of North America, covering Chesapeake Bay, the Hudson River and past Cape Cod. He looked along the coast of Maine and continued up to Newfoundland and the Strait of Belle Isle having named Pamlico Sound, inside the Carolina Outer Banks, the Verrazano Sea in the belief that it was the Pacific. His two other voyages also added to France's knowledge of North America, but his hitherto friendly experience with natives did not prepare him for the hostile reception he received when he tried to land in the Antilles – he was murdered and eaten by cannibalistic Caribs in 1528.

There was by now a significant school of navigation and boat-building in Normandy and Francis appointed Jacques Cartier to lead a two-ship expedition to sail across the Atlantic to the north and find a route to Cathay. He left St Malo in April 1534 and sailed up the Strait of Belle Isle, along the Gulf of St Lawrence, reconnoitred the Gaspé Peninsula and Anticosti Island. On returning the King sponsored a second voyage with three ships with which Cartier explored the St Lawrence up to where Quebec is now, created a base and then on by boat to the rapids below Montreal. With reputedly gold, copper and silver for the taking further inland, Cartier sailed as second-in-command a third time in 1541 with several hundred colonists. They did not survive the devastating Canadian winter and no further attempt to explore North America was made by France for 50 years; indeed, both France and Spain lost interest in America north of Florida. But geographers realized the importance of the St Lawrence seaway in opening up a main artery into North America and La Nouvelle France was loudly proclaimed on charts and maps with all the force and vigour of Christianity's right to take over the land and convert any who were deemed savages.

By 1603 Samuel de Champlain, who had cut his nautical teeth in command of a ship from Cadiz to the West Indies in 1599, sailed to Canada as an agent to exploit the fur trade. He followed Cartier's route exploring the St Lawrence and finally founded a French settlement at Arcadia, carrying out surveying and charting and, returning again from France in 1608, founded the first white settlement at Quebec. He remained convinced of a sea-route through Canada along the St Lawrence, across the great lakes and down a further river to the west for the rest of his life.

For 60 years France concentrated on the European wars, but in 1666 a man of energy and intellect, Robert Cavelier, Sieur de la Salle, emigrated to Canada. (Canada is an Indian word meaning village, something of a geographical understatement!) He learned a dozen Indian languages, secured money from

France and was granted a seigneury on the St Lawrence by rapids near Montreal which he wryly named Lachine, as close as he was ever to get to the Orient. By 1682 he had explored south along the Mississippi from its source in present-day Minnesota to where this mighty river exits into the Gulf of Mexico and boldly declared the whole watershed as part of King Louis' Empire, naming it Louisiana. La Salle persuaded the King to finance his return to found a colony. His four ships sailed into the Gulf of Mexico but through bad navigation landed on the Texas coast, and never made it to the Mississippi. He perished in Texas, butchered by the remaining 20 of his frustrated followers. But New Orleans became a French colony as a direct result of La Salle's extraordinary exploratory efforts.

The English followed a similar ambition to the French by initially setting up trading, then colonizing the north and south of North America. Sir John Hawkins was perhaps the first of a series of legalized pirates; privateers sailing with letters of marque or royal authorization. He had started to trade slaves from West Africa, selling to the Spanish settlers in the West Indies, antagonizing the Portuguese who considered this 'commerce' their monopoly, and the Spanish who considered the Caribbean their trading monopoly.

His third voyage, with his young cousin, Francis Drake, culminated in the capture of Queen Elizabeth I's ship, on loan, at San Juan de Ulloa, Mexico, in 1568 and marked the start of a long period of hostility and war between Britain and Spain. He sailed on a two-and-half-year circumnavigation in 1580. His success at sea brought him to the post of Treasurer, in 1577, and, in 1589, Comptroller of the Navy, and with these two most important posts he redesigned the Elizabethan navy with new ships, 'lower charged' with more guns, faster and more seaworthy. These became the tools for English expansion of trade and influence, challenging and demolishing Spanish maritime ability.

Drake was then granted a privateering commission to take five ships to plunder and harass the Spanish possessions on the West Coast of South America. This meant breaking into the Pacific through the Strait of Magellan, which the Spanish thought unlikely. He achieved this at great cost, putting down a mutiny, and executing one of the gentlemen sailors who had invested in the voyage. Sailing north he ransacked the cities of Peru and Chile, attacking any Spanish ship he met, and to this day mother's in those countries threaten their young children with *El Draco* if they don't behave. The expedition included intercepting the annual treasure ship on her way from Acapulco to the Philippines, and returning with so much Catholic altar plate, golden crucifixes and silver that his ship *Golden Hind* barely made it back to Plymouth.

These voyages excited English interest in colonizing the Americas. Richard Hakluyt, of Welsh extraction, attended Christ Church Oxford, learned six languages and studied all the maritime accounts of the time to publish, in 1589, one of the best-loved accounts in maritime literature, *The Principal Navigations, Voiages, Traffiques and Discoveries of the English Nation*. Obsessed by geography, although he never travelled west of Bristol, he canvassed every explorer he could and amassed a vast library of relevant manuscripts. His writings – much while serving in the Church at Westminster Abbey, where a copy of the first two volumes of his accounts are in the Archives, voicing the conviction that the ills of England's poor could be relieved by immigration to the American colonies – inspired the Queen to encourage her people to make the voyage. The first British colony was financed by Sir Walter Raleigh at Roanoake and was named Virginia after Queen Elizabeth, who gave him the patent in 1580. John Donne, tactfully before he became Dean of St Paul's Cathedral, reflected an attitude to the westward interest of the time in his famous, but bawdy poem in which he compares the discovery of his mistress's body with a voyage to America: 'And sailing toward her India, in that way, Shall at her fair Atlantick Navell stay'.

Financial reward was a strong influence, too, for the men who could put up the money. Any newly discovered lands automatically belonged to the Crown, and men such as Sir Thomas Smythe, director of the East India Company, Sir

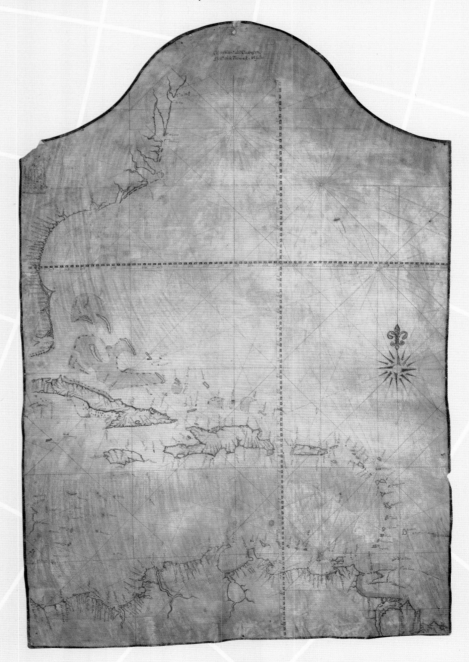

| ANONYMOUS SPANISH CHART OF THE CARIBBEAN, *C.* 1750 | The Caribbean is shown on a Spanish parchment sailing portolan chart, but is unusual as the zero meridian for longitude is centred on the Azores, at Corvo (Cuerbo) rather than Santa Cruz de Tenerife, in the Canary Islands, but with both latitude and longitude scales shown. There is a legend (A to G) north of Florida which refers to the Florida Keys, red ink is used to mark major ports, but hydrographic features are only shown on the eastern seaboard of North America, and soundings shown in detail in the Bahamas. (Courtesy of The Hispanic Society of America, New York)

Ferdinando Gorges, Sir John Popham, Lord Chief Justice, saw the opportunities for rich reward in vast new plantations in Virginia, but needed a royal charter. Queen Elizabeth I had given such a charter to the East India Company in 1600, and James I similarly granted one to the London Company formed by its backers in 1606. Ordinary Britons, whose life then was still little short of feudal, tied to the land and pressured to conform to one religious belief, heard of America as a land of free opportunity and provided the motivated manpower to colonize it.

Three ships set sail in 1606 to America, following the north Atlantic trade winds and currents via the Azores, then the West Indies to found a discreet settlement north of the Spanish in Florida and south of the French in Canada. Finding their way into Chesapeake Bay, up the James River they called their settlement, to honour their patron, Jamestown. They survived, just. Within seven months they had exhausted the supplies they had brought with them, tried to barter with the Indians, steal their land and food, but within two years their numbers were reduced from 105 to 38. They were on the verge of giving up and preparing to leave for England when, by chance, a relief ship arrived with new blood and food. They persevered and found a new crop that they could cultivate. By wood-smoking it they created a cash crop in Virginian tobacco. By 1619, a governor was appointed, Sir George Yardley, who set a precedent and lived there amongst the settlers. He couldn't cope with all the duties and asked for two representatives from each borough to meet with him. A new form of organisation, independent of England, was burgeoning – democracy, forming the basis of the two-house system to become in time the Congress of the United States.

The topography of Virginia and the Carolinas is such that there are fingers of land out into the Atlantic that gave a natural waterfront and each plantation became its own sea-port. River charts were needed, of course, for these but the main ports still developed, as by the 1760s rice and indigo were grown and shipped.

The other ingredient the settlers needed to create a plantation economy was heavy labour, and slaves provided the answer. The Portuguese have the doubtful credit of the first enslavement of the African Black in 1444. The Spanish systemized it and the English expanded it, shipping the first slaves from Africa to Virginia within 12 years of the first settlement, paradoxically in a vessel name *Jesus of Lubeck*. The 'trade' to supplement the white indentured servants built up from 300 blacks over the first 40 years to 60,000 a decade by the 1680s. The Atlantic Ocean supported a triangle of trade that sailing ships were able to fulfill. For the British this meant sailing out of London or Bristol and later Liverpool to the African west coast with cheap trading goods, such as worn out muskets, iron goods and trinkets. These were bartered for slaves, who were then crammed into the same holds as all the other merchandise, such as pepper and gold dust, and shipped along the notorious 'Middle Passage' to the sugar plantations in the Caribbean and Brazil. From thence sugar, molasses, rum, fruit and hardwood were carried back to England.

For the Americans this meant a voyage from ports such as Newport, Boston or Charleston to West Africa with rum and iron goods for barter, calling along the Ivory, Gold and Slave Coasts, back across the Atlantic with a cargo of slaves along the Middle Passage to the Caribbean, and even to the Mosquito Coast and Honduras, then reloading with sugar, molasses and perhaps Spanish coin (some obtained through piracy) to North American eastern seaboard ports between Charleston and Boston. While the slave trade flourished in the South, building the vessels to carry them flourished in the disapproving northern seaports. Other transatlantic routes took fish and furs from Canada to Britain, and tobacco, indigo, naval stores and cotton was carried from the southern American ports to Britain, and a return trip loaded with manufactured English products. The dependence of the British economy on slavery into the eighteenth century was demonstrated by the fundamental purpose of the mutinous voyage of HMS *Bounty* in 1789, to bring breadfruit from Tahiti to the West Indies as a cheap staple food for the sugar labourer – the Black slave.

Two years after the Jamestown landing a settlement was established in 1609 on an island 500 miles due east of Charleston when a party of English colonists, under the mariner Sir George Somers, sailing for Virginia was shipwrecked there. Three survived and set up their existence with far more ease than they could have at their intended destination. To be called the Bermudas, attributed to a Spanish navigator, Juan de Bermúdez, who was shipwrecked there in about 1503, the islands' position, initially known as Somers Islands were uncertain. Called by Shakespeare 'the vex'd Bermoothes', their position was still questioned in 1653 by the English poet Andrew Marvell who wrote,

> Where the remote Bermudas ride
> in the ocean's bosom unespied

Another ship arrived there in 1612. These settlers were surprised to come across the three survivors, who already knew of ambergris (a derivative of the sperm whale used in the perfume industry) which became the major export and allowed the island economy to flourish so that by 1614 there were over 600 colonists.

The third English colony came about through religious dissent. The Virginia Company of London gave these Pilgrims a charter, but couldn't afford any financial assistance. A hundred dissenters and a crew of 49 sailed the *Mayflower*, a ship of 180 tons, which hitherto had plied wine in the Mediterranean. Incompetent navigation took her 200 miles north of her intended destination in Virginia, to Cape Cod Bay. Landing on 21 December 1620, they called their settlement, founded by their leader William Bradford, Plymouth in Massachusetts. He chronicled,

> Being thus passed the vast ocean, and a sea of troubles … They had now no friends to welcome them, nor inns to entertain or refresh their weatherbeaten bodys, no houses or much less townes to repaire too … it was muttered by some that if they got no place in time they would turn them and their goods ashore (and return) … But may not and ought not the children of these fathers rightly say – Our Fathers were Englishmen which came over this great ocean, and were ready to perish in this wilderness, but they cried unto the Lord, and he heard their voice and looked on their adversities, ETC.

The route to North America was established, even if the ships were small, the journey dangerous and survival across the Atlantic uncertain. The settlements that became known as the Middle Colonies – New York, Pennsylvania, Maryland, Delaware – were set up with the only common links between them being the English language, English Common law, a desire to start a new life, and a common seaboard. The few and primitive roads connecting them meant that they felt closer to London than to each other.

The *Atlantic Neptune*

Lieutenant Joseph-Frederick Wallet des Barres is most respected for producing the folio of charts known as the *Atlantic Neptune* and published in 1777. The term 'Neptune' was widely used in the eighteenth century to signify a set of charts, as the term 'Atlas' refers to a set of maps. King George III's copy of the *Atlantic Neptune* was presented to the UK Hydrographic Office and is held in their archives.

Des Barres was Swiss and had emigrated to England in about 1752, studying at the Royal Military Academy at Woolwich, and gained a commission in the Royal American Regiment in 1756. He played his part in the fall of Quebec that gave control of the whole of Canada to Britain, surveying and preparing charts of the St Lawrence during the winter before the fall of the town with Cook and Samuel Holland, a former Dutch Army Surveyor who had taught Cook army surveying techniques that he adapted for sea surveys. Afterwards they surveyed the town and sounded the harbour and approaches, and Cook both helped and learned from des Barres during the surveys of Halifax and Nova Scotia.

Holland was appointed Surveyor General of British North America, and with prodding from the Admiralty he and other surveyors who had worked for the Board of Trade and Plantations handed over their work to des Barres. Cook himself was instructed by the Admiralty to survey Newfoundland. With victory in the Seven Years War came the need to survey a very extensive coastline. Des Barres was engaged by the Admiralty to survey the Bay of Fundy and Nova Scotia. This took 10 years, which included two years charting the highly dangerous Sable Island, 90 miles southeast of Nova Scotia at the edge of the continental shelf where wave heights are amplifed by the swiftly shallowing sea bed. He returned to London in 1774 where, at the instigation of Earl Howe and the imminent prospect of war with the American colonies, he had the charts engraved (on copper plates) and printed for use by the British fleet. His work as a marine artist was capable, too, reflecting much of his flair, and is much sought after by collectors.

However, des Barres was reluctant to attribute the other charts combined into the *Neptune* to those who made them. The sequence seems to have been as follows: Holland worked on the mainland from the town of Quebec down the St Lawrence river and along the western shore of the Gulf to the Strait of Canso; he also charted the islands of St Jean, Cape Breton and Magdalene. Des Barres surveyed Sable Island and traversed the coast of Nova Scotia from the Strait of Canso to the Bay of Fundy and as far as the Saint John river on the south coast of New Brunswick. From the Saint John River to Passamaquoddy Bay the survey was conducted by Edward Wright and Thomas Hurd, acting under Holland. Southwards, at least as far as New York, the coast was surveyed by Holland and his deputies, Sproule, Blaskowitz, Grant and Wheeler. Further south still Gauld was responsible for the charts of Florida, Louisiana and Jamaica; the collection includes about two dozen of his draughts and a few by James Smith who worked in the Bahamas and West Indies.

These five attractive navigational views of the landfalls and approaches to New York of the 1770s, painted by des Barres and included in the *Atlantic Neptune*, demonstrate his deft artistic skill that he put to such practical use. (UKHO © British Crown Copyright)

Colonies were established for other reasons, too. William Penn set up Pennsylvania because that was the way Charles II decided to settle a debt of £16,000 to his admiral father, and Maryland was established by one of Charles's ambassadors turned Catholic as a haven for Catholics in America.

So spread the English colonies in the seventeenth and eighteenth centuries, and by 1733 there were 13 with independent organization – in effect, separate nation-states with an allegiance to the English Crown.

Meanwhile the French wanted to develop the hinterland and saw the strategic value in containing the British within the coastal area by building, at the end of the 1740s, a series of forts down the Ohio valley joining their colonies in Canada to the Mississippi. With continuing war between England and France in Europe, conflict in North America was inevitable. The Atlantic was key to both British and French aims through blockade and landing investing armies. Charting the coastline and harbours was essential.

In 1758 James Cook was appointed to the highly respected position of Sailing Master to HMS *Pembroke*, a 60-gun ship of the line. Many masters during the eighteenth and nineteenth centuries preferred to remain as such, since naval officers during times of peace would be placed on half-pay, but masters remained on full pay.

Cook met J F W des Barres and Samuel Holland during the St Lawrence campaign of the Seven Years War, and after the surrender of Louisbourg in 1758 Cook's invaluable help to Holland on the plan of the city and its fortification impressed Captain Simcoe of the *Pembroke* who got them both to prepare charts of the Gulf of St Lawrence and, with Cook now sailing master of HMS *Mercury*, the dangerous job of sounding the St Lawrence River for use during General Wolfe's intended attack on Quebec. During the winter of 1758–59 in Halifax, Cook learned more of mathematics and draughtsmanship from Holland and Simcoe, and probably from des Barres, who was working on captured French charts – an important source of information. Then, in 1759 he took over as sailing master of HMS *Northumberland*, part of Admiral Lord Colville's fleet, and in 1762, as part of the preparations for the capture of Placentia Bay in Newfoundland, he surveyed the harbour. This brought him to the attention of Captain Graves, Governor of Newfoundland and Labrador, who engaged Cook to help in charting these coasts.

The war with France ended in 1763 and the British acquired the whole of Canada. Spain, who had belatedly sided with France, ceded Florida to the British, but gained Louisiana. As part of the peace plan, the islands of St Pierre and Miquelon were to be handed over to the French as their fishing base. However, William Pitt wanted them thoroughly surveyed first, with the proviso that the French built no forts there, then followed by a complete survey of Newfoundland: Cook was given the task.

At this point in the history of settlement in North America it seemed to the British that the colonies needed to be re-organized with a central, controlling London authority, and that they should pay for their successful defence against the French, and for future safety. The colonies, already largely autonomous, wanted more independence. Familiarity with the British army on the ground had bred a realization that the American fighting a more open form of war was actually a better soldier than the stiff British army pattern of set-piece battle. The British Parliament also declared the lands beyond the fledgling colonies to be Crown Property, trying to prevent the existing colonies spreading their manpower too thinly, and being unable to defend the land against the nascent

danger from the French in the Mississippi and the Spanish in New Spain. The colonists had, during their fighting, both grown up with the a sense of their own military self-confidence, and glimpsed the new lands to the west which they had fought for and now wanted to inhabit. A clash was inevitable. With the passing of a simple retail tax, the Stamp Act, the American colonies erupted in revolt.

In 1764 Cook's former captain, Hugh Palliser, was appointed Governor of Newfoundland and he gave Cook the use of his schooner *Greenville* for a four-year survey of the west and south coasts of the island. As many did, Cook was able to publish these charts privately for profit. His methodical chart-work came to the attention of the First Lord of the Admiralty, the Earl of Sandwich, who would appoint Cook to command the first voyage of exploration into the Pacific. Cook used a theodolite, trained in this by the Royal American Regiment Engineers at Quebec and the title of Cook's chart of the west coast of Labrador, '*An exact trigonometrical survey of the West Coast of the Island of Newfoundland taken by Order of Commodore Pallisser, Governor of Newfoundland, Labradore etc etc by James Cook 1766*', and signed *James Cook*, shows that the surveys were based on mainland triangulation, although it is puzzling that he didn't show the trigonometrical station positions, which we know, for example, in the case of Murdoch Mackenzie senior's earlier survey of the British Isles.

During this time Cook was ably helped by William Parker and Michael Lane and the resulting surveys were incorporated into Robert Sayers' 1775 *North American Pilot*. Such was their accuracy that they continued in use until Commander James Kerr's Newfoundand survey of 1864. Sayers' Fleet Street London business was ultimately absorbed into the private chart-sellers, Laurie and Whittle, who became one of the foremost suppliers of charts of the nineteenth and twentieth centuries to the Merchant Navy, the 'Bluebacks', so called because of their blue lining.

The eighteenth century produced many great marine surveyors. Cook must be the best known but there is another who is described in an Admiralty Hydrographic Department Professional Paper of 1950 as 'selfish, friendless and uncompromising,' yet 'for all his faults, stands pre-eminent'. Lieutenant Joseph-Frederick Wallet (or Walsh) des Barres (1721–1824) was not an explorer like Cook, nor had he the intellectual approach of Dalrymple, but his skill and adaptability as a surveyor and a draughtsman are outstanding. He campaigned with Wolfe on the St Lawrence, prepared charts of the river in the winter before the Quebec enterprise, and after the fall of the citadel, surveyed the town and environs, and sounded the harbour and basin.

After the Peace of Paris in 1763, Rear-Admiral Sir Richard Spry, Commander-in-Chief of all His Majesty's Ships and Vessels of War in North America wanted charts of the coasts of Nova Scotia and the American colonies, and des Barres spent the next 10 years surveying them. He returned to England in 1774 and was immediately engaged, at the insistence of Earl Howe, on the publication of his charts of the American coast. Howe was anxious to have the reliable government surveys published with urgency to replace the existing inaccurate, privately printed charts; the outbreak of the American War of Independence added weight to his arguments. The outcome was an unparalleled series of engravings of views and charts that appeared first in 1777 and then in several editions over a period of 10 years as the *Atlantic Neptune*.

Des Barres was appointed Governor-General of Cape Breton Island, at the

| SPANISH CHART OF
FLORIDA, *C.* 1769 | Taken
from a captured Spanish folio of
13 original manuscript charts
dating *c.*1769 held in the British
Admiralty Library, this chart of
Florida and part of Havana is a
sophisticated attempt to chart the
Florida keys, with shoals shaded
in yellow; reefs and keys, and
shallow water shaded light green.
The lines shown are in three sets:
the surveyors' diagonal graticule,
the rhumb lines for lines of
bearing and courses to steer, and
the squares of latitude and
longitude (again, as was the
Spanish custom at the time, with
the zero meridian of longitude
based on the Spanish island of
Tenerife, in the Canary Islands).
(Admiralty Library Manuscript
Collection MSS 351)

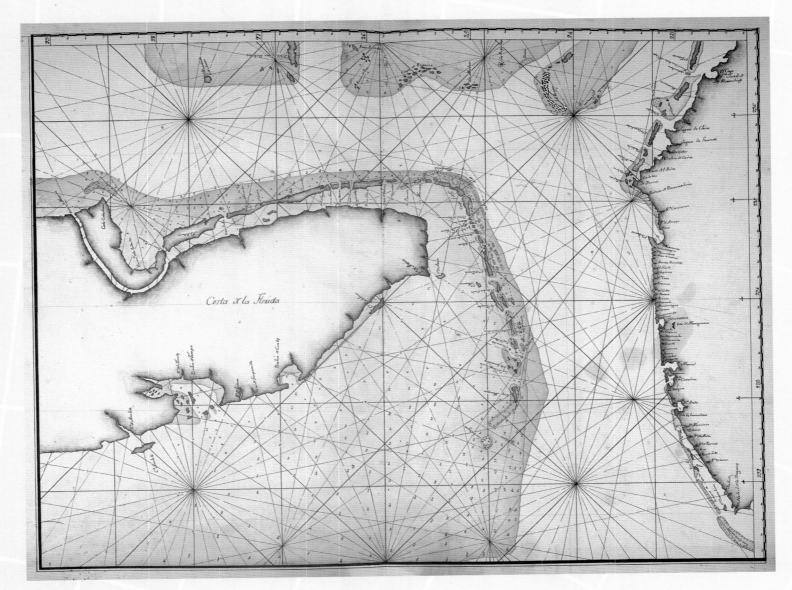

north of Nova Scotia in 1784, and the young Lieutenant Thomas Hurd worked under him as Surveyor General, until dismissed by des Barres who, in turn, was relieved by the British Government. Des Barres was then given the governorship of Prince Edward Island in 1892, which he successfully carried out for 10 years, by which time he was 90 and Captain Thomas Hurd was Hydrographer to the Navy. Hurd, understandably smarting from his dismissal 30 years earlier, had the satisfaction of buying the original 251 copper plates of the *Neptune*, which des Barres had tried to get the Admiralty to buy for £40,000, for 2 guineas each. When, in 1940, the UK was desperate for metal, 40 tons of engraved copper plates were handed over by the UK Hydrographic Office for melting down, but the 64 des Barres plates were retained, and in 1946 presented to the USA and Canada as appropriate. Des Barres died a month short of his 103rd birthday, seeing out those at the Admiralty who had disputed his chart payment.

The US merchant and military navy were reliant on the Admiralty charts for many decades after the War of Independence and the Depot of Charts and Instruments was set up within the Department of the Navy by order of the Secretary of the Navy in 1830. Initially, its job was to provide and maintain a stock of charts. It metamorphosed under many guises until 1866 when it became the Hydrographic Office. Matthew Maury was the driving force in US charting. Joining the US Navy in 1825 he devoted himself to the study of navigation and published a treatise on navigation after the circumnavigation of the USS *Vincennes* in 1838. By 1842 he was running the Depot of Charts and Instruments and took on the job of Superintendent of the US Naval Observatory, founded in 1833. He received regular reports of winds and currents from a wide range of sailing masters and his charts and sailing directions were respected world-wide. He was a prime mover in the first international conference on oceanography, held in Brussels in 1853, at which he represented the USA and his uniform system of reporting oceanographic data was adopted by all maritime nations. His chart representing the sea-bed profile of the Atlantic paved the way for the transatlantic cables, but he faced a dilemma with the start of the American Civil War. He resigned from the US Navy and took a commission as a Commander in the Confederate Navy. He was initially denied an amnesty when the Civil War was over, working in Mexico for a time, and then living in England. He returned to the USA in 1868 and passed the rest of his life in Virginia, a professor of the Virginia Military Institute, Lexington.

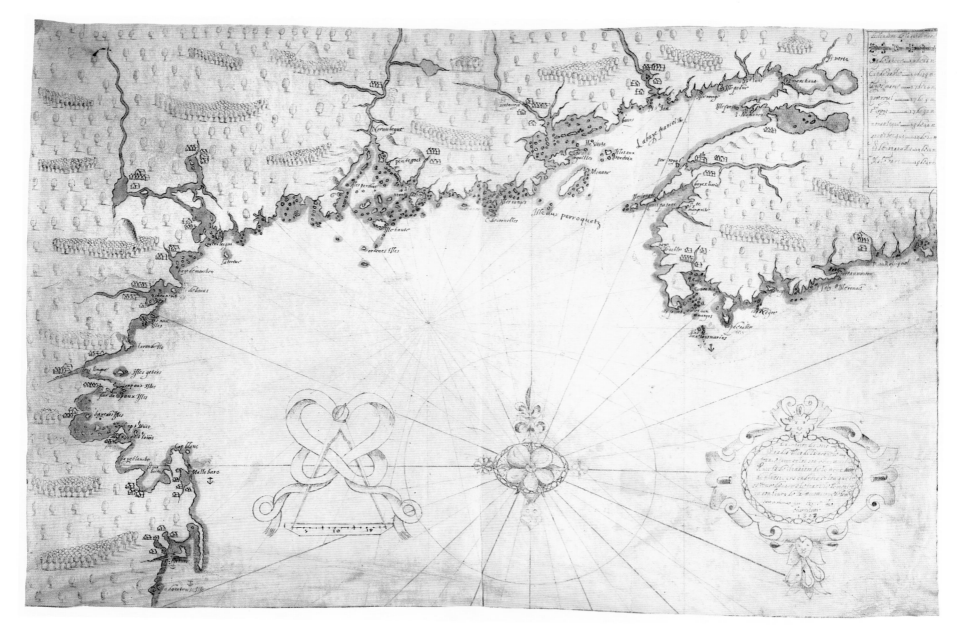

| **FRENCH CHART OF NOVA SCOTIA TO CAPE BLANC BY SAMUEL DE CHAMPLAIN, DATED 1607** | Samuel de Champlain's name is indissolubly linked with French Canada, founding both Arcadia and Quebec in 1608. In 1607 he surveyed and charted large parts of Canada as part of his expedition to find a settlement as agent under the French King, Henry IV, for the fur trade monopoly. This is a facsimile of the original vellum chart by him held in the Library of Congress, and covers the south-west part of Nova Scotia, the Bay of Fundy, called La Baye François by Champlain, to Cape Cod, named as Cape Blanc. The site of Boston is shown at Baye Longue, and in the middle of the coast is present-day Bangor and Penobscot Bay. To the top right of the chart is a table of Champlain's longitude calculations. (Library of Congress)

| MARITIME MAP OF ROANOKE, VIRGINIA, 1585 | John White was both governor and the recording artist who sailed with the settlers to Sir Walter Raleigh's ill-fated settlement of Roanoke. His very fine map of 1585 showing the settlement of Virginia was later published by Theodore de Bry, in Thomas Hariot's account of the abortive attempt to found a colony in Virginia, which gives us some understanding of the extreme difficulties all the early settlers faced.

Latin was the *lingua franca* of charts then and the points of the compass, giving North (*Septentrio*) to the right, are in that language. (Library of Congress)

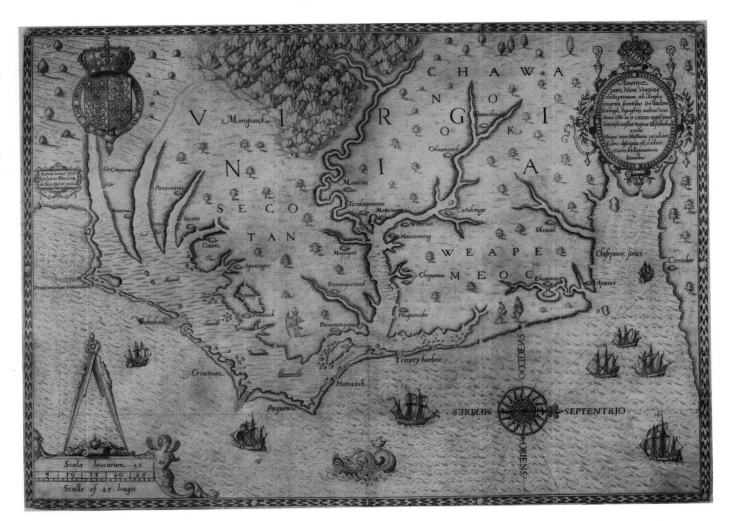

| A PLAN OF PORT ROYAL IN CAROLINA, *C*.1740 | An example of sea-borne talent, the chart of Francis Swaine, probably a ship's master, provides a guide to the approaches to the harbour of Port Royal, about 30 miles north of Savannah and 30 miles south of Charleston, through the channel with '19 and 20 feet at low water'. Most important is the reference to good drinking water and the two proposed sites for forts. Dated *c.* 1740, the attractively painted sailing ships show an armed navy cutter towing a dismasted French prize with jury-rigged sails. In the harbour mouth lies a 24-gun Royal Navy frigate, probably Swaine's own ship, at the marked anchorage. (Admiralty Library Manuscript Collection MSS 369/34)

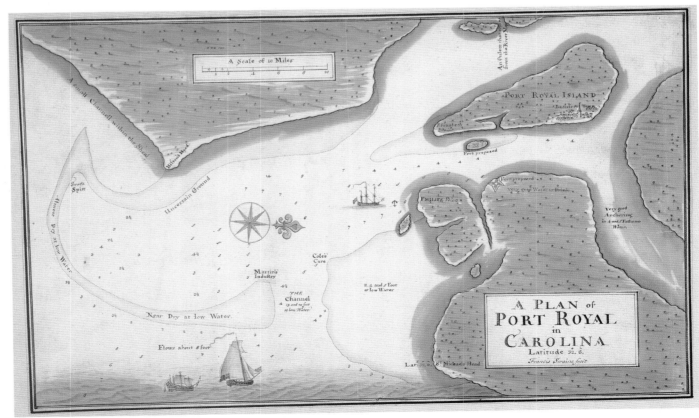

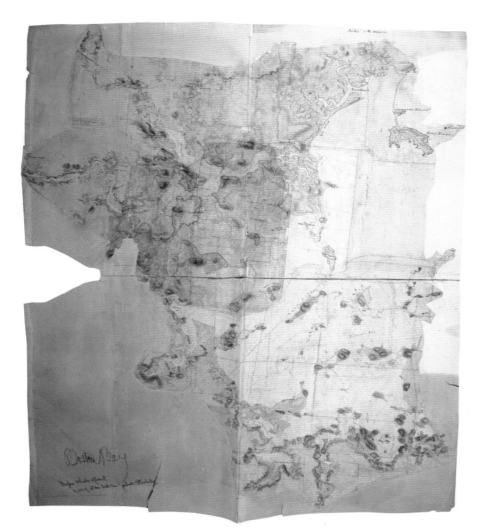

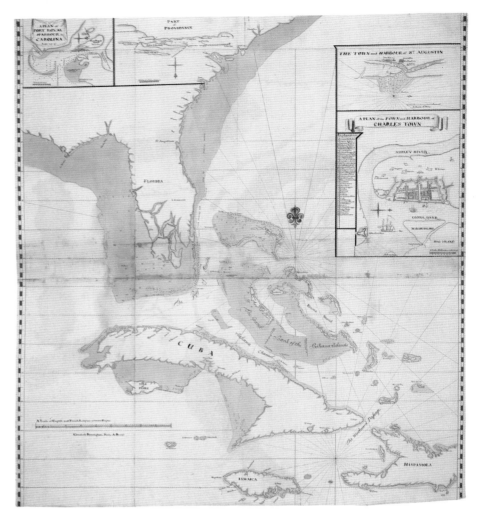

| BOSTON BAY BY MESSRS WHEELER & GRANT BY ORDER OF THE LORDS COMMISSIONERS FOR TRADE AND PLANTATIONS, *C.*1750 | Boston in the eighteenth century was the most important sea-port in North America and good charts were essential. This manuscript chart shows a careful and complex survey of the approaches to Boston harbour and the topography around, by J Grant and T Wheeler, both deputies of des Barres and Samuel Holland, and contributed to the surveys over the 10 years it took to complete the *Atlantic Neptune*. It includes information on shoals and depths, and a comparison between true (geographical) North and magnetic north, in this case of 6º 40' E (although this looks as though it has been added later). The lattice grid lines can be seen that were used to form a framework on which to draw the coastal features. This chart would have provided the basis of the printed charts the Royal Navy needed to safely navigate to port during the War of Independence of 1776 to 1783. It is also of interest today, with Cambridge College marking Harvard University founded in 1636, as it shows the tidal areas to the west of Beacon Hill and around Charles Bay, and the shoals to the east of Beacon Hill, prior to being filled in for building. Governor's Island, Bird Island and Apple Island are all now part of Logan Airport, Noddles Island is east Boston and Dorchester Head is south Boston. (Admiralty Library Manuscript Collection MSS 369/28)

| THE ATLANTIC COAST OF NORTH AMERICA FROM SOUTH CAROLINA TO FLORIDA, INCLUDING THE EASTERN CARIBBEAN, BY ELIZABETH BERMINGHAM, 1727 | This is the earliest known chart of North America by a woman that the author has come across and, intriguingly, nothing can be found about her. Hopefully, showing the narrow Bahama Channel and the Bahama Bank, it was used for the more innocent transatlantic trade, carrying sugar or rum up to Charleston from the Caribbean island producers. This is an elegant, well executed chart, albeit she seems to have copied the four inset harbour plans of Port Royal and Charleston in South Carolina, New Providence in the Bahamas (with a scale in the old English measure of chains{1 chain = 22 yards}) and St Augustine in Florida, from Hermann Moll's famous 'Beaver' Map of North America of 1715, although the Charleston plan (with a scale of 80 perches = 2 furlongs {400 yards}) has nearly twice as many names, indicating Bermingham's familiarity with the town. (Courtesy of The Hispanic Society of America, New York)

| CHART OF THE 'GOLF' OF HONDURAS, 1769 |

The pilot of the Spanish frigate *Venus* drew this chart of the 'Golf' of Honduras in 1769, with the ship's track shown close to the coast. Honduras had been claimed by Hernando Cortes on behalf of Spain in 1525, and gold was believed to be abundant there. This chart is part of a collection of captured Spanish charts of the Americas bound at the British Admiralty into one volume. It is based on a zero meridian of longitude at Tenerife. With an attractive compass rose showing North, a vignette of the frigate herself and reefs and rocks shown with a + (an early example of this symbol that has endured since), rhumb lines have still been used to help in the construction of the chart, in addition to latitude and longitude. (Admiralty Library Manuscript Collection MSS 351

| MARITIME MAP OF JAMAICA BY JOHN SELLERS, 1672 |

Jamaica comes from the name given by the original indigenous peoples, the Arawaks, *Xaymaca* meaning 'Island of Springs'. Columbus sighted it on his second voyage and it became a Spanish colony in 1509. African slaves were imported to replace the indigenous population who had quickly died out. An English naval force under Sir William Penn (the admiral father of colonist William Penn) captured it in 1655 and, unlike many of the other Caribbean islands, which were fought over and changed hands between the various European colonial contestants, remained under British rule until 1962. By the early seventeenth century the island became the base for buccaneering principally against the Spanish, and became so normalized that a code of laws, the Jamaica Discipline, had been adopted to decide the division of the prize ships captured, drinking hours and the treatment of women.

John Seller's maritime map is dedicated to Sir Joseph Williamson. It combines navigational information, including shoals, rocks and soundings along the south, with geographical information such as the division of the island by English settlers and is part of Samuel Pepys' copy of Seller's *Atlas Maritimus* of 1675. (Pepys Library, Magdalene College, Cambridge)

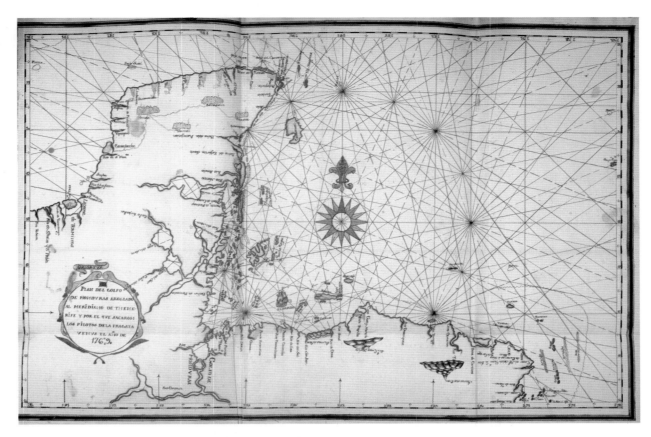

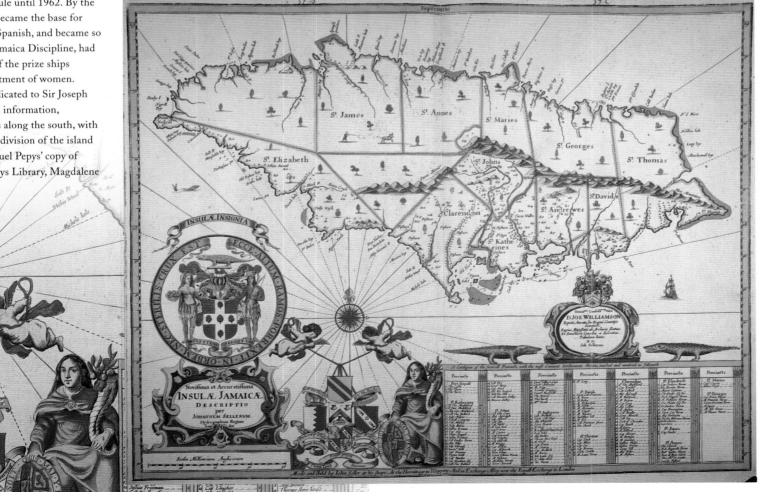

| CHART OF PLYMOUTH BAY BY DES BARRES IN THE *ATLANTIC NEPTUNE, C. 1770* | The town of Plymouth, shown snugly protected by the 'Long Beach' bar of land, is where the settlers from their English namesake town had landed in the famous little ship, *Mayflower*, in error some 200 miles from their intended landfall in Virginia. It is shown to have developed somewhat in the intervening 150 years on this exquisite chart, part of des Barres' *Atlantic Neptune*, which adopts a zero meridian of longitude based on Greenwich. Des Barres also gives more sophisticated tidal information (e.g. spring tides 14 feet; common tides 10 feet), using tidal stream arrows to indicate strength and direction of flood and ebb tides. This is one of the earliest charts to show both magnetic and true North – an important difference to adjust for in the ship's heading. A difference of a not unusual magnetic variation of 5° east or west would put a ship over 6 miles to port or starboard of her intended destination after she had sailed a hundred miles. (Library of Congress)

| MARITIME MAP OF NEW JERSEY BY JOHN SELLER | Detail from John Seller's maritime map of New Jersey, one of the British Secretary to the Navy, Samuel Pepys', working portfolio of charts, showing New York in 1677. It is interesting to compare the skyline with that of Bernard Ratzer's (opposite page) nearly 100 years later. (Pepys Library, Magdalene College, Cambridge)

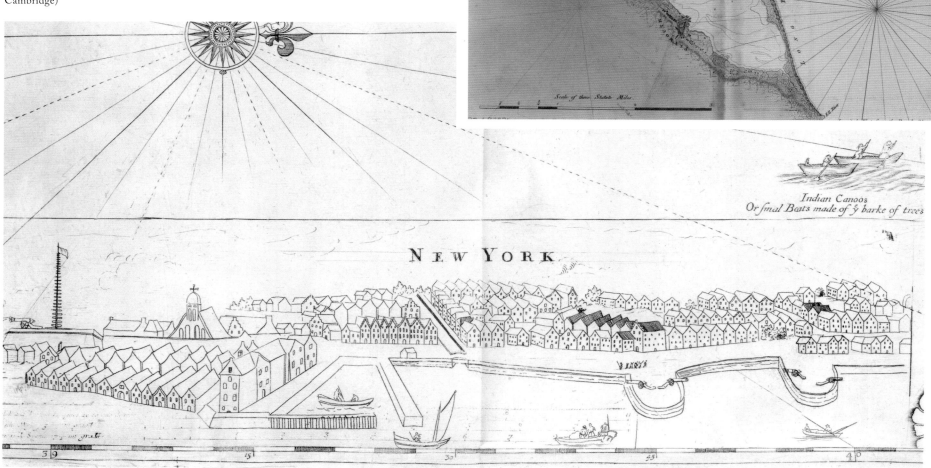

| **LIEUTENANT RATZER'S 1776 SURVEY OF NEW YORK** | Like George Washington, Lieutenant Bernard Ratzer (*fl.* 1756–1777) of the Royal American Regiment trained as a surveyor and was one of a number of the British Corps of Engineers of mixed European origin, such as des Barres and Holland, who surveyed the American Atlantic colonies. He defined the borders between New York and New Jersey, although this didn't stop the continual bickering as with so many borders across the Americas. New York was held by the British until it was handed over after the Peace of Paris in 1783.

Published by the London chart-sellers Faden and Jefferys in 1776 it stands as one of the best examples of Ratzer's fine draughtsmanship and accuracy with detailed topography inland showing the streets, fields and farms and the first grid pattern of street blocks, now familiar world-wide as a marque of New York. With a graceful cartouche dedicating the chart to the Governor of New York at the top left, and an impressive view of New York below to be utilized as a navigational elevation, showing what were then the tallest buildings – the church spires – and smoke wafting unconcernedly from a careened sailing ship having her timbers re-pitched. (© The Admiralty Collection®)

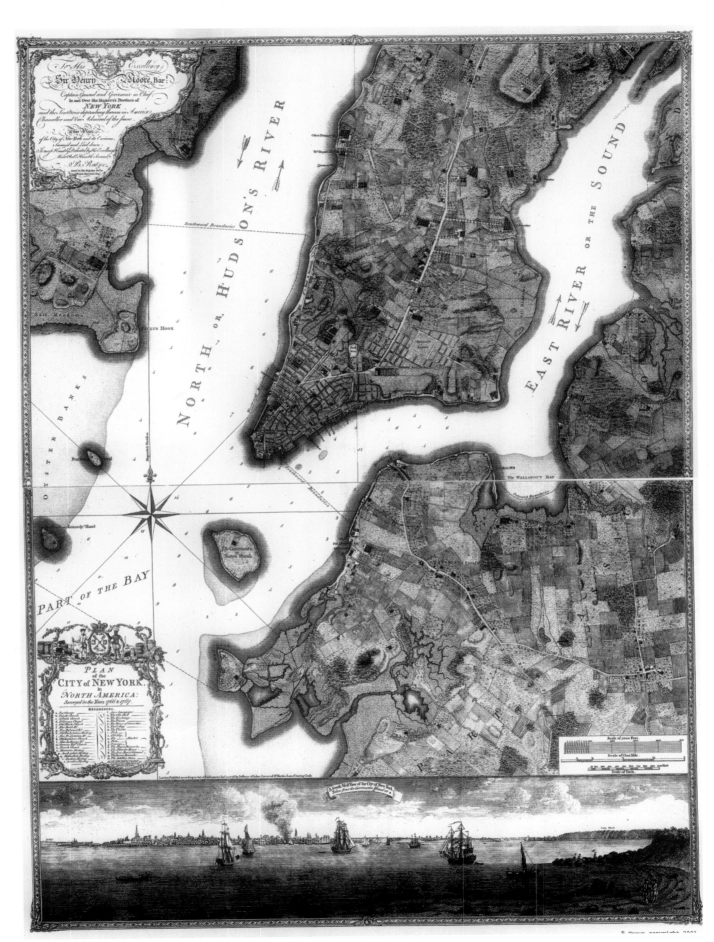

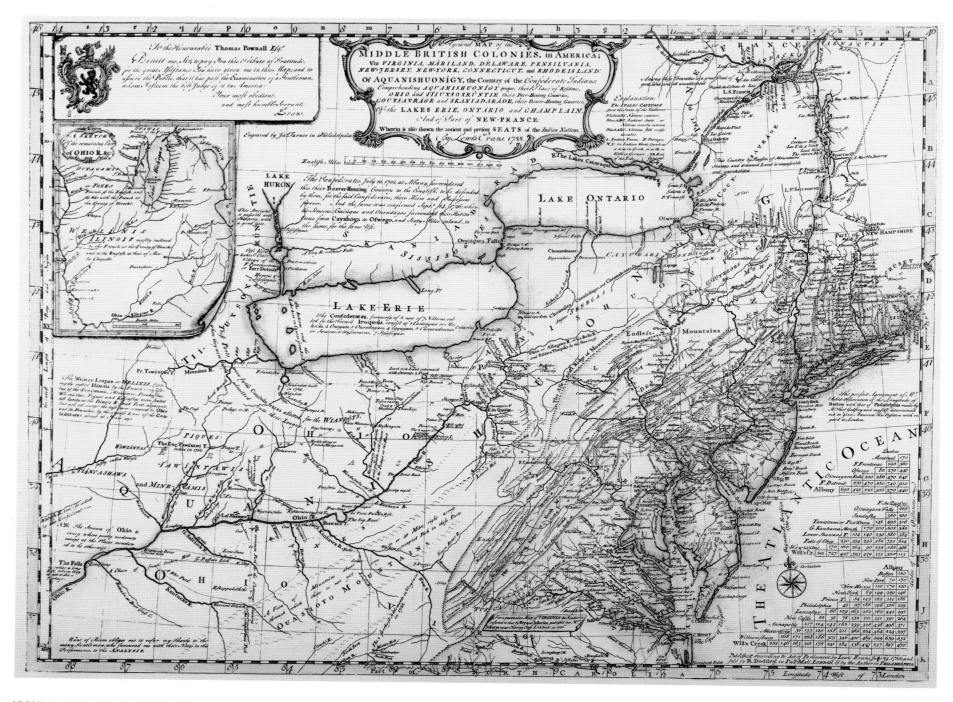

| MAP OF THE MIDDLE BRITISH COLONIES BY LEWIS EVANS, 1755 | The belief in a route across America, as a feasible alternative to the North-West passage, to the Pacific along the St Lawrence Seaway, and somehow across the Great Lakes is understandable from Lewis Evans's highly influential map of the 'Middle British Colonies' in North America completed in 1755 after four years of travelling and surveying (and hand coloured in the style of the time by the UKHO). The result has been described as the most ambitious and splendid map produced before Independence and, used for many years in boundary disputes, it was published by Benjamin Franklin, who ran a printing works for a time with his uncle, David Hall, in Philadelphia. The imperative of finding a way across was emphasized by presidential initiative when Meriwether Lewis and William Clark's expedition later found and mapped a river crossing of the continent after Independence.

Evans dedicated this map to Thomas Pownall, who, always known as Governor Pownall, was at various times Governor of Massachusetts, New Jersey and South Carolina. He tried hard to avert the War of Independence, arguing against the British Government's opposition towards the Colonists' contention of 'no taxation without representation'. He later published his own accounts of North America using Evans's maps. (© The Admiralty Collection®)

| RIGHT | **ENTRANCE TO THE ST LAWRENCE RIVER, *C*.1725** | The St Lawrence Seaway was the key to entering Canada, the Great Lakes and the interior of the American colonies. Whomsoever controlled it largely controlled North America. Early French charts of the approaches to Quebec were very useful in British hands, and this early eighteenth-century manuscript chart with a scale of '*soissante liege marinnes*' (60 marine leagues), though with significant inaccuracies, was helpful. The shape of Newfoundland to the right is refreshingly different but wrong. Although the Île d'Anticosty (Anticosti) and Île de Magdaleine and Prince Edward Island are reasonably placed and shaped, that of Nova Scotia is distorted and dangerous with little comparison to the actuality. Coste de la Cadie is presumably Acadia of today. The original orientation of this chart was with North pointing downwards, hence the upside down scale. Compare it with Cook's Newfoundland sketch on page 119. (Admiralty Library Manuscript Collection MSS 368/7)

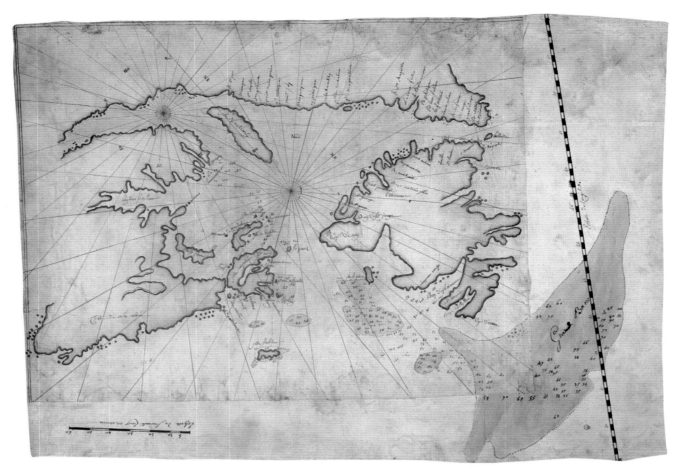

| BELOW | **FRENCH CHART OF THE APPROACH TO QUEBEC, 1758** | This French '*plan de la Grande Riviere*' by Germain Goynard in 1758 is one that Captain Cook was able to improve on for the capture of Quebec in 1759, strategically positioned in the interior of Canada some 300 miles from the sea. (Admiralty Library Manuscript Collection MSS 368/13)

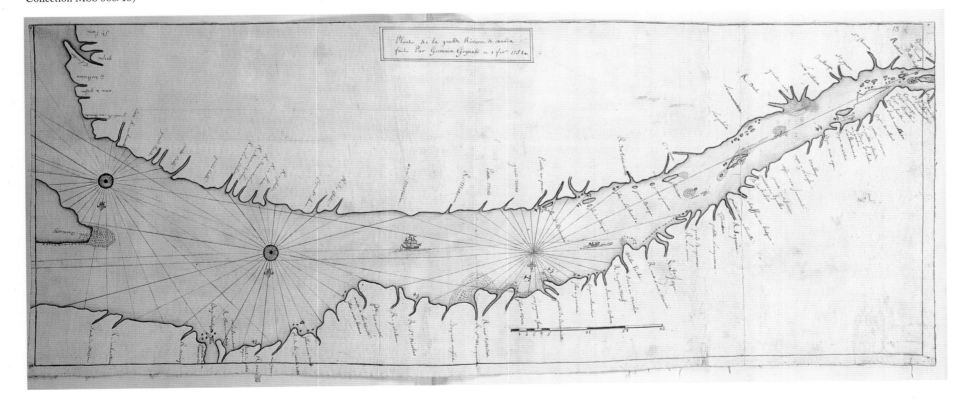

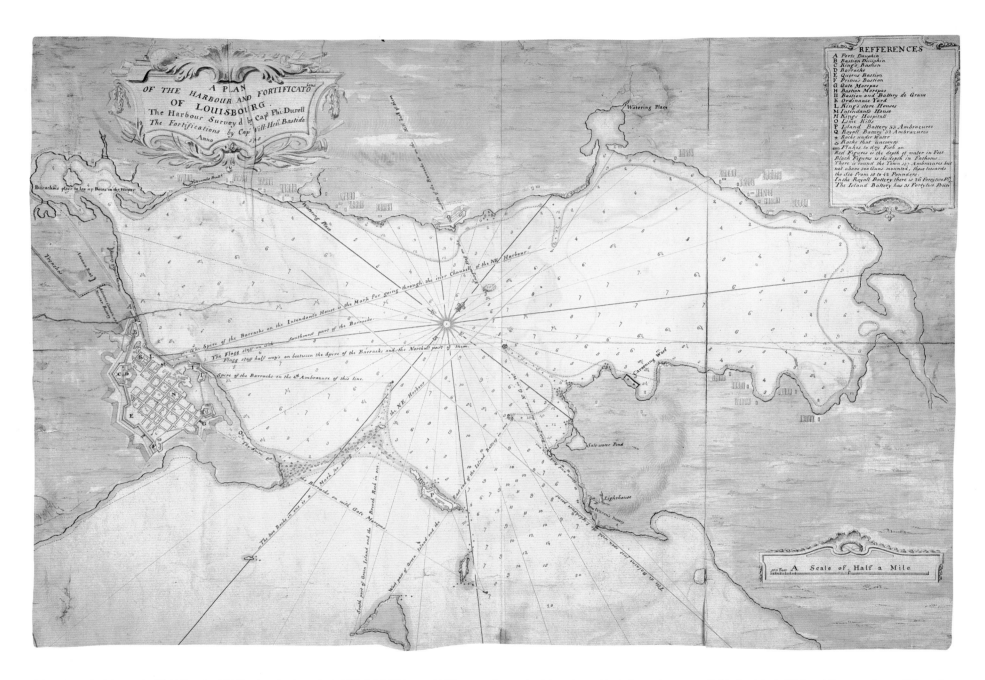

| **SURVEY OF THE FORT AND PORT AT LOUISBOURG, NOVA SCOTIA, 1745** | The French built a huge fort at Louisbourg on Cape Breton Island, strategically placed to control the approaches to the St Lawrence Seaway, to Quebec, and hence was the key to the defence of the whole of French Canada. In 1745 the Governor of Massachusetts, William Shirley, got together a band of settlers and with the aid of five British warships laid siege to Louisbourg. The French capitulated within five weeks. Captain Phillip Durell carried out this survey of the harbour in 1745, assisted by Captain William Henry Bastide on the fort. Three years later at the treaty of Aix-la-Chapelle, Louisbourg was handed back to the French. But the chart was by this time at the Admiralty and its information was available for Admiral Edward Boscawen's expedition of 157 warships and transports, which re-took Louisbourg in 1758 during the Seven Years War. It was now really only a matter of time before Quebec fell.

The chart itself was carefully prepared and has detailed clearing bearings to enable a safe approach into the harbour, and depths in feet in red, and in fathoms in black. Rocks and watering places are marked, even where to dry fish, with details of gun emplacements and the fort itself. In short, the information was there to assist the landing of marines and guns. (Admiralty Library Manuscript Collection MSS 368/42)

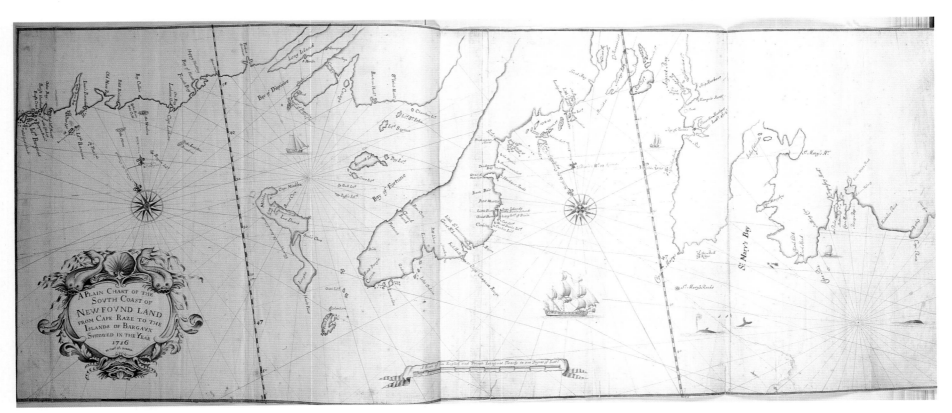

| ABOVE | **CHART OF PLACENTIA, NEWFOUNDLAND BY CAPTAIN DURELL, 1716** | Captain Thomas Durell's chart is a work of great patience and determination and would have been used in London to engrave a chart of the area used for fishing and whaling. The names of the bays often add a poignant touch to the scene, named after emotional events – Bay of Despair, Mistaken Point, Happy Meeting and Bay of Fortune are some – and the scattering of French names along the coastline is evidence of French fishing interest there, too. Placentia Road and harbour would make up one of Captain Cook's earlier surveys made in 1762. Durell was unable to determine longitude accurately to make a Mercator projection and he had to cope with a plane chart projection, using a 'portolan' approach to the construction of his chart with three sets of rhumb lines. In consequence, the two latitude scales differ slightly as he tried to draw a coastline that compensated for the Earth's curvature drawn on to a flat, plane surface. Indeed, careful comparison shows a difference of 1½ miles between the two vertical scales, although the left-hand one agrees with the scale Durell drew in English leagues, with 3 miles to a league. The detail is pleasing and artistic, showing an attractive cartouche, spouting and swimming whales (which were hunted in the area) and different types of ship (including probably his own frigate). (Admiralty Library Manuscript Collection MSS 368/23)

| RIGHT | **'SKETCH OF THE ISLAND OF NEWFOUNDLAND DONE FROM THE LATEST OBSERVATIONS BY JAMES COOK 1763'** | With the ending of the Seven Years War, formalized by the Peace of Paris in 1763, England gained Canada, Nova Scotia, Cape Breton, Florida, Senegal, St Vincent, Tobago, Dominica, Grenada and the huge triangular slab of land that is Newfoundland with ports and access to the cod-rich fishing grounds adjacent. Cook had already contributed hugely to the charting of the highway into the centre of Canada and the Great Lakes, the St Lawrence Seaway. Admiral Lord Colville's report to the Secretary of the Admiralty writing of 'Mr Cook's Genius and Capacity' in carrying out this survey was recommendation enough for his appointment to survey Newfoundland. This was an enormous undertaking, surveying an island bigger than Ireland with 6000 miles of coastline, and this 'sketch' by Cook shows the British claim to the fishing rights along the coast. He completed the whole survey at the end of the summer of 1767.

Rear-Admiral Sir William Wharton, Hydrographer to the Navy 1884–1904, and who had surveyed in the same areas as Cook wrote of his surveys, 'the best proof of their excellence is that they are not yet fully superseded by the more detailed surveys of modern times. …Their accuracy is truly astonishing.' (Admiralty Library Manuscript Collection MSS 368/21)

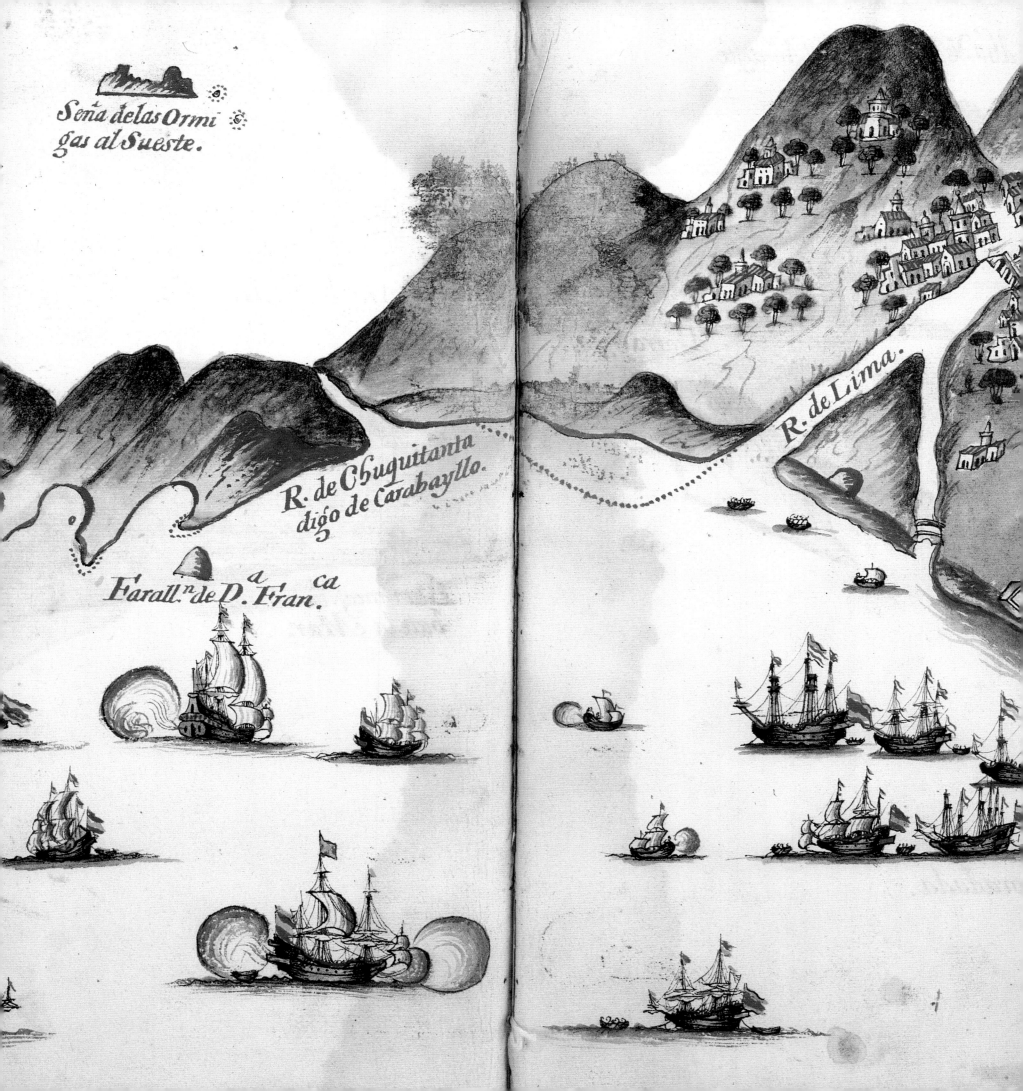

Seña de las Ormi
gas al Sueste.

R. de Chuquitanta
digo de Carabayllo.

R. de Lima.

Farall.n de D.ª Fran.ca

CHAPTER IX

The West Coast of America

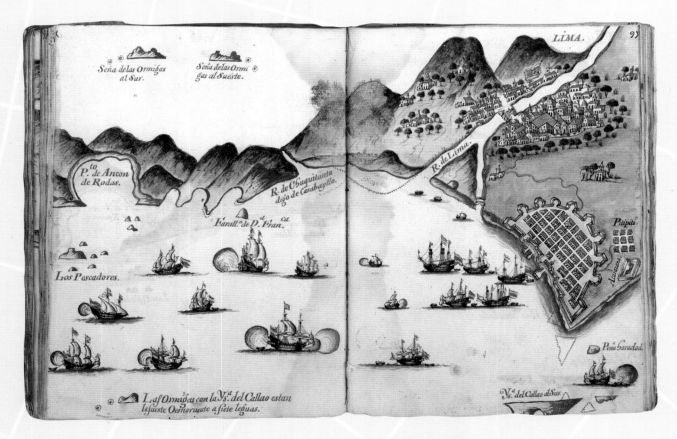

| LEFT DETAIL & ABOVE | **COASTAL CHART OF CALLAO, LIMA IN PERU, 1684** | By 1535 Pizarro and his conquistadors had founded Lima, now the capital of Peru, and Callao, its port about 8 miles to the west, became one of the key ports on the long stretch of coast at the foot of the Andes mountains. This is one of the attractive coastal charts from the *Derroterro* held by the Hispanic Society of America, showing the fortified port of Callao in 1684. The red dotted lines mark shoals and rocks, while the Spanish Pacific Fleet, if not at anchor off Callao, seem to be engaged in gunnery practice. (Courtesy of The Hispanic Society of America, New York)

SOUTH AMERICA

THE charting of South America followed a different sequence to that of North America. South America was dominated by the Spanish and Portuguese and the coastal outline was set down long before the shape of the west and north coasts of North America were known. Extending 4600 miles (7400 kilometres) from the Isthmus of Panama to Tierra del Fuego, and 3000 miles (4830 kilometres) at its widest part, the natural topography of the Andes range of mountains, the second highest in the world and reaching to heights of nearly 23,000 feet (7000 metres), was a forbidding barrier to expansion overland, and the route around Cape Horn with its intricate passage through the maze of islands at the tip of Patagonia became crucial. These islands needed to be charted accurately so that the best route through could be ascertained. With a never ceasing prevailing, but contrary, westerly wind, it could take weeks to weather the Horn; some never did, as sails were rent and freezing crews became worn out.

Probably the earliest chart that gives any real appreciation of the west coast of the Americas and an indication of the enormous distance across the Pacific to Asia is the chart by the Genoese Battista Agnese. He produced over a hundred manuscript atlases, usually with 8 to 10 charts in each. Recognized for their beautiful artistic execution, they reflected the world as was understood around the 1550s.

Spanish domination of South America was quick, ruthless and total and Battista Agnese's chart (below right) of the Pacific Ocean shows much of what they later took: the Strait of Magellan, the coast of Peru, so brutally explored by Francisco Pizarro's conquistadors and conquered from 1531 in three short years, the Pacific coast of Central America and Mexico explored by the Spanish after 1520, on up to California, explored by Francisco de Ulloa in 1539–40, and by Juan Rodriguez Cabrillo in 1542–43, correctly shown as a peninsula and with important seaport names along the coasts. Interestingly, near the head of the Gulf of California shown in red, assumed to be because Ulloa, who discovered the Colorado River with its reddish tinge had named it the Vermilion Sea, is a Spanish narrative which annotates one of the earliest suggestions of depth 'Vermilion Sea' where the channel at high water is marked with a depth of 11 *brazas*; at low water 8. A *braza* was a Spanish fathom.

A sense of how the Spanish opened up the sea routes to the west, on the Asiatic side of the Pacific, following the route of the treasure ships laden with plundered gold and silver to the Philippines to pay for the spices and silks is revealed. The coast is shown up to Canton and beyond, along with Java, Timor and some of Borneo, Palawan, and the Moluccas – the Spice Islands that brought such wealth to the Portuguese and then the Dutch – and the Philippines. Ceylon is known by its earlier name of Taprobana, but shown by Sumatra. Singularly absent is any sign of Japan, Korea and China to the north, and New Guinea, Australia and New Zealand to the south.

The Spanish takeover of South America was relentless. By 1533 Ecuador was taken, colonies were soon established along the northern coast of Colombia at Santa Maria in 1525 and Cartagena in 1532, which became one of the most important sea ports in South America.

South of Peru, from the Spanish perspective, Pedro de Valdivia successfully invaded Chile in 1545 and in the same year the infamous silver mines at Potosoi in the Bolivian Andes were found, drawing the Spanish over in hordes,

and providing the largest source of income for the Spanish in South America. In a decade the Spanish had overcome jungle and mountain to take the entire western half of the continent, but at a terrible cost to indigenous culture. In 1541–42 Francisco de Orellana had, in a harrowing 2000-mile journey, sailed and identified the Amazon River. But the Spanish left Brazil, the largest part of the continent to the Portuguese; there was little mineral wealth and the colonies that developed there grew on agriculture and hardwoods.

The natural indentation to the south of Brazil at the Rio de la Plata (River Plate) gave an easy entry into the continent. Buenos Aires was founded in 1536 and in Paraguay the Jesuits had established themselves more strongly than other parts of the continent with a network of missions that traded and lived harmoniously with the Indians – to be cruelly put down with the expulsion of the Jesuits by the Spanish in 1767. The domination of South America by the Spanish meant that, maintaining secrecy to prevent foreign intrusion, very few charts were published. Those that came into the possession of another nation were highly prized.

On 29 July 1681 the British buccaneer, Bartholomew Sharp, took the Spanish ship *Rosario* off the coast of modern Ecuador. Amongst the haul was a *derroterro* or Spanish book of sea charts and sailing directions covering the coast from Acapulco to Cape Horn, put together in Panama in 1669, which was to blow open the secrets of the approach to the Spanish settlements. After a remarkable voyage to the West Indies, making him the first Englishman to round Cape Horn west to east, Sharp took his 'jewel' to London (his other 'jewel', as he describes in his account, was 'a young lady of about 18 years of age, a very comely creature'). The charts were copied and made available by William Hack, 'a platt-maker from Wapping' and known today as one of the Thames School of chartmakers. Translated from the Spanish by Philip Dassigny a copy of the *Wagoner of the Great South Sea* was presented in 1682 by

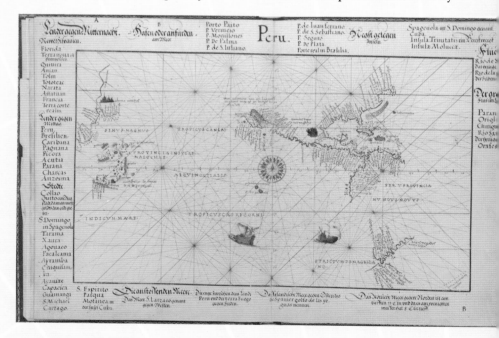

| **BATTISTA AGNESE'S PORTOLAN OF THE PACIFIC, *C.* 1550** | This plane projection portolan includes central and south America with the Strait of Magellan, and on the Asiatic side of the Pacific the coast from Taprobana (Ceylon) to Canton in China, along with Portugal's trading region: Java, Timor and a little of Borneo, Palawan, the Spice Islands and the Moluccas, and Spain's Philippines. (© The National Maritime Museum, London)

Sharp to Charles II in time to receive an acquittal for piracy. Charles made him a captain in the navy, but tiring of this Sharp went back to piracy in the West Indies. They were the first reasonably accurate charts of the Pacific to be seen in England, providing very useful 'intelligence' for British sea rovers from an expanding maritime nation and were partly instrumental in opening up this coast.

An excellent example of a *derroterro*, the *Derrotero general del Mar del Sur*, is held in the Hispanic Society of America archives. Compiled in 1684 in Panama it contains 146 coastal charts, mostly double paged, illustrating the prominent ports and geographical landmarks from the Ensenada de San Roque (today's Baja in California) to the Strait of Le Maire, which is Tierra del Fuego. Distance scales are not much shown, but the notes give the distances from one point to another with detailed directions to sail into port, such as Guayaquil in Ecuador.

Little more was done as the basic design of the continent was well enough understood, but the Spanish began to realize the need for a more uniform set of charts of the coasts. Alejandro Malaspina, who had commanded the *Descubierta* (Discovery) on a world voyage in 1790–91 and whose charts around Nootka in North America were generously shared with George Vancouver, took on the task, charting almost the entire South American coast in the 1790s. When Alexander von Humboldt embarked on his five-year exploration of the Orinoco region and then the Andes from northern Colombia to Peru, his scientific studies of the geology, climate, botany and zoology founded today's scientific geography, and the very least that could be done for him was to name the beneficial current that flows up the west coast of South America after him.

The discarding of the Spanish colonial yoke set the scene in the early part of the nineteenth century, achieved in major part by one of Britain's most skilful and proficient Admirals, Lord Thomas Cochrane, who in turn commanded the navies of Chile, Brazil and Peru and beat the Spanish navy.

In 1831 Lieutenant Robert Fitzroy was given command of HMS *Beagle* with instructions to complete the surveying and charting of South American waters that had been started in 1825. It was perceived by the Foreign Secretary, George Canning, that South America would provide excellent investment opportunities for Britain. Trade needed ships and ships needed charts. Fitzroy had proved his abilities surveying for two years in South American waters when he took over command of the *Beagle*, aged 23, after Captain Pringle Stokes shot himself. A dedicated if literal Christian, believing every word in the Bible as written, Fitzroy had passed out top of the Royal Naval College at Portsmouth, and was already showing exceptional ability. As the son of Lord Charles Fitzroy and grandson of the Duke of Grafton, and with Lord Castlereagh as an uncle, he had aristocratic clout and influence which he wielded with effect for himself and the Service. He could afford to have the *Beagle* fitted out in large measure in mahogany, and he could purchase the odd ship or two to complete the task in hand.

Arguably the more famous figure in this unique voyage that was to have such epoch-making repercussions for man's understanding of his origins, although only victualled on board and unpaid, was Charles Darwin. He was very unlike Fitzroy. Perhaps the attraction of opposites made their enforced but successful companionship, sharing the Captain's Cabin for a five-year voyage, possible for Fitzroy. The Captain, as had become customary since James Cook's first voyage with Sir Joseph Banks, realized how useful it would be to have a competent naturalist for the voyage.

The second purpose of the *Beagle*'s voyage was to establish accurate meridian traverse points by time with the chronometer, stopping on a four-year voyage at selected land sites that would be as equidistant as possible and to see how much time variation there was at the end. In the event, they exceeded a world traverse of 24 hours by 33 seconds.

HMS *Beagle* was a 10-gun brig (technically a brig-sloop) of 242 tons and 90 feet in length. They were known disparagingly by the 'orthodox' navy as 'coffins', yet were regarded with great affection by those who served in them. With a beam of 25 feet she accommodated a ship's company of 74 – just. Darwin later wrote to Professor Henslow, who had so encouraged Darwin in his natural interest in Botany, 'The absolute want of room is an evil that nothing can surmount'.

Many of Fitzroy's crew were to become well known later in their field. His first lieutenant was John Wickham, who took command for a further voyage in the *Beagle* to carry out the detailed surveys of the northern and western coasts of Australia until illness forced him home. John Lort Stokes made an invaluable contribution to the surveys, living on board the *Beagle* from Midshipman to Commander for some 18 years. Finally making full admiral, he also made invaluable surveys of New Zealand and the English Channel and was shortlisted for the job of Hydrographer of the Navy. James Sulivan, the second lieutenant, went on to admiral and famously led the naval squadron in 1854 to attack Bomarsund during the Crimean War. Robert McCormick was the hot-headed surgeon who also sailed as geologist under Captain Sir James Clark Ross in HMS *Erebus* in the 1839–43 exploration of Antarctica. He was generally disliked and Dr Benjamin Bynoe, who became a close friend of Darwin's, took over in Rio de Janeiro.

Such voyages, following the precedent set during Cook's Pacific explorations, took an artist, and Augustus Earle, who had already spent 20 years recording remote scenery around South America, Australia and New Zealand was chosen. He was 38 years old but his health deteriorated, and he left the ship in Montevideo in December 1832. Luckily for posterity, Fitzroy was able to engage Conrad Martens in Rio de Janeiro whose attractive colour washes provided the visual record of the voyage. Apart from the crew needed to work the ship – the master and two mates, the boatswain, carpenter, 34 seamen and six boys – there was a complement of eight marines to help enforce discipline. For scurvy prevention Fitzroy took pickles, dried apples, lemon juice, Kilner and Moorsums preserved meats, vegetables and soup. In addition there were three natives from Tierra del Fuego whom Fitzroy had picked up on his previous two-year voyage around South America, brought back to England to 'educate' and planned to return them to their land to spread Christianity.

The *Beagle* sailed from London to Plymouth in 1831 where she was to finish refitting. The delays were frustrating for all but finally she sailed on 27 December after two attempts to clear Plymouth Sound against contrary winds had forced her back. Darwin was chronically seasick. The other difficulty was Fitzroy's exacting standards. He drove himself hard, and expected all others to do likewise. The wardroom code to find out Fitzroy's mood was to ask on taking over the watch, 'Has much hot coffee has been spilled this morning?' Darwin wrote home, 'if he does not kill himself, he will do a wonderful quality of work …' – prophetic words indeed. But no one questioned Fitzroy's superb seamanship, so necessary at Cape Horn where the winds never die and get funnelled on their circular quest around the roaring forties of the Southern Ocean. When he was feeling happy Fitzroy 'was all charm and consideration'.

Darwin was very popular and Sulivan later affectionately wrote of him,

I can confidently express my belief that during the five years in the Beagle he was never known to be out of temper, or to say an unkind or hasty word to anyone … this combined with the admiration of his energy and ability, led to our giving him the name of 'the dear old Philosopher'.

In July 1832 the *Beagle* anchored off Montevideo ('I see a mountain'; so-named in 1520 by Magellan) and for the next two years Fitzroy carried out detailed surveys of South America from the south bank of the Rio de la Plata (River Plate) down the coast to Cape Horn. Wickham, Lort Stokes, and the master, Mr Osborne, worked day and night under Fitzroy's supervision in two, small-decked boats and later a tender paid for personally by their Captain. Fitzroy had realised he couldn't finish such an ambitious survey with just one ship and he used his own funds to buy or charter local ships and boats to do the work. In addition he got Wickham to take one of the ships he bought, a whaling schooner named *Unicorn* and renamed the *Adventure*, to survey and chart the Falkland Islands.

By 1834 both the *Beagle* and *Adventure* were in Valparaiso, Chile. Fitzroy, by now desperately worn down by the constant need to keep ahead of the job, contending with the terrible weather and worrying about the ship's safety, took to the shore to organize the drawing up of the charts. When the mail brought him news that the Admiralty would not reimburse him the £3000 he had spent on extra ships, he became very depressed and, placing Wickham in command, resigned. Dr Bynoe managed to get Fitzroy back to himself; the *Adventure* was sold and the charts were sent to Sir Francis Beaufort, Hydrographer of the Navy. There is a constant correspondence between Fitzroy and Beaufort, which reflects his despair of that time. The official correspondence reads as from one competently in charge of the situation, but the unofficial correspondence relates Fitzroy's worries and self-doubt to Beaufort, who acted as a father-figure sending advice and encouragement.

Fitzroy now needed to survey northwards up the coast of Chile, and he purchased another boat, a 35-ton vessel called *Constitucion*, sending Sulivan in her. By September 1835 the South American survey from 47° S, including the Gulf of Guayaquil in Ecuador, the whole of the coast of Chile and Peru was complete with 'no port or roadstead omitted'. The old Spanish charts, unsurprisingly since they were made without the benefit of Harrison's chronometer, were as much as 25 miles in error. Sulivan had surveyed half the coast of Chile, and the coast of Peru was undertaken by Mr Osborne.

The long voyage home took them around the world stopping for about seven days at each selected land-site to check the meridians with the 22 chronometers held on board for that purpose. The significance of the Galapagos Islands visit, which was the first land stop to check the longitude position was profound and lead to the eventual publication of Darwin's *The Origin of the Species* in 1859. The *Beagle* finally arrived at Greenwich in November 1836.

NORTH-WEST COAST OF AMERICA

While the early exploration of the West Coast of North America was considered by the Spanish to be very much their preserve, they were slow to follow up their territorial domination of South America and the Gulf of Mexico. Pushing across the enormous distances from communities in Florida and the nearest settlement to California at Acapulco in Mexico was not easy.

By the middle of the eighteenth century the coastline from Acapulco north-eastwards was still sketchy and from Cape Mendocino almost unknown. The British Admiralty took the matter in hand, if only to define British territorial ambitions in North America, and the man who would help them achieve this was George Vancouver.

Born in June 1757 in the ancient East Anglian port of Kings Lynn in Norfolk, Vancouver was the youngest son of a monied Anglo-Dutch family. He joined the navy at the age of 13 as an able seaman; and was fortunate to serve under Captain Cook on his second voyage of discovery (1772–75). Vancouver impressed Cook and he sailed again under him, aboard HMS *Discovery*, for his third voyage, the aim of which was to find the fabled North-West passage from the Pacific Ocean across or through North America to the Atlantic.

Although Cook's exploratory surveys were necessarily less meticulous than his earlier work around Newfoundland, which had used triangulation as the basis, Vancouver would have learned much from Cook's methods. Typically Cook would carry out coastal surveys built up from running fixes, founded largely on dead reckoning from astronomical fixes. Horizontal fixes were used from intersecting points on the coast and distances were measured by pendulum

California Island

It was inevitable in the centuries after the discovery of America and the route around Cape Horn into the Pacific, that, given the enormous size and inaccessibility of the Pacific, there should be considerable misinformation and muddle as to what was actually there. In particular the distances involved in crossing were greatly underestimated and the number and position of the many Pacific islands was inaccurate. One of the larger conjectured islands was that of California, in the distant past thought to be part of the Garden of Eden. But early Spanish charts, and the maps of Mercator, Ortelius, De Wit and others of the Dutch cartographic 'school' showed it correctly as a peninsula. However, in 1602 a Spanish Carmelite Friar made a chart showing California as an island, and this was taken by the Dutch. It was soon copied by others, for example John Speed included it in his Atlas, and was accepted as fact in chart and map reproductions. In the early seventeenth century a Spanish Jesuit, Father Kino, explored the coast and proved that California wasn't an island. Gradually the actuality was correctly shown, until the accurate and painstaking work of Captain George Vancouver revealed the coast in detail in 1793–95.

timed gunshot or by subtending masts. Latitude and coastal traces were made with remarkable accuracy, but longitudes relying on lunar tables, in common with most navigation before Harrison's chronometer (carried on Cook's second voyage) were as much as a degree in error. Cook organized careful records of tides and currents, either from discrepancies between dead reckoning and observed positions, or, in calm weather, noting drift with reference to an anchored boat. Vancouver would also have been taught Cook's methods of keeping his crews healthy on such long voyages – mainly through antiscorbutic measures, such as eating samphire (sea-grass), fruit and berries when available, the boiled bark of fir tree, scrupulous cleanliness between decks and the three-watch system of running the ship while underway.

Cook had reached the north-west coast of America in 1778, entering a deep fjord-like inlet. The locals were most friendly, and tried to imply with the word 'Nootka' a large island, in fact 286 miles long, around which they could sail. Cook took it to be the local name and called it Nootka Sound. There was a plentiful supply of fresh water, seafood and game and wood for repairs. The crew caught some of the numerous sea otters swimming there, and, after Cook's death in Hawaii, the ships homeward bound called into Macao for much needed supplies, a rest and refit. The crew were able to get huge prices for the sea otter pelts, and unwittingly opened up a new market for which many former naval officers set up trade. The most notorious was former Royal Navy Lieutenant, John Meares, who traded in his commercial vessel, the *Nootka*. The Spanish had been exploring northwards from Mexico since 1774, and took formal possession of Nootka in 1789. When Meares's two ships sailed into the Sound they were seized by the Spanish and sent to the Viceroy in Mexico. Meares returned to Britain in 1790 and presented a memorial to Parliament which described, and exaggerated, his treatment by the Spanish. Events escalated and naval mobilization was ordered in Britain. A major crisis built up between the two countries. Vancouver, by now established with a strong record for seamanship and navigation, had been appointed as first lieutenant of a new *Discovery* of 340 tons and was fitting her out in the Thames for a voyage to the Pacific. Overnight he was provided with a crew of pressed men, appointed in command and sent to join the Channel Fleet. Spain backed down and diplomatic channels produced the Nootka Convention, whereby buildings and land seized at Nootka were to be returned to Britain. Vancouver was ordered by the Admiralty to action the agreement, and to then carry out a detailed survey of the Pacific American coast and, continuing a long-held vision, to find the North-West passage, for which Parliament, recognizing the commercial importance of such a link, offered a prize of £20,000.

The Admiralty's instructions to Vancouver of 1790 were clear: 'The King having judged it expedient that an expedition should be immediately undertaken for acquiring a more complete knowledge than has yet been obtained; you are, in pursuance of his Majesty's pleasure … to repair to the north-west coast of America.'

Vancouver, in the introduction to his journal, phrased his purpose more romantically: 'For the glorious task of establishing the grand keystone to that expansive arch, over which the arts and the sciences should pass to the furthermost corners of the earth.'

HMS *Discovery* left Britain on 1 April 1791. Vancouver had with him a back-up ship, HMS *Chatham*, a small, armed, two-masted brig, commanded by Lieutenant William Broughton, to act as tender. HMS *Daedelus*, captained by

Lieutenant Richard Hergest, sailed later as a store ship to meet *Discovery* at Nootka Sound, and deliver the final territorial plan to be agreed by the diplomats. The ships followed the 'Cook's tour', by now established as a route via the Canary Islands, round the Cape of Good Hope across the Indian Ocean and on to Australia, then New Zealand, into the South Pacific then north to the coastline of North America, thus avoiding the difficulties of rounding Cape Horn. Vancouver had chosen his crew well. The first lieutenant was Zachary Mudge, who drew some beautiful sketches of the more remarkable sights they encountered. Broughton later captained the sloop *Providence*, with Mudge as his first lieutenant, the same 400-ton sloop of war that Captain William Bligh had in 1793 successfully brought the breadfruit from Tahiti to Jamaica. Lieutenant Peter Puget took over command of the *Chatham* when Broughton was sent home with important despatches relating to the Nootka Sound situation. Archibald Menzies, the surgeon, was also appointed as botanist at Sir Joseph Bank's behest. Lieutenant Joseph Baker was to draw the last chart of the expedition, appropriately naming the final feature Port Conclusion. All their names, with those of Royal, Admiralty and political personalities, were immortalized on the charts of Vancouver.

Siting the North American coast at last, by present day Mendocino on 18 April 1792 at 40° N as instructed, Vancouver commenced the laborious running survey northwards. The routine he used was based on Cook's, with his own refinements. With favourable visibility he would reach or run along the coast, or tack depending on the wind's direction, keeping in sight of the shore. Night they would spend in the offing, well clear of coastal dangers, but close enough to regain the land for the next day's work. Every course alteration was noted, every speed change logged; innumerable compass bearings and horizontal sextant angles of shoreline and inshore features were taken; the crew were always heaving the lead inshore to record the depth, and the nature of the sea bottom; all this was noted on a running plot so that nothing was missed.

After 19 weeks, and 1400 miles of coastline, they reached Cape Flattery, named by Cook and considered one of the four most vicious headlands in the world, to investigate the Strait of Juan de Fuca, situated between Vancouver Island and Washington State, named after a Greek pilot employed by the Spanish in 1592 to sail through this supposed strait into the Atlantic. Here Vancouver organized a different surveying technique. A shoreside observatory was set up to take sun sights, which would check the rates of the new chronometers. Accurately knowing the time enabled the longitude position of the coast to be determined. Local magnetic variation with regard to the true bearing of heavenly bodies was measured. From the anchored ships two or more boats, with one of the lieutenants in charge, provisioned for up to three weeks, would row the coastline, stopping from time to time so that the surveying officer could take various hand-held compass bearings to measure the intricate serpentines of the coast. The tangent angle of off-lying islands combined with the other angles gave position lines and thus the relative positions to the shore. At night they slept either in the boat or ashore, depending on the suitability of the land, and the potential danger of attack from hostile natives. Typically, in one 23-day survey, the boat crew rowed over 900 miles to achieve a surveying advance of 65 miles northwards on the chart.

It rained hard and it rained often. By the second surveying season, they had learned from experience and made awnings of painted canvas as tents, and bags for provisions to provide two hot meals a day of wheat flour and portable soup, and a discretionary issue of grog. This could be supplemented by hunting and fishing, and on the eve of the King's birthday one boat's crew were able to feast on 'Bear Steaks, stewd Eagle, and roasted Muscles, with as much glee as a City Alderman attacks his Venison'. Courses and speeds all had to be recorded; then upon return all this information would be transferred to the fair working sheet by Lieutenant Baker who worked steadily on board the mother ship. Admiralty Inlet and Puget Sound were charted in this fashion. At Burrard Inlet, Vancouver took charge of a boat, naming the inlet after a shipmate in HMS *Europa* out in the West Indies, Sir Harry Burrard, commended for bravery in rescuing five shipmates from a hurricane. Today the city of Vancouver lies along its shores, where Vancouver in June 1792 was surprised to meet two Spanish ships on survey. They offered to work with Vancouver, but seemed unable to take the pace, parting amicably after three weeks, after sharing their own survey of Juan de Fuca inlet and more, which Vancouver distinguished on his own chart in red, an early forerunner of mutual exchange between nations of navigational information.

When, in 1792, Vancouver's survey around what was to be called Vancouver Island was almost completed, *Discovery* ran aground, on rocks, and as the tide fell started to heel over dangerously to starboard. Mudge has caught this moment dramatically in his illustration, showing natives in their canoes looking on in amazement. The crew had to prop her up with spars and even oars to prevent collapse on to her beam ends. With the next rising tide she was safely floated off, thanks to the crew's drive and calm weather.

Vancouver was to rendezvous at Nootka with *Daedelus* to top up on stores and to get the latest word on the diplomatic situation with the Spanish. He was to receive a sharp reminder of the unpleasant situation in the Sandwich Islands (Hawaii) when told that the *Daedelus* captain, Lieutenant Hergest, and the astronomer to join Vancouver's team, Mr Gooch, had been murdered there. Captain Quadra was in charge of the Spanish ships at the base at Nootka Sound, and was extremely friendly to Vancouver, firing a 13-gun salute on his arrival, sending food daily and entertaining the men. That said, Quadra would not hand over all the land seized, although he offered to re-site to another position away from Nootka. Vancouver actually named the island Vancouver and Quadra Island, as can be seen on the illustration showing Vancouver's chart of the area (page 133), to mark the harmony between them. On 12 October 1792 he left Nootka Sound to head via Monterey to meet with the Spanish and where Quadra would continue to act as the generous host, then to winter in the Sandwich Islands.

Mudge was sent home on a fur trader with despatches via Macao, and on 19 October Vancouver explored a river pointed out to him by a Boston trader, Captain Robert Gray, in the trading vessel *Columbia*. On their survey north Vancouver had inexplicably decided not to investigate this entrance; possibly because of the dangerous rip tide over a shallow sand bar that made the entrance extremely tricky. One of the crew wrote in his journal, 'I never felt more alarmed and frightened in my life.' Possibly Vancouver also felt that it looked unpromising in the light of his instructions from the Admiralty 'not to pursue any inlet or river further than it shall appear navigable by vessels of such burden as might safely navigate the Pacific Ocean'. He had missed the Fraser River, too, never returning to survey it. *Discovery*, with the shallower draught *Chatham* following, tried to lead over the sand bar against a strongly ebbing tide. *Discovery* hauled off for the night but *Chatham* got through, and a survey

100 miles up river was made by ship's boat. At what was called Point Vancouver, Broughton took possession in His Britannic Majesty's name, although arguably Gray had been into the Columbia River first, and perhaps could have claimed the river for America. This was to prove a decisive point in the Oregon Boundary dispute between Britain and the USA 50 years later. But Broughton's seamanship was of the highest quality, and his choice by the Admiralty to carry out further exploration and surveying of the north-west Pacific in HMS *Providence*, starting in 1795, around Japan was a good one.

In the spring of 1793, Vancouver continued surveying at Nootka and on to Restoration Cove. Across the northern continent, down the Bella Coola River walked Alexander Mackenzie, exploring for the North West Company. He was the first white man to cross North America north of Mexico, and reached the sea by the North Bentinck Arm at near latitude $52^{1}/_{2}°$ N on 20 July, just four days after *Discovery*'s boat party had left. What a historic meeting was missed; it would have been on a par with Stanley and Livingstone at Lake Tanganyika in Africa some 80 years later. By the end of the summer survey season they had covered the Prince of Wales archipelago, and south to the west coast of Queen Charlotte Islands. Vancouver sailed south again via Monterey to the Sandwich Islands for the winter.

Returning north again in the spring of 1794, Vancouver investigated Cook's Inlet in Alaska to see if this would lead into the Atlantic. In bitterly cold weather with the cabin temperature down to $-14°$ C and large ice chunks in the tidal waters to avoid, he showed that it did not, and continued surveying eastwards along the Alaskan coast, seeing many Aleut Indians who hunted the sea otter for the Russians. Vancouver's health was starting to fail during this third season, and he could not take to the boats. Everyone was tiring and after the final survey of Cape Decision, at the point where all the claims of a North-West passage could be laid to rest, to Port Conclusion, near the southern end of Baranoff Island on 18 August he fittingly announced the work complete.

Had any river or opening in the coast existed near either the 43rd or 53rd parallel of north latitude, the plausible system that has been erected (of a north-west passage) would most likely have been deemed perfect; but unfortunately for the ingenuity of its hypothetical projectors, our practical labours have thus far made it totter.

The following day they made for Nootka to prepare the ships for the long haul home. This took nearly two months and on 16 October 1794 they departed the north-west coast for the last time, stopping at Valparaiso.

The longest coast survey, with 10,000 miles rowed in small boats and over 65,000 miles of intricate labyrinthine coastline accurately charted and recorded was finished. Vancouver had been instructed to survey the coast to the south of Valparaiso, but, with ship's hull and rigging suffering from more than three years' service at sea, the final voyage to England still to be made, Vancouver's health worsening and the crew deeply weary, they made for the Horn and into the Atlantic. 'He that would go to sea for pleasure' the old proverb had it, 'would go to hell for a pastime'.

Those who came later, even after more than 100 years, and used Vancouver's charts either for navigation or further surveying, such as Rear Admiral Charles Wilkes who surveyed Puget Sound in 1841 for the US Navy, were unfailingly impressed by their accuracy. A lasting memorial was decided in 1868 by the founding fathers of a new city, naming it Vancouver.

| RIGHT | **BATTISTA AGNESE'S WORLD MAP WITH MAGELLAN'S CIRCUMNAVIGATION TRACK, *C*.1520** | Battista Agnese drew the circumnavigation of Magellan's ship on this map showing the world as it was then understood, *c*.1520. Ferdinand Magellan was the first European to cross the Pacific – albeit combining his earlier voyage to the Moluccas (Spice Islands) in 1511–12 with his voyage to find a route to the Orient around the southern tip of South America of 1519–21. (UKHO © British Crown Copyright)

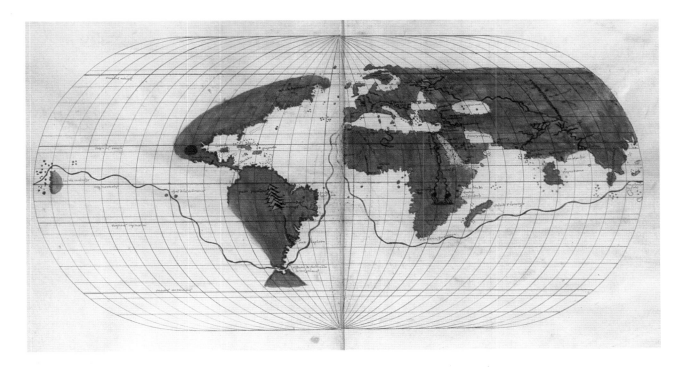

| **CHART OF GOOD LUCK BAY AND BAD BAY IN THE MAGELLAN STRAIT BY SAILING MASTER ROBERTSON, 1767** | Captain Samuel Wallis's skills as a navigator led to his appointment in 1766 to command HMS *Dolphin* in company with the sloop *Swallow*, commanded by Philip Carteret. Captain Wallis's sailing master was George Robertson, who was assisted by the mate, Mr Butler, who drew these plans of Good Luck Bay and Bad Bay. Recorded in 1767, during the long beat against the prevailing westerly winds through the Magellan Strait that separates the southern tip of South America's mainland in Chile from Tierra del Fuego, they are three of a total of some 25 plans showing various anchorages and ports, held in the UK Hydrographic Office archives. Without the shorter route through the strait, vessels would have to sail a further 500 miles south, west then north-west to head into the Pacific. These charts are quite 'intimate' in that they are drawn to a large scale, in fathoms (6 feet) or cables (equal to 200 yards) and would form a useful basis for Robert Fitzroy's later much longer and more comprehensive South American surveys. (UKHO © British Crown Copyright)

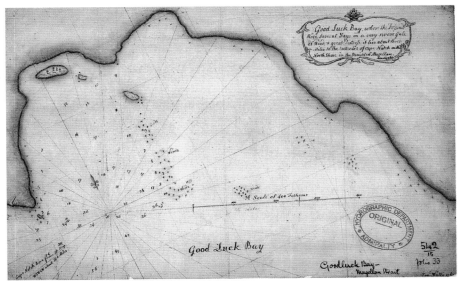

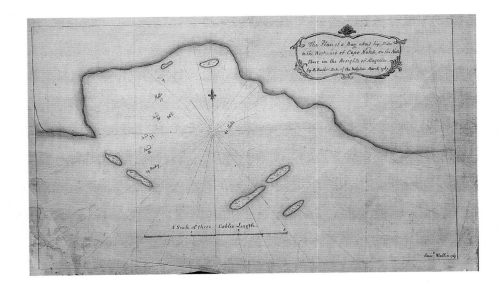

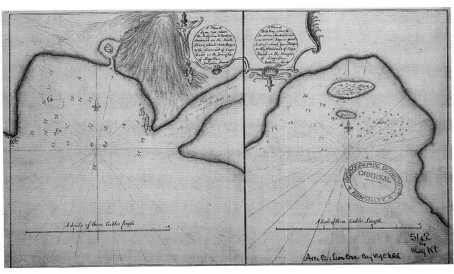

| WOODCUT MAP SHOWING THE SETTLEMENT OF DARIEN FROM 'MEMOIRS OF DARIEN' BY FRANCIS BORLAND, 1715 | One of Scotland's greatest calamities, draining, according to contemporary reports, half of her wealth, was the expedition to Darien, situated in southern Panama. It was a failed nationalistic venture organized by a fervent Scotsman, Patterson, with the intent of starting a Scottish Empire independent of England, settling 4000 Scotsmen with but a handful of women in a 'New' Caledonia. They sailed in 1699, taking four months to cross the Atlantic into the heart of Spain's American empire – an audacious plan that was broken by the mosquitoes, the jungle and the Spanish. It has been said that the Union of Scotland and England was forged by the jungles of Darien.

This crude woodcut nonetheless vividly shows the harbour, the site of the settlement, where the Spanish anchored and the bay from which they attacked and where the helpful local Indians lived. It is from a contemporary account of 1715 of the expedition by one of the settlers, Francis Borland. (Reproduced by courtesy of the Royal Geographical Society with IBG, LIBR: 566.B)

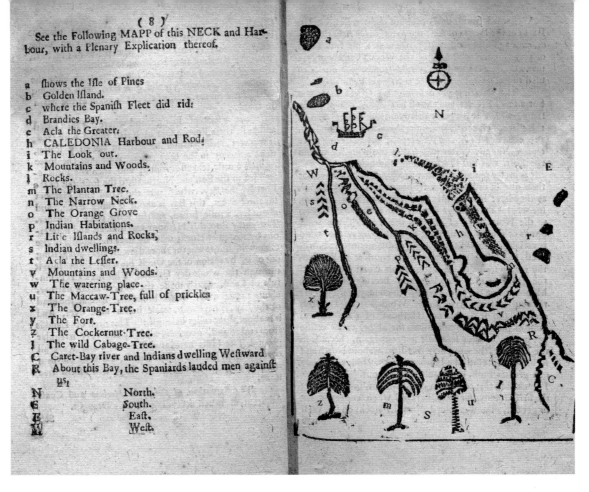

| WILLIAM HACK'S WRITTEN DESCRIPTION AND CHART OF PANAMA | This extract is taken from the original manuscript account of the chartmaker William Hack and covers the period 1680–1686 of accounts of voyages, probably made for the Admiralty, along with plans of harbours and coastal elevations. They include the original journal of Captain Bartholomew Sharp describing, as a crude ship's log or Remark Book, his actions, along with navigational advice. Three other manuscript volumes by Hack have been transferred from the Admiralty Library to the British Library. The chart is a crude but important one from William Hack's book of South American buccaneers who harried the Spanish Main (used in the broadest sense to mean the Spanish mainland possessions in South America, and then latterly to refer to the Caribbean). Sharp's track is shown sailing around Panama Bay. (Admiralty Library Manuscript Collection MSS 4 p108 & 109)

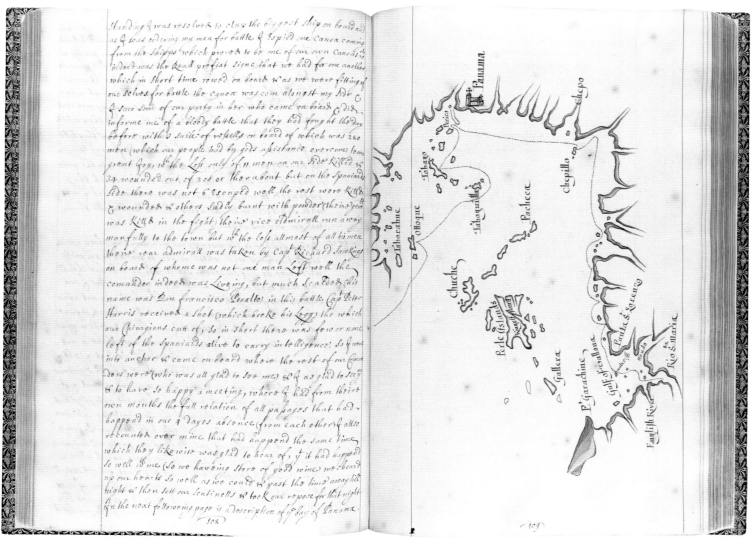

| **MAP OF NORTH AMERICA, 1761** | John Rocque, of Huguenot ancestry, worked for many years in London, for which his maps are best known. He had developed mapping skills surveying the estates of the landed gentry and worked in Ireland for a time. His 1761 map of North America (hand-coloured by the UKHO in the style of the time) taken from various army surveys, provides us with a wonderful snapshot, showing the known and the 'intirely unknown' of the time. He gives many interesting snippets of information for land and sea: where Drake claimed New Albion for his Queen, Elizabeth I on the west coast; the possible Pacific outlets for the supposed strait across North America; the route of the Spanish treasure ships, following the trade winds from Santa Cruz to 'the Havana'; the extent of the Newfoundland cod fishing banks;

details of the hurricane season in the Caribbean and the boundaries showing the uneasy territorial claims of the rival European superpowers – France, England and Spain – and the North American Indians' shrinking boundaries, too. Rocque has written historical anecdotes and advice for ships about available victuals and water alongside various islands; for example how Nova Scotia was settled by 3000 families from Spithead, Portsmouth, England in 1749.

The complete ignorance of the American Pacific coast shown here, and the possibility of a North-West passage awaiting discovery from the Pacific side, was the catalyst for England to send Cook, and then Vancouver to explore and chart the coastline in detail. (© The Admiralty Collection®)

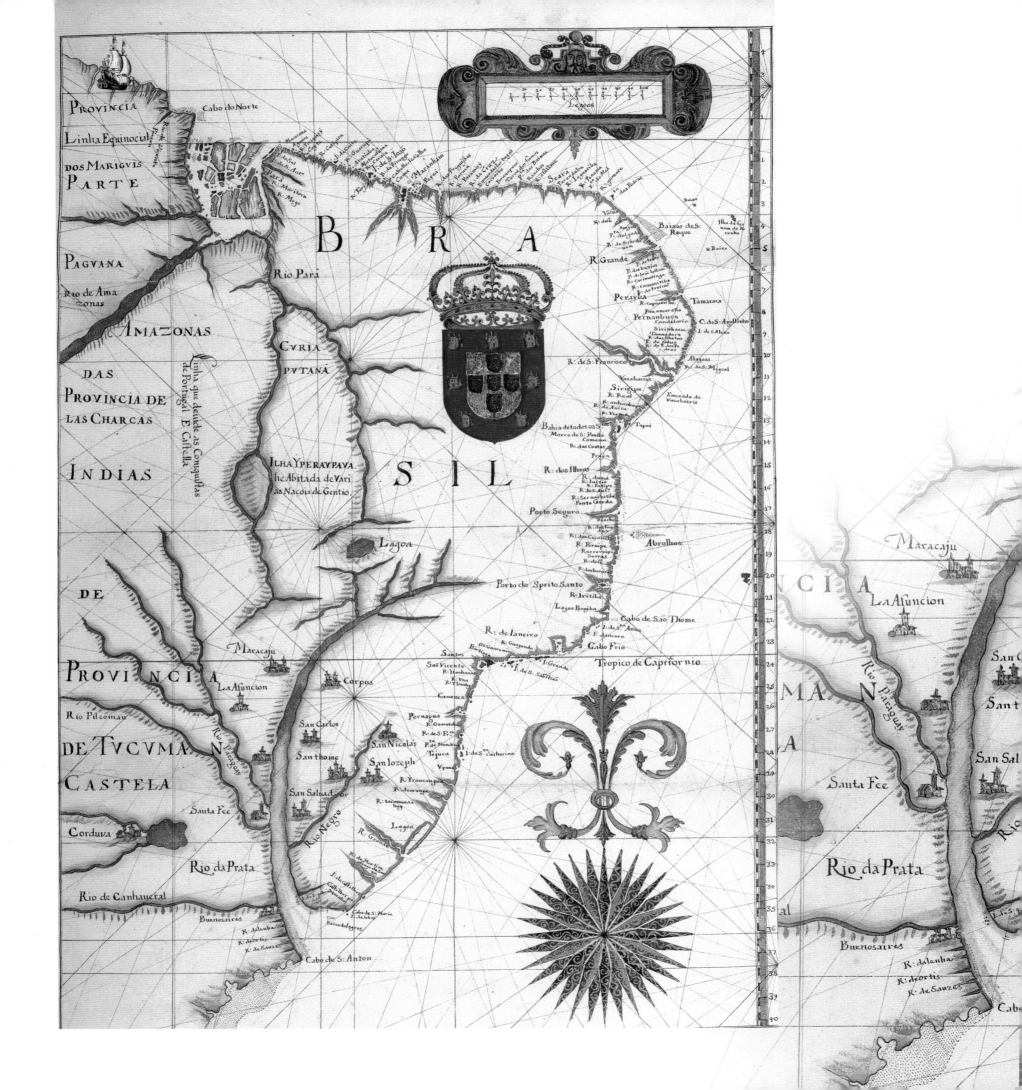

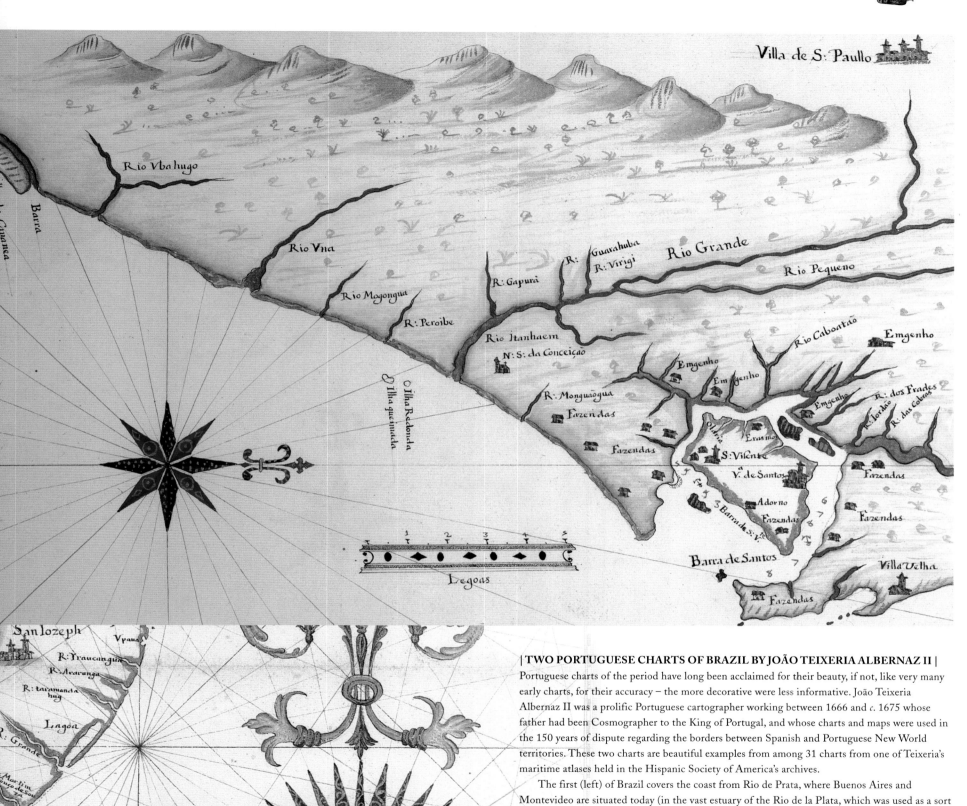

Villa de S. Paullo

Rio Vbahugo

Rio Vna

Rio Mogongua

R: Peroibe

R: Gapurà

R: Guarahuba

R: Virigi

Rio Grande

Rio Pequeno

Rio Itanhaem

N: S: da Conceição

R: Monguaogua

Fazendas

Fazendas

Rio Caboatão

Emgenho

Emgenho

Em genho

Emgenho

Emgenho

R: dos Frades

R: Jordão

R: das Cobras

Olitia

Erasmos

S: Visente

V: de Santos

Adorno

Fazendas

Barra de S: V:

Barra de Santos

Fazendas

Fazendas

Villa Velha

Fazendas

Ilha da Cananea

Barra

O Ilha Redonda

O Ilha guennada

Legoas

San Iozeph

Vpaua

R: Yraucangua

R: Araruoga

R: taramanda hug

Lagoa

R: Grande

| TWO PORTUGUESE CHARTS OF BRAZIL BY JOÃO TEIXERIA ALBERNAZ II |

Portuguese charts of the period have long been acclaimed for their beauty, if not, like very many early charts, for their accuracy – the more decorative were less informative. João Teixeria Albernaz II was a prolific Portuguese cartographer working between 1666 and *c.* 1675 whose father had been Cosmographer to the King of Portugal, and whose charts and maps were used in the 150 years of dispute regarding the borders between Spanish and Portuguese New World territories. These two charts are beautiful examples from among 31 charts from one of Teixeria's maritime atlases held in the Hispanic Society of America's archives.

The first (left) of Brazil covers the coast from Rio de Prata, where Buenos Aires and Montevideo are situated today (in the vast estuary of the Rio de la Plata, which was used as a sort of nautical super-highway into the interior) in the south, northwards to the mouth of the Amazon. With an attractive north compass rose, cartouche and scale in '*Legoas*', all, as is the coastline, picked out in real gold, this is 'the most beautiful and complete chart by Teixeria'.

The second chart (above) is with a larger scale showing about 150 miles of the coast from just north of Curitiba in Brazil, with the island of Cananea (known today as Cananéia) up to the natural port of Santos, near present day São Paulo, and São Vicente, the first European settlement along this coast, is shown too. It has the beginnings of useful hydrographical information with soundings (in *Brassa*) and anchorages shown, and the range of low mountains parallel to the coast are drawn with charm. (Courtesy of The Hispanic Society of America, New York)

| ABOVE | **NAVIGATIONAL VIEW OF FINGER POINT, CHATHAM ISLAND IN THE GALAPAGOS ISLANDS, 1846** | Captain Henry Kellett stopped at the Galapagos Islands in 1845 on his way north to the Arctic in HMS *Herald*, as part of the Franklin-search team, and this attractive navigational view of Higher Rock from Finger Point on Chatham Island was made. Today administered by Ecuador, it is one of the six larger islands straddling the Equator (thus their importance in fixing an accurate meridian traverse points for Longitude on Robert Fitzroy's circumnavigation) in the Galapagos group made famous by Darwin's great discovery of natural selection by studying the finches found there. (UKHO © British Crown Copyright)

| ABOVE RIGHT | **CHART OF KEALAKEKUA BAY IN HAWAII BY EDWARD RIOU, 1779** | Edward Riou drew this chart as a midshipman under Captain Charles Clerke of HMS *Discovery*, accompanying HMS *Resolution* on Cook's third and last voyage. It shows Kealakekua Bay in Hawaii, the bay where Cook was killed in 1779. It reflects the surveying influence of Cook through Clerke in the style and careful recording of navigational information. Riou went on to become one of the navy's finest frigate captains, distinguishing himself, but killed, at the Battle of Copenhagen in 1801. (UKHO © British Crown Copyright)

| RIGHT | **VIEW OF NOOTKA SOUND, NORTHWEST AMERICA, 1794** | An engraved view of part of Nootka Sound from Vancouver's published account of his voyage of exploration. Both *Discovery* and *Chatham* reached the Thames in October 1795 after a voyage of four years and nine months. The account was written with his brother's help after his return to England, because his health further deteriorated as a result of his enormous efforts during the voyage. Vancouver died in 1798. (UKHO © British Crown Copyright)

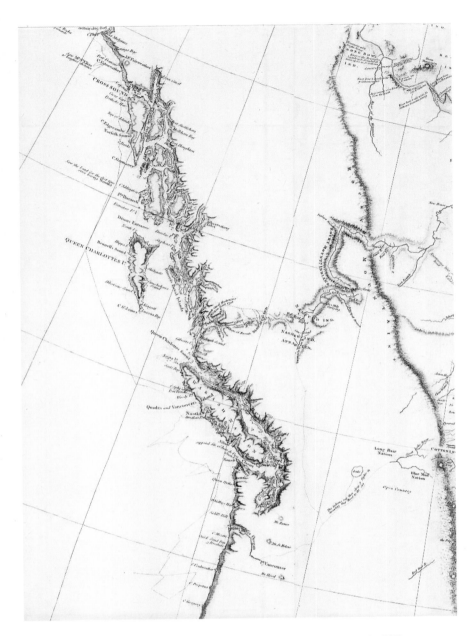

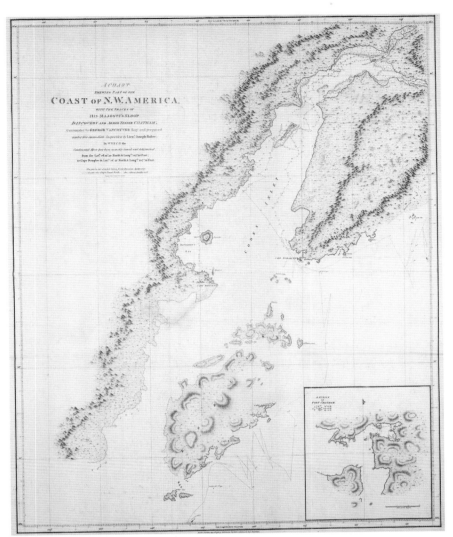

| ABOVE | **VANCOUVER'S CHART OF THE PACIFIC COAST OF NORTH AMERICA, 1792** | The published Admiralty chart from Captain George Vancouver's original survey includes Queen Charlotte Islands, at the time thought to be one large island, and Vancouver Island with Nootka Sound, the scene of the controversy between England and Spain that, but for Vancouver's diplomatic solution, threatened to lead to war. Vancouver and his team were able to include the coastal mountain range around 60 miles inland, some peaking at over 13,000 feet, which dominate the view, but would not of course include the land between. The site of the city of Vancouver, named after the hydrographer, can be seen on the chart. (UKHO © British Crown Copyright)

| ABOVE | **VANCOUVER'S CHART OF COOK'S INLET, ALASKA, 1794** | Vancouver produced a detailed pioneer survey of the north Pacific coast of America of such accuracy that, in part, it remained in use up to the 1970s. He was able to greatly improve on Cook's chart of the remote inlet in Alaska named after him that leads to the modern city of Anchorage. The Admiralty chart shown here, engraved and published from Vancouver's original survey, and with hatching and contour work and a wealth of navigational information, set a new surveying standard, but with a functional beauty, too. Credit must also go to the capable officers, such as Puget, Broughton, Mudge, Baker, Hanson, Whidbey and Johnstone, he had working under him, who in turn went on to command ships and carry out key surveys across the world. (UKHO © British Crown Copyright)

Australia or

British

New Holland

New

Terra

Australis

Gulph

of

Carpentaria

Arnhems Land

Chart
showing such parts of
Terra Australis
and its vicinity, as were discovered
or examined by the following vessels—

Schooner Francis of 60 tons burthen, in 1798,
Sloop Norfolk of 25 tons, in the years 1798, and D.
Schooner Cumberland of 29 tons burthen in 1803,
and by
His Majestys ship Investigator in 1801.2. and 3,
by M. Flinders, Commander.

The original charts are constructed upon a scale of four inches to a degree of longitude, from which this abridgment was made whilst
a prisoner at the Isle Mauritius.

The dotted parts of the different tracks were run during night.

The arrows show the direction and strength of the winds.

The coasts represented by the plain single line are
copied from other detailed authorities: the
shaded coasts only being seen
by me.
1804

The Antipodes (Australia and New Zealand)

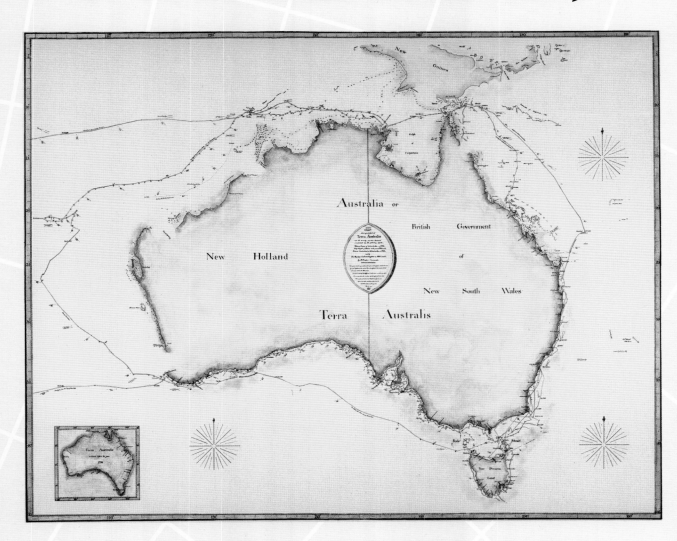

| LEFT DETAIL & ABOVE | **CHART OF CAPTAIN FLINDERS' CIRCUMNAVIGATION OF AUSTRALIA** | Captain Matthew Flinders completed his circumnavigation of Australia in 1803. The published chart, copied and hand coloured from Flinders' original held in the UKHO Archives, shows the combined tracks of the surveys he carried out in various ships from 1798. (© The Admiralty Collection®)

THE land mass of Australia was guessed at by the early geographers, drawn as a huge continent centred on the South Pole and thought to be there by inference, to balance the known continents centred around the North Pole. This view went back to the Greeks in Ptolemy's writings, but was overturned by the medieval church in favour of the literal flat Earth interpretation from the Bible, and *Terra Australis Incognita* disappeared from charts. The explorations of the fifteenth and sixteenth centuries re-introduced the idea and by the early sixteenth century the land mass was shown joined to South America and extending up to 60° S, and in the Pacific Ocean extending almost up to the Equator.

Remotest of the settled continents, Australia is the flattest with an average elevation of just under 1000 feet, and just 6 per cent of the country above 2000 feet high – mostly the Great Dividing Range which extends from Cape York in the north to Victoria in the south-east. Low-lying coastal plains extending 40 miles inland enclose a vast interior, known as the outback, which is largely desert or semi-desert. The coastline is fairly regular with the two large bights, the Gulf of Carpentaria in the north and the Great Australian Bight to the south, which gave rise to the belief that the continent was divided into two large islands. The Great Barrier Reef of living coral – the world's largest natural organism – runs southwards from Cape York for 1250 miles and provides a natural breakwater for sea-going traffic down the east coast.

The name Australasia was first coined by the French historian des Brosses in his *Histoire des navigations aux terres australes* in 1756, and referred to the part of the Indian Ocean lying south of Asia, taking the old word for the south wind, Auster.

From Europe, explorers, square-riggers and, later, surveyors would 'run the easting down' from the Cape of Good Hope to Australia along the roaring forties. If heading round the north of the continent they had to contend with the Torres Strait, one of the most difficult straits to sail through in the world, and graveyard to many of the early ships.

The strait took its name from the Spanish navigator, Luis Vaez de Torres, who was the first to record the 80–90-mile wide stretch of dangerous waters, sailing through in 1606 to Manila. He had first recorded his sighting of Australia as a group of islands to the south during the expedition in 1605 under de Quiros, with Torres as second-in-command sent by Phillip III of Spain.

Several Dutch navigators discovered various parts of the northern and western coasts of Australia, and in 1622 the company of the Dutch ship, *Leeuwin*, sighted Cape Leeuwin, the south-west corner of Australia, at which point it was realized that the land tended eastwards. In 1642 Antony Van Diemen, the Governor-General of the Dutch East India Company, chose the Dutch explorer, Abel Tasman, to command an expedition to the 'Great South Land' to confirm whether it was part of the great southern continent or an island. Tasman sailed from Batavia to Mauritius and from there headed due south, before turning east at the roaring forties (about 40° S). He came across Tasmania, named it Van Diemen's Land, sailed through the two islands of New Zealand and on a second voyage followed the northern coast of Australia westward to 22° S.

William Dampier, had skirted the north in two voyages commissioned by the Admiralty around 1700. Although rightly known for his epic surveying achievements along the western coast of North America in 1791–1794, Captain George Vancouver's contribution to the charting of Australia on the outward voyage ensures his inclusion in the record of Australia's surveyors. On 26 September 1791, while on his way to British Columbia to search for the North-West passage, he sighted Cape Chatham and examined the south-west coast of Australia for a distance of 300 miles, discovering and charting King George Sound, then sailing on to New Zealand, where he charted Dusky Bay. Vancouver was not without a cartographical sense of humour. He explored further into the bay than Captain Cook who had named it 'No-body knows what'. Vancouver got to the far end and named it, 'Some body knows what'.

The colonies' overthrow of British rule in America created one particular problem: what to do with the 'criminal classes'. Although the death penalty could be given for most forms of theft, the courts usually preferred to show leniency and transport the convict overseas. Sir Joseph Banks, president of the Royal Society, had led the scientific party in Cook's first voyage, when he had not only circumnavigated New Zealand, but explored and charted about 1000 miles of the east coast of Australia, too. Banks's interest in the Antipodes never waned and he suggested that a colonial penal settlement be started in New Holland. The Admiralty regarded Australia as a potential southern naval base and source of some of the essential raw materials for Britain's ships involved in trade expansion in India, China and the Spice Islands – flax for sails, hemp for rope and spruce for masts.

The First Fleet of 11 ships under the first Governor, Captain Arthur Philip, bravely sailed on 13 May 1787, with 443 sailors and 800 convicts, to a land that had not been visited since Cook 17 years before. They were to found, as an experiment never attempted before or since, a colonial jail, 16,000 miles from the mother country on a little-known continent. Upon reaching the coast of New South Wales, Philip discounted Botany Bay, originally recommended by Banks, as unsuitable and choosing instead to set up the penal colony inside Port Jackson (Sydney Harbour) at Sydney Cove.

Governor Philip returned to England in 1792. After six weary years the colony was established. In 1795 Captain John Hunter was 'persuaded' to take on the job. He was a most respected surveyor, having sailed out to Australia as captain of HMS *Sirius*, as part of the original fleet of 11 ships. The survey of Port Jackson (named by Cook after the First Secretary of the Admiralty) including the nearby penal settlement at Sydney Cove (named after the British Home Secretary, Viscount Sydney) had been Hunter's first duty after the safe arrival of the fleet. Lieutenant William Bradley of the *Sirius* had drawn the original chart in 1788, which was published in Hunter's journal in 1793 and was subsequently published by the Hydrographic Office as an inset to the chart of the east coast of Australia. Hunter had also added further detail to Cook's work on the coast of New South Wales, and improved charts of the islands to the south of the Solomon group.

On 15 February 1795, HMS *Reliance* set sail from England to take John Hunter out to Australia. Matthew Flinders, a competent navigator, was chosen as master's mate. He jumped at the chance to join such an exciting voyage and, as he wrote in his account,

> the author, who was then a midshipman, and had not long returned from a voyage to the South Seas, was led by his passion for exploring new countries, to embrace the opportunity of going out upon a station which, of all others, presented the most ample field for his favourite pursuit.

Flinders would be away from England for six years.

His younger brother, Samuel, was also on board as a midshipman. The ship followed the usual route across the Atlantic, keeping clear of the French with whom Britain was at war, stopping at the Canaries to re-provision, on to Rio de Janeiro. Arriving at Sydney to a settlement that was coarse and unruly, Flinders realized that very little charting had been made of the coasts. Only three ports and a small section of coast amounting to about 100 miles had been surveyed.

George Bass was a surgeon and naturalist in the *Reliance*. He formed a friendship with Flinders and a mutual interest in exploration of the coasts near-by Port Jackson. They started in a little boat called *Tom Thumb* and learned the rudiments of landing through surf and 'dealing' with natives. Governor Hunter was concerned by the threat of French expansion and needed to know if Van Diemen's Land was part of the mainland or separated. The lasting answer to the French threat was to set up a colony there which was to lead to the tragic extermination of the native aborigines. Flinders had learned the rudiments of surveying from Bligh, under whom he had served as a midshipman during the successful voyage to take breadfruit from Tahiti to Jamaica in HMS *Providence* in 1792. For the rest he was entirely self-taught, so this work does not stand comparison for accuracy with that of his predecessor, Cook, or of Captain Philip Parker King (son of the later Governor, Philip Gidley King) who followed him. Even so, his fieldwork was extensive and painstaking. Over the next six years Flinders and Bass established that Van Diemen's Land was a separate island which they circumnavigated in the 25-ton sloop, HMS *Norfolk*, built at Britain's own prison, 'devil island' (Norfolk Island); Bass giving his name to the strait between the island and the mainland. Flinders named many places on his charts around Sydney, complimenting the personalities of his time – the Duke of Portland, Alexander Dalrymple, and the Chappell Islands after the girl into whose family he was to marry, and so on.

Flinders returned to England in August 1800, a mature, experienced lieutenant filled with a personal ambition – to chart the waters around Australia. To this end he contacted Sir Joseph Banks with his proposal. Writing politely in the third person, 'The interests of geography and natural history in general, and of the British nation in particular, seem to require, that this only remaining considerable part of the globe should be thoroughly explored.' Flinders extended his vision of an exploratory mission:

> A further knowledge of the strait between New Holland and New Guinea (Torres Strait), and of the south coast of the latter, are perhaps desiderata of importance, and might possibly be explored during the circumnavigation of New Holland without much lost time; and during these intervals when the examination of the coasts might be thought too dangerous [during the Southern monsoon period when winds blew stormy], that extensive group the Feegee or Bligh's Islands would afford ample employment, as well as refreshment, to the crews.

How cruelly was fate to ruin this idyllic vision he had of surveying and circumnavigating Australia and returning straight away with his completed working charts. The Great Australian Bight to the south and the Gulf of Carpentaria to the north indicated that the continent could well be two large landmasses with a sea between them. The potential prospect of the French colonizing the western half spurred the Admiralty into accepting Banks's support to Flinders' proposal. The East India Company was interested, too, for the potential of an alternative route to India. They stumped up additional payments for the officers and scientists in the form of 'table money'; they wanted to share the information.

A plan was put before Lord Spencer, First Lord Commissioner of the Admiralty. Even though there was a fragile peace with France agreed by the Peace of Luneville (ratified later by the Treaty of Amiens) and most suspected that war would flare up again, the Admiralty enthusiastically backed the plan. Once King George III had sanctioned the scheme, the 100-foot, three-masted sloop *Xenophon* was renamed HMS *Investigator* and fitting out for the voyage began. A passport of immunity was arranged with the French, which was mutually granted to the French expedition that left in October 1800 under Captain Nicolas Baudin commanding *Le Géographe* and *Naturaliste*. Rumour had reached the Admiralty as early as 1799 of the preparations of the French captain's voyage, so the *Lady Nelson*, captained by Lieutenant John Murray was sent out 'hurriedly' to complete the surveys of southern Australia and forestall any French landings. Murray was a competent rather than a brilliant surveyor but gained a just renown from his discovery of Port Phillip and also for his work in company with Flinders. The Admiralty's archives include 10 of the *Lady Nelson*'s charts.

The French aims added impetus to the project, but the immunity allowed Flinders to take fewer and lighter guns, with more room for exploration equipment and stores. In a similar way to Bligh's *Bounty* and Cook's *Endeavour*, the cabins had to be redesigned to take the botanical samples that Joseph Banks wanted, and areas organized for the scientific work of surveying, drawing charts and recording the flora and fauna. The crew of 80 and the scientific party were chosen, the latter comprising an official landscape painter, William Westall; an astronomer, John Crosley; a mineralogist, John Allen; a naturalist, Robert Brown; a gardener from Kew Gardens, Peter Good; and an artist, an Austrian painter, Ferdinand Bauer. William Alexander, who was the artist on Lord Macartney's 'embassy' to open up trade with China in 1792 was preferred but was too ill. Bauer is now considered to be one of the greatest natural history artists that ever lived. He had botanized for 18 months in Greece, and settled near Oxford to illustrate a book, *Flora Graeca*, with 1500 sketches. These had brought him to the attention of Banks. The botanical studies the French produced on the voyage were also of the highest standard.

Flinders realized the significance in fixing the positions of the ship and shoreline of the effect of magnetism on the compass bearings they used. Variation, the difference between geographic and magnetic north, was understood and allowed for, but deviation caused by the varying magnetic influence of the ship's own metal wasn't appreciated. Flinders swung the ship to find out what the deviation was for various headings and was able to apply this amount to the binnacle compass bearings he took.

To minimize or annul the magnetic influence Flinders devised iron bars that were placed in the best position around the binnacle to achieve this. His solution is used today and is known as Flinders' bars.

Sighting Cape Leeuwin on 6 December 1801, Flinders headed eastwards along the south coast surveying much of the Great Australian Bight. As they progressed, to Flinders personal chagrin, they lost Mr Thistle, the sailing master, and seven of the crew when one of the ship's boats was swamped in the tide rip. He named the point Cape Catastrophe. They continued and discovered Port Lincoln, the finest natural harbour in Australia. The coast then indented into a gulf some 48 miles across. Flinders named it Spencer Gulf, after the First Lord of the Admiralty, and taking shelter from a vicious storm in the lee of an island he was pleased to find it overrun with kangaroo, providing fresh meat. In

James Cook's Three Voyages of Discovery

FIRST VOYAGE (1768–1771)

By 1768 James Cook, at 39 seasoned by his surveying experience in Canada and Newfoundland, was commissioned, promoted lieutenant and given command of HM Bark *Endeavour*, a Whitby collier with shallow draught, broad 30-foot beam to a 100-feet length, ideal for surveying, and a best speed of 7 knots. Sturdily built with remarkable sea-keeping qualities and a large capacity, she could carry the 98 men (including the scientific party appointed by the Royal Society), stores and equipment needed for a two-year exploration. His 'offical' mission was to carry out observations of the transit of Venus across the Sun from the island re-discovered by Samuel Wallis – Tahiti.

France was keen to annex what territories she could in the Pacific. Britain, having now driven the French out of both North America and India, 'owned' one eighth of the known world and sought more. Behind the ostensible reason for Cook's first Pacific voyage was another purpose: to found a new continent. The Dutch knew of New Guinea and parts of north, south and west Australia, which gave credence to the belief, supported by huge tracts of land shown on earlier charts and maps that there was a vast southern continent to counter-balance the Northern Hemisphere land masses, that was temperate, extended to South America and New Zealand and occupied most of the South Pacific. Before Cook, Abel Tasman had touched Tasmania in 1642 and the west coast of New Zealand. Otherwise, there was only the explorations of Wallis and Lord Byron to go by.

Cook sailed from Plymouth in August 1768 stopping at Madeira and Rio de Janeiro for fresh water and provisions, then rounded Cape Horn in unusually calm weather, taking advantage of this to chart the islands and to find a new channel.

He arrived at Tahiti on 13 April 1769 and the transit was duly observed, the island charted, and after six weeks he sailed taking a local chief, Tupia, both as a guide and translator, charting many islands in what he called the Society Islands 'because of their contiguity'.

He had been ordered by the Admiralty to penetrate as far as latitude 40º S in search of the Southern Continent, and he sailed south for close on 1500 miles, enduring the roaring forties, turned north-west for smoother waters, then west-south-west for three weeks until on 7 October he sighted an east coast promontory of New Zealand, which he circumnavigated in 1769–70, an incredible 2400-mile voyage.

He headed west and made a landfall at the southeasterly corner of Australia, Point Hicks. Turning north, he carried out a running survey, anchored in Botany Bay, and continued north until he was hemmed in by the Great Barrier Reef. During the night of 11/12 July 1770 the *Endeavour* hit a coral reef and almost sank. Cook managed to pull her off by ditching buoyed guns, ballast and gear. After careening the *Endeavour* at today's nearby Cooktown to repair the hull, he decided to settle the question of whether or not Australia was attached to New Guinea. His discoveries in Australia led to the foundation of the first British colony in New South Wales a mere 18 years later.

He broke through what he called the 'Labyrinth' to sail the notorious maze of shoals and reefs of the Torres Strait, discovering and charting the Endeavour Strait and sailing on to Batavia (Djakarta), one of the most disease-ridden ports in the world. Cook lost 23 men from sickness, with, at one low point, only 12 men fit enough to work the ship. On 12 July 1771 he made Chatham after a voyage of 2 years 11 months.

The Admiralty now regarded Cook as the greatest navigator, explorer and surveyor of the age, a public relations asset, a good reflection on their Lordships at the Admiralty, and an excellent agent for British expansion. It was not long before he was appointed for a second voyage.

SECOND VOYAGE (1772–1775)

South of latitude 40º S was still largely unexplored and the British wanted to claim any southern continent before the French or Spanish. On 13 July 1772 Commander Cook started the second voyage of 3 years and 18 days in HMS *Resolution* with HMS *Adventure*, captained by Tobias Furneaux.

Cook had previously used lunar observations to work out his longitude, which involved lengthy tables, but he now had K4, a copy of John Harrison's H4 chronometer. From the Cape of Good Hope, Cook steered south-east to criss-cross where the French explorer Lozier Bouvet had reported land, thought to be the tip of the Antarctic, then tried to find the land Kerguelen and Crozet reported in the Indian Ocean, and struck south to 60º to the longitude of the East Coast of Australia. He proved that there was no inhabitable 'great southern continent' within the one third of the world's circumference he had covered.

He set course for New Zealand, refitted, and sailed further eastwards checking between 41º and 46º S, after which he made for Tahiti to rest and refit. He then steered west to the Friendly Islands (Tonga), discovered by Tasman in 1643, altered course to the south, becoming the first known explorer to cross the Antarctic Circle, reaching 71º 10' South on 30 January 1774. He decided on another season of Pacific exploration to the north to chart a number of islands including Roggeveen (Easter) Island, then back to New Zealand for a final refit before heading home via Cape Horn, discovering the South Sandwich Islands and re-discovering South Georgia.

THIRD VOYAGE (1776–1779)

On 25 June 1776, aged 46, promoted Post Captain and elected a fellow of the Royal Society, Cook commenced his third Pacific voyage. He took HMS *Resolution* again, with *Discovery* (Captain Charles Clerke) to find the North-West passage. The voyage this time was blighted from the start with a skimped refit. He got to Nootka Sound on the north-west coast of

Canada, surveyed the Alaskan peninsular, sailed through Bering Strait to 70° 30' N, but was blocked by an impassable ice wall. Cook returned to Hawaii to refit where a rapturous welcome greeted him as a god on his first landing on the main island, but this so strained the island's limited resources that relations deteriorated sharply on his return to repair storm damage. Cook was stoned to death in August 1779 during a fracas on the beach. Bligh, Cook's 23-year navigator of distinction, completed the survey of the Alaskan and North Russian coasts which showed that the North-West passage was as elusive from the Pacific as from the Atlantic.

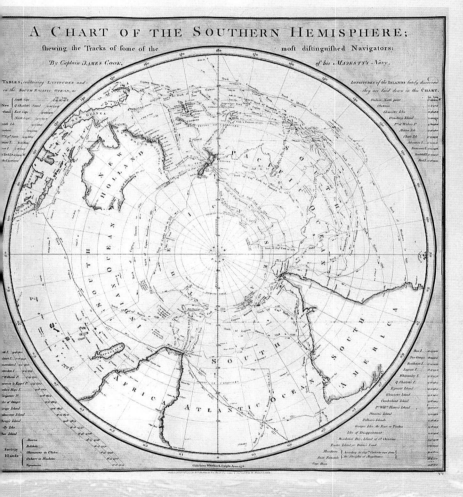

| ABOVE | Cook's chart of the Southern Hemisphere, which appears on his knee in the famous 1776 portrait by Nathaniel Dance, summarizes not only the tracks of his first two voyages, but also the voyages of some of his predecessors. The jigsaw puzzle that is the view of land and sea centred on the South Pole has begun to take its modern shape, although very little of the Antarctic continent was yet laid down. (UKHO © British Crown Copyright)

| LEFT | *The Triumph of the Navigators, Endeavour* July 13th 1771, by Robin Brooks.

gratitude he named it Kangaroo Island. He spent just six days surveying the area of the future site of Adelaide, as the prospect of winter weather urged him to press on, and strangely missed the Murray River. Had he surveyed it the whole history of the development of the country would have followed an altogether different pattern.

He missed the Yarra River, too. This was disappointing as one of the key purposes of the voyage was to substantiate the supposition that there must be considerable rivers to 'drain' the inland areas and a river mouth could provide the necessary infrastructure for a settlement. On 8 April 1802 to their surprise, and by extraordinary chance, they met Captain Baudin in Encounter Bay, near today's Adelaide. Cautiously clearing for action as they closed *Le Géographe*, Flinders ordered a boat to be lowered and went across. Stopping only for a circumspect discussion and exchange of information over two days, Flinders then sailed on to make Sydney.

Baudin had sighted Cape Leeuwin in May 1801 and by the 30th he was anchored in Géographe Bay, about 130 miles south of the present-day position of Perth, Western Australia. From there he headed north to take on supplies at Timor, then returned south to survey the southern coast of Van Diemen's Land in January 1802. He then made his way along the south coast in the opposite direction to Flinders patriotically naming bays and inlets with French names – Golfe Josephine (Gulf St Vincent), Golfe Bonaparte (Spencer Gulf), and a broad selection of army marshals.

After the meeting with Baudin, Flinders account relates that at 1 o'clock on 9 May 1802, they passed through the Sydney Heads, came to anchor and reported to the Governor, Captain Philip Gidley King, that *Investigator* had surveyed the south coast of Australia for five months, logged 20,000 miles from England and 6000 miles from Cape Leeuwin to Port Jackson. In fact his surveying was so accurate that his work is still the basis of the Admiralty charts.

He had put in to Port Jackson to re-provision and refit *Investigator* and discussed the continuing assignment with King. He would chart what Cook had called 'the labyrinth'; the Great Barrier Reef, filling in the details of the survey so perilously garnered some 32 years earlier. This would be followed by the challenge of the Torres Strait. Next he would survey the 'Gulph of Carpentaria' and then complete the Australian continent circumnavigation along the north and north-west coasts. They anticipated finalizing this phase within a year, but Flinders' prime constraint was to complete the eastern coast of the Gulf of Carpentaria before the supposedly on-blowing north-west monsoon gave him a tricky lee shore from around November.

On the second part of the expedition Flinders wanted to investigate Hervey Bay, at Great Sandy Island, about 200 miles north of Brisbane, and getting towards the southerly start of Cook's nightmare 'labyrinth', the Great Barrier Reef, north to South Head, and verify Cook's survey. Cook had not had the advantage of the chronometer, and Flinders was able to accurately determine the distance and position across the bay. As the coast northwards tended to the west, Cook's error compounded so that at Cape York it was over half a degree; 35 miles in one of the world's most dangerous straits. Flinders corrected this.

The Torres Strait was relatively unknown. Following Torres' passage in 1606, the existence of the strait had been kept secret by Spain for reasons of national advantage. Only a few other sailors had traversed them: Cook in 1770 and Bligh in the *Bounty*'s 23-foot open launch in 1789; Captain Edwards with four boats to Timor three years after Bligh; Bligh again on his successful breadfruit expedition from Tahiti to Jamaica, and two merchantmen in 1792.

Flinders task now was to survey Cape York and the passage through the strait. It was believed that accurate charts would cut up to five weeks off any commercial passage through the Pacific to India.

Flinders was half expecting to find the Gulf of Carpentaria was a sea that split Australia into two parts. Only the Dutch had explored the gulf before Flinders, and Tasman had been there a long time before, in 1644. Flinders took 10 days to cover the gulf and concluded correctly, but for the wrong reasons, as he missed another three rivers, that Australia was not split by a sea. He also reported that this was not a suitable place for a settlement.

He later wrote a memorandum which would eventually reach the Admiralty with Mr John Aken, who had been released from incarceration with Flinders by the French on Mauritius. It explained the background to Flinders' work, and included a chapter entitled, 'Of the restitution of the name Australia, or Terra Australis, to the extensive country which has lately gone under the name of New Holland'. The Dutch had given the name New Holland in the seventeenth century, and Cook on his first Pacific voyage had in 1770, named and claimed all the land to the east of longitude 135° E for King George III and named what was virtually half of the continent as New South Wales. Flinders rightly concluded it was one land mass and this begged a single name for the whole area. Besides his scientific and practical contribution to understanding and remedying a ship's own magnetism, Flinders's lasting achievement was to name and establish the extent of the sixth continent – Australia.

In 1817 the French launched a far more scientifically oriented voyage with Louis-Claude Desaulses de Freycinet, who had served in Le Géographe under Baudin in his Australian expedition of 1800–04. With the support of Louis XVIII, Freycinet took L'Uranie around the world, stopping at New South Wales in 1819 long enough to explore the Blue Mountains, but little else.

The use of the Torres Strait by passenger ships to and from Sydney and British India and Singapore created a need for a port in northern Australia and the maps and charts of Captain Philip Parker King were made in consequence during a number of hazardous expeditions between 1817 and 1822 along the western, northern and north-eastern coasts of Australia, discovering amongst others the excellent harbour of Port Essington on the Cobourg Peninsula. King completed the work of Flinders left unfinished due to the rotten condition of the Investigator. Some of his plans of northern Australia are of such high standard that they remain in use with few amendments to the present day.

Admiral Sir Francis Beaufort decided that the north-west, the Gulf of Carpentaria and the Bass Strait between Tasmania and southern Australia, where many ships were running into unforeseen dangers, should be more accurately surveyed than the hitherto running surveys had provided. Captain John Lort Stokes took over HMS Beagle from Captain Robert Fitzroy and charted 300 miles of coastline to the north-west in 1837. The key to colonization was in the rivers and Lort Stokes, following his Admiralty instructions, surveyed up 90 miles of what he named Fitzroy River after his old commander. Lort Stokes survived an attack with a spear to carry out the Gulf survey including two rivers, one he named after Flinders and the other after Queen Victoria's consort, Albert. He was loaned the colony's survey vessel, Vansittart, to help complete the Bass Strait survey. Beaufort sent out two other survey vessels, the Bramble and the Fly, to relieve Lort Stokes after six years, commanded by Captain Francis Blackwood. The Beagle herself had completed 18 years' con-

tinuous service in South American and Australian waters.

As the number of ships sailing south from Cape York to Sydney increased so the need for a safe channel either around or through, as Cook described it, the labyrinth within the Great Barrier Reef became paramount. Blackwood took on the difficult task of charting the outer part of the Great Barrier Reef northwards to New Guinea, along with 140 unexplored miles of that coast in three surveying seasons from 1843, including the 'Blackwood Channel' whose entrance he marked by the reef on Raine Island with a 64-foot high stone tower, built by convict quarrymen and masons brought up from Sydney. This allowed a vessel to choose the best route depending on her ability to fix latitude, the ship's draught, and sailing qualities, between the inner, King's Route (surveyed by Philip Parker King) or keeping outside of the reef with Bligh's entrance to what is now called the Great Northeast Channel into the Torres Strait.

By mid-1847 a 500-ton frigate, HMS Rattlesnake, relieved Blackwood, captained by an experienced surveyor, Owen Stanley. He completed the Torres Strait survey over a two-year period, finding eight channels, and had on board a young surgeon, T H Huxley, whose thesis on jellyfish was published by the Royal Society. He left the navy after the Admiralty refused to publish further work, was elected a Fellow, and was appointed Professor of Natural History and Palaeontology at the Royal School of Mines in London in 1854. He was a vociferous supporter of Darwin for most of his working life but looked back on his naval life with gratitude as

> the opportunities for scientific work, to me, personally, the cruise (around New Guinea) was extremely valuable. It was good for me to live under sharp discipline; to be down on the realities of existence by living on bare necessities: to find how extremely well worth living life seemed to be when one woke from a night's rest on a soft plank, with the sky for a canopy, and cocoa and weevily biscuits the sole prospect for breakfast; and more especially, to learn to work for the sake of what I got for myself out of it, even if it all went to the bottom and I along with it.

Unfortunately it was the first Maori War of 1845–58 that provided the impetus for improving on Cook's extraordinary running fix survey of the coastline of New Zealand. Lort Stokes, in command of a 5-gun paddle-steamer, HMS Acheron, started the work providing charts of the approaches and sheltered anchorages for the settlements beginning in the Bay of Islands, Auckland and Wellington, and with Otago and Canterbury soon to follow. This task continued until 1851, the year of the Great Exhibition in London and the Australian gold rush, and was finally completed in 1856 by Pandora, a brig, and the charts were immediately made available to the New Zealanders.

The completion of surveys of the eastern waters, in response to the huge numbers of gold-speculating ships, under Captain Denham, took from 1852 to 1860 and laid down a safe route, called, as one might expect, the Denham Route, which cut the sailing time to Singapore and India by a fifth, charting an immense area embraced by New South Wales, New Zealand, the Kermadec group, Tonga, Fiji, New Hebrides and New Caledonia, an approximate quadrilateral of sides totalling 6000 miles, and recognized as a nine-year Herculean achievement by the Royal Geographical Society.

There were many smaller but valuable contributions to complete the picture, but it was mainly finished and was the precursor to the former British colonies setting up their own hydrographic surveying service.

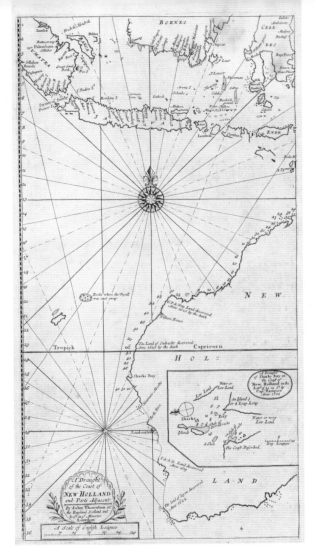

| WILLIAM DAMPIER'S CHART OF SHARKS BAY, 1701 |
During his voyage around the world of 1683 to 1691 Dampier landed on the western and north-western coasts of Australia in January 1688, and kept meticulous surveys, charts and records of the flora and fauna which he published as *A New Voyage Round the World*, which was a bestseller in 1697 and 1699. As a result he was commissioned in 1699 by the Admiralty to captain HMS *Roebuck* to find the Great Southern Continent, again exploring around Australia and New Guinea and giving his name to what is now called Dampier Strait and the Dampier Archipelago. But he got the impression that Australia was made up of islands and this gave rise to the idea of a strait down the middle of Australia that persisted for the next century until clarified by Flinders' meticulous circumnavigation.

Dampier's chart of Sharks Bay of 1701 and the coast northwards was drawn and published by John Thornton, well-known for his successful folio of charts sold as *The English Pilot*. Dampier's description of the Aborigines he encountered along the coast inspired Swift's 'Yahoos' in *Gulliver's Travels*. (UKHO © British Crown Copyright)

| JOHN THORNTON'S CHART OF DAMPIER'S VOYAGE TO NEW GUINEA | Dampier got John Thornton to draw out his voyage as captain of HMS *Roebuck* in 1699–1700 during which he was to sail to New Guinea and around Australia. This original (and unique) chart held in the UKHO archives and drawn on vellum from Dampier's own work, shows his track from England, past the Cape of Good Hope and along the west coast of New Holland. He couldn't find any natural harbours or fresh water, and had to make for Timor where he refitted and re-provisioned. He was a far better navigator than captain and, after some survey work off New Guinea, the crew mutinied over his harsh conduct. He returned to Timor and headed home, but the *Roebuck* was suffering and sank by Ascension Island. Fortunately a passing East Indiamen took them off. Dampier was court-martialled for his treatment of the crew, had to forgo his pay for the whole voyage, and was declared unfit to serve again in any of HM Ships.

The chart's zero meridian of longitude is based on the Lizard, whose lighthouse is often the first and welcome sight to returning ships at the south-west tip of England. Dampier kept copious notes on navigation (trade winds and magnetic variation are noted on the chart), flora, fauna, geology and anthropology and, despite his buccaneering times, is regarded by many as the first to attempt a scientific approach to exploration. (UKHO © British Crown Copyright)

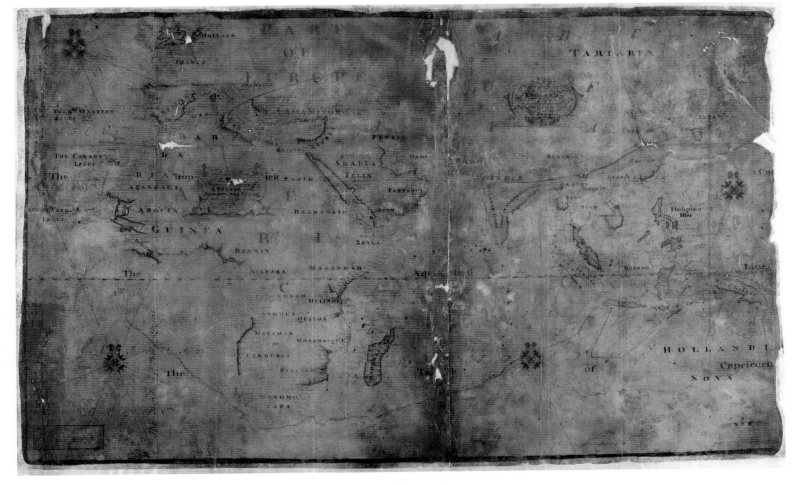

| VANCOUVER'S CHART OF THE SOUTH-WEST OF NEW HOLLAND |

Vancouver's chart of the south-west of New Holland displays his careful and accurate approach to surveying. The chart at the lower left of the group shows the reach named by Vancouver as 'Somebody knows what' in New Zealand. (UKHO © British Crown Copyright)

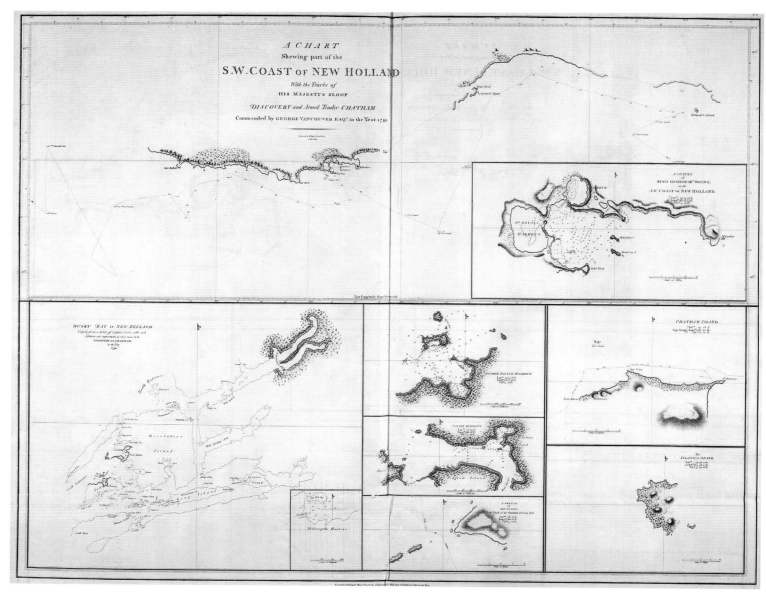

| CHART OF COOKSTOWN, AUSTRALIA BY RICHARD PICKERSGILL |

Cook, on his first voyage, explored over 1000 miles of the east coast of Australia. Inside the Great Barrier Reef he hit bottom and HMS *Endeavour* was in danger of sinking – prevented by a large lump of coral that, remaining in place, stopped sea water flooding inboard below the water line. He made it to what is now called Cookstown, where the ship was careened up-river and the damage repaired while the ship lay on her side as high above the tide line as they could get her. This chart is by 20-year-old Richard Pickersgill, Master's Mate, who had sailed with Samuel Wallis, and, although naïve compared to Cook's professional drawings, shows his love of charting and survey work which, in part, earned him promotion to Lieutenant on HMS *Resolution* for Cook's second voyage. (UKHO © British Crown Copyright)

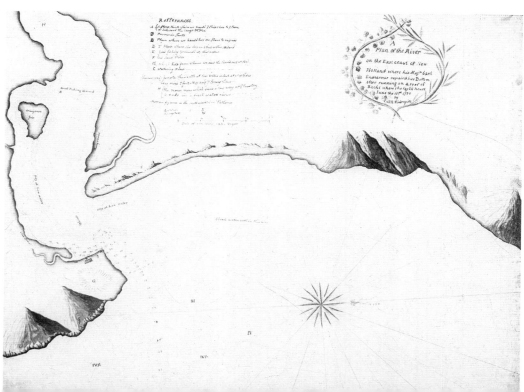

| CAPTAIN COOK'S CHART OF HIS CIRCUMNAVIGATION OF NEW ZEALAND, 1769–70 | This chart from Cook's published account shows the track of HMS *Endeavour* in 1769 and 1770, during which he carried out a 2400-mile circumnavigation of New Zealand, mostly based, because of near continuous gales, on running surveys. It was recently hand coloured by the UKHO. His work is of such a high standard that the New Zealand navy only withdrew his last chart from their portfolio nine years ago. His first voyage proved that New Zealand was two islands, and not part of the Great Southern Continent. (© The Admiralty Collection®)

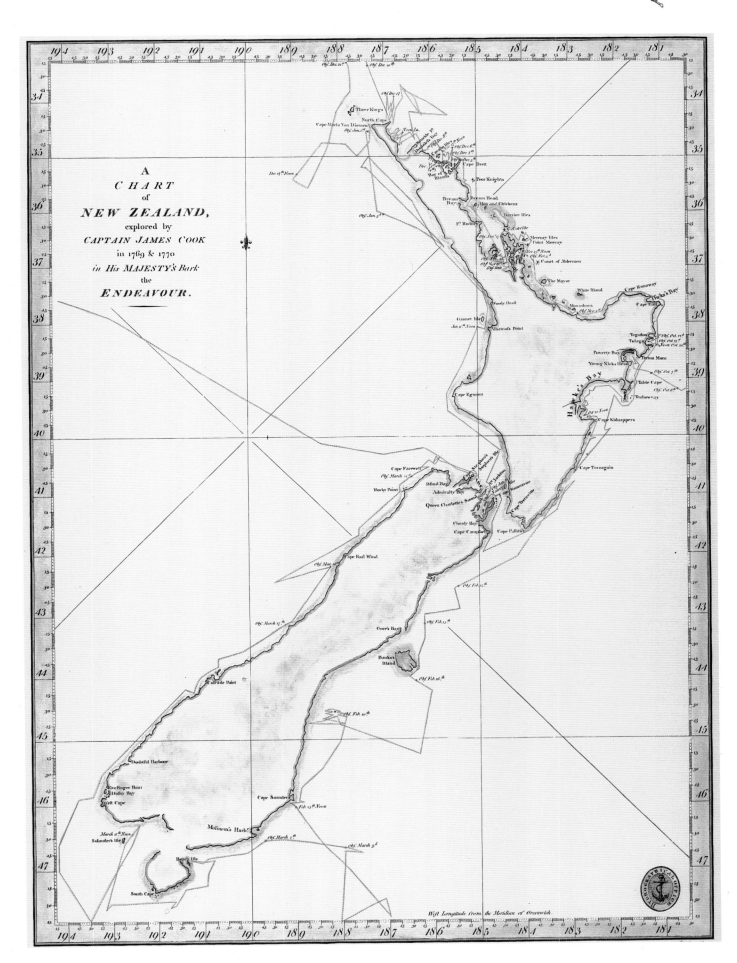

A CHART of NEW ZEALAND, explored by CAPTAIN JAMES COOK in 1769 & 1770 in His MAJESTY'S Bark the ENDEAVOUR.

| **SURVEY OF PORT JACKSON, 1822** | Lieutenant John Septimus Roe drew up this survey of Port Jackson in New South Wales in 1822. Roe joined the navy aged 15 and learned surveying during three years in HMS *Horatio* between 1814 and 1817 in the North American, Home and East India stations. He then served under Captain Philip Parker King in Australia 1817–1823 and returned again in 1828 as Surveyor-General. He spent the rest of his life there until his death aged 81, surveying for the next 42 years. He explored and surveyed much of the northern and southwestern coasts and was one of the first to land in the Swan River, and his surveys led to the settlement of Perth and the founding of the seaport at Freemantle. (UKHO © British Crown Copyright)

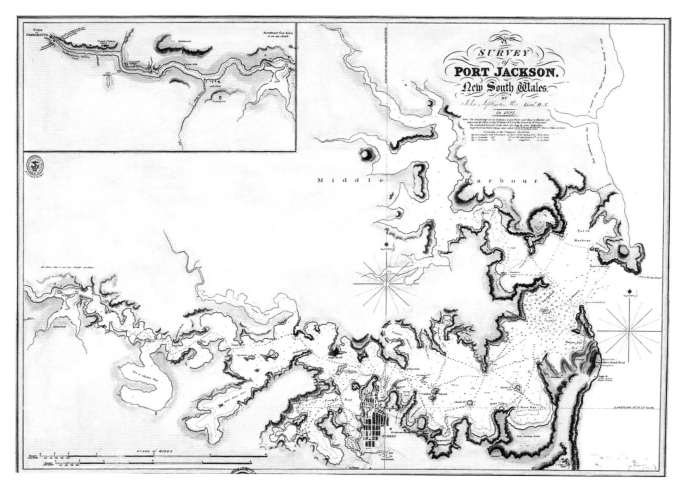

| **TERRE NAPOLEON, AUSTRALIA, BY FREYCINET** | France's two greatest maritime exploratory endeavours, the expedition under Nicolas Baudin in *Le Géographe* and *Naturaliste* (to be replaced by *Le Casuarina* for inshore work) of 1800–04 and Louis-Claude Desaulses de Freycinet commanding *L'Uranie* of 1817–20 were principally a voyage of discovery, sanctioned by Napoleon, and a voyage of science, sponsored by King Louis XVIII.

The first voyage, with 22 scientists, was undoubtedly hopeful of establishing a French foothold on what Freycinet, then a lieutenant, had put on the chart as Terre Napoleon. The meeting with Flinders in Encounter Bay, near today's Adelaide, forestalled any further ideas, although the survey of Port Jackson, then an isolated and comparatively defenceless settlement, was likely to have been for invasion.

Ironically, as Baudin was naming the southern Australian coastal features in French, Flinders was busily doing the same in English. Freycinet's chart reflects the poise and beauty inherent in French charts and, in terms of cartographic skill, was perhaps better than Flinders'. However, without the assistance of the English during Baudin's five-month stay, the French expedition, which enjoyed diplomatic immunity, would have been in trouble. (UKHO © British Crown Copyright)

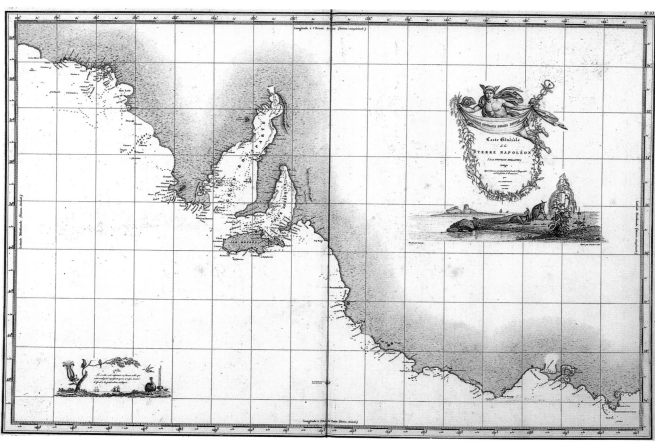

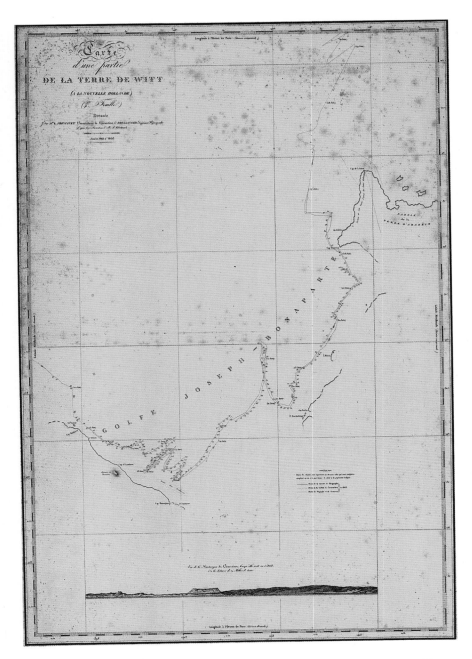

| **GULF OF TERRE DE WITT, AUSTRALIA BY FREYCINET** | Freycinet's chart of the Golfe Joseph Bonaparte shows the tracks of both survey vessels, *Le Géographe* and *Le Casuarina* during the 1801–04 voyage as they progressed clockwise around Australia, with soundings and anchorage positions marked. The names Baudin gave in this vicinity have stuck, for example Mount Casuarina, shown at the bottom of the chart in elevation, and nearby Cape St Lambert, are those still used today. (UKHO © British Crown Copyright)

| **CAPTAIN FLINDERS' MANUSCRIPT CHART OF THE NORTH-WEST COAST OF THE GULF OF CARPENTARIA** | Flinders carried out his surveys of the Australian coast with incredible determination. Having lost many of the original charts on his first attempt to take them to England he redrew many of them from memory while a prisoner of the French in Mauritius. In Flinders' own words, 'The two original rough charts of this part of the north coast of Australia, were lost in the shipwreck of the *Porpoise*, wherein we had embarked to return to England, I had embraced the leisure, afforded by a close imprisonment in this island, to reconstruct the parts lost, before the recollection of them had become too faint, this was done in Jan. 1804, but the scale then used being of 4 inches only to a degree of longitude, and the continuance of my detention not allowing me to prosecute the examination of Australia actively, I have constructed these parts afresh, upon the present scale, and I hope with increased accuracy. It must, however, be still remembered, that although almost every projection is fixed by bearings and observations, the intermediate parts are mostly filled in from memory. My books record 43 observed latitudes, between Jan. 2 and Mar. 6 1803, together with 871 bearings and angles taken on board, and 720 with a theodolite onshore, besides other observations, and these form the basis of the chart, as will be more particularly explained in a memoir. Matthew Flinders. Isle of France. Oct. 9 1805.' (UKHO © British Crown Copyright)

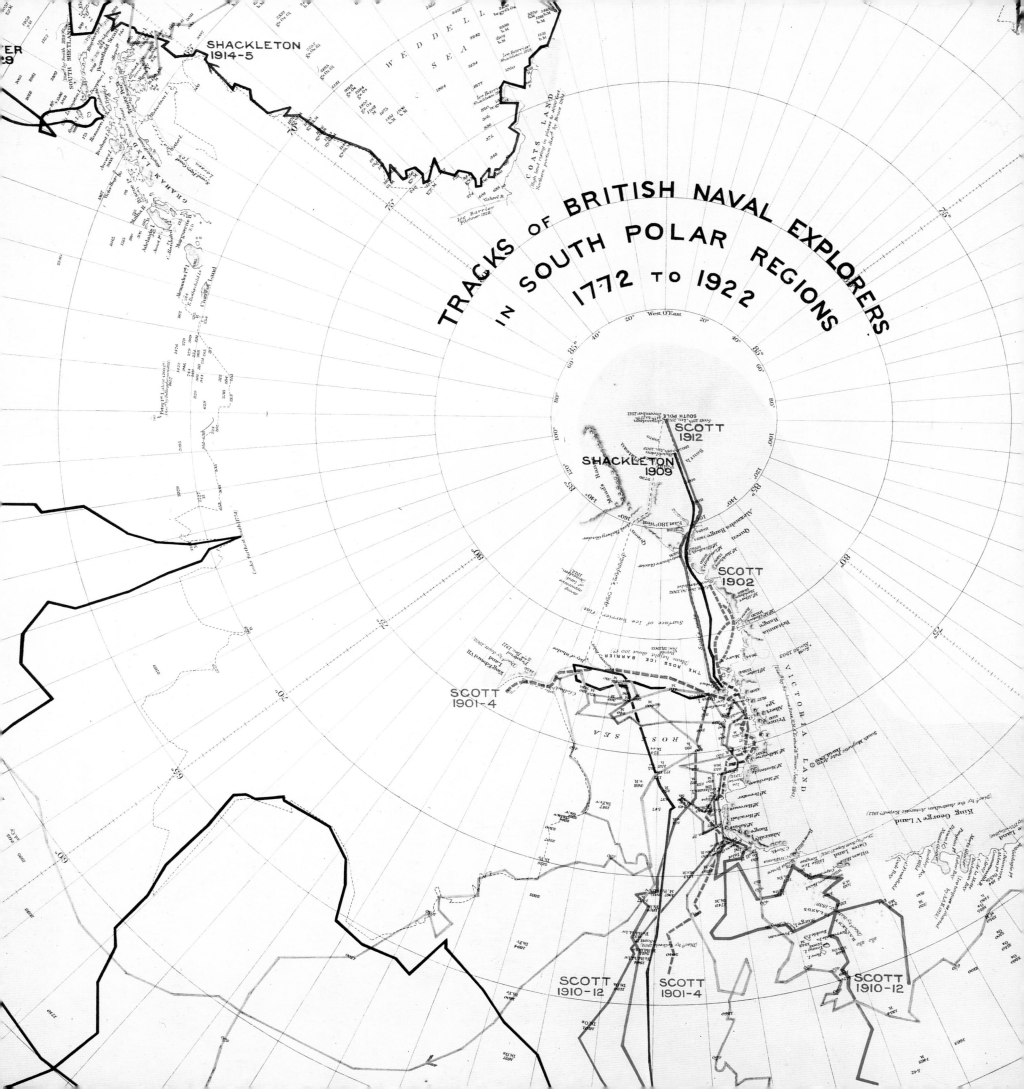

TRACKS of BRITISH NAVAL EXPLORERS
IN SOUTH POLAR REGIONS
1772 TO 1922

SHACKLETON
1914-5

SCOTT
1912

SHACKLETON
1909

SCOTT
1902

SCOTT
1901-4

SCOTT
1910-12

SCOTT
1901-4

SCOTT
1910-12

WEDDELL SEA

COATS LAND

ROSS SEA

VICTORIA LAND

THE ROSS ICE BARRIER

KING GEORGE V LAND

The Antarctic

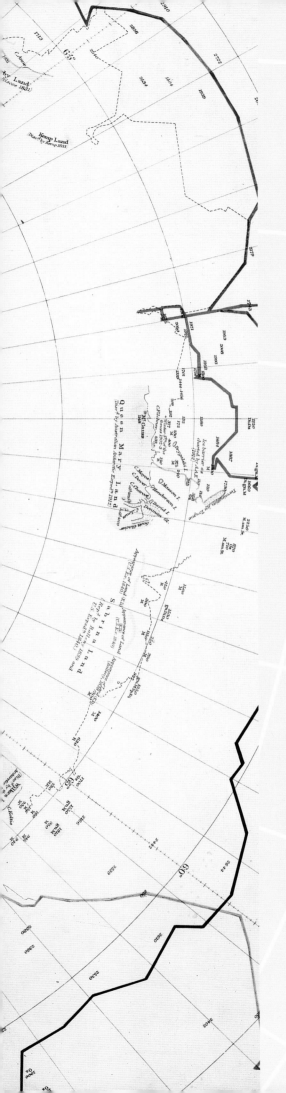

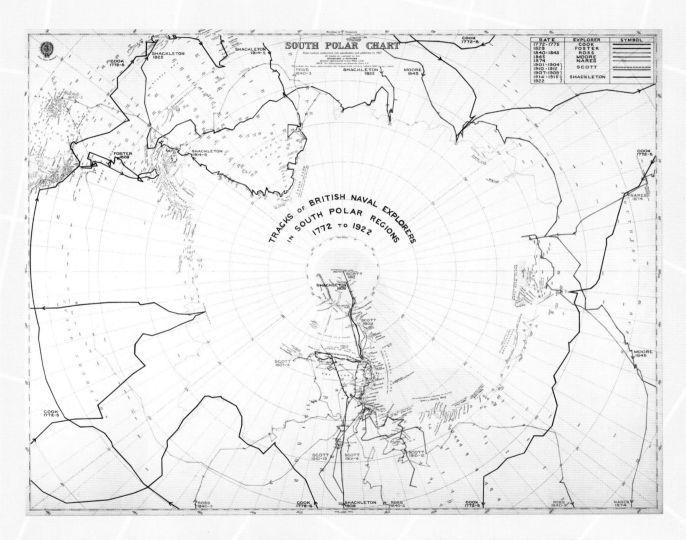

| LEFT DETAIL & ABOVE | **CHART SHOWING ANTARCTIC AND TRACKS OF BRITISH EXPLORERS, 1927** | An example of a printed Admiralty chart originally printed and published in 1927 with, somewhat jingoistically, overprinting to show the ships' tracks of British naval explorers between 1772 and 1922. It does give an interesting snapshot of the state of discovery of the Antarctic and a useful overview of where the main British explorers voyaged, such as Captain George Nares as commanding officer of HMS *Challenger* in 1874. The small corrections noted at the bottom of the chart give the updates as more information came into the Hydrographic Office, as it then was, from a variety of sources, including merchant shipping, whalers and fishing vessels. (UKHO © British Crown Copyright)

THE Greeks thought that there had to be a solid land mass around the South Pole to balance that around the North. By the time of Henry the Navigator whose organization of expeditions around Africa, starting with Bartolomeu Diaz in 1487, changed the age of speculation to the age of exploration, it seemed possible that a continent could exist that covered this massive area.

The quest to find *Terra Australis Incognita* started in earnest. The maps and charts of sixteenth- and seventeenth-century cartographers such as Henricus Hondius and Frederic de Wit neatly filled the space with a large land mass and it began to be accepted as reality that a rich and fertile region with natives willing to trade existed. The relatively recent discovery of the Piri R'eis maps (see Chapter I) have opened up some intriguing possibilities by the American Historian, Charles Hapgood, that there was much earlier knowledge of the Southern Continent. He has stated with some conviction that the Turkish Admiral's depiction follows remarkably the actual Antarctic land mass perimeter. This was only verified through the mile-thick polar ice cap by sonar soundings during the International Geo-Physical Year of 1957. Again Gavin Menzies argues evidentially that one of the Chinese fleets of 1421 had reached the Falkland Islands, and plotted parts of Antarctica, and that these are the source the Piri charts.

The Antarctic is the fifth largest of the earth's seven continents, and, because of its thick ice cover, is the highest, with an average elevation of about 7500 feet (2300 metres). It contains about 90 per cent of the world's fresh water and is more than 95 per cent ice covered; the depth of ice over the South Pole is a staggering 9000 feet (2772 metres). Now largely contained within latitude 66° 33' S, the definition of the Antarctic Circle is made by the point at which the sun never rises during the winter, and never sets during the summer. It seems, through geological evidence, that the continent has two sources. The larger eastern part, with remains of fossils and coal, floated tectonically from its tropical position when part of one huge land mass of Gondwanaland broke off 300 million years ago; the smaller western part would appear to be an archipelago of islands continuing southwards from the spine of South America, with a trans-Antarctic mountain ridge between the two resulting from tectonic collision. The other chief features are the two large indentations into the land, the Ross and Weddell Seas and their ice shelves – launch pads for so many trans-Antarctic expeditions. Antarctica's total area is about 5.5 million square miles (14.2 million square kilometres) in summer, but during the winter it doubles in size swollen by the freezing sea ice that forms at its periphery.

However, the maritime boundary of Antarctica is not at the coastline of the continent but at the Antarctic Convergence, which is a sharply defined zone in the southern extremities of the Atlantic, Indian, and Pacific Oceans between latitudes 48° and 60° S. In this zone, the colder waters flowing north from Antarctica meet with warmer waters moving south. The convergence marks a definite physical difference in the oceans in terms of temperature, chemical composition and marine life. For these reasons, the water surrounding the Antarctic is considered an ocean in itself, known as the Southern Ocean.

The highest point on the continent is Vinson Massif at 16,864 feet (5140 metres); the lowest point appears to be the Bentley sub-glacial trench at 8200 feet (2499 metres) below sea level in West Antarctica. This trench is covered with more than 9840 feet (3000 metres) of ice and snow. Lower points may exist under the ice, but they have not been discovered.

The UK Hydrographic Office *Sailing Directions* is a compendium of nautical information for the mariner, a mix of fascinating background and factual but essential advice hard-won from the dangerous experiences of our sailing forbears. It describes the Southern Ocean in dry informative tones that understate the drama of these waters. At the northern limit of the ocean at 56° S you can sail eastwards with the prevailing fetch, circumnavigating the world at this latitude for 12,000 miles without interruption. Nothing stops the seas, pushed on by the prevailing westerly winds, except the constriction forced by the Antarctic Peninsula, named Graham Land and Palmer Land, that curves up, topped by the South Orkney and South Shetland Islands, towards Tierra del Fuego some 600 miles north and creating huge waves that challenge every vessel that ventures into that area. The sailor heading south into the Atlantic Convergence will notice the sharp drop in water and air temperature. Fog and mist often mark this delineation, as Captain Cook was the first to testify, and many whalers and sealers have since found to their cost. This, then, is the inhospitable scenario that has attracted national expeditions for reasons of patriotism, greed or curiosity.

Alexander Dalrymple had strongly supported the idea of a Southern Continent while Hydrographer to the East India Company. In 1766 the Royal Society's proposal that he should lead an expedition to the South Pacific, was denied by the Admiralty in favour of a naval officer, and in 1768 Captain James Cook sailed in command of what would become his first great voyage of discovery. Voyages by single- or two-ship explorations progressively chipped away at the size of the unknown. Jean Bouvet de Lozier discovered the ice-covered island that bears his name in 1739 – at less than 1000 miles from land in any direction the loneliest place on the planet – and Yves Joseph de Kerguelen-Tremerac, similarly in 1771, prefaced the first serious attempt by Cook's voyage of 1772 to 1775, to prove or disprove the Southern Continent's existence.

Cook's real discovery, having probed south to 71° 10' S 106° 54'W (which still stands today as the furthest position south of any vessel at that longitude), was that any land that did exist beyond would be so inhospitable as to preclude either trade or colonization. But he did discover within the Antarctic area part of the South Sandwich Island Group and South Georgia. The plentiful numbers of seal attracted English and American hunters, who hunted them to near extinction, but contributed significantly to the charting of the islands and landfalls in that area. In 1819 an English sealer, William Smith, master of the brig *Williams* from Blyth in Scotland, found the South Shetland Islands near to the tip of the Antarctic Peninsula, which he patriotically called New South Britain. In 1820 mountains were seen on the peninsula by Edward Bransfield and an American, Nathaniel Palmer, after whom this land was named. In 1819 the Czar, Alexander I, appointed Thaddeus Fabian von Bellinghausen to command a two-ship Antarctic circumnavigation in the sloop *Mirny*, in company with the *Vostok*, following Cook's track. He finished Cook's survey of South Georgia and surveyed the South Sandwich Islands. He noted his sighting of the cliffs of Queen Maud Land, but received very little recognition for his work.

Looking at a chart of the Antarctic shows two major indentations that bring the coast to within 700 miles of the South Pole, giving advantage to expeditions to land as close into the Antarctic as possible. These seas have been named after the two men who were to make significant contributions to the exploration of the Antarctic – Weddell and Ross. James Weddell was a man of significant ability and within six years of joining the Royal Navy was made Master, as advanced as you could get as a warrant officer. He may have hoped to emulate Cook and become a commissioned officer, but with the ending of the Napoleonic War in 1815 he knew that promotion was unlikely when the only way up to Admiral from Post Captain was through time and 'natural wastage' at the top. Weddell took his chance with the Merchant Navy and by 1819 was sailing his new command, a 75-foot, two-masted brig, *Jane*, fitted out to take seals and whales, south to investigate whether the much reported Aurora Islands existed; in which case he would chart them and capture seals. He took a chronometer with him, unusual for the time when most whalers and sealers preferred dead reckoning and latitude sights and applied the old seamen's proverb, 'trust a good lookout more than a bad reckoning'.

Weddell sailed to the Falkland Islands to winter, which had become a haven for English, US and French whalers. While lacking any shore-side entertainment the islands provided water, peat (for cooking fires), fish and birds, with cattle in the East Falklands. Weddell collected information on the islands, tides, currents, safe anchorages, and navigational dangers. The reports of seals on the South Shetland Islands started a rush of seal hunting in 1821. Weddell made a good profit and bought a small consort, a fore-and-aft-rigged cutter, *Beaufoy*, and with her he returned to the Southern Ocean for another season.

In the story of his experiences, *A Voyage Toward the South Pole*, he recounts an uncanny parallel to the experience of Selkirk's abandonment by Dampier on the island of Juan Fernandez when he found an American, Captain Charles Barnard, who, in 1814, had been taken by a British crew he had rescued after their vessel was shipwrecked. They had abandoned him for two years on New Island, to the west of the Falkland Islands. In 1821 Weddell's two vessels joined up with Barnard's ship, *Charity*, and sailed for the South Shetlands, where the breeding grounds were being thinned out by as many as 1000 men from 43 US and British sealers. Others were scouting to find untapped seal beaches and in consequence the South Orkneys were discovered by the Englishman George Powell aboard the *Dove* and Nathaniel Palmer of the *James Munroe*.

Weddell embarked on his third voyage in *Jane* with *Beaufoy*, but with a new captain – Matthew Brisbane, a Scot and efficient commander who worked well with Weddell but was to be shipwrecked three times and brutally murdered on the Falklands. They reached the South Orkneys in early 1823, passing by the South Shetlands, aware that these grounds had been all but stripped bare of seals in four seasons of frenetic activity. Weddell knew he had to search new areas and this allowed him to pursue his surveying abilities. He tried to find shoals reported between Patagonia and the Falklands, still marked on the Admiralty chart today with ED (Existence Doubtful) beside the Aigle reef. Very few seals were found at the South Orkneys and the two small vessels searched north through fog, cold and icebergs towards the South Sandwich Islands. Weddell altered course to the south-east and, with the men on rationing, they sailed south on longitude 30º W and broke free of the hellish iceberg-ridden seas to an area in which the noon sighting of the sun showed them to be at 71º 24' S. Weddell continued south until the wind blew fresh from the south. He had to make a hard decision and turn around, but he had sailed further than any man into the sea he called George the Fourth Sea but which was changed to his name, to a new southerly latitude of 74º 15' S. The world recognized his achievement, apart from the French explorer, Dumont d'Urville: reaching a less impressive 63º 23' S, he dismissed Weddell's success as the attempts of 'a simple seal hunter' and branded him a liar.

Weddell had, however, been fortunate with the weather. The sealers and whalers discovered great variation in the amount of ice in the Weddell Sea from season to season. The nature of the Antarctic iceberg differs from its Arctic sister. Up to 9780 feet (3000 metres) thick, the mean flow of the ice is a continuous but slow northward movement away from the Pole. Pieces break off with thunderous claps at the edges forming icebergs sometimes miles across. The continuous and mostly uninterrupted prevailing westerly wind blows these ice islands counter-clockwise until they pack up into the entrapping arm of the Antarctic Peninsula. They slowly bump and grind northwards until clear of the land where they are either picked up by the easterly winds and current to extend a virtually impenetrable pack-ice barrier north-eastwards until guided up by the northerly Falkland current, or carried on to the east by the prevailing current and wind. From summer to winter the northerly extent of the pack ice varies on average from around 65º S in January to 55º S in July, but the immense flat-topped icebergs can get as far as the tip of the Cape of Good Hope and on the back of the northerly Falklands current up to the River Plate estuary in Brazil, and even to the southerly edge of New Zealand.

In 1830 John Biscoe, employed by the Enderby Brothers to hunt seals and explore and write up what he found as a treatise, circumnavigated the Antarctic continent, discovering Enderby Land, Adelaide Island, the Biscoe Islands, and Graham Land on the west side of the Antarctic Peninsula. Another voyage combining sealing and discovery was made by Peter Kemp, Captain of the *Magnet*, in 1833–34, discovering Heard Island and Kemp Land. John Balleny, in *Eliza Scott* and *Sabrina*, discovered the Balleny Islands and Sabrina Coast.

The scientific motive to verify the predicted position of the earth's magnetic south pole in the Antarctic led to three major national expeditions and attendant patriotic fervour. The French went first in 1838 lead by Dumont d'Urville. He tried to penetrate as far south as possible within the Weddell Sea, but was ultimately unsuccessful. His second attempt did find the area now known as Adelaide Land, still a French area of influence today.

Concurrently, the Americans had sent Lieutenant Charles Wilkes, in the wake of Weddell, to the Antarctic south of Tasmania. Although from English parents, Wilkes joined the US Navy after three years in the Merchant, aged 20. Ferdinand Hassler, who founded the US Coast and Geodetic Survey, tutored him. He served in two surveying expeditions from 1826 to 1833 and was appointed Head of the US Navy Depot of Charts and Instruments in 1834, out of which grew the Hydrographic Office. US Congress approved plans for a national expedition to explore the South Atlantic and South Pacific to promote US whaling and fishing interests and in 1838 Wilkes sailed in the USS *Vincennes* in command of a six-ship expedition. He was to follow 'the track of Weddell as closely as practicable, endeavouring to reach a high southern latitude'. Starting in the Samoa Island Group, which would have given them the opportunity to hone their surveying skills in warmer climes, they set out on the Antarctic exploration hoping to sail as far south as possible between longitudes 160ºE and 45ºE. In bad weather, having left Tierra del Fuego in the *Porpoise* and *Sea Gull* late in the season during February 1839, while two of his other ships the *Peacock* and *Flying Fish* headed further west, ordered by the US Navy Department to 'stretch towards the southwards and westwards as far as the 'Ne Plus Ultra' of Cook. ('No man farther,' was shouted by an exuberant Midshipman George Vancouver, aged 16, who had climbed out on the bowsprit as the *Resolution* went about to head north again during Captain Cook's second

Whaling

The earliest recorded whale hunting was by the Basques of Northern Spain in the tenth century, hunting the Atlantic right whale (*Balaena glacialis*). As the whale numbers dropped, the whaling grounds shifted during the sixteenth century to Newfoundland. The English Muscovy Company organized the first British expedition in 1610 to operate out of Barents' 1596 discovery of Spitzbergen. But by the early eighteenth century, over-hunting forced whalers to move north to the Davis Strait, and a large fishery was created on Disco Island, mainly run by the Germans and Dutch.

Around this time the British North American colonies established whaling as a major industry centred on an island, improbably small in relation to the global hunting grounds – Nantucket, off the coast of Massachusetts, peppered with towns and ports with English names, and on the mainland at New Bedford. Seeking oil to light the lamps of homes throughout the world, these whalers followed the Cachalot *(Physeter catadon)* or sperm whales, reckoned to give better oil than the right whale, all the way down the American coast to Brazil. With the first British whaler rounding Cape Horn in 1787, the Americans swiftly followed to pursue the right whale north to Japan and, by 1840, further along the Kamchatka coast as far as the Bering Strait.

By 1820 more than 70 whale ships were berthed in Nantucket harbour, and representative of these was the *Essex*, of 238 tons displacement and 87 feet in length; three masted with square-rigged sails, but fore-and-aft rigged at her head and stern. She was to become the most famous whale ship in the USA after she was sunk near the Equator, 1500 miles west of the Galapagos Islands in the Pacific, by an enraged sperm whale; an event that inspired the central theme of Herman Melville's book *Moby-Dick*.

By 1846, the peak of American whaling, 20,000 were involved in the industry with 736 ships registered as whalers that sailed from 70 Atlantic coast ports. Typically in the nineteenth century a whaling voyage such as that of the *Charles W Morgan* would circumnavigate the world, leaving New Bedford in June 1849 and not returning until May 1853. Although the average whaling voyage by now was two-and-a-half to three years, the longest recorded was attained by the whale ship *Nile* sailing from New Bedford, Connecticut in May 1858 and returning 11 years later in April 1869 – amongst many major events, she had completely missed the American Civil War.

Southern commerce raiders nearly wiped out the New England (Union) American whaling industry during the Civil War of 1861–65, and from around 1870 the centre of American whaling had shifted to San Francisco, to suffer enormous setback during the winter of 1871 when the entire fleet was crushed by ice. Demand for Sperm oil dropped when paraffin superseded the oil for fuelling lamps.

Whales were by then caught in other parts of the Pacific; north along the west coast of South America and west across the Indian Ocean to the grounds around Zanzibar and the Seychelles.

However, for the first half of the twentieth century, as stocks were hunted out in the Northern Hemisphere, whaling was concentrated in the Antarctic, to the phytoplankton-rich seas at the convergence that twists between 50º and 60º S around that continent, giving abundant pastures for the baleen and blue whales that proliferate there during the feeding phase. In 1904 a large land-based whaling station was set up on the island of South Georgia by the Norwegians under a British licence. Its presence later saved the lives of Shackleton and his crew. Whalers and sealers had, almost by default, discovered and explored much of the Antarctic (and Arctic), such as James Weddell, Peter Kemp, John Biscoe, William Smith and others, fitting surveys in between whale hunting to fill in the gaps on the chart.

The invention of the harpoon gun by a Norwegian in the 1860s, the advent of steam-driven metal-hulled ships and then, in 1920, the factory ship transformed the hunting of whales into an industry that has now threatened the very survival the whale population. The International Whaling Commission started the necessary job of regulating the whale catch, but proved ineffective as the quotas had assumed an unrealistically high whale population. While most of the original whaling countries have ceased hunting, a few continue and environmental organisations such as Save the Whale Foundation and Greenpeace have worked to abolish whale hunting. Many countries such as the USA and Great Britain have banned whale meat import, reducing its use as pet food, and more countries joining the ban may ultimately save the species.

voyage of exploration of the South Seas in 1774). With his crews unwell and badly clothed Wilkes sighted land along a 1500-mile tract on the present Knox and Sabrina Coasts of Australian Antarctic Territory at, what is called Wilkes Land after him, and naming the region for the first time the Antarctic Continent. But he failed in his endeavour and Cook and Weddell's achievements in this respect stood.

The third nationalistic endeavour was initiated by the British Admiralty who appointed Captain James Clark Ross to command HMS *Erebus* and *Terror*. Ross was one of the most experienced of all Royal Navy Officers in polar exploration. He had joined the navy aged 12 and, patronized by his uncle,

Sir John Ross, had served out the last three years of the Napoleonic War in the Baltic, the White Sea and the North Sea. The navy, under its Second Secretary Sir John Barrow, was to have a century of peace, and, much reduced, was primarily engaged in anti-slavery, anti-piracy, colonial protection and exploration. Ross's first polar experience in 1818 was one of a series of expeditions to the Arctic to find the North-West passage under his uncle and subsequently under William Parry. He would achieve enduring fame as the man who found the magnetic north pole.

With this wealth of experience Ross was probably the most obvious choice to lead such an expedition. He was instructed to carry out a magnetic survey towards the South Pole, stopping at St Helena, the Cape of Good Hope and Kerguelen Islands and on to Tasmania setting up magnetic observatories.

Specially strengthened, the ships were able to force a way through the Antarctic pack ice in what is now called the Ross Sea for the first time, discovering the Ross Ice Barrier and penetrating southwards close to the 180° meridian to a new furthest position south of 78° 04' S, and charted and claimed the coastline he found, Victoria Land, for Britain in 1841. He returned in 1842 and found the Ross Ice Shelf, and again in 1843 discovering and charting islands off the northern tip of the Antarctic Peninsula, naming them perhaps a little vaingloriously, but his effort was extraordinary, the Ross Island Group. He added significantly to the charting and understanding of the continent, and pointed the way to the shortest route to the South Pole. But Ross was not able to double his achievement and find the south magnetic pole, which today meandering with time, is some 1600 miles from the geographical South Pole, but firmly inland.

Not much more happened for 50 years. As in the Arctic a poor understanding of the causes scurvy and the need for anti-scorbutics hampered exploration.

The famous scientific voyage of HMS *Challenger* in 1874, the first steam vessel to cross the Antarctic Circle in her circumnavigation of the world, dredged up useful evidence of the continent's geo-physical structure. The possibility of setting up a whaling industry led to Scottish and Norwegian expeditions which, while failing to make profitable catches, added to the knowledge of the Weddell Sea coast. Likewise in the Ross Sea, the Norwegian, Henrik J Bull, landed on Victoria Land, at Cape Adare in 1895. The venture failed but bizarrely his team found lichen, the first evidence of plant life in Antarctica. Whaling climaxed in the 1930–31 season with the massive slaughter of 31,000 blue whales, reducing them to a pathetic 2 per cent of their original numbers.

The International Geographical Congress of 1895 decided to prioritise the exploration of the Southern Continent ushering in the so-called 'heroic period'. A series of expeditions, reliant on the sea to springboard them to their start point, were basically land orientated, and, while focussing on bringing back scientific information, reflected the nationalistic fervour of the time. Expeditions set out from Belgium (Adrien de Gerlache de Gomery who charted the Gerlache Strait, Danco Coast, named the Palmer Archipelago and sighted Alexander Island), Sweden (Otto Nordenskjöld, who was the first to sled in the Antarctic, exploring the Weddell Sea coast south to 66° S), Scotland (Oceanographer, William Spiers Bruce, who discovered part of the Caird Coast and conducted deep-sea soundings of the Weddell and Scotia seas), France (Jean-Baptiste Charcot, who charted the sea south to Adelaide Island and Alexander Island, discovering Charcot Land during two expeditions in 1903–05 and 1908–10), Germany (Wilhelm Filchner, who discovered the Luitpold Coast and Filchner Ice Shelf between 1910 and 1912). These events would have been dramatic enough, but a series of headline grabbing expeditions then seized the public attention.

The example of the Norwegian Carsten E Borchgrevink, who showed that it was possible to spend a whole winter in the Antarctic, in fact in Victoria Land, led to Britain's first nationalistic enterprise when the navy's Captain Robert Falcon Scott overwintered in *Discovery* at Ross Island and hauled sledges southwards to 77° 59' S at the foot of the great glacier system leading up to the polar plateau. These sledging expeditions required navigation which was not dissimilar to navigating at sea, taking sun and star sights (adjusting for the observer's height above sea level), and, when visible, bearings of the mountain ranges to fix a position. Sir Ernest Henry Shackleton, who had been one of the crew on Scott's first journey, led his own expedition from 1907 to 1909, sledging to within 97 miles of the South Pole and discovering 500 miles of unknown mountain ranges flanking the Ross Ice Shelf.

Early in 1911 Scott returned to Ross Island in the *Terra Nova* to try to become the first man to reach the South Pole. His party's courage is legendary, but some ill-advised decisions, such as trying to sled with ponies, and insufficiently spaced food dumps, allowed the Norwegian, Roald Amundsen, very much better prepared with skiing skills and experience gained at the North Pole, a much swifter journey to the South Pole where he raised the Norwegian flag first. Scott and his party perished on the return journey in an unusually harsh Antarctic winter.

The last of the nationalistic expeditions was to show perhaps even greater courage when Shackleton's Imperial Trans-Antarctic Expedition of 1914–1917 was crushed in their ship *Endurance*. After a one-month walk and sailing across the ice of the Weddell Sea to Elephant Island, Shackleton, Frank Worsley, the navigator and three others made an extraordinary 700-mile sailing voyage to South Georgia in one of *Endurance*'s sea boats, an epic that vies with the famous 3500-mile open-boat journey of the discarded Captain Bligh of HMS *Bounty*; neither captain lost a man and both showed extraordinary powers of determination and leadership. Shackleton landed on the uninhabited side of South Georgia, climbed over the mountain to the Whaling Station, an epic that fit and well-equipped mountaineers today find a struggle, got to Chile and returned to rescue the remainder of the crew with a loaned Chilean vessel.

A look at these documents of past endeavour must surely make one appreciate the early explorer's courage and determination to find new lands, for whatever reason, although those explorers could not have foreseen the effect that first link with an unknown land would have on the indigenous inhabitants, their culture, their way of life.

Today navigation and the provision of navigational information are shared world-wide and highly sophisticated – and becoming impersonal and detached from the raw reality beyond the sheltered ship's bridge. Today's sailor can use the latest advanced electronic, microchip and electro-magnetic technology availing itself of GPS, computers, radar, sonar, gyroscopic compasses, with electronic inputs of ship's speed and course, to automatically give a constantly up-dated position on an electronic chart produced by either a scan of the up-to-date paper chart or an electronic composition from sophisticated data bases gathering electronic information from a multitude of sources world-wide (known as a Raster Navigational Chart). The computerised chart display can combine an actual radar picture, giving a computerised best course to steer and warnings of navigational hazards and obstructions.

It is all a far cry from the hand-held tools of navigation used with a secret vellum or paper chart, where sailors needed experience, skill and intuition to guide them safely across oceans and into the haven. But a modern mariner must still learn the old ways, for if the electronic equipment fails, then he is reliant on the same skills, tools and intuition that sailing masters have evolved and used for centuries.

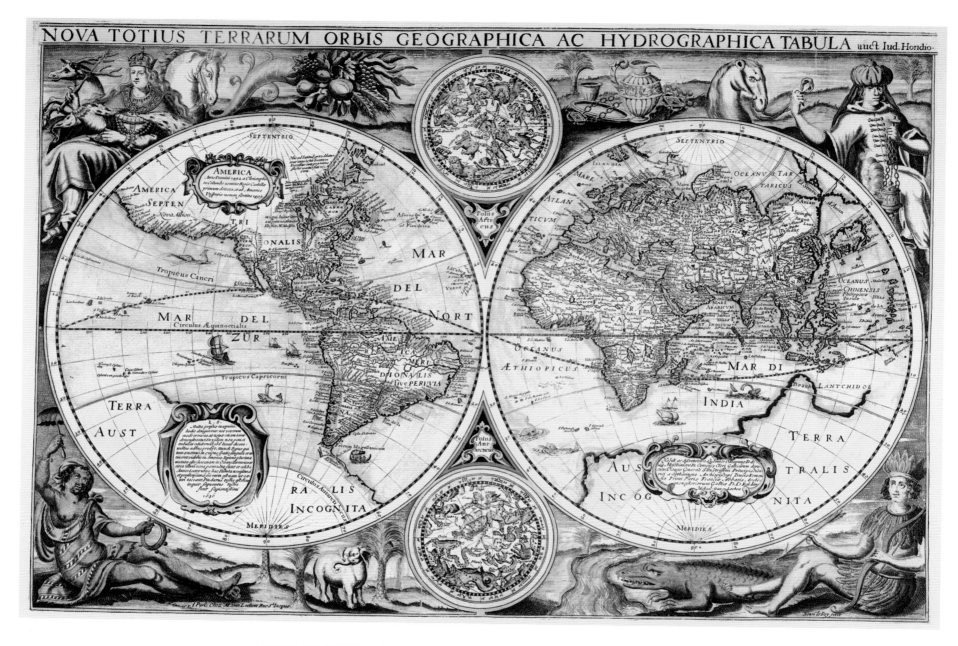

| HENRICUS HONDIUS WORLD MAP, 1636 | Henricus Hondius's World Map of 1636, copied by Henri Le Roy (coloured in the style of the time by the UKHO), shows the Southern Continent as a vast, counterbalancing land mass, ripe for exploration and colonization, joined to what little was then known of Australia. Peoples of the four corners of the Earth and the two celestial charts with stars outlined as the constellation animal they had been given (helping navigators remember the layout of the heavens to find the crucial stars for an astro-navigational fix) are all depicted.

Henricus Hondius was the grandson of Jodocus, one of the most renowned engravers of the period, who worked in Amsterdam, and for a time in London, where he met leading scientists and geographers of the day and engraved the plates of *The Mariner's Mirrour*. He bought up many of Mercator's Atlas plates, and this map is based on those. (© The Admiralty Collection®)

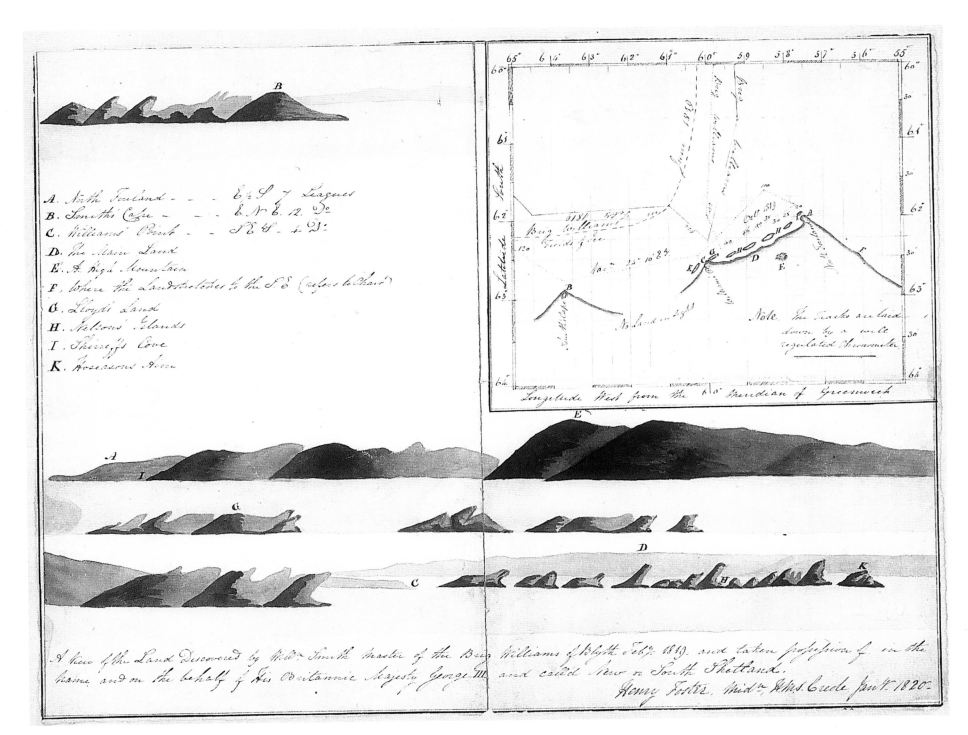

A. North Foreland - - - - E¼S 7 Leagues
B. Smith's Cape - - - - E.N.E. 12 Do.
C. Williams' Point - - - S.E.S. 4 Do.
D. The Main Land
E. A High Mountain
F. Where the Land stretches to the S.E (refers to Chart)
G. Lloyd's Land
H. Nelson's Islands
I. Shirreff's Cove
K. Roseason's Arm

A View of the Land Discovered by Will.m Smith Master of the Brig Williams of Blyth Feb.y 1819. and taken possession of, in the name and on the behalf of His Britannic Majesty George III and call'd New or South Shetland.
Henry Foster, Mid.r H.M.S. Creole Jan.y 1.t 1820.

| COASTAL VIEW OF THE NORTH-WEST SHORE OF THE SOUTH SHETLAND ISLANDS, 1820 |

New South Britain, now the South Shetland Islands and still a British territory, stands some 500 miles south of the tip of the American continent. William Smith, master of the brig *Williams*, discovered the group of islands on 19 February 1819. The brig had been blown off course while on a trading voyage round the Horn. Smith reported his discovery to Captain Shirreff, Senior Naval Officer on the West Coast of South America, but Shirreff was doubtful until Smith's second chart made at another landing in October.

Convinced, Shirreff hired the *Williams* under Edward Bransfield, press-ganged into the Royal Navy, as so many then were, from his previous civilian job as Master of the *Arromanche*, to undertake surveys in this new territory between January and March 1820. He had some immortal compensation with the naming of Mount Bransfield and Bransfield Strait. Contending with prevalent fog he wrongly charted the central part of the group as a continuous landmass, but, unhindered by commercial considerations, he surveyed with creditable accuracy the rest of the group of islands that stretch as an archipelago from the north coast of Graham Land, the finger of land extending north towards America, which he discovered as well, to Clarence Island and Livingston Island with 11 days at George's Bay in King George Island, now Chilean, and the longitude he established of the anchorage still holds good.

This chart with coastal views, although a rough attempt to show the north-west shores of South Shetland, is the first recorded view of this forbidding land. Probably a copy twice removed, it was made for the Admiralty by Henry Foster, midshipman of HMS *Creole* on 20 January 1820 for inclusion in the engraved charts to be published of this area. The expanses of the 'Main Land' at D are probably due to the influence of Smith's collaborator, William Goddard, who was certain this was part of the Southern Continent. The slaughter of the entire seal population left the islands to scientific explorers and nine years later Henry Foster commanded the *Chanticlear* (*sic*) in the first scientific expedition there to establish latitude and longitude accurately, for which he used pendulum observations. (UKHO © British Crown Copyright)

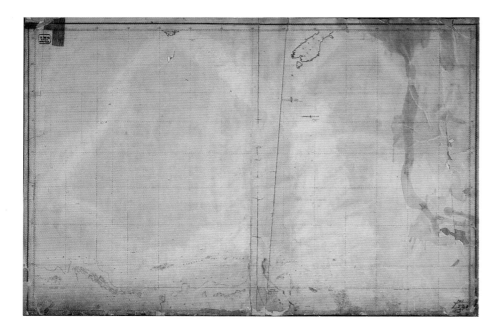

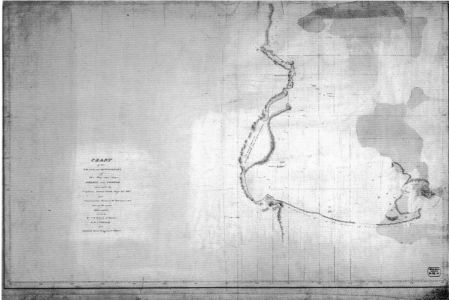

| ABOVE | **TWO CHARTS OF CAPTAIN ROSS'S EXPLORATION OF THE ANTARCTIC** | The first of the 'great' British explorations of the Antarctic continent was made by Captain James Clarke Ross in HMS *Erebus*, in company with Commander Francis Crozier of HMS *Terror*. These two original manuscript surveys of five from the expeditions in the UK Hydrographic Office are drawn by the second sailing master of *Terror*, Mr J E Davies, as a back-up copy to Captain Ross's. Between 1840 and 1843 *Erebus* and *Terror* tried three times to penetrate the ice barrier to the South Pole. In the summer of 1840–41, sailing from Van Diemen's Land (Tasmania) southwards from New Zealand at around 180° longitude, encountering the Antarctic coast as shown at Mount Sabine, and deliberately eastward of the landfalls of d'Urville and Wilkes, Ross passed the Admiralty Range and the twin volcanoes named after his ships and came within a remarkable 12° (720 nautical miles) of the Pole, returning to winter at Van Diemen's Land. (UKHO © British Crown Copyright)

| RIGHT | **CHART SUMMARIZING THE TRACKS OF EXPLORATION OF THE ROSS SEA** | Fascinatingly, we can safely surmise that Captain Ross took this printed Admiralty Chart of the South Shetland and South Orkney Islands with him on his three voyages of discovery between 1840 and 1843. It shows the tracks and knowledge gained from previous Antarctic explorations between 1819 and 1838 with names that read like a roll call of the Antarctic greats – Biscoe, d'Urville, Foster, Bellinghausen, Weddell and others, but has Ross's actual 1843 ship's track drawn on between 23 December 1842 and 13 February 1843. It presents the discovery of the Gulf of Erebus and Terror, at the northern tip of Graham Land, with the worrying occurrence of pack ice. (UKHO © British Crown Copyright)

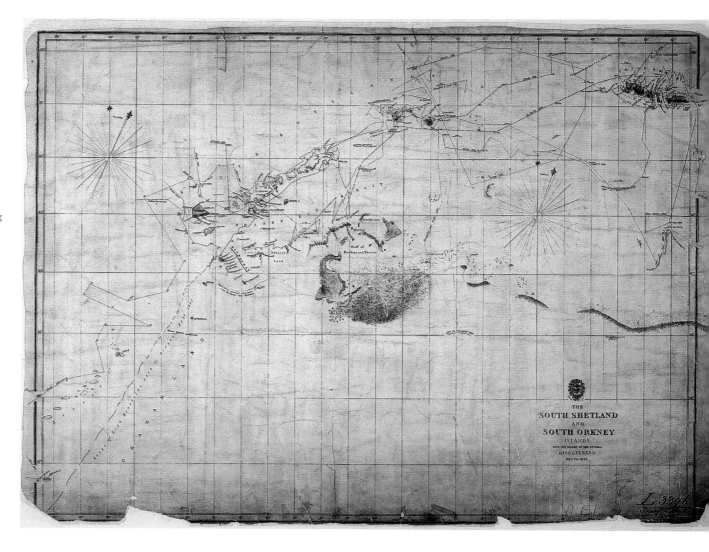

| MAP SHOWING CAPTAIN SCOTT'S SLEDGE JOURNEY AND HIS SHIP'S TRACKS 1910–1913 | This printed map, published by Stanfords of London, has incorporated the survey and ship's tracks of the *Terra Nova* shown in the manuscript chart (page 157, top right) with Scott's sledge journey to create a record of all topographical aspects of the expedition of 1910–1913. (UKHO © British Crown Copyright)

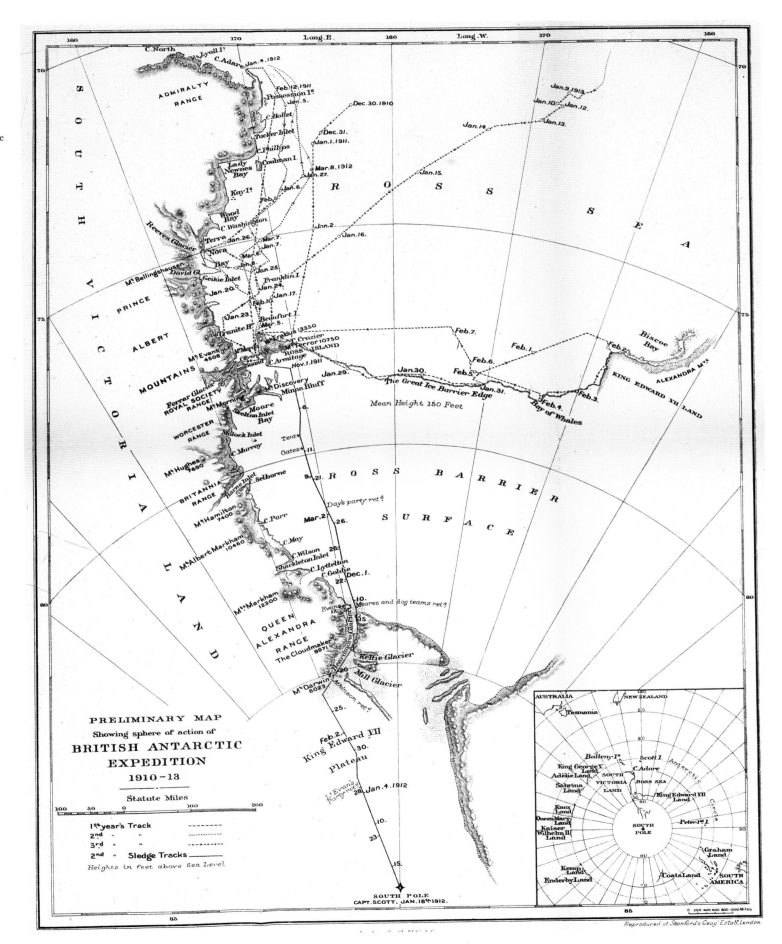

PRELIMINARY MAP
Showing sphere of action of
**BRITISH ANTARCTIC
EXPEDITION
1910–13**

Statute Miles

100   50   0   100   200

1st year's Track   --------
2nd   "   "   ···············
3rd   "   "   ─·─·─·─·─·
2nd   "   Sledge Tracks ─··─··─··─

Heights in feet above Sea Level

SOUTH POLE
CAPT. SCOTT. JAN. 18th 1912.

Reproduced at Stanford's Geog'l Estab.London.

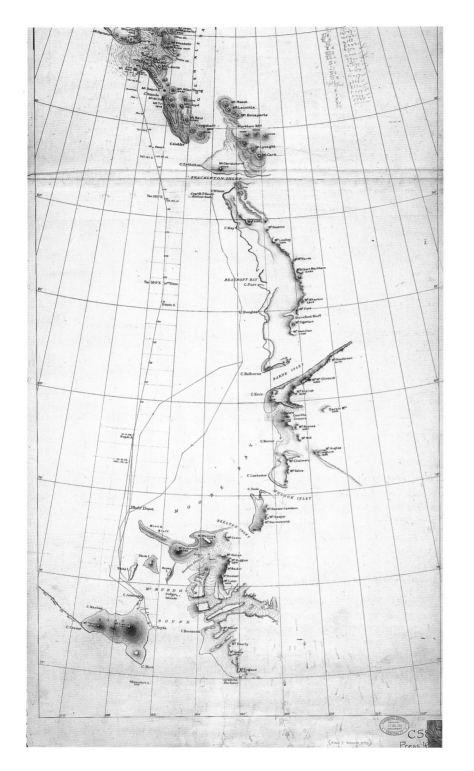
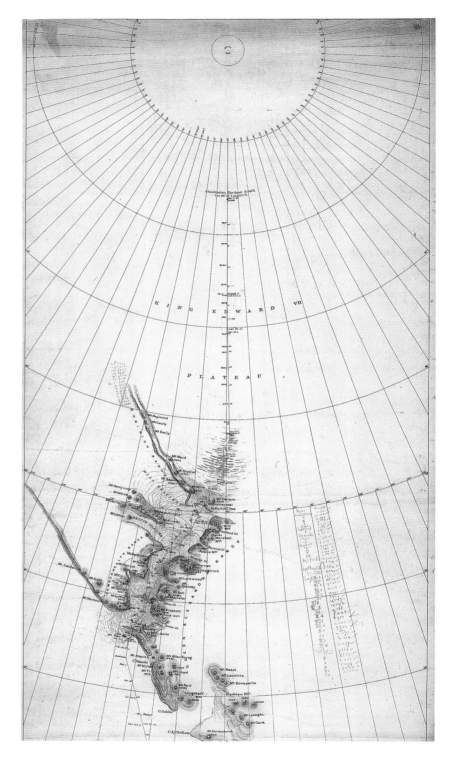

| MANUSCRIPT CHARTS SHOWING SHACKLETON'S TRACK TO THE SOUTH POLE | Sir Ernest Henry Shackleton's first polar expedition got to a furthest latitude of 88° 23' S at longitude 162° E on 9 January 1909, which he recorded here as at 10,050 feet above mean sea level. These manuscript charts (he navigated his way as he would have done on sea), in the Hydrographic Office collection, show Shackleton's track from November 1908 to January 1909, with very good topography and glacier survey work, recorded *en route*. He also shows Scott's furthest south position, presumably for posterity's comparison. The set of figures, hand written to the right of Queen Alexandra Range, refer to various peaks and their height, while the figures to the left of the Dominion Range show the average height along King Edward VII plateau. His party discovered the magnetic pole, and showed that to reach the geographical pole was mainly a matter of organization. (UKHO © British Crown Copyright)

| CAPTAIN ROBERT FALCON SCOTT | Captain Scott in daytime dress uniform by Harrington Mann, aged about 41.

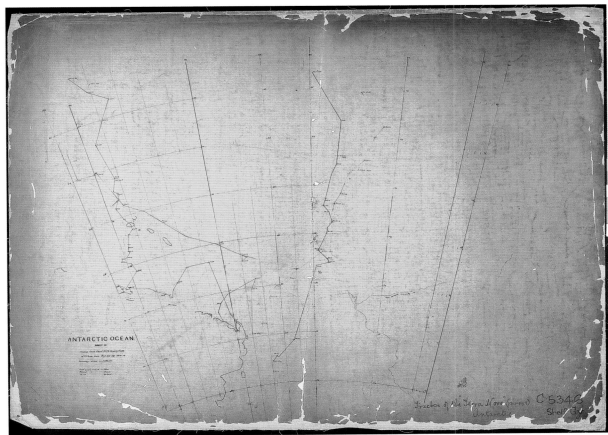

| TRACK OF CAPTAIN SCOTT'S SHIP, *TERRA NOVA*, 1911–13 | While Scott was making his courageous attempt to get to the South Pole (first), his base ship, the steam yacht *Terra Nova*, was carrying out wide surveys on the western shores of the Ross Sea, discovering Oates Land during the summer of 1911 and adding it to the chart. Four detailed original manuscript charts held originally by the Admiralty, now at the UKHO, are by Lieutenant Harry Pennell, Scott's commander of the *Terra Nova* (who has the Pennell Bank in the Ross Sea named after him) and show the detailed surveying of the Ross Sea made by the ship's crew, including the Great Ice Barrier and King Edward Land from Cape Crozier to Cape Colbeck, the north coast of South Victoria Land between Smith Inlet and Robertson Bay and Oates Land discovered by the *Terra Nova*. This chart shows the tracks of each of the three summers of exploration between 1911 and 1913, returning each winter to New Zealand. (UKHO © British Crown Copyright)

| SURVEY CHART OF SHACKLETON'S EXPEDITION OF 1914–17 BY LIEUTENANT COMMANDER WORSLEY | Frank Worsley RNR was responsible to Shackleton for the safe, efficient running and navigation of the *Endurance*. He drew up the charts of their progress and new discoveries. Eight pencil sketch survey charts in the UKHO are originals by him made during the epic expedition in 1914–17. This chart shows his astro-navigational fix where the *Endurance*, captured by the ice in the Weddell Sea drifted northward, crumpled and sank. The party was marooned on the ice and ultimately landed on Elephant Island in the South Shetlands. Another of the charts shows the remarkable voyage in the open boat to South Georgia. Although Shackleton didn't succeed in crossing the Antarctic, Worsley's charting of Coats Land and the previously unknown Caird Coast, including information on the nature and direction of the edge of the pack ice, marine and wildlife and the drift of the *Endurance* in the Weddell Sea was invaluable as it supplemented the earlier discoveries in the vicinity by Charles Bruce and Wilhelm Filchner. Worsley was sailing master and hydrographer in the *Quest* on Shackleton's last voyage in 1921, and jointly led an expedition to Franz Joseph Land in the Arctic in 1925. (UKHO © British Crown Copyright)

Bibliography

Admiralty Charts and Publications, *Admiralty Distance Tables*, NP350, 1978

Admiralty Charts and Publications, *Admiralty Ocean Passages for the World*, NP136 – 4th Edition, 1987

Admiralty Charts and Publications, *The Mariner's Handbook*, NP100, 1979

Admiralty Charts and Publications, *The Sea Pilot*, various volumes

Barrow, Sir John, *The Mutiny of HMS Bounty*, 1831, republished by the Folio Society, 1976

Bathurst, Bella, *The Lighthouse Stevensons*, HarperCollins, 1999

Beaglehole, J C, *Exploration of the Pacific*, 1966

Brewer, *Dictionary of Phrase and Fable*, Galley Press

Brown, Michelle P, *The Painted Labyrinth*, The British Library, 2003

Burgess, Anthony, *The Book of Tea*, Flammarion, 1992

Campbell, Tony, *Portolan Charts from the Late Thirteenth Century to 1500*

Colledge, J J, *Ships of the Royal Navy*, Greenhill Books, reprinted 2003

Conner, Daniel & Miller, Lorraine, *Master Mariner*, Douglas & Macintyre, 1978

Cook, Dr Andrew S, *Contribution to The World of the East India Company*, Boydell Press in association with National Maritime Museum and University of Leicester

Cooke, Alistair, *Alistair Cooke's America*, BBC, 1973

Cortazzi, Hugh, *Isles of Gold: Antique Maps of Japan*, Weatherhill Inc., 1983

Courtney, Nicholas, 'Gale Force 10', *Review*, 2002

Crane, Nicholas, *Mercator, The Man who Mapped the Planet*, Weidenfeld & Nicolson, 2002

Dafter, Ray, *Guernsey Wrecks*, Matfield Books, 2001

Dampier, William, *A Voyage to New Holland*, Alan Sutton Publishing Ltd, 1981

Dawson, Cdr L S, *Memoirs of Hydrography*, Henry Keay, 1885, reprinted in single vol. 1969

Day, Vice-Admiral Sir Archibald, *The Admiralty Hydrographic Service*, Her Majesty's Stationery Office, 1967

Douwma, Robert, *Admiralty Charts and Selected Maps Catalogue 28*, 1984

Evans, G N D, *Uncommon Obdurate – The Several Public Careers of JFW Des Barres*, Peabody Museum of Salem, Massachusetts,1969

Farrington, Anthony, *Trading Places*, The British Library, 2002

Fisher Susann, *Address at the 54th AGM of the Royal Institute of Navigation, 25th October 2000*

Fleming, Fergus, *Barrow's Boys*, Granta Books, 1998

Franklin, Rear-Admiral Sir John, *Journey to the Polar Sea*, Republished by Könemann, 1998

Freycinet, L, *Voyage autour du Monde*, Paris, 1825

Greenhill, Basil, *The National Maritime Museum*, Philip Wilson Publishers Ltd & Summerfield Press Ltd, 1982

Gurney, Alan, *Below the Convergence*, Norton & Co., 1997

Hapgood, Charles, *Maps of the Ancient Sea Kings*, Adventures Unlimited Press, 1966

Harley, J Brian & Woodward, David, *The History of Cartography Vol I*, University of Chicago Press, 1987

Harvey, Robert, *Cochrane – The Life and Exploits of a Fighting Captain*, Constable & Robinson Ltd, 2000

HM Stationery Office, *Admiralty Manual of Navigation Volumes II and III*, 1955

Hollett, David, The *Conquest of the Niger by Land and Sea*, PM Heaton Publishing, 1995

Hough, Richard, *Captain James Cook*, Hodder & Stoughton, 1994

Howse, Derek & Sanderson, Michael, *The Sea Chart*, David & Charles (Publishers) Ltd, 1973

Hudson, Alice & Cohen-Stratyner, Barbara, *Heading West, Touring West*, New York Public Library, 2001

Hughes, Robert, *The Fatal Shore*, Collins Harvill, 1987

Huntingford, G W B, *The Periplus of the Erythrean Sea*, The Hakluyt Society, 1980

Huxley, Elspeth, *Scott of the Antarctic*, Weidenfeld & Nicolson, 1977

Huxley, Julian, *Huxley's Diary of the Voyage of HMS Rattlesnake*, Chatto & Windus, 1935

Hydrographic Department, Admiralty, *Professional Paper 13*, London, 1950

Hydrographic Department, Admiralty, *Admiralty Manual of Hydrographic Surveying*, 1938, revised 1948

Imago Mundi Volume 48, The British Library, 1996

Journal of Navigation, Volume 54 No. 2, Cambridge University Press, May 2001

Kemp, Peter, *The Oxford Companion to Ships and the Sea*, Oxford University Press, 1976

King, Dean, *A Sea of Words*, Henry Holt and Company, 1997

King, Dean, *Harbors and High Seas*, Owl Books, 1996

Lavery, Brian, *Building the Wooden Walls*, Conway Maritime Press, 1991

Lubbock, Basil, *The China Clippers*, James Brown & Son, 1919

MacLean, Alistair, *Captain Cook*, Fletcher & Son Ltd, 1972

McClintock, Captain Francis, *The Voyage of the 'Fox' 1847*, Republished by Könemann, 1998

Menzies, Gavin, *1421*, Bantam Press, 2002

Milton, Giles, *Nathaniel's Nutmeg*, Hodder & Stoughton, 1999

Milton, Giles, *Samurai William*, Hodder & Stoughton, 2002

Moorehead, Alan, *Darwin and the Beagle*, Hamish Hamilton Ltd, 1969

Moreland, Carl & Bannister, David, *Antique Maps*, Longman, 1983

Morriss, Roger, *Guide to British Naval Papers in North America*, Mansell Publishing Ltd, 1994

Natkiel, Richard & Preston, Antony, *Atlas of Maritime History*, Bison Books Ltd, 1986

Padfield, Peter, *Maritime Supremacy and the Opening of the Western Mind*, John Murray (Publishers) Ltd, 1999

Peron, F and Freycinet, L, *Voyage de decouvertes aux terres australes*, Paris 1807-16

Philbrick, Nathaniel, *In the Heart of the Sea*, HarperCollins, 2000

Potter, Jonathan, *Collecting Antique Maps*, Jonathan Potter Ltd, 1988

Randier, Jean, *Marine Navigation Instruments*, translated from the French & published in the UK by John Murray (Publishers) Ltd, 1980

Rice, Dr Tony, *Voyages of Discovery*, Scriptum Editions, 2000

Ritchie, Rear-Admiral G S, *The Admiralty Chart*, Hollis & Carter Ltd, 1967

Ritchie, Rear-Admiral Steve, *As it Was*, GITC, 2003

Rodger, N A M, *The Wooden World*, Collins, 1986

Ross, Sir James Clark, *A voyage of Discovery and Research to Southern and Antarctic Regions (1839-43)*

Shackleton, Sir Ernest, *South*, William Heinemann, 1919

Sider, Sandra, *Maps, Charts, Globes: Five centuries of exploration*, The Hispanic Society of America, 1992

Smith, Richard J, *Chinese Maps*, Oxford University Press, 1996

Sobel, Dava & Andrewes, William J H, *The Illustrated Longitude*, Fourth Estate Ltd, 1998

Stefoff, Rebecca, *The British Library Companion to Maps and Mapmaking*, The British Library, 1995

Taylor, E G R, *Mathematics and the Navigator in the 13th century*, Institute of Navigation

Taylor, E G R, *The Haven-finding Art*, Cambridge University Press, first published 1956, augmented edition 1971

The Times Concise Atlas of the World, 1993

Thomson, George Malcolm, *The North-West Passage*, Martin Secker & Warburg Ltd, 1975

Tibbetts, G R, *Arab Navigation*, The Royal Asiatic Society of Great Britain and Ireland, 1971

Van der Merwe, Pieter (et al), *South – The Race to the Pole*, National Maritime Museum, 2000

Wallis, Helen & Tyacke, Sarah (ed.), *My Head is a Map*, Francis Edwards and Carta Press, 1973

Waters, David, *The Art of Navigation in England in Elizabethan and Early Stuart Times*, National Maritime Museum, 2nd edition, 1978

Whitfield, Peter, *New Found Lands*, The British Library, 1998

Whitfield, Peter, *The Charting of the Oceans*, The British Library, 1996

Whitfield, Peter, *The Image of the World*, The British Library, 1994

Wilde, Antony, *The East India Company*, HarperCollins, 1999

Williams, Glyn, *The Prize of all the Oceans*, HarperCollins, 1999

Williams, Glyn, *Voyages of Delusion*, HarperCollins, 2002

Woolley, Benjamin, *The Queen's Conjuror: The Life and Magic of Dr Dee*, HarperCollins, 2001

Index

Figures in italics refer to captions.